Latino Literature

Edited by Sara E. Martínez

Foreword by Connie Van Fleet

Genreflecting Advisory Series

Diana Tixier Herald, Series Editor

Libraries Unlimited
An Imprint of ABC-CLIO, LLC

A B C  C L I O

Santa Barbara, California • Denver, Colorado • Oxford, England

Library of Congress Cataloging-in-Publication Data
Latino literature : a guide to reading interests / Sara E. Martínez, editor ; foreword by
  Connie Van Fleet.
    p. cm. — (Genreflecting advisory series)
  Includes bibliographical references and indexes.
  ISBN 978-1-59158-292-2 (alk. paper)
  1. American fiction—Hispanic American authors—Bibliography. 2. Hispanic American fiction (Spanish)—20th century—Translations into English—Bibliography. 3. Hispanic American fiction (Spanish)—21st century—Translations into English—Bibliography. 4. American literature—Hispanic American authors—Bibliography. 5. Hispanic American literature (Spanish)—20th century—Translations into English—Bibliography. 6. Hispanic American literature (Spanish)—21st century—Translations into English—Bibliography. 7. Readers' advisory services—United States. I. Martínez, Sara E.
  Z1229.H57L38   2009
  [PS153.H56]
  016.863008'09287—dc22   2009026355

13 12 11 10 9   1 2 3 4 5

This book is also available on the World Wide Web as an eBook.
Visit www.abc-clio.com for details.

ABC-CLIO, LLC
130 Cremona Drive, P.O. Box 1911
Santa Barbara, California 93116-1911

This book is printed on acid-free paper ∞
Manufactured in the United States of America

For Alma Inez and José Emiliano con mucho amor

Contents

Chapter 4—Latina Romance and Love Stories (*Cont.*)

Chapter 5—Mysteries and Suspense *Brandi Blankenship & Sara E. Martínez* 151

Chapter 6—Fantastic Fiction: Science Fiction, Fantasy, Paranormal, and Magical Realism 215

Chapter 7—Young Adult Fiction *Jessica Reed* 235

Foreword

When I first began teaching readers' advisory nearly twenty years ago, few such courses gave explicit attention to literature for ethnic and cultural populations. After a few iterations of the course, it seemed natural and perhaps even essential to devote a class session to multicultural works. In addition to reading in a variety of genres, students read works reflecting the rich diversity of literary perspectives, expanding their knowledge of literature and their ability to offer service to readers.

At that time, most multicultural fiction was limited to mainstream or literary fiction; most of the books the students selected were classics or award winners—works recognized for extraordinary merit. This was virtually the only type of ethnic literature readily available to them. Although these classics offer valuable reading, they do not always reflect the diversity of reading tastes in any group. It is a fairly predictable pattern for minority literature to become accepted and available in a wide variety of popular literary formats only after meritorious works have been recognized and, not coincidentally, the market for such work has grown to a sustainable level.

There is no longer a single "multicultural" session in my class. Students are required to read at least one work that reflects the minority experience, but the selection may represent any of the genres we read in any of the formats in which they are available. And, as this guide illustrates, students have a wide variety of increasingly accessible works from which to choose. We rejoice in the availability of this literature, but its growing presence and complexity may be a bit overwhelming for librarians who are trying to keep current.

Latino Literature: A Guide to Reading Interests will prove an interesting and useful guide for librarians as they serve a rapidly growing Latino segment of their service population and introduce other library users to Latino culture. Typical of the Genreflecting series, the organization of the chapters, the chapter introductions, and the annotations provide an overview and structure of the literature that will be useful in collection development, as well as in organization and marketing of collections, programming, and individual readers' advisory guidance.

A key feature of this book is the recognition that "Latino" covers a lot of ground (figuratively and literally). Just as Native American sensibilities and experiences vary by tribe, so country of origin has a profound influence on Latino authors, their work, and their readers. Identification of that origin will enhance the ability of a readers' advisor to find a good match between reader and book. Inclusion of the content of these annotations in the *Readers' Advisor Online* database will enable searching in a manner that is not always possible in traditional catalogs, but is meaningful to readers.

I am delighted to welcome this addition to the Genreflecting series. As I have noted in several professional publications, people who live "on the hyphen" in the United States have a unique perspective that not only engages those who share their unique cultural experience, but informs those of us who approach understanding from a different viewpoint and background. Sara Martínez, coordinator of the Hispanic Resource Center for Tulsa City-County Library, shares her knowledge, enthusiasm, and experience in this timely guide.

I became convinced Sara would be the perfect editor for this guide after she gave a vivacious booktalk featuring Latina literature in one of my readers' advisory classes. All of the chapter authors she brought together for this project were in that section. I am proud—justifiably, I think—of the contributions of that extraordinary group and delighted to share their work with a wider audience.

Sara and her *compadres* have given us a useful, well-researched, and well-organized guide. More important, they have managed to convey their enthusiasm for this literature and for readers' advisory service. Their lively style and engaging wit make this an entertaining as well as informative read. *¡Disfruta!*

Connie Van Fleet, Professor
School of Library and Information Science
University of Oklahoma–Norman

Acknowledgments

Un millón de gracias, a million thanks to Barbara Ittner for her infinite patience and wisdom; to Dr. Connie Van Fleet for her faith in me and enthusiastic support of this project. I am very grateful to Tracy Warren, who was a rock during this process and brought unfailing energy to the painstaking detail work needed to create the subject tags and the glossary. *Muchísimas gracias* to Marianne Stambaugh for letting me rely on her expertise with the English language and always being willing to take another look at awkward wording (like this). I owe a big *gracias* to my coworkers at the Martin Regional Library for their spirit of *compañerismo*. I also appreciate the Tulsa City-County Library System management, especially CEO Linda Saferite, Division Director Suanne Wymer, and Martin Library's branch manager Amy Stephens, as well as former branch managers and supervisors Richard Parker, Christy Chilton, and Theresa Fowler for their support—TCCL is a great place to work!

Latino Literature:
A Guide to Reading Interests

En gustos se rompen géneros

Introduction

It's been over ten years since Eduardo Valenzuela (1997) asked why there were no Latinos in outer space, lamenting the dearth of Hispanic actors on science fiction TV shows and movies. Since then, Edward James Olmos has commanded *Galactica*, Jessica Alba has kicked a lot of butt, and Richard Rodriguez's Spy Kids have navigated science fiction territory with the ease of anyone used to navigating two languages. Once worried about being in the future at all, it looks like Latinos ARE the future! As Julia Alvarez states in *Once Upon a Quinceañera*, "Hispanic teens are . . . 'a bellwether for one of the most important trends shaping the future of the United States-the growth of the US Hispanic population. Clearly, the future is theirs and they know it'" (Alvarez 2007, 70). That future is evident in all areas of popular culture, including books and reading.

And who should win the Pulitzer Prize for fiction in 2008 but a second generation Dominican American with a novel about a *Star Wars*, comic book, video game–loving nerd? Junot Díaz's *The Brief Wondrous Life of Oscar Wao* looks very much like the great Latino novel—"a big messy collage of tradition and media influences. It will dialogue with the past but will also establish a link with the chaotic present we inhabit" (Augenbraum and Stavans 2006, xx–xxi).

Past, present, and future. Literature by Latino authors has been a part of the U.S. literary landscape all along, but only recently has begun to play a more vital, visible role as the community itself becomes more visible. Latinos have received a lot of attention and scrutiny since they became the largest "minority" group in the United States. Publishers have certainly begun to sit up and take notice. The Association of American Publishers (AAP) created a Publishing Latino Voices for America Task Force. Its Web site states that, "The Latino population is large . . . and growing . . . and youthful. Latinos have real buying power in the United States . . . and primarily speak English" (AAP 2008).

It is important "to recognize that a Hispanic presence has been integral to the United States for centuries" (Stavans 2005, 455). "The Mexican," aka Gustavo Arellano, brags that

> the oldest city in the United States is St. Augustine, Florida, founded by Spaniards in 1565, twenty-one years before the English crown ever bothered to explore the Americas. The oldest American capital is Santa Fe, founded in 1609, over 150 years before the United States *was even born* and 250 before the United States eventually conquered what's now the Southwest from Mexico. (2007, 30)

It is also important to remember, in the context of the Latino community as a whole and its place within U.S. society, that

> [w]hether through colonial conquest, war, national security concerns, or Cold War geopolitics, U.S. activities in the regions have had an impact on the immigration of Latin peoples to the United States . . . there has been a long-standing relationship between the peoples of Latin America and the Caribbean and the people of the United States—a relationship that has hardly been innocent. (Stavans 2005, 454)

Furthermore, although Latino immigration to the United States has come from many different countries and cultural traditions, "a common ground can be found in an alliance that celebrates and respects both differences and affinities . . . based on . . . solidarity and the communion of contemporary cultural experiences" (Colmeiro 2001, 49).

The Latino experience is both old and new again—from the Mexican Americans who have inhabited the Southwest since before the pilgrims landed on Plymouth Rock to those immigrants dying to cross every day. The Latino experience is multicolored—from Christina and her life as a blonde to Celia Cruz, the Afro-Cuban queen of salsa. The Latino experience is multilingual—from English to Spanish to Spanglish and back again.

Scholar and founder of Arte Público Press Nicolás Kanellos, who has done more than anyone to conserve and catalog the Hispanic presence in and impact on U.S. culture and history, describes Hispanic literature this way: "It is a literature that proclaims a sense of place in the United States while it also erases borders and is transnational in the most postmodern sense possible" (2003, 1). The *Encyclopedia of Latino Popular Culture* recognizes that the "innovative forms of expression resist categorizing as distinct genres" (Chávez Candelaria et al. 2004, 440). Martin-Rodriguez asserts that in this literature, "borders tend to become contact zones rather than geographical markers, cultures are understood as processes and not as essentially predefined, writers become (of necessity) transcultural mediators, and languages infiltrate other languages in everyday and literary practices" (2003, 123).

A word about the concept of transculturation. This term was coined by Malinowski in the context of anthropological studies: "We should study both sides of contact and consider that phenomenon as integral as a transculturation, in other words a process in which each new element merges, adopting modes that have already been established and at the same time introducing its own exotic styles and generating new fermentation" (Ortiz 1983, xxxiv; my translation). In other words, when two cultures meet, both evolve into something new and unique. Immigrants don't just "acculturate" or "assimilate"; they change, but they also bring change. This concept is important to Latino literature.

For our purposes, we define Latino literature in the broadest possible sense as an *international* literature (in the spirit of the International Latino Book Awards and the Latin Grammys) written by authors from the American continents and their European colonizers, which includes U.S. Latino authors and authors from Latin America, the Caribbean, Spain, and Portugal.

Purpose

We wrote this book for anyone interested in Latino literature, especially Latino readers. It is definitely NOT a comprehensive history of Latino literature, but rather a guide for librarians and others as they seek to better serve the Latino community.

We wrote this book to

- acknowledge Latino books and authors;

- remind Latinos about our literary heritage and future;

- introduce Latino literature and the Latino perspective to all readers;

- help people who read for fun find books they'll enjoy;

- assist librarians in providing readers' advisory services;

- serve as a collection development tool for libraries; and

- shed new light on this body of literature for teachers, students, and scholars.

Audience

Latino Literature is intended primarily as a readers' advisory guide for use by and with adult readers. Other guides to Latino authors do exist, but their focus is primarily academic; thus there is a need for a guide such as this one, which focuses on reading interest and includes popular works. Latino library usage is healthy: "In the largest and most representative study to date on Latinos and library use, the Tomás Rivera Policy Institute (TRPI) reports a largely positive perception by Latinos regarding public libraries, library resources and staff" (Flores and Pachon 2008, 1). The publishing industry is also aware of the need to better serve our demographic, as evidenced by the AAP's Latino Voices for America project, "working to find innovative and exciting ways to broaden the awareness of the diverse array and availability of titles by Latino voices in both (the publishing) industry and the reading public" (Schroeder 2008, 2).

We have dedicated one chapter to young adult fiction, because growing up as a second generation immigrant is integral to many Latinos' experiences. The books covered in this guide appeal to readers of all cultural and ethnic backgrounds. Romance readers who are fans of Candace Bushnell are sure to have a blast with Alisa Valdes-Rodriquez's Dirty Girls, armchair travelers will find adventure titles here, and anyone who likes a Hillerman whodunit will undoubtedly enjoy following Sonny Baca's exploits. Throughout their multiple perspectives and experiences, a common human bond is the thread that unites all these works.

Scope and Criteria for Selection

The authors included here range from Latinos born in the United States and naturalized U.S. citizens to Latin American, Spanish, and Portuguese authors whose works are available in English translations. We also included some non-Latino authors whose works prominently feature Latino protagonists and/or subject matter. The works included are limited to those written originally in English or available in English translation. Some publishers have made an effort recently to publish especially popular authors' works simultaneously in English and Spanish versions. This is the case for García Márquez's latest work, for example, *Memorias de mis putas tristes/Memories of my Melancholy Whores*. Some authors who write originally in Spanish, such as Carlos Ruiz Zafón, are even having the English-language translation published before the original Spanish. These are anomalies, however. In most cases, it should be evident in the entry which version is the original.

As mentioned previously, although we focused on popular reading interests for adults and most of the titles covered are novels written specifically for adults, there is a chapter on young adult literature (chapter 7), one that covers memoirs and autobiographies (chapter 8), and one on narrative nonfiction (chapter 9).

Finally, the emphasis is on works first published from 1995 through 2008. It was difficult to say *ya basta!* as new and interesting books showed up on my desk every day, but we finally *puso fin* at around 775 titles. The time period covered coincides with the explosion of interest in and creation and publication of genre literature by Latino authors. Some classic older works have been included, especially those that have been recently reissued with updated translations. Some earlier titles are included without an annotation, to provide a complete list of works in a series.

Methodology and Selection

Latino Literature represents the efforts of five librarians who enjoy particular genres or who are interested in Latino authors. I invited them to contribute chapters based on a template that outlined the major components. As primary author, I tried to preserve the individual voices of each of the contributors, while still providing consistency throughout the guide.

The approach used here has been broadly inclusive rather than selective, but the book still covers only a sampling of Latino literature. Because there are fewer titles and only a handful of Latino authors who are well known in any genre, the primary goal was to identify appropriate titles and categorize them to facilitate access.

A number of strategies were used to find suitable titles. We consulted award lists for each of the genres, as well as more generalized lists that recognize work by Latinos. We also used general, genre-specific, and multicultural readers' advisory sources—in books, databases, and the Internet—as starting points for selection. We are very interested in presenting the diversity of genres, authors, and themes to create a balanced sampling of titles available to readers.

Of course, new books are being published all the time, and it is important to keep up on new publications. Information on major publishers of Latino literature in the United States and journals that make a point of reviewing Latino literature are covered in the appendix.

Organization and Format

The selected titles have been categorized by subgenre—for example, historical fiction or crime fiction—and are often further subdivided by theme or popular reading interest, such as fiction about the Spanish Conquest or police procedurals. Some subgenres not plentiful enough in representation and cross genres are noted in the subject listings. Examples of these include *chica* lit and street lit. Cross-references to similar genres can often be found in the chapter introductions.

Foreign authors' national origin (if known) is indicated in parentheses after their names, for example: García Márquez, Gabriel (Colombian) and Valdés, Zoé (Cuban). U.S. American Latino authors' heritage is also indicated in parentheses, for example: Cisneros, Sandra (Mexican American) and Goldman, Francisco (Guatemalan American). When more specific appellatives are available, they are included: Chicano/a for Mexican Americans with an activist bent; Nuyorican for Latino authors, usually Puerto Rican or Dominican, from New York City; Tejano for Latino authors, usually Mexican American, from Texas; Californiano/a for Latino authors from California; and New Mexican for Latino authors from New Mexico. A Marielito is someone who came to the United States in the Mariel boatlift from Cuba in 1980.

In each entry, the English title of the work is followed by the Spanish title in parentheses (if the book was published in Spanish), with that publication date. When known, the translator's name is provided. Some authors, for example Ariel Dorfman, translate their own books. Usually we have annotated the original edition; if a newer edition was annotated, the original publication date is noted in parentheses.

Entries for award-winning titles or authors are identified by an award icon 🏆 in front of the name or title, and the awards are listed at the end of the entry.

The title and bibliographic information are followed by a short annotation and a sample quotation from the book, to give readers a glimpse of the author's writing style. Where applicable, key features that might interest potential readers are identified (especially strong language, violence, sexual situations, and unique narrative characteristics).

The subject lists for the entries developed naturally. After examining the keywords applied by our various contributors, we developed a controlled vocabulary and standardized the keywords or subject headings applied to each title.

Also included are recommendations for similar titles, usually from within the genre. Remember that you can also access titles with the same subject by using the subject index.

How to Use This Book

When working with readers, remember that every reader is unique. Don't expect that Latinos will be the only ones interested in these titles. On the contrary! Make use of these titles all year-round; don't save them for Hispanic Heritage month. Any month is a good time for a display on "Latino Detective Mysteries" or "Latino Romance." Remember to include Latino titles in other genre displays and lists. Great reads like these are great in any season.

Because titles in this guide are organized by genre, subgenre, and theme, the best way for a readers' advisor to identify "read-alikes" for a specific title is to look for that title in the author/title index, and then check to see which titles and authors are near that entry in the index. If the book in question is not included here, try to find out its genre or subgenre, and then consult the appropriate chapter or section. As mentioned, for most titles annotated, we list "related reads" (under the label "Similar titles"). Finally, you might check the list of subjects for the title and then consult the index for other titles on that subject.

As a collection development tool, this book provides a source to check for titles in areas where your collection may have gaps. For example, are you lacking in Latino mysteries? Is your general fiction collection weak on Latino authors? What about the science fiction collection? With this guide, the collection development specialist can quickly identify authors and titles to fit specific niches in the collection.

A Word about Terminology

Throughout this book, we have used Spanish words and terms somewhat liberally to convey the flavor of particular titles. Although such expressions as *compadre* are known to most people, and the English translation is often included parenthetically after the Spanish words, this is not always the case. Sometimes the English meaning can be gleaned from the context of the annotation. Readers who do not fully understand all Spanish words and expressions are advised to consult the glossary for further explanation of Spanish terms.

We have been guided by José Cuello's explanation in using terms *Latino* versus *Hispanic* and other ethnic identity terminology:

> Usage depends on individual choice. While one Mexican-American may reject all other labels, another may also call himself a Chicano, Latino, and a Hispanic at various times or even simultaneously without feeling any conflict although each one of these terms has a political charge to it. (2008)

For purposes of full disclosure, I identify myself as a Latina and a Chicana, but often suffer the term *Hispanic* in deference to what the dominant Latino (OK, Hispanic) community in Tulsa prefers.

In Conclusion

With this volume, we hope to extend reading pleasure to as many people as possible by making connections across cultural divides to bring new authors to those who may not have previously considered them. We hope that people who like to read will find books in the Latino cultural experience presented here that they will thoroughly enjoy.

Literature by Latinos is complicated. But it is also exciting and fun. So hang on to your *sombreros* and jump in!

References

Alvarez, Julia. 2007. *Once Upon a Quinceañera. Coming of Age in the USA.* New York: Viking.

Arellano, Gustavo. 2007. *Ask a Mexican.* New York: Scribner.

Association of American Publishers (AAP) 2008. Publishing Latino Voices for America Task Force Web site, at www.publishers.org/main/Latino/attachments/Hispanic_data.doc (accessed June 22, 2008).

Augenbraum, Harold, and Ilan Stavans, eds. 2006. *Lengua Fresca. Latinos Writing on the Edge.* New York: Houghton Mifflin.

Chávez Candelaria, Cordelia, Arturo J. Aldama, and Peter J. García, eds. 2004. *Encyclopedia of Latino Popular Culture.* Westport, CT: Greenwood Press.

Colmeiro, José F. 2001. "The Hispanic (Dis)Connection: Some Leads and a Few Missing Links." *Journal of Popular Culture* 34, no. 4 (spring): 49. Available at http://search.ebscohost.com/login.aspx?direct=true&db=afh&AN=6105157&site=ehost-live (accessed October 26, 2007).

Cuello, José. 2008. *Latinos and Hispanics: A Primer on Terminology.* REFORMA Gold Library Resources. Available at www.reforma.org/refogold.htm#cuello (accessed June 29, 2008).

Flores, Edward, and Harry Pachon (Tomás Rivera Policy Institute). 2008. *Latinos and Public Library Perceptions.* Dublin, OH: OCLC Online Computer Library Center.

Kanellos, Nicolás. 2003. *Hispanic Literature of the United States: A Comprehensive Reference.* Westport, CT: Greenwood Press.

Kevane, Bridget A. 2003. *Latino Literature in America.* Westport, CT: Greenwood Press.

Martin-Rodriguez, Manuel M. 2003. *Life in Search of Readers: Reading (in) Chicano/a Literature.* Albuquerque: University of New Mexico Press.

Ortiz, Fernando. 1983. *Contrapunteo del tabaco y el azúcar.* Havana, Cuba: Editorial de Ciencias Sociales.

Schroeder, Patricia Scott. 2008. *Latino Voices 2008–2009.* New York: Association of American Publishers.

Solé, Carlos A., ed. 1989. *Latin American Writers.* New York: Scribner.

———. 2002. *Latin American Writers. Supplement 1.* New York: Scribner.

Stavans, Ilan, ed. 2005. *Encyclopedia Latina: History, Culture and Society in the United States.* Danbury, CT: Scholastic Library Publishing.

Valenzuela, Eduardo A. 1997. "No se habla Español in Outer Space." *Hispanic* 10, no. 4 (April). Available at http://search.ebscohost.com/login.aspx?direct= true&db=afh&AN=9705061317&site=ehost-live (accessed June 22, 2008).

West-Duran, Alan, ed. 2004. *Latino and Latina Writers*. New York: Scribner.

Chapter 1

General Fiction

La crema y la nata

Introduction

Many Latino fiction titles fall into the category "general fiction." They do not fit easily into any specific genre, but do share certain elements: a desire for stylistic innovation and excellence; an effort to push, and often cross, the boundaries of genre and language; and an exploration of the Latino experience—not necessarily in a realistic manner. We have assigned those titles to this chapter.

Alternatively, these titles often share genre elements—such as a historical background, a romantic relationship, or the use of magic—and could be assigned to a specific genre, but that would miss the point of their main appeal, which lies in that stylistic dexterity, manipulation of language, and playfulness with the time and space continuum.

We've included immigrant stories in this section—individuals, families, and their surrounding communities participate in the transculturation process; generational conflict is usually present here. Humorous novels can be found here also—the *pícaro* lives by his or her wits, and outright nonsense reigns. Other novels tinged with black humor cast a cynical eye at ugly reality.

Some books often classified as "general fiction" are not covered in this chapter. Not included here are titles classified as "magic realism," a strong force in Latino literary history. Instead, these are grouped with other speculative fiction titles (science fiction, fantasy, and paranormal) in Chapter 6, albeit in a separate section.

Also not included here are historical fiction titles in which the historical setting serves as a focal point or plays a prominent role, even if the writing can be considered "literary." Those titles are in Chapter 2.

Finally, novels telling the stories of female protagonists from a woman's perspective, for a largely female reading audience, are in Chapter 3.

Appeal

Titles in this chapter appeal to readers who enjoy a challenge, because these authors love to experiment. Those who like to view the world from new and different perspectives also feel welcome here.

Organization

The chapter is divided into three sections, beginning with "Classics" and ending with "Anthologies and Collections." The vast majority of titles in this chapter are listed alphabetically by author in the second section, "Contemporary Mainstream Fiction."

Classics

The titles included in this section are true masterpieces, groundbreaking works, and award winners now available in new editions and/or translations. Here you will find benchmark works by such legendary writers as Jorge Amado, Julio Cortázar, and Manuel Puig.

Amado, Jorge (Brazilian).

Gabriela, Clove and Cinnamon. (*Gabriela, cravo e canela*, 1958). **Translated by James L. Taylor and William Grossman. New York: Vintage International, 2006 (1962). ISBN 0307276651. 425pp.**

> Gabriela, a lowly migrant worker from the cacao-growing region of Brazil, is discovered by bar owner Nacib Saad. She becomes his cook and later his wife, an affront to "decent society," and ultimately, an agent of change for this hypocritical, straitlaced community.

> > *In that year of 1925, when the idyll of the mulatto girl Gabriela and Nacib the Arab began, the rains continued long beyond the proper and necessary season.* (5)

> **Key features:** Sexual situations

> **Subjects:** Brazil—Ilheus; love stories

> **Similar titles:** *Eleven Minutes* by Coelho is also set in Brazil and features strong women grappling with love and sex.

Arguedas, José María (Peruvian).

Deep Rivers. (*Los ríos profundos*, 1958). **Translated by Frances Horning Barraclough. Austin: University of Texas Press, 1989 (1978). ISBN 0292715331. 248pp.**

> This is the story of a young boy in Peru growing up between two worlds, two cultures—dominant Spanish and subjugated Indian. Ernesto's father is a country lawyer, who leaves Ernesto to be brought up by the Indian servants until he enters the Catholic boarding school at age fourteen.

I thought the plaza would explode with sound. But the vibrations expanded slowly, at spaced intervals-growing stronger, piercing the elements, transmuting everything into that Cuzco music that opened the doors of memory. (13)

Key features: First person narration; narrative uses Quechua rhythms and syntax; includes introduction by John V. Murra, afterword by Mario Vargas Llosa, and glossary of Quechua and Spanish terms

Subjects: Andean Indians; Peru; Quechua language

Similar titles: Most of Vargas Llosa's novels are set in Peru; *Balún Canán* by Castellanos is another novel set in an indigenous community and told from a child's perspective.

🏃 Asturias, Miguel Angel (Guatemalan).

The President. (*El señor presidente,* 1948). Translated by Frances Partridge. Prospect Heights, IL: Waveland Press, 1997 (1963). ISBN 0881339512. 286pp.

A cruel Latin American dictator is determined to crush all those he suspects support his overthrow. Citizens are brutalized by his methods, suffering psychological and physical ravages.

No one knew where he was, for he occupied several houses in the outskirts of the town; nor how he slept—some said beside the telephone with a whip in his hand; nor when—his friends declared he never slept at all. (10)

Subjects: dictatorships; dreams; repression; torture

Similar titles: *The Color of Summer* by Arenas, *The Hive* by Cela, and *A Place Called Milagro de la Paz* by Argueta are other novels that deal with life under repressive regimes and use a collective point of view.

Awards: Nobel Prize for Literature, 1967

Cortázar, Julio (Argentinian).

Hopscotch. (*Rayuela,* 1963). Translated by Gregory Rabassa. New York: Random House, 1987 (1966). ISBN 0-394-75284-8. 564pp.

Horacio Oliveira, an Argentine expatriate, lives a bohemian existence in Paris. The parallel story tells of Horacio's return to Buenos Aires. The novel is constructed so that it could be read in either of two possible sequences, either straight through or following an alternate chapter order laid out at the front of the book; hence the title.

Would I find La Maga? Most of the time it was just a case of my putting in an appearance, going along the Rue de Seine to the arch leading into the Quai de Conti, and I would see her slender form against the olive-ashen light which floats along the river as she crossed back and forth on the Pont des Arts, or leaned over the iron rail looking at the water. (3)

Key features: nonlinear structure that provides alternate reading options

Subjects: Argentina—Buenos Aires; classics; expatriates—Argentina; France—Paris; love stories

Similar titles: *Palinuro of Mexico* by del Paso, *The Best Thing That Can Happen to a Croissant* by Tusset, and *The Lamentable Journey of Omaha Bigelow* by Vega Yunqué are other novels that follow Cortázar's path by using stream-of-consciousness narration and that experiment with the very structure of the novel; they also feature bohemian protagonists.

de Queirós, Eca (Portuguese).

The Crime of Father Amaro: Scenes from a Religious Life. (*Crime do padre Amaro,* 1876). **Translated by Margaret Jull Costa. New York: New Directions, 2003 (1962). ISBN 0811215326. 471pp.**

With a new translation and a Mexican movie version, this nineteenth-century Portuguese classic takes on new life in the twenty-first century. It tells the story of a young Catholic priest who lets himself be slowly corrupted, losing what slim vocation he had had, and the consequences that follow, especially for the young woman who has become the object of his lust.

> *Canon Dias was said to be rich; he owned rented properties near Leiria, gave turkey suppers and had some fine wine in his cellar. However, the main fact about him—much commented on and gossiped over—was his longstanding friendship with Senhora Augusta Caminha.* (10)

Subjects: Catholic Church; classics; corruption; murder; Portugal; priests—Catholic

Similar titles: Corrupt priests are also at the center of *By Night in Chile* by Bolaño.

The Maias. (*Maias,* 1888). **Translated by Margaret Jull Costa. New York: New Directions, 2007 (1965). ISBN 9780811216494. 628pp.**

This overlooked classic follows the fortunes of the Maia family, members of the decaying elite in Lisbon. Down to the last two males—grandfather Afonso and Carlos—the family struggles to carry on. Carlos becomes a doctor and indulges in the pastimes of the aristocracy, until he falls in love with a woman who threatens to bring scandal and downfall to the family

> *[T]here was the legend, according to which the walls of Ramalhete had always proved fatal to the Maias, although, as he himself admitted sagely, he felt somewhat ashamed even to mention such superstitious nonsense in the age of Voltaire, Guizot, and other liberal-minded philosophers.* (3)

Subjects: aristocracy; love affairs; Portugal—Lisbon

Similar titles: *A World for Julius* by Bryce Echenique also features the decadent aristocracy; Antunes's novels explore Portuguese history and society in the twentieth century.

del Paso, Fernando (Mexican).

Palinuro of Mexico. (*Palinuro de México,* 1977). **Translated by Elizabeth Plaister. Normal, IL: Dalkey Archive Press, 1989.**

This is the story of Palinuro, Estefania, and Walter, who are cousins and/or lovers and/or friends. A Joycean novel about everything and nothing, the novel features language and the telling of stories in which everything, including the kitchen sink, or a beloved mirror, takes on personality and substance. The study of medicine forms a narrative thread through the novel, as does the process of growing up and attending university in Mexico. Each chapter is structured differently—using different styles and different narrators, thus keeping readers on their toes.

In effect, Uncle Esteban, who had long white hands which could trace master operations in the air and, with two arabesques link the iliac artery of John Abernethy, the English surgeon who a hundred years previously had invented this very operation to the awe of posterity; this Uncle Esteban, as we were saying, had also dreamed of one day becoming a doctor. (3)

Key features: Stream of consciousness; multiple perspectives; nonlinear, heterogeneous structure

Subjects: families; love stories; medical school; Mexico

Similar titles: *Rayuela* by Cortázar and *A World for Julius* by Bryce Echenique are other experimental novels told from multiple perspectives.

Lezama Lima, José (Cuban).

Paradiso: A Novel. (Paradiso, **1968). Translated by Gregory Rabassa. Normal, IL: Dalkey Archive Press, 2000 (1974). ISBN 156478228X. 466pp.**

Asthmatic José Cemi grows up in a bourgeois family in the Cuba of the first half of the twentieth century. As he develops his worldview as a writer and artist, he discusses existential questions about the nature of love, sexuality, and art with family and friends.

Her old age was like another form of youth, more penetrating in its transparency, its lightness. She would jump from dreams into daily life without establishing differences, as if moving off by herself, walking on the waters. (22)

Subjects: classics; coming-of-age; Cuba; families

Similar titles: *A World for Julius* by Bryce Echenique is another novel told from a child's perspective about an aristocratic family and society; *Palinuro of Mexico* by del Paso is a similarly existential, coming-of-age tale told in a stream-of-consciousness style.

Puig, Manuel (Argentinian).

Kiss of the Spider Woman. (El beso de la mujer araña, **1976). Translated by Thomas Colchie. New York: Vintage International, 1980 (1978). ISBN 0-679-72449-4. 281pp.**

Molina, a homosexual who loves the movies, and Valentin, a revolutionary idealist, share a jail cell in the oppressive Argentina of the 1970s. Their friendship/relationship develops as they pass the time by Molina describing old movie plots.

Her stockings glitter, that kind they turned inside out when the sheen went out of style, her legs look flushed and silky, you can't tell if it's the stockings or her skin.

Look, remember what I told you, no erotic descriptions. This isn't the place for it. (4)

Subjects: Argentina; classics; homosexuals; men's friendships; prison; rebellion

Similar titles: *The Movies of My Life* by Fuguet also uses movies as a plot device; *The Inhabited Woman* by Belli features revolutionary struggles; and *The Way of the*

Jaguar by Stork and *González and Daughter Trucking Company* by Escandón are also prison narratives.

Rivera, Tomás (Mexican American).

🐾 *. . . and the Earth Did Not Devour Him.* (*. . . y no se lo tragó la tierra,* 1971). Translated by Evangelina Vigil-Piñón. Houston, TX: Arte Público Press, 1995 (1987). ISBN 155885083X . 152pp.

In fourteen poetic vignettes, this novel is narrated from the point of view of an anonymous son of migrant farmworkers.

> *At times he tried to remember and, just about when he thought everything was clearing up some, he would be at a loss for words. It always began with a dream in which he would suddenly awaken and then realize that he was really asleep.* (83)

Key features: Stream-of-consciousness and some first person narration; bilingual format

Subjects: Chicanos; migrant farmworkers

Similar titles: Other novels narrated from a child's point of view include *Deep Rivers* by Arguedas and *Balún Canán* by Castellanos; other books that explore the plight of migrant farmworkers include *Crossing Vines* by Rigoberto González, *The Circuit* by Jiménez, and *Barefoot Heart: Stories of a Migrant Child* by Elva Treviño Hart.

Awards: Quinto Sol Prize, 1970

Contemporary Mainstream Fiction

A broad sampling of Latino literary works currently being published comprises this section. As mentioned previously, some contain genre elements, such as magic or a historical setting, but this is not the focus of the stories.

Alarcón, Daniel (Peruvian American).

Lost City Radio. (*Radio Ciudad Perdida,* 2007). Translated by Jorge Cornejo. New York: HarperCollins, 2007. ISBN 9780060594794. 257pp.

Norma is a radio announcer who reads, on the air, the names of people gone missing during the civil war in an unnamed Latin American country in the not-too-distant future. All the towns and *pueblos'* traditional names have been replaced with numbers. Norma is shaken out of her comfortable, if lonely, routine by the arrival of a boy from the jungle bringing a list of missing people from his village—including one of the aliases used by her own missing husband.

> *For local news, she relied on the station's policy, which was also the government's policy: to read good news with indifference and make bad news sound hopeful. No one was more skilled than Norma; in her vocal caresses, unemployment figures read like bittersweet laments, declarations of war like love letters.* (8–9)

Key features: First person; multiple perspectives

Subjects: censorship; *desaparecidos;* dystopias; loneliness; missing persons; radio hosts; repression; war; widows

Similar titles: *When the Ground Turns in Its Sleep* by Sellers-García is another book that looks at a society after the trauma of violent, dehumanizing conflict along with an obsession with names, ancestors, and finding links of blood or humanity; Saramago's *The Cave* presents a similar futuristic and dystopian tone.

Arenas, Reinaldo (Cuban Marielito).

The Color of Summer or the New Garden of Earthly Delights. (El color de verano, 1991). **Translated by Andrew Hurley. New York: Viking, 2000. ISBN 0-670-84065-3. 417pp.**

After fifty years, life on this fictional island is as absurd as the carnival held to commemorate those years lived under the dictator Fifo, in this parody of Cuba under Castro.

> *[H]e orders the people of Cuba to stage an act of repudiation against the poetess, while secretly ordering his trained sharks and diligent midgets to do everything in their power to block her flight. The act of repudiation begins with the appearance of a group of eminent poets who are still on the Island, some of whom have been brought back to life especially for this event.* (5)

Subjects: Cuba; dictatorships—Castro; homosexuality; humor

Similar titles: *Palinuro of Mexico* by del Paso and *The Return of the Caravels* by Antunes are other novels that play with time and structure under absurd premises.

Argueta, Manlio (Salvadoran).

🎖 *Little Red Riding Hood in the Red Light District. (Caperucita en la zona roja,* 1977). **Translated by Edward Waters Hood. Willimantic, CT: Curbstone Press, 1998. ISBN 1-880684-32-2. 237pp.**

Alfonso, student, poet, and erstwhile revolutionary, and Ant, his *campesina* lover, struggle for survival during the repressive, brutal period of El Salvador's civil war, told through the allegory of the fairy tale.

> *It is a sudden decision. It's inexplicable that I would abandon this hole in the wall after spending so much time here, surrounded by small objects, a book, a night stand, discarded ball point pens, old shoes.* (3)

Subjects: allegory; El Salvador; fairy tales; love stories; revolutionary struggles

Similar titles: *My Tender Matador* by Lemebel, *Swallowing Stones* by St. Aubin de Terán, and *The Farming of Bones* by Danticat are novels that also bring home the brutality of life under repressive regimes. *Bitter Grounds* by Benitez also takes place during El Salvador's civil war.

Awards: Winner, Casa de las Americas, 1977

Arriaga, Guillermo (Mexican).

The Night Buffalo: A Novel. (Búfalo de la noche, 2006). **Translated by Alan Page. New York: Atria Books, 2006. ISBN 9780743281850. 228pp.**

When his best friend, Gregorio, commits suicide, Manuel is haunted by guilt (and possibly by Gregorio). A sinister Mexico City is the backdrop for the dark triangle among Manuel, Gregorio, and Tania, a situation tainted by mental illness and betrayal.

> *We needed to get a sense of the territory again. Especially me: I didn't want to walk back to the edge of the abyss. Out of luck, respect, or maybe just mere courtesy, he didn't ask me about Tania, even though I'm sure we both thought of her in each of our silences.* (2)

Key features: First person narration

Subjects: madness; Mexico—Mexico City; romantic triangles; suicide

Similar titles: *Any Wednesday I'm Yours* by Santos-Febres and *Sultry Moon* by Giardinelli are other novels that explore the dark side of the human psyche that comes out when the sun goes down.

Bolaño, Roberto (Chilean).

2666. (*2666*, 2004). Translated by Natasha Wimmer. New York: Farrar, Straus & Giroux, 2008. ISBN 9780374100148. 898pp.

Bolaño intended that this work be published in five separate installments. The interweaving plotlines converge in Santa Teresa, aka Ciudad Juarez, in Mexico. The major plotlines follow certain professors on the trail of the German novelist Archimboldi, an African American reporter from the States who is investigating a boxing match but is sidetracked by *las muertas de Juárez* (the murdered women of Juarez), and a police detective looking into the serial murders of these women.

> *Then Pelletier could think back on the day when he first read Archimboldi, and he saw himself, young and poor, living in a* chamber de bonne, *sharing the sink where he washed his face and brushed his teeth with fifteen other people who lived in the same dark garret, shitting in a horrible and notably unhygienic bathroom that was more like a latrine or cesspit, also shared with the fifteen residents of the garret, some of whom had already returned to the provinces, their respective university degrees in hand or had moved to slightly more comfortable places in Paris itself, or were still there-just a few of them-vegetating or slowly dying of revulsion.* (4)

Key features: Stream-of-consciousness and avant-garde style; violence

Subjects: college professors; factories; *maquiladoras*; police detectives; reporters; students; U.S.–Mexico border; violence against women; writers—fiction

Similar titles: Another author who broaches the difficult subject of the Juarez murders is Gaspar de Alba, in *Desert Blood*.

The Savage Detectives. (*Los detectives salvajes*, 1998). Translated by Natasha Wimmer. New York: Farrar, Straus & Giroux, 2007. ISBN 9780374191481. 577pp.

Juan García Madero is a student in Mexico City during the 1970s who fancies himself a poet, especially once he is inducted into the "Visceral Realists" group. Once he is vetted, he becomes *compinches* (or *cohorts*) with Arturo Belano and Ulises Lima. The three embark on a search for the missing poetess and founder of their movement, Cesárea Tinajero, which leads them to the Sonoran Desert. On the way, we follow Belano and Lima on their world travels as they *taquean* (make fun of) Latin America's great *literatos* and sacred cows.

> *It was all very simple. Belano shook my hand and told me that I was one of them now, and then we sang a ranchera. That was all. The song was about the lost towns of the north and a woman's eyes. Before I went outside to throw up, I asked*

them whether the eyes were Cesárea Tinajero's. Belano and Lima looked at me and said that I was clearly a visceral realist already and that together we would change Latin American poetry. (7)

Key features: Multiple first person narrators

Subjects: humor; literary movements; Mexico—Mexico City; Mexico—Sonoran Desert; poetry; road trips

Similar titles: *Palinuro of Mexico* by del Paso also deals with complex subjects in a playful way.

Bonilla, Juan (Spanish).

The Nubian Prince. **(*Los príncipes nubios*, 2003). Translated by Esther Allen. New York: Metropolitan Books, 2006. ISBN 0805077812. 258pp.**

Spanish *pícaro* Moises tells readers about his job "rescuing" beautiful men, women, and children from marginal, poverty-stricken circumstances to work in the international sex trade. He and a former protégé/lover race against each other to see who can bring in a famously endowed fighter called The Nubian Prince. Will Moises ever confront the not-so-beautiful reality of his situation?

My job was to seek beauty, to plunge my hands into the world's muck and bring up pearls. I cleaned those pearls, made them presentable, prepared them to acquire the value that was rightfully theirs. I traveled to places where poverty had hidden these treasures; I searched them out with infinite patience and rescued them. That's what I mean by saving lives. (4)

Key features: First person narration; sexual situations

Subjects: black humor; ethics; immigrants; prostitution; refugees; sex trade

Similar titles: *El Indio Jesús* by Chávez Ballejos is another novel in which the protagonist must live by his wits.

Braschi, Giannina (Nuyorican).

Yo-Yo Boing! **Pittsburgh, PA: Latin American Literary Review Press, 1998. ISBN 0935480978. 205pp.**

Lively conversations and monologues by a Puerto Rican writer living in New York City comprise this book. Many of the conversations take place at home with her lover, who is also her literary rival; others take place at parties and gallery openings. Some are philosophical and weighty; others, scatological and silly. The dialogues are written in Spanglish, taking the reader back and forth from English to Spanish and everywhere in between.

"¡Y si estoy leyendo, why do I have to get up para hacerte el gran favor de abrirte la puerta. Do I look like a doorman. Besides, you have the keys and they fit, they sure do. You just have to learn how to handle them." (36)

Key features: First (and second) person; stream of consciousness; sexual situations

Subjects: New York—New York City; Puerto Ricans; writers—fiction

Similar titles: Other works that experiment with language and tackle the constant challenge that is communication between people are *Budapest* by Buarque, *Lengua*

fresca edited by Augenbraum, and *Loosing My Espanish* by Carrillo; the last two titles also use Spanglish.

Buarque, Chico (Brazilian).

Budapest. (Budapeste, 2003). **Translated by Alison Entrekin. New York: Grove Press, 2004. ISBN 0-8021-1782-1. 183pp.**

A successful Brazilian ghost writer, master at learning languages and married to a movie star, drops everything to travel to Budapest and learn Hungarian. This novel examines this man's existence (or not?) as ghost and writer, between languages and between lover and wife.

> *It should be against the law to mock someone who tries his luck in a foreign language. One morning, when I accidentally left the metro at a blue station exactly like hers, with a name similar to that of the station near her place, I called from a phone booth and said: There I am arriving almost. I instantly suspected I'd made a blunder, because my teacher asked me to repeat the sentence.* (1)

Subjects: Brazil; ghost writers; Hungarian language; Hungary—Budapest; languages

Similar titles: *The Movies of My Life* by Fuguet also features a stranger in a strange land; *Yo-Yo Boing!* by Braschi also tackles the constant challenge of communication between people.

Castellanos Moya, Horacio (Salvadoran).

🏵 *Senselessness. (Insensatez,* **2004). Translated by Katherine Silver. New York: New Directions, 2008. ISBN 9780811217071. 142pp.**

The alcoholic narrator takes on the onerous and potentially lethal task of editing a report for the Catholic Church about atrocities committed in the previous decade by the military and generals who continue in power in an unnamed Central American country.

> *[E]njoying the brilliant morning among these hundreds of Indians decked out in their Sunday dress of so many festive colors, among the most salient being that joyous cheerful red, as if red had nothing to do with blood and sorrow but was rather the emblem of happiness for the hundreds of domestic servants enjoying their day off in the large square.* (67–68)

Key features: First person, stream-of-consciousness narration

Subjects: alcoholics; atrocities; Catholic Church; Central America; writers—fiction

Similar titles: *The Art of Political Murder* by Goldman also deals with the Catholic Church, the military, reports on human rights abuses, Central America, and atrocities; this novel also brings to mind the classic *Under the Volcano* by Lowry, which is also narrated by an alcoholic.

Awards: PEN Translation Fund award, 2007, to Katherine Silver

Castillo, Ana (New Mexican).

The Guardians: A Novel. **New York: Random House, 2007. ISBN 9781400065004. 211pp.**

Regina, a handsome *cincuentona* widow of over fifty, keeps busy raising her mystical and solitary high school aged nephew, Gabo, after his mother dies. Regina receives a suspicious phone call about her brother, who disappeared while crossing back and forth over the border into Mexico. She enlists Miguel, Gabo's sympathetic teacher, to help her look into what could be a dangerous situation.

> *I do not know what Rafa is talking about his son becoming a gringo. These lands, this unmerciful desert—it belonged to us first, the Mexicans. Before that it belonged to los Apaches. Los Apaches were mean, too. They knew how to defend themselves. And they're still not too happy about losing everything, despite the casinos up by their land.* (5)

Key features: Multiple first person narration—Regina, Gabo, Miguel, and Abuelo Milton

Subjects: Mexican Americans; stigmata; teachers; undocumented immigrants; U.S.–Mexico border; widows

Similar titles: *The Journal of Antonio Montoya* by Collignon also features a single woman raising teenagers in New Mexico; the <u>Texana Jones Series</u> by Allana Martin also takes place in the U.S.–Mexico border region.

Cercas, Javier (Spanish).

The Speed of Light. **(***La velocidad de la luz,* **2005). Translated by Anne MacLean. New York: Bloomsbury, 2006. ISBN 1596912146. 278pp.**

The Spanish writer/protagonist loses his focus after the success of his first novel. He seeks to reconnect with a Vietnam vet named Rodney, who was a teaching assistant, friend, and mentor in the Midwestern United States when they were both at university. But Rodney is missing, and suddenly it becomes vital for the narrator to find out what happened to him in order to recover his own lost vision.

> *Now I lead a false life, an apocryphal, clandestine, invisible life, though truer than if it were real, but I was still me when I met Rodney Falk.* (3)

Key features: First person narration

Subjects: college professors; friendship; Illinois; Spain—Barcelona; veterans—Vietnam War; writers—fiction; writing

Similar titles: *No Matter How Much You Promise to Cook or Pay the Rent . . .* by Vega Yunqué and *Gods Go Begging* by Véa are other novels that feature Latino veterans of the Vietnam War.

Chávez Ballejos, Gilberto (Mexican American), and Shirley Hill Witt.

El Indio Jesús. **Norman: University of Oklahoma Press, 2000. ISBN 0-8061-3230-2. 257pp.**

El Indio Jesús is a multitalented man from Albuquerque who uses his gifted friends to help the needy and thwart an unfeeling system. Jesús provides the common thread that weaves his quirky friends' stories together, stories that play out along the U.S.–Mexico border.

> *As sure as farts follow* frijoles, *El Indio Jesús found himself in the custody of the police at fairly predictable intervals. There was always that phase of his life cycle.* (9)

Subjects: Chicanos; humor; New Mexico; undocumented workers; U.S.–Mexico border

Similar titles: *The Lamentable Journey of Omaha Bigelow* by Vega Yunqué and *The Adventures of Don Chipote* by Venegas are other humorous novels featuring a peripatetic antihero.

Coelho, Paulo (Brazilian).

Eleven Minutes. (*Onze minutos*, 2003). **Translated by Margaret Jull Costa. New York: HarperCollins, 2004. ISBN 0-06-058927-2 (cloth); 0-06-058928-0 (pbk.). 273pp.**

Maria, a young girl from a small town in Brazil, has become disillusioned with love and sex. She embarks on the profession of prostitute, ending up in Switzerland, where she meets Ralf, an artist who has also given up on love. Maria's story is told in the third person, alternating with diary entries that document her journey of self-discovery and ponderings on sex, love, and their ultimately sacred nature.

> *It began to seem to Maria that the world was too large, that love was something very dangerous and that the Virgin was a saint who inhabited a distant heaven and didn't listen to the prayers of children.* (5)

Key features: Sexual situations; some epistolary style narration; edition contains bonus material

Subjects: artists; Brazil; love stories; prostitutes; Switzerland—Geneva

Similar titles: *Gabriela, Clove and Cinnamon* by Amado is another novel set in Brazil about strong women, love, and sex.

The Zahir: A Novel of Obsession. (*O Zahir*, 2005). **Translated by Margaret Jull Costa. New York: HarperCollins, 2005. ISBN-10: 0-06-08251-9; ISBN-13: 978-0-06-08251-9. 298pp.**

This fable about obsession and the nature of love, faith, and self-knowledge takes the reader from Paris to Kazakhstan while the narrator, a famous journalist, searches for his missing wife, aided by her translator, who also may have been her lover.

> *He is married himself and although he doesn't like my books (So he isn't as ignorant as he looks! He knows who I am!), he can put himself in my shoes and imagine what I must be going through.* (6)

Subjects: France—Paris; journalists; Kazahkstan; love stories; men and women

Similar titles: The <u>Regalo Grande Series</u> by Arana also explores the relationship between Christian faith and love.

Cordova, G. (New Mexican).

Big Dreams and Dark Secrets in Chimayó: A Novel. **Albuquerque: University of New Mexico Press, 2006. ISBN 082634075X. 307pp.**

Flaco Salvador Cascabel Natividad is the quintessential alcoholic macho of Chimayó, New Mexico. While pinned down by a tree in a freak accident, Flaco relives his life and the absurd choices he has made and actions he has taken; at the same time, he looks forward to his funeral, burial, and a possible afterlife.

Christmas became like drinking Mexican mescal without the worm: uncultured and tasteless. But he was a Chimayoso-creative, resourceful, and chingón, *a small genius, at that, but nevertheless a small genius is still a genius.* (21)

Subjects: alcoholics; New Mexico—Chimayó

Similar titles: The <u>Guadalupe Trilogy</u> by Collignon is also set in rural New Mexico and touches upon macho culture, especially *A Santo in the Image of Cristobal García*, which features end-of-life musings, as does *The Death of Artemio Cruz* by Carlos Fuentes.

Cortázar, Julio (Argentinian).

Final Exam. (Examen, **1986). Translated by Alfred MacAdam. New York: New Directions, 1999 (1985). ISBN 0811214176. 237pp.**

The night before taking the final exams that signify the end of their university career, Juan and Clara walk the streets of a surreal Buenos Aires that is wrapped in mysterious fog. During their trek they encounter strange happenings and people being shadowed by a ghostly figure, who may be a former lover of Clara's.

Completely distracted, incapable of focusing on Eglantine (she intended to read it on her own, as she did so many books she never ended up reading), she again stared at Andrés back, at Stella's hair, at the Reader's indifferent face. She was surprised to find herself using her fingers to explore the contents of the package, moving along like an insect over the cold, wrinkled surface of the cauliflower. (13)

Key features: Stream-of-consciousness narrative style

Subjects: Argentina—Buenos Aires; college students

Similar titles: *Any Wednesday I'm Yours* by Santos-Febres and *Night Buffalo* by Arriaga are other novels with nocturnal settings and a dark tone.

Danticat, Edwidge (Haitian American).

🏵 *The Dew Breaker.* **New York: Knopf; 2004. ISBN 1-4000-4114-7.244pp.**

Each chapter presents a different perspective from victims, family members, and lovers of the "dew breaker." This man was a torturer (*tonton macoute*) in Haiti and fled to New York after the fall of the Duvalier regime, bringing the torturous history of the Caribbean with him to the United States.

He scratches his chin and the scar on the side of his face, but says nothing. In this light the usually chiseled and embossed-looking scar appears deeper than usual, yet somehow less threatening, like a dimple that's spread out too far. (16)

Subjects: immigrants—Haitian; love stories; New York—New York City—Brooklyn; torture

Similar titles: *In the Palm of Darkness* by Montero also deals with the *tontons macoutes* in Haiti; *Tango for a Torturer* by Chavarría also features a torturer hiding out. *By Night in Chile* by Bolaño and *The Inquisitors' Manual* by Antunes are novels whose protagonists are at the end of their lives and had collaborated with dictatorships as younger men.

Awards: Booklist Editor's Choice Best Fiction, 2004

de Azevedo, Kathleen (Brazilian).

Samba Dreamers. **Tucson: University of Arizona Press, 2006. ISBN 0-8165-2490-7; ISBN-13: 978-0-8165-2490-7. 304pp.**

Two Brazilians in Los Angeles, Rosea Socorro Katz and Joe Silva, struggle to survive in the States while longing for Brazil.

> *Joe struggled to make his way through airport, clawing through the raw and vivid memories that always blended into his present sadness, as they did now, when the memory of Sonia turned into a craving for* biscoito de polvilho, *which he knew he would never taste again.* (2–3)

Key features: Glossary

Subjects: Brazil; Brazilian Americans; California—Los Angeles; expatriates—U.S.; immigrants—Brazilian

Similar titles: Other novels that feature immigrants struggling in big cities are *Paradise Travel* by Franco and *Let It Rain Coffee* by Cruz.

Díaz, Junot (Dominican American).

🎗 *The Brief Wondrous Life of Oscar Wao.* **(*La breve y maravillosa vida de Oscar Wao,* 2008). Translated by Achy Obejas. New York: Riverhead Books, 2007. ISBN 9781594489587. 340pp.**

Oscar de León, aka Oscar Wao, wrestles with the family curse or *fukú* that came from the terrible times in the Dominican Republic during the Trujillato, which catches up with him in New Jersey as a nerdy teen. Oscar's friend Yunior—his sister's on-again, off-again *novio*—narrates with a chatty style and an urban, *cholo* voice that's firmly embedded in Latino Spanglish usage.

> *For Oscar, high school was the equivalent of a medieval spectacle, like being put in the stocks and forced to endure the peltings and outrages of a mob of deranged half-wits, an experience from which he supposed he should have emerged a better person, but that's not really what happened-and if there were any lessons to be gleaned from the ordeal of those years he never quite figured out what they were.* (19)

Key features: First person narration

Subjects: dictatorships—Trujillo; Dominican Republic; families; New Jersey—Paterson

Similar titles: *Caramelo* by Cisneros has a similar chatty tone and also uses footnotes full of cultural factoids; *In the Time of the Butterflies* by Julia Alvarez and *The Farming of Bones* by Danticat also portray Haiti and the Dominican Republic under the dictator Trujillo.

Awards: 2008 Pulitzer Prize for Fiction; National Book Critics Circle Award; Anisfield-Wolf Book Award; Dayton Literary Peace Prize

Donoso, José (Chilean).

The Obscene Bird of Night. **(*El obsceno pájaro de la noche,* 1970). Translated by Hardie St. Martin and Leonard Mades. Boston: David R. Godine, 1995 (1970). ISBN 1567920462. 438pp.**

The narrator, Humberto Peñaloza, is a mute who takes on many different personas —from deformed baby fetus to dog to repressed nun. He tells the story of wealthy politician Don Jerónimo de Azcoitía. Azcoitía is determined to carry on the family name and goes to grotesque extremes to achieve this purpose. His heir is a deformed, unnatural freak, so Azcoitía creates an artificial world for him, surrounding him with other freaks.

> *He probably wouldn't recognize me, changed as I am into Iris's dog, stripped of everything of the Humberto I used to be, except the still-active principle of my eyes. I'm just another old woman, Don Jerónimo, I'm Iris's dog, let me rest, don't harass me, I've already served you.* (62)

Key features: First person narration

Subjects: families; freaks; nuns; South America

Similar titles: *Palinuro of Mexico* by del Paso is narrated from a similarly convoluted point of view; *One Hundred Years of Solitude* by García Márquez and *A World for Julius* by Bryce Echenique also feature aristocratic families in decay.

Dorfman, Ariel (Chilean).

The Nanny and the Iceberg. (*La nana y el iceberg,* 2000). **New York: Farrar, Straus & Giroux, 1999. ISBN 0374218986. 357pp.**

Gabriel McKenzie travels to Chile to reconnect with his reprobate father in an effort to learn his secrets to a successful love life. As the son of a notorious Don Juan, Gabriel is ashamed of being a virgin. Meanwhile, Gabriel's nanny—the last surviving member of a Patagonian Indian tribe—and the ghost of Ché Guevara help him protect the iceberg cut out of Antarctica to be towed to Spain for the World's Fair, commemorating the five hundredth anniversary of Columbus's voyage.

> *Except that what had just happened to Cristóbal McKenzie was written all over him, every pore in his body was singing the royal flush of consummation, the fuck happiness of a young man who has just learned on his first night of love that the best way to discover your own body is by exploring someone else's.* (29)

Key features: First person narration (in the form of a suicide note); sexual situations

Subjects: Chile; Guevara; Ernesto "Che"; humor; sex; virgins

Similar titles: *The Color of Summer* by Arenas features another absurd commemoration.

Duarte, Stella Pope (Mexican American).

Let Their Spirits Dance. **New York: Rayo, 2002. ISBN 0060186372. 312pp.**

A dysfunctional Chicano family makes a road trip from Phoenix to Washington, D.C., at the mother's behest. Alicia feels compelled by the voice of her dead son to touch his name on the Vietnam Veterans Memorial Wall.

> *Still, in 1968, truth was suspended in midair, and the passion vine forced blooms into the cold, gray days of November. Each blossom lived one day. All that beauty for just one day.* (1)

Subjects: families; road trips; Vietnam Veterans Memorial Wall

Similar titles: *Caramelo* by Cisneros also features road trips and Chicano families; *No Matter How Much You Promise to Cook or Pay the Rent . . .* by Vega Yunqué explores the

Vietnam War and its toll on families; *Esperanza's Box of Saints* by Escandón presents another mother on a quest thanks to her deceased offspring.

Espinoza, Alex (Mexican American).

Still Water Saints. (*Los santos de Agua Mansa, California,* 2007). **Translated by Liliana Valenzuela. New York: Random House, 2007. ISBN 9781400065394. 242pp.**

A twenty-first-century Chicana *curandera*, Perla Portillo, runs the Botánica Oshún in this small town near Los Angeles. During her daily routine she encounters, counsels, and supplies her customers with remedies of all types, some of them magical. Some of the more striking stories feature overweight Clara, undocumented teenager Juan—who is working as a male prostitute—and transgendered Azucar. Eventually, Perla must confront her own choices in life and her future possibilities in an uncertain world.

> *She imagined the* botánica's *counters and walls as outstretched arms, beaded with amulets and ankhs and silver medallions, those arms then becoming her own, gathering her customers in. She thought about wisdom that stretched on and on, beyond the sky, beyond that and into death.* (11)

Key features: First and third person narration

Subjects: *botánicas*; California; *curanderas*; *pueblos*

Similar titles: *Doña Flor and Her Two Husbands* by Amado, *Bless Me, Ultima* by Anaya, and *Like Water for Chocolate* by Esquivel also present unconventional women working magical remedies.

Fernández, Roberto G. (Cuban American).

Holy Radishes! **Houston, TX: Arte Público Press, 1995. ISBN 1-55885-075-9. 298pp.**

In this parody of the Cuban Diaspora, snooty Cuban aristocrats must toil as laborers in a Florida radish factory when they immigrate to the United States.

> *The theme music signaled that the show was over for today and that her husband, Nelson, would arrive in an hour. He worked as a stocker for Rosser and Dunlap Trucks and Rigs. It was the first real job he had found after arriving from Xawa; he held on to it, happily stagnant despite having once been the head of his father's vast business empire.* (9)

Subjects: Florida; humor; immigrants—Cuban

Similar titles: *Empress of the Splendid Season* by Hijuelos also portrays a Cuban aristocrat who becomes a working-class immigrant in the United States.

Raining Backwards. **Houston, TX: Arte Público Press, 1997. ISBN 1558852239. 208pp.**

In this absurd novel, Cuban American families in Miami have a hard time becoming accustomed to life in Florida—one lovesick sister is obsessed with becoming a cheerleader for the Miami Dolphins, a brother becomes pope, another brother is a revolutionary, and the mother is a "ditzy plaintain magnate."

> *The sea bivalve was pulled to the center of the stage by her escort. Upon deposit of the sea shell, the trumpets and cymbals echoed through the room, announcing the*

arrival of her Majesty the Queen of the Sea. Connie emerged from her silicon cell in unison with a shower of bubbles that engulfed her splendid silhouette like falling autumn leaves. (29)

Subjects: Cuban Americans; families; Florida—Miami; transculturation

Similar titles: *The Color of Summer* by Arenas also portrays crazy Cubans; *War by Candlelight* by Alarcón and *Shorts* by Fuguet portray similar clashes between cultures.

Franco, Jorge (Colombian).

Paradise Travel. (Paraíso travel, 2001). **Translated by Katherine Silver. New York: Farrar, Straus & Giroux, 2001. ISBN 0-374-22977-5; ISBN-13: 978-0-374-22977-5. 228pp.**

Marlon Cruz tells the story of his trip to New York with his *pareja* Reina—his *compañera*, companion, and common-law wife. He weaves his tale of being lost and separated from her in the big city with the story of his and Reina's life in Medellín, Colombia.

> *But you also have to figure in my anger, and when I went out that night I never imagined I was going to get lost in the world's biggest, most intricate labyrinth, doomed to having as my last memory that angry expression on Reina's face, her yelling at me like my mother used to when I was little: Marlon Cruz, don't you go out!* (4)

Subjects: Colombia—Medellín; immigrants—Colombian; New York—New York City

Similar titles: *Let It Rain Coffee* by Angie Cruz and *Samba Dreamers* by de Azevedo also feature immigrants in the big city.

Fuentes, Carlos (Mexican).

Inez. (Instinto de Inez, 2001). **Translated by Margaret Sayers Peden. New York: Farrar, Straus & Giroux, 2002. ISBN 0-374-17553-5. 150pp.**

Gabriel Atlan-Ferrara, an Italian maestro conductor, and Inez Rozensweig-Prada, a Mexican opera singer, carry on a love affair over many decades beginning in London during World War II. The chapters that follow their affair are interspersed with chapters about the love between the first man and the first woman, *neh-el* and *ah-nel*. These two eternal relationships are linked by a mysterious crystal seal.

> *He wanted to have the crystal seal in his hand so that he could hold it and squeeze it until he destroyed it; hold it the way he wanted to hold her, tighter, tighter, until she choked, communicating a fiery urgency, making her feel that in love—his for her, hers for him, theirs for each other—there was a latent violence, a destructive danger, that was the final homage of passion to beauty. To love Inez, to love her to death.* (15)

Subjects: divas; historical fiction; Italians; love stories; Mexicans; music; orchestra conductors

Similar titles: *The Wake* by Glantz and *Deep Purple* by Montero are novels whose plots also center on music and love. *The Law of Love* by Esquivel also features a pair of eternal lovers.

Fuguet, Alberto (Chilean).

The Movies of My Life. (*Las películas de mi vida*, 2003). Translated by Ezra E. Fitz. New York: Rayo, c2003. ISBN 0060534621. 287pp.

Beltran Soler, a Chilean seismologist who spent his formative years in California, reviews his life through the prism of significant movies. He does this while taking an intermission from life in a Los Angeles hotel during a layover on his way to Tokyo.

> *It's best to arrive in Los Angeles at night. If you get there during the day, it's too easy to see the truth: the city doesn't have angels, dreams, or stars. But if you arrive at night, the idea of sleeping vanishes, no matter how tired you are, and you feel—if only for a moment—privileged. You feel that it's not just by chance that you're here, where movies are born.* (53)

Key features: First person narration; dialogue written in the style of movie scripts

Subjects: California—Los Angeles; Chile; movies; seismologists

Similar titles: *The Matter of Desire* by Paz Soldán also features Latin Americans living in the United States; *Tokyo Doesn't Love Us Anymore* by Lóriga is a similarly experimental novel.

🎬 García Márquez, Gabriel (Colombian).

Love in the Time of Cholera. (*El amor en los tiempos del cólera*, 1985). New York: Knopf, 2003. ISBN 1-4000-3468-X. 368pp.

In Caribbean South America, Florentino Ariza falls in love with Fermina Daza, wooing her for three years by writing her passionate letters, but she marries Dr. Juvenal Urbino. After she is widowed half a century later, Florentino renews his suit.

> *She never knew when the diversion became a preoccupation and her blood frothed with the need to see him, and one night she awoke in terror because she saw him looking at her from the darkness at the foot of the bed. Then she longed with all her soul for her aunt's predictions to come true, and in her prayers she begged God to give him the courage to hand her the letter just so she could know what it said.* (58–59)

Subjects: historical fiction; Latin America; letters; love stories; physicians

Similar titles: *Tarzan's Tonsillitis* by Bryce Echenique also follows the evolution of love through a lifetime of correspondence.

Awards: Nobel Prize for Literature, 1982

Memories of My Melancholy Whores. (*Las memorias de mis putas tristes*, 2004). Translated by Edith Grossman. New York: Random House, 2005. ISBN 140004460X. 115pp.

A journalist who has never married requests a virgin for his ninetieth birthday at his favorite brothel, Rosa Cabarcas's whorehouse. He promptly falls in love with the child and strives to write a memoir about the experience, a "relationship" that lasts a year and inspires him to wax poetic on the nature of love, the carnal expression of which he has always made a point of paying for.

> *I have begun with my unusual call to Rosa Cabarcas because, seen from the vantage point of today, that was the beginning of a new life at an age when most mortals have already died.* (5)

Subjects: bachelors; Colombia; old men; prostitutes; virgins

Similar titles: Another novel about old men remembering sexual encounters is *Deep Purple* by Montero; *Sultry Moon* by Giardinelli is a different take on an older man's "relationship" with a young girl.

Glantz, Margo (Mexican).

The Wake. (*El rastro*, 2002). **Translated by Andrew Hurley. Willimantic, CT: Curbstone Press, 2005. ISBN 1-931896-23-2. 123pp.**

In a Mexico City suburb, Nora relates her emotions about, reactions to, and memories of Juan, her old lover/friend/enemy/husband, beneath and behind the social exigencies of wake, funeral, and memory that accompany his death. This surreal, lyrical novel is written in the style of a symphony.

> *His face is livid, I suppose that's only natural, it's simple enough, he's dead, the faces of dead people have no color, their heart has stopped beating, that's right, I tell myself, that's right, he's dead.* (2)

Key features: First person narration

Subjects: death; hearts; life; Mexico; music; musicians

Similar titles: *Deep Purple* by Montero is another novel that revolves around music and sex.

González, Rigoberto (Mexican American).

Crossing Vines. **Norman: University of Oklahoma Press, 2003. ISBN 080613528X. 216pp.**

Grape pickers in present-day California's Caliente Valley endure hard times, discrimination, labor abuse, and the threat of immigration raids. Meanwhile, their family life is plagued by situations involving infidelity and domestic violence, in this poetic look at one day in their lives.

> *Since the housing project was susceptible to blackouts, she had learned to do a number of things while partly blinded, guided only by the mercy of moonlight. She had learned to recognize, for example, the number keys on the telephone.* (3)

Subjects: California; family relationships; Mexican Americans; migrant farmworkers

Similar titles: . . . *and the Earth Did Not Devour Him* by Tomás Rivera is the seminal novel about the plight of migrant farmworkers.

Grandes, Almudena (Spanish).

The Wind from the East. (*Los aires difíciles*, 2002). **Translated by Sonia Soto. New York: Seven Stories Press, 2007. ISBN 9781583227466. 541pp.**

Seeking refuge from their torturous lives full of passion, betrayal, death, and possibly murder, three people—Sara Gómez Morales, Juan Olmedo, and Maribel—coincide at an apartment building in Andalucía, where they find friendship in unexpected places.

> *He would put his arms right round her until he was touching his own sides with his fingertips, and hold her tight as if he wanted to absorb her, carry her inside him, merge with her so that they were a single body, but he was always very careful not to hurt her. (35)*

Subjects: brothers; families; godparents; murder; Spain

Similar titles: *The Farewell Angel* by Martín Gaite also features the themes of friendship and growth; mentally challenged siblings also play an important role in *Two Brothers* by Atxaga.

Gutiérrez, Pedro Juan (Cuban).

Dirty Havana Trilogy. (*Trilogía sucia de La Habana,* **1998). Translated by Natasha Wimmer. New York: Farrar, Straus & Giroux, 1998. ISBN 0374140162. 392pp.**

This novel is told in three stories that take place in Havana, where journalist Pedro Juan lives on the edge. Pedro Juan and his friends and neighbors witness the city's decay, while in the name of survival, they sink to decadent, seedy depths. (This is not a formal series, although all of his novels feature a protagonist very much like the author.)

> *That's the way it is in the Caribbean. It'll be sunny, then all of a sudden the wind picks up and it starts to rain and you're in the middle of a hurricane. I needed some rum, but there was no way to get it. I had money, but there was nothing to buy. I lay down to sleep. I was sweaty and the sheets were dirty, but I like the smell of my own sweat and dirt. It turns me on to smell myself. (6)*

Key features: First person narration; sexual situations

Subjects: Cuba—Havana; journalists; prostitutes

Similar titles: *The Color of Summer* by Arenas is also set in a decaying Havana, but with a humorous tone.

Insatiable Spiderman. (*El insaciable hombre araña,* **2002). Translated by John King. New York: Carroll & Graf, 2002. ISBN 0786716657. 163pp.**

The further misadventures of Pedro Juan as he pursues a life as an existentialist writer in contemporary Havana, a life that is gritty and lonely even though he is surrounded by desperate seekers like himself.

> *Perhaps that's what saved me: the drunken bouts, the women, letting out my rage, throwing everything in the shit, not expecting anything from anyone. And writing. (6)*

Key features: First person narration; sexual situations

Subjects: Cuba—Havana; sex; writers—fiction

Similar titles: *Dirty Blonde and Half-Cuban* by Wixon is another sexually explicit novel set in a decadent Havana.

Islas, Arturo (Mexican American; Californiano).

La Mollie and the King of Tears. **Albuquerque: University of New Mexico Press, 1996. ISBN 0826317324. 200pp.**

When he breaks his leg on the day the comet Kahoutek crosses the earth's path, Louie tells his story as he waits for treatment in the emergency room. He tells the tale of his love for La Mollie to a scholar who happens to be at the hospital doing research, tape recorder in hand. Louie is constantly amazed at La Mollie's love for him in spite of their great differences—she being a classy woman and he, a poor slob.

> *La Mollie's always saying how much she wishes she had my skin. It's that Yaqui Indian blood of mine-skin for a lifetime, man-tough, smooth, ready. The sun don't wrinkle it. It sandblasts new every single day. Ever hear of a Yaqui needing a facelift? (5)*

Key features: First person narration

Subjects: California—San Francisco—1970s; Chicanos; hospitals; love stories; musicians

Similar titles: *Forever True* by Alberro and *On Fire* by Sylvia Mendoza are also about love between people from different social classes.

Jennings, Phillip (U.S. American).

Goodbye Mexico. **New York: A Tom Doherty Associates Book, 2007. ISBN 9780765316615. 348pp.**

Jack Armstrong is working for the CIA in Mexico City when a friend he thought had died three years earlier shows up. This friend wants to involve him in an off-the-wall plot to assassinate the president of Mexico to precipitate the takeover of Mexico by Cuba.

> *There would come a time when the next beer or the next became a catalyst and he would go from Gearheardt to raving madman; this was usually signaled by his taking a pistol from his shoulder holster and scaring the crap out of anyone nearby. (13)*

Subjects: assassination; CIA; Cuba; Mexico—Mexico City

Similar titles: *A Good Day to Die* by Coltrane contains a similarly absurd plot involving the CIA and Cuba.

Kozameh, Alicia (Argentinian).

259 Leaps, the Last Immortal. **(*259 saltos, uno inmortal,* 2001). Translated by Clare E. Sullivan. San Antonio, TX: Wings Press, 2007. ISBN 9780930324872. 166pp.**

This novel is composed of 259 short poetic sections/chapters that a former political prisoner narrates about her experiences as a prisoner and an exile.

> *This is Los Angeles: so wouldn't it be better to adopt a less warlike, more beach-friendly vernacular? Let's say: resist. Will you have to resist the image that the new light creates? (3)*

Key features: Second person, stream-of-consciousness narration

Subjects: Argentina; California—Los Angeles; exile; experimental fiction; political prisoners

Similar titles: *Kiss of the Spider Woman* by Puig is another novel about political prisoners in Argentina; *González and Daughter Trucking Compny* by Escandón is also a novel about women in prison, but with a much lighter tone.

Lemus, Felicia Luna (Mexican American).

Like Son: A Novel. **New York: Akashic Books, 2007. ISBN 9781933354217. 267pp.**

Born Francisca in Southern California, Frank is a lesbian who is living as a man. He becomes reacquainted with his or her father, who leaves his son or daughter a photo of the bohemian 1920s Mexican feminist Nahui Olin. This photo serves as a touchstone throughout Frank's later adventures, including a move to New York City, a tempestuous love affair with Nathalie, and surviving the September 11, 2001, terrorist attacks on the twin towers.

> *My father, Francisco Cruz, the ultimate drama queen. Eventually, he would die on Father's Day. At sunrise. With me at his side. Seriously. He was such a theatrical bastard. This being the case, it came as little surprise when, although we'd been estranged since I was a kid, he called out of the blue to announce both his impending death and his desire for a lunch date.* (13)

Subjects: California—Los Angeles; lesbians; love stories; New York—New York City; obsession; Olin, Nahui; September 11, 2001

Similar titles: *The Lamentable Journey of Omaha Bigelow* by Vega Yunqué features a humorous take on obsessive love in New York City, and *Paradise Travel* by Franco deals with Latino survival in New York City.

Marías, Javier (Spanish).

🎗 *A Heart So White.* (*Corazón tan blanco,* **1992). Translated by Margaret Jull Costa. New York: New Directions, 2000. ISBN 0-8112-1452-4. 279pp.**

Juan, a translator, narrates this story, which takes place in Spain. His father, Ranz, married Juan's mother after his first wife—her sister—committed suicide. Juan's wife (Ranz's daughter-in-law, *pues*) is the only one able to draw the story out of Ranz. Meanwhile, Juan muses on the mysteries of love, adultery, and the struggle to unite with another.

> *I did not want to know but I have since come to know that one of the girls, when she wasn't a girl anymore and hadn't long been back from her honeymoon, went into the bathroom, stood in front of the mirror, unbuttoned her blouse, took off her bra and aimed her own father's gun at her heart, her father at the time was in the dining room with other members of the family and three guests.* (3)

Key features: First person narration

Subjects: adultery; betrayal; Cuba—Havana; family secrets; fathers and sons; suicide; translators

Similar titles: *Don Rigoberto's Notebooks* by Vargas Llosa also looks at the difficult relationship between fathers and sons; *Budapest* by Buarque has a similarly psychologically tense tone.

Awards: International IMPAC Dublin Literary Award 1997

Martín Gaite, Carmen (Spanish).

🌶 *The Farewell Angel.* (*La reina de la nieves,* **1994). Translated by Margaret Jull Costa. London: Harvill Press, 1999. ISBN 1860463576. 309pp.**

Leonardo Villalba, just released from prison, learns that his parents have been killed in a car wreck. He then begins a journey of self-discovery that takes him back to his grandmother's house on the coast, La Quinta Blanca, in Spain, now owned by a reclusive writer with mysterious ties to his family. There Leonardo lives out a version of the Hans Christian Anderson story, *The Ice Queen,* seeking the one who can withdraw the sliver of ice from his own heart through the power of story.

> *The more daring of the village boys would sometimes scale the Quinta's thick, moss-covered walls, not so much in order to steal fruit from the orchard as to wander, with a mixture of fear and fascination, amongst the statues, arbours and box-lined labyrinths that filled the vast, neglected garden where the birds sang strange songs and where even the sight of a frog hopping, a snake slithering or a lizard scampering would make you feel oddly unsettled.* (4–5)

Subjects: allegory; death; ex-convicts; fairy tales; family secrets; grief; Spain

Similar titles: *Little Red Riding Hood in the Red Light District* also uses a fairy tale as an allegory, and *In Perfect Light* by Sáenz shares a similar theme of coming to terms with deceased parents.

Awards: Spanish National Prize for Literature, 1994

Martínez, Tomás Eloy (Argentinian).

The Tango Singer. (*El cantor de tango,* 2004). Translated by Anne McLean. New York: Bloomsbury, 2004. ISBN 1-58234-601-1; ISBN-13: 978-1-58234-601-1. 246pp.

Bruno Cadogan, a grad student at NYU, is writing his dissertation on Jorge Luis Borges and the origins of the tango. He travels to Buenos Aires to find and hear the elusive singer Julio Martel—a quest that takes him into the dark corners of Argentina's history.

> *When we least expected it, he unleashed his voice. It was incredible. I was floating in mid-air, and when the voice fell silent, I didn't know how to detach myself from it, how to get back to earth.* (5)

Key features: First person narration; notes

Subjects: Argentina—Buenos Aires; Borges, Jorge Luis; music—tango

Similar titles: *The Matter of Desire* by Paz Soldán also features grad students and professors; *Inez* by Carlos Fuentes and *Deep Purple* by Montero have music as a central theme or motif, and *The Speed of Light* by Cercas also puts a grad student in an ethical dilemma after uncovering dark secrets.

McGahan, Jerry (U.S. American).

A Condor Brings the Sun. San Francisco: Sierra Club Books, 1996. ISBN 0871563541. 266pp.

Pilar, a Runa Indian from Peru, holds in her heart twenty-three stories handed down from ancestors that sometimes speak to her. Forced to flee her Wasi *pueblo* to escape the Senderistas, she meets a grad student, Arnie, while on the lam. Arnie is in Cuzco studying bears. Pilar narrates the first half of the novel; Arnie, the second.

> *Nearby was the magic, the illas my mothers had hidden in the hands of the stone man. When there is power in the savage place, it shows in the light. The ichu grass is gold, and there is no orange in it, nothing warm like the light in cooking fires. The spears are cold like starlight that shivers in night's sky.* (12)

Key features: First person narration

Subjects: biologists; human–animal relationships; interethnic relationships; mothers and daughters; Peru; Runa Indians; *Sendero Luminoso*; Shining Path

Similar titles: *When the Ground Turns in Its Sleep* by Sellers-García also explores the intersection of U.S. and Latin American cultures; *Malinche* by Esquivel, *The Flower in the Skull* by Alcalá, and *The Inhabited Woman* by Belli feature indigenous women as protagonists.

Medina, Pablo (Cuban American).

The Return of Felix Nogara. **New York: Persea Books, c2000. ISBN 0892552514. 278pp.**

After thirty-eight years of exile in the United States, Felix Nogara returns to his birthplace to reclaim his personal history on the fictional Caribbean island of Barata after the demise of its Castro-style leader.

> *Felix Nogara returned to the island of his birth on a rainy Thursday that marked the thirty-eighth anniversary of his leaving. It was February and a norther' was sweeping through Miami with a cool wind and a heavy air that smelled sweet with ozone and decay.*(3)

Subjects: exile; Caribbean Americans; Florida—Miami; New York—New York City

Similar titles: *Dirty Blonde and Half-Cuban* by Wixon features a Cuban American's adventures in Cuba; *The Color of Summer* by Arenas takes place in a parody of postrevolutionary Cuba.

Mestre-Reed, Ernesto (Cuban American).

The Second Death of Única Aveyano. **New York: Vintage Books, 2004. ISBN 1400033160. 259pp.**

At the end of a long life, Única Aveyano battles leukemia. Awaiting death, she looks back on four generations of her family and their life in Cuba and as immigrants to the United States.

> *On the beach there was an early-morning jogger who would later tell those in charge at the nursing home and the police investigators that he thought it strange that a bald naked old woman was steadfastly making her way across the wide stretch of sand towards the water, leaning on a long crooked staff, determined as a prophet crossing the desert towards Jerusalem, but that this was a crazy town and that he had seen crazier things before so he didn't stop her.* (20)

Subjects: aging; Cuba; death; families; Florida—Miami; immigrants—Cuban

Similar titles: *In the Name of Salomé* by Julia Alvarez, *The Colonel Has No One to Write Him* by García Márquez, *The Cigar Roller* by Pablo Medina, and *The Death of Artemio Cruz* by Carlos Fuentes are other end-of-life narratives.

Montero, Mayra (Caribbean: Cuban; Puerto Rican).

Deep Purple. (*Púrpura profundo,* 2000). Translated by Edith Grossman. New York: HarperCollins, 2003. ISBN 0-06-093821-8. 182pp.

After Agustín is forced to retire from his job as music critic for a paper in San Juan, Puerto Rico, he decides to tell the stories of his many affairs with virtuosos and soloists, thus exploring the relationship between music and sex.

> *Saying good-bye to one's profession is like saying good-bye to sex, one clings to it, I cling to this brief piece of writing as if it were a woman's body, the last I will ever embrace in my life.* (1)

Key features: Sexual situations

Subjects: critics; musicians; sensual fiction; sex; writing

Similar titles: *Memories of My Melancholy Whores* by García Márquez is another novel about old men remembering sexual encounters; *Inez* by Carlos Fuentes is also about music and sex.

The Last Night I Spent with You. (*Última Noche que Pasé Contigo,* 1991). Translated by Edith Grossman. New York: HarperCollins, 2000. ISBN 0-06-095290-3. 115pp.

After their daughter leaves home to marry, Celia and Fernando, a middle-aged married couple, take a cruise. Being out of their routine milieu brings up memories of past indiscretions, and the atmosphere of the cruise incites them to explore the edges of "death and desire"—accompanied by the strange and solitary Julieta. The chapter titles taken from sensual boleros set the tone for the erotic and dangerous action therein.

> *That was when I thought of Elena, thought about the dream I had on her wedding night, and closed my eyes. I held Celia close and she rubbed her belly against mine, encouraged by the dim light and the attitude of the other couples, more or less our age, who were encouraged in turn by seeing us. Then she licked my ear and repeated the phrase.* (2)

Key features: Sexual situations

Subjects: Caribbean; cruises; death; love stories; sensual fiction; sex

Similar titles: *A Simple Habana Melody* by Hijuelos, *The Messenger* and *Deep Purple* by Montero, as well as *The Tango Singer* by Tomás Eloy Martínez are all novels with music and love as dominant themes and motifs.

The Red of His Shadow. (*Del rojo de su sombra,* 1992). Translated by Edith Grossman. New York: HarperCollins, 2001. ISBN 0-06-621059-3. 159pp.

Based on true happenings, this is the story of a young Haitian voodoo priestess, Mistress Zulé, who leads her people on a Gagá ritual trip that takes place in Dominican sugar cane fields during the Holy Week. She does fearful battle with her former lover and now rival priest, Similá Bolosse, a formidable, bloodthirsty opponent who has bathed in the blood of 100 goats and has the *tontons macoutes* at his disposal.

> *But everyone saw in her face the reddened marks of the flame, the cut lips, the wild eyes she had when a mystery mounted her for a long time, many times, and with a good deal of rancor.* (3)

Key features: Glossary

Subjects: Dominican Republic; Haitians; love stories; supernatural; voodoo

Similar titles: *The Dew Breaker* by Danticat also features the fearsome *tontons macoutes* and *The Farming of Bones* by Danticat also delves into the schizophrenic dynamic between Haiti and the Dominican Republic.

In the Palm of Darkness. **(*Tú, la oscuridad,* 1995). Translated by Edith Grossman. New York: HarperCollins, 1995. ISBN 0-06-018703-4. 183pp.**

In the Caribbean nation of Haiti, on the far side of the island of Hispaniola (an island the country shares with the Dominican Republic), Victor Grigg and his Haitian guide Thierry Adrien take turns narrating the story of an ill-conceived trip to search for rare species of frogs. Their quest brings the scientist Grigg into the Haitian world of *macoutes* and zombies during the terrifying regime of Papa Doc Duvalier. Each chapter is preceded by short descriptions of a different frog species that has mysteriously disappeared somewhere around the world.

> *My father was named Thierry, like me, and he had a very difficult job, the most difficult one ever known: He was a hunter, he was what they call a* pwazon, rat, *that is what those hunters were called.* (10)

Subjects: frogs; Haiti; scientists; zombies

Similar titles: *Dead Easy* by Bicos also features scientists in danger; *The Farming of Bones* by Danticat takes place amid the terror in Haiti and the Dominican Republic.

Muñoz, Braulio (Peruvian American).

The Peruvian Notebooks. **Tucson: University of Arizona Press, 2006. ISBN 0816525064. 271pp.**

Antonio Alday Gutiérrez immigrates to the United States and becomes Anthony Allday. To the family back home, he brags about making the big time, when in reality he works as a lowly security guard. At the same time, he boasts about fictional wealth and high society in his home country to his acquaintances and potential friends in the United States. When reality begins to threaten his fantasy creation, will Antonio go to deadly lengths to protect it?

> *The opportunity to change his name and become someone else altogether—a process that at the beginning was imperceptible but in the long run turned out to be fundamental and irrevocable—did not even enter his mind while he was still dealing with the world in Tacora.* (9)

Key features: Epistolary style narration recounted as journal entries in Braulio's notebook

Subjects: epistolary fiction; immigrants—Peruvian; murder; Pennsylvania

Similar titles: *The Crime of Father Amaro* by de Queirós is another story about going to extreme lengths to protect falsehood.

Nicholson, Joy (U.S. American).

The Road to Esmeralda. **New York: St. Martin's Press, 2005. ISBN 0-312-26863-7. 346pp.**

Slacker couple and ugly Americans Nick, a would-be writer, and his girlfriend Sarah travel to the Yucatan hoping for a simple vacation from the exigencies of life in the States. They are brusquely brought into contact with the sinister side of life in Mexico when they get involved with *narcotraficantes*.

> *Having grown up believing every person in Mexico envied and emulated the free, rich citizens of the United States, Nick hadn't been prepared for snobbery a la Mexicana. Who would have guessed the low-rent perception of American citizens by Mexico's middle class? Any Mexican who owned a sport jacket or even a blender exclusively admired Europeans. (34)*

Subjects: drug trafficking; Europeans; Mexico—Yucatán; police corruption; tourists—American; writers—fiction

Similar titles: Traven's classic novel *The Treasure of the Sierra Madre* is the quintessential tale of North Americans brought low in Mexico; Carlos Fuentes quotes Ambrose Bierce in *Old Gringo* to the effect that a sure way to commit suicide is to be a gringo in Mexico.

Paz Soldán, Edmundo (Bolivian).

The Matter of Desire. (*Materia del deseo*, 2001). **Translated by Lisa Carter. New York: Houghton Mifflin, 2001. ISBN 0618395571. 214pp.**

Professor Pedro Zabalgo returns to Bolivia to research his revolutionary father's legacy and to escape romantic entanglements at the university where he teaches in the United States. Pedro's research is complicated by more romantic entanglements, despotic *políticos*, and the enigmas he finds in his uncle's crossword puzzles and his dad's one novel.

> *It was strange to arrive and know more about the country than its inhabitants did, incapable as they were of suspecting the magnitude of the crisis that was coming. . . . Carolina kept talking, I amused myself making anagrams out of her name, Aanilorc: a planet in Star Wars. Oilancar: a brand of car oil. (20)*

Key features: First person narration

Subjects: Bolivia; crossword puzzles; professor–student affairs; University of California–Berkeley

Similar titles: *The Shadow of the Wind* by Ruiz Zafón also contains puzzles and enigmas. *The Movies of My Life* by Fuguet also features Latin Americans in the United States; *The Tango Singer* by Tomás Eloy Martínez also features a U.S. university professor and students in Latin America.

Pérez, Loida Maritza (Dominican).

Geographies of Home. **New York: Viking, 1999. ISBN 0-670-86889-2. 321pp.**

After a disappointing stint at college, Iliana decides to return home to her Dominican immigrant family, where her strict Seventh Day Adventist father and magical mother wrestle with their wayward, tragic, second-generation offspring and other demons.

> *Raised in a religion which condemned as pagan the piercing of body parts, she had imagined that, were her mother's clogged holes pried open, she would transform into a sorceress dancing, not secretly on a Sabbath when*

> *she stayed home by feigning illness, but freely, unleashing impulses Papito's religion had suppressed.* (3)

Subjects: immigrants—Dominican; magical realism; New York; religion—Seventh Day Adventists

Similar titles: *Let It Rain Coffee* by Angie Cruz and *The Brief Wondrous Life of Oscar Wao* by Díaz also feature Dominican families in the United States.

Poniatowska, Elena (Mexican).

🏆 *The Skin of the Sky.* (*La piel del cielo,* **2001**). **Translated by Deanna Heikkinan. New York: Farrar, Straus & Giroux, 2004. ISBN 0374265755. 322pp.**

Lorenzo de Tena grows up with the twentieth century in Mexico, the illegitimate son of a simple *campesina* and a Mexico City businessman. He becomes a brilliant Mexican astronomer, studying at Harvard and returning to Mexico to direct the National Observatory. There Lorenzo becomes frustrated by the provincial attitudes and beliefs of those around him. As he strives for excellence, he learns that he may have to make painful sacrifices in his personal life.

> *The de Tena family was not rich, although they lived as if they were. They would not have changed the course of their lives for anything in the world, but no one was to know that Tila turned Joaquín's and Manuel's collars and cuffs inside out and that they owed her three months' salary.* (30)

Subjects: astronomers; Harvard University; Mexicans in the United States; Mexico—Mexico City

Similar titles: *The Matter of Desire* by Paz Soldán wrestles with a similar theme of returning to the home country after studying in the United States.

Awards: Premio Alfaguara 2001

Quesada, Roberto (Honduran).

The Big Banana. **Translated by Walter Krochmal. Houston, TX: Arte Público Press, 1999. ISBN 1558852557. 248pp.**

Honduran immigrant Eduardo Lin, an aspiring actor, has some comical adventures with the subway and apartment living in New York City while scrimping to send money home by working at a construction company. Back home, his girlfriend/fiancée longs for him but has a major crush on James Bond; she may even try to catch up to him in the Big Banana.

> *Good fortune never was with Eduardo as far as these beds on wheels go. At 74th and Roosevelt in Queens in the morning hours it's impossible to get a seat, and people finish their dreams standing: they hang from the straps like swaying bats.* (6)

Key features: Sexual situations

Subjects: actors; Bond, James; Hondurans; New York—New York City

Similar titles: *Paradise Travel* by Franco features another Latino immigrant on the loose in New York City.

Restrepo, Laura (Colombian).

🌶 *Delirium.* (*Delirio*, 2004). Translated by Natasha Wimmer. New York: Doubleday, 2007. ISBN 9780385519908. 320pp.

After returning to Bogotá from a four-day business trip, Agustina's doting husband finds her staying in a hotel and out of her mind. He determines to find out what happened to her while he was away. This involves finding out about some surprising and sinister secrets of her life before she met him—about her strict, upper-class family and her *narcotraficante* ex-boyfriend.

> *My wife's unhinged mind is a dog snapping at me, but at the same time its barking is a call for help, a call to which I'm unable to respond. Agustina is a hurt and starving dog who wants to go home but can't, and the next minute she's a stray dog who can't even remember it once had a home.* (2)

Key features: First person narration; multiple voices

Subjects: college professors; Colombia; drug trafficking; madness

Similar titles: *Lies* by De Hériz is also about family secrets and a woman taking time out; *The Wind from the East* by Grandes also features a woman taking time out.

Awards: 2004 Premio Alfaguara; 2006 Grinzane Cavour Prize (Italy)

Ríos, Julián (Spanish).

Loves That Bind. (*Amores que atan o belles letters*, 1995). Translated by Edith Grossman. New York: Vintage International, 1998. ISBN 0-375-40058-3. 244pp.

When the narrator's lover leaves him for a month, he occupies the time apart by writing her a letter every day. Each letter tells the tale of a former lover who shares similarities with heroines from classic twentieth-century novels.

> *As inconstant as the moon, her body also changed its form, and occasionally I was deceived when I attempted to fix certain specific details. And so I recalled a roguish birthmark on her chin that was really on her cheek.* (7)

Key features: First person epistolary style narration; sexual situations

Subjects: Europe; literary heroines; love stories

Similar titles: *The Notebooks of Don Rigoberto* by Vargas Llosa and *Inez* by Carlos Fuentes are other novels that examine the differences between carnal and ideal lovers.

Rizik, Marisela (Dominican American).

Of Forgotten Times: A Novel. (*El tiempo del olvido*, 1996). Translated by Isabel Z. Brown. Willimantic, CT: Curbstone Press, 2004. ISBN 1-931896-00-3. 215pp.

This story of mothers, daughters, and lovers takes place in a fictional small island nation very like the Dominican Republic. When Lorenza chooses a man out of loneliness instead of love, she sets in motion a chain of events that have dire consequences for her daughter and possibly even for her granddaughter. These women's lives are made miserable by the sadistic, perverted, power-hungry general who runs the nation (very like Trujillo).

> *Rolanda Parduz exercised many important roles within The Council. She interpreted dreams and studied the phases of the moon to determine when to plant rice and fruit. Traditionally, the Parduz women would select the man that would father their daughters from dreams.* (7)

Subjects: Caribbean; dictators; love stories; mothers and daughters

Similar titles: *The Brief Wondrous Life of Oscar Wao* by Junot Díaz and *In the Name of Salomé* and *In the Time of the Butterflies* by Julia Alvarez also portray life and love in the Dominican Republic under Trujillo's iron-fisted rule.

Sáenz, Benjamin Alire (Tejano).

In Perfect Light. New York: HarperCollins, 2005. ISBN 9780060779207. 328pp.

Therapist Grace Delgado takes on Andrés Segovia's case as a favor to a friend. Andrés is a violent offender with a strange, sad story of parental loss from his childhood. His older brother took the remaining family members back to Mexico after their parents' death in a suspicious car accident. In helping him, Grace may find answers to her own personal misery.

> *She kept running her hands over them, sheet by sheet, trying to smooth them out, her ironing hand as useless as the roots of a dead tree. You could never uncrease a piece of paper once it had been folded. Not ever.* (16)

Subjects: child abuse; families; Mexico—Juárez; sexual abuse; Texas—El Paso; therapists; violence

Similar titles: *The Farewell Angel* by Martín Gaite also features adult orphans; *Dr. Neruda's Cure for Evil* by Rafael Yglesias and *Blake's Therapy* by Dorfman explore Latinos' experiences with psychotherapy.

Santana, Patricia (Mexican American).

Ghosts of El Grullo. Albuquerque: University of New Mexico Press, 2008. ISBN 9780826344090.290pp.

After the death of her mother, Yolanda Sahagún, a student at the University of California at San Diego, travels to her parents' ancestral *pueblo* of El Grullo in Mexico on a quest to understand herself and keep her increasingly estranged family from falling apart.

> *Possibly there was blood present, but I was only a year old when we returned to the house, and Mamá never mentioned this to me. We know of the brutal hangings from the tree because the ánimas—what you call ghosts—cannot rest.* (13)

Subjects: California—San Diego; families; ghosts; immigrants; México—Jalisco

Similar titles: *When the Ground Turns in Its Sleep* by Sellers-García is another novel about a second generation immigrant returning to his parents' home country to find himself.

Sellers-García, Sylvia (U.S. American).

When the Ground Turns in Its Sleep. New York: Riverhead Books, 2007. ISBN 9781594489549. 325pp.

When Nítido Amán travels to Guatemala on a quest to understand his dead father's life, he is inadvertently mistaken for a new priest the village is expecting. He falls into the role as a convenient way to learn the *pueblo's* secrets; but he learns more than he bargained for about the painful past and torturous present of Río Roto and the phantom village of his parents, Naranjo.

> *I'd pictured the river as a clear ribbon lining the green hills, an image that later seemed roughly as prescient as the hundreds of other slight and colossal suppositions that had driven me there. Instead I saw the brown waters ripping trees from the banks and a car pinned to the skeleton of a flooded bridge.* (3)

Key features: First person narration

Subjects: Guatemala; Guatemalan Americans; massacres; *pueblos*

Similar titles: *The Heiress of Water* by Barron and *Little Red Riding Hood in the Red Light District* by Argueta also ponder the legacy of the Central American civil wars; *The Yellow Rain* by Llamazares takes place in a similar phantom *pueblo*.

Soto, Gary (Mexican American).

Silver Mendez Series.

Three novels follow the *suerte*, good and bad fortune, of this Chicano poet/survivor/philosopher king as he wrestles with middle age and *machismo*. Silver always demonstrates his capacity for survival and the ability to find the humor in even the most trying circumstances.

Nickel and Dime. Albuquerque: University of New Mexico, 2000. ISBN 0-8263-2185-2. 189pp.

Silver Mendez makes his first appearance in this novel, in which the three interwoven stories are told from each protagonist's point of view. Down-and-out Chicanos in Oakland—Roberto Silva, a laid off bank security guard; Gus Hernandez, Roberto's retired coworker; and Silver Mendez, Chicano poet—find ways to survive being homeless during the unforgiving climate of the 1990s.

> *He lamented that the money belonged to other people, some of them feebleminded, sourpusses, income-tax cheats, or would-be killers in glossy red pumps. Some belonged to misers stingy even in offering a smile.* (1)

Subjects: California—Oakland; Chicanos; homelessness; poets—fiction

Similar titles: *El Indio Jesús* by Chávez Ballejos also feature some *pícaro* Chicano *amigos*; *The Adventures of Don Chipote* by Venegas follows the adventures of down-and-out Mexicans.

Poetry Lover. Albuquerque: University of New Mexico Press, 2001. ISBN 0826323197. 206pp.

> Chicano poet Silver Mendez has been invited to present at a literary conference in Spain, but lacks the wherewithal to attend. He attempts to scrape together the necessary funds while struggling with difficult situations, including death, romance, and family troubles.

> > *Money was on Silver's mind when he left his mother's house the next morning, a heaping bowl of shredded wheat piled in his stomach and scouring, he visualized, the insides of his guts.* (11)

> **Subjects:** Chicanos; love stories; poets—fiction; widows

> **Similar titles:** *The Best Thing That Can Happen to a Croissant* by Tusset has a similar humorous slacker tone, and *How to Be a Chicana Role Model* by Serros also features Chicano writers.

Amnesia in a Republican County. Albuquerque: University of New Mexico, 2003. ISBN 0-8263-2931-4. 200pp.

> Chicano poet Silver Mendez recovers from a bout of amnesia to find himself teaching English at a conservative college, where he is mixed up in a series of uncomfortable and unfamiliar situations, including an affair with the college president's wife and drug dealing on campus.

> > *Then a second flash lit his memory: he was from Oakland, he owned a Volkswagen up on cement blocks, and his mother, a woman with scalded hands and a temper that matched her occupation, worked in an industrial laundry, washing the duds of convicts in the Alameda County Jail.* (4)

> **Subjects:** amnesia; California; Chicanos; colleges; poets—fiction

> **Similar titles:** *The Quixote Cult* by Genaro González presents another Chicano on campus.

St. Aubin de Terán, Lisa (European American).

Swallowing Stones. New York: HarperCollins, 2005. ISBN 978-0-06-078104-0. 512pp.

> After surviving cancer, Oswaldo Barreto Miliani recounts his long life as a guerrilla fighter and strategist. His story takes the reader through the significant revolutionary struggles of Latin America and other hot spots around the world.

> > *My body may look old and wasted on the outside now, but it has been old and wasted on the inside since I was in my twenties. Thanks to the high-tech methods taught by CIA instructors worldwide, every inch of my flesh has been tampered with and prematurely aged.* (11)

> **Key features:** First person narration

> **Subjects:** revolutionary struggles; spies; torture; Venezuela

> **Similar titles:** *The General in His Labyrinth* by García Márquez and *By Night in Chile* by Bolaño are other fictional memoirs; *The Cigar Roller* by Pablo Medina is another novel centered on an old man's memories.

Stork, Francisco X. (Californiano).

The Way of the Jaguar. Tempe, AZ: Bilingual Press, 2000. ISBN 0927534932. 270pp.

Ismael Diaz reconstructs the sequence of events that brought him to death row. As he writes his story, Ismael encounters other inmates, who turn him on to the "Way of the Jaguar," with which he can tap into the power of his Aztec ancestors and challenge even Death herself—*la mismísima Pelona.*

> *Armanda with her brown glistening beauty, squeezing out of and demanding from ecstasy the very last drop of joy that this world can give. Armanda, even in those final days in El Paso ravaged by loss and addiction, even so, beautiful in a way that is hidden to all but those who wait for beauty patiently-stalk it even-regardless of the pain.* (18–19)

Key features: First person narration; epistolary writing

Subjects: prison—death row; prisoners; Texas

Similar titles: *González and Daughter Trucking Company* by Escandón, *Kiss of the Spider Woman* by Puig, and *Big Dreams and Dark Secrets in Chimayó* by Cordova are other prison narrative novels.

Suárez, Virgil (Cuban American).

Going Under. Houston, TX: Arte Público Press, 1996. ISBN 1558851593. 155pp.

Xavier Cuevas, a YUCA (Young Urban Cuban American) insurance sales-man, is set on the path to success, until life is disrupted when his gringa wife leaves and he suffers a big setback at work. He then suffers an iden-tity crisis that inspires him to get in touch with his roots with the help of a *santera,* a traditional healing woman.

> *You busted your back, he thought, working hard to serve and understand one,* la americanada, *as he called it, and the other,* lo cubiche, *the source of his livelihood, which he protected and respected. ¿Qué es la vida? Caja de sorpresas. Hoy felicidad, mañana tristesa [sic].* (18)

Subjects: Cuban Americans; divorced men; Florida—Miami

Similar titles: The protagonists in *Sex and the South Beach Chicas* by Piñeiro are fe-male YUCAs, and those in *Tristan and the Hispanics* by Jose Yglesias are second generation Cuban Americans.

Tagliavini, Gabriela (Argentinian).

The Colors of Memory. (Los colores de la memoria, 1999). New York: Herodias, 2001. ISBN 1-928-74617-9. 204pp.

Carla, a bitter old woman, looks forward to death from leukemia. When "the kid" asks her to help find his father in Los Angeles, she runs away from the hospital in Mexico, deciding to use the trip to search for her lost love of long ago and not expecting much to come of either quest.

> *I guess I trusted someone once. A man. Okay, he wasn't just a man. At least not to me. He was a liar, a thief. Not a big thief, though; he stole*

> *stories. He wasn't a good liar either. He said his name was Dmitri, but I never
> knew if it was true. As the years passed, I realized the more you live, the more you
> hate. I hate thousands, probably millions, of things, but I hate him more than
> orange.* (7–8)

Key features: First person narration

Subjects: old age; orphans; road trips

Similar titles: *The Wake* by Glantz is also structured around a woman's memories; *The Second Death of Única Aveyano* by Mestre-Reed is another end-of-life narrative.

Troncoso, Sergio (Mexican American).

The Nature of Truth. **Evanston, IL: Northwestern University Press, 2003. ISBN 08101199119. 259pp.**

Grad student Helmut Sanchez is working with a German professor when he stumbles on information that leads him to believe the professor was guilty of atrocities during World War II. German Chicano Sanchez takes it upon himself to mete out justice, but then must face his own conscience.

> *The air inside was cold and damp. In front of him, two lines of students were ready
> to check out books under the mosaic of the Goddess of Knowledge behind the
> circulation desk. Another line was at the copy machines, which flashed and droned
> like dragons trapped in a box.* (10)

Key features: Sexual situations

Subjects: college professors; graduate students; Nazis; World War II

Similar titles: *The Name of a Bullfighter* by Sepúlveda is another novel that has post–World War II consequences as plot motivators; *The Tango Singer* by Tomás Eloy Martínez and *The Matter of Desire* by Paz Soldán also feature grad students and their research.

Valdés, Zoé (Cuban).

Yocandra in the Paradise of Nada: A Novel of Cuba. **(*La nada cotidiana,* 1995). Translated by Sabina Cienfuegos. New York: Arcade Publishing, 1997. ISBN 1-55970-362-8. 157pp.**

Yocandra was born with the Cuban revolution and raised on its ideals. As adults, she and her friends—the Traitor, the Nihilist, the Lynx, and the Gusana—contend with the absurd bureaucracy that results when these high ideals meet dirty reality and begin to rot.

> *It's that militant nutcase from agricultural school who always used to stick me
> with weekend guard duty just to piss me off and keep me from meeting boys.* (18)

Key features: First person narration; sexual situations

Subjects: allegory; Cuba—Havana; humor; love triangles; sensual fiction; tropical socialism

Similar titles: *The Color of Summer* by Arenas is also full of Cuban absurdity; while *Dirty Blonde and Half-Cuban* by Wixon is another novel about survival in postrevolutionary Cuba.

Vargas Llosa, Mario (Peruvian).

🏶 *The Notebooks of Don Rigoberto.* (*Los cuadernos de Don Rigoberto,* 1997). Translated by Edith Grossman. New York: Farrar, Straus & Giroux, 1997. ISBN 0-374-22327-0. 259pp.

Lucrecia is Don Rigoberto's young second wife. The novel opens as his son, Alfonso or Fonchito, visits Lucrecia to ask her not to be angry with him after she has been thrown out of the house, accused of committing an indiscretion with him. The cherubic, albeit precocious, Fonchito's visits with Lucrecia, Don Rigoberto's notebooks full of fantasies and descriptions of erotic episodes involving Lucrecia (episodes that may or may not have happened), and anonymous love letters to Don Rigoberto all add spice and tension to their erotic triangle.

> She saw her reflection in the foyer mirror: her expression had regained its composure, but a light blush tinged her cheeks, and her breast rose and fell in agitation. With an automatic gesture she closed the neckline of her dressing gown. How could he be so shameless, so cynical, so perverse, when he was still so young? (6)

Key features: some epistolary style narration in the notebooks; sexual situations

Subjects: love triangles; sensual fiction; stepchildren

Similar titles: *Sultry Moon* by Giardinelli also features sexual obsession with a precocious youngster.

Awards: Best Fiction 1998—New York Times Notable Books; Library Journal Best Books

The Real Life of Alejandro Mayta. (*La historia de Mayta,* 1984). Translated by Alfred MacAdam. New York: Farrar, Straus & Giroux, 1998. ISBN 0374525552. 310pp.

Alejandro Mayta is a guerrilla fighter. Mayta's childhood friend narrates this novel seeking to understand Mayta and his place in the sequence of violent events and uncertain times in Peru.

> The real Peru was in the mountains and not along the coast, among the Indians and condors and the peaks of the Andes, not here in Lima, a foreign, lazy, anti-Peruvian city, because from the time the Spaniards had founded it, it had looked toward Europe and the United States and turned its back on Peru. (19)

Key features: First person narration

Subjects: civil war; guerrilla warfare; guerrilleros; Peru—Lima; revolutionaries

Similar titles: *Swallowing Stones* by St. Aubin de Terán and *Lost City Radio* by Alarcón are other novels about the guerrilla and guerrilleros.

Vega Yunqué, Edgardo (Nuyorican).

No Matter How Much You Promise to Cook or Pay the Rent, You Blew It Cauze Bill Bailey Ain't Never Coming Home Again: A Symphonic Novel. New York: Farrar, Straus & Giroux, 2003. ISBN 0-374-22311-4. 638pp.

Vidamía Farrell is the result of the union between her sensitive, sad Anglo father and her uptight, Puerto Rican, overachieving mother. The author presents a rich portrait of all the family members, friends, and musicians who make up life in New York City as they come together to create the unique but familiar person that is Vidamía Farrell.

> *She didn't meet her father until the age of twelve, when she learned that once upon a time her father had sat in the middle of a Vietnamese rice paddy, under a shower of steel, cradling the broken and forever useless body of her uncle, Joey Santiago of Rivington Street on the Lower East Side of New York City, whom she would never meet since time and space didn't allow for such stratagems.* (3)

Key features: Stream-of-consciousness narration

Subjects: blended families; families; Irish Americans; New York—New York City—Lower East Side; music—jazz; musicians—fiction; Puerto Ricans; race relations; veterans—Vietnam War

Similar titles: *The Wake* by Glantz and *Inez* by Carlos Fuentes are other novels with strong musical motifs; the protagonist in *Gods Go Begging* by Véa is also a Vietnam veteran.

Venegas, Daniel (Mexican).

The Adventures of Don Chipote or, When Parrots Breast-Feed. (*Las aventuras de Don Chipote o Cuando los pericos mamen,* **1998). Translated by Ethriam Cash Brammer. Houston, TX: Arte Público Press, 2000 (1928). ISBN 1558852972. 160pp.**

First published in Los Angeles in 1928, this novel portrays the plight of Don Chipote, who has come to the United States to sweep dollars off the streets of gold so he can save his family from hunger in the *pueblo.* Through a series of comic misadventures, accompanied by his dog and his faithful sidekick Policarpo, Don comes to find the truth of the matter: "Mexicans will make it big in the United States . . . WHEN PARROTS BREAST-FEED" (160).

> *Let's leave Don Chipote and family, sleeping naked as jaybirds, spread-eagle and snoring like there's no tomorrow, and turn our attention to some distance from his shack.* (23)

Key features: Introduction by Nicolás Kanellos

Subjects: California—Los Angeles; Chicanos; humor; immigrants—Mexican

Similar titles: More adventures with down-and-out Mexicans can be found in *El Indio Jesús* by Chávez Ballejos and *Nickel and Dime* by Gary Soto; *Dante's Ballad* by González Viaña also features a trusty animal sidekick.

Vila-Matas, Enrique (Spanish).

Montano's Malady. (*El Mal de Montano,* **2002). Translated by Jonathan Dunne. New York: New Directions, 2007. 9780811216289. 235pp.**

Writer José Cardoso Pires is so obsessed with his work that he is having difficulty distinguishing between literature and reality. He narrates this novel in five parts, musing on the nature and difficulty of writing fiction and on the betrayal of the form, but also the betrayals of his wife and best friend. Along the way, he travels to literary places and mixes literary personages into his narrative.

> *He almost certainly had to be fantasizing, perhaps childishly trying to conceal his anguish at his unfortunate inability to write. But in his slightly disturbed look there was a strange hint of truth.* (7)

Key features: First person narration

Subjects: literature; literary critics; metafiction; obsession; writers—fiction

Similar titles: *The Savage Detectives* by Bolaño and *Budapest* by Buarque are other novels that look at the nature of fiction, art, and life.

Wixon, Lisa (U.S. American).

Dirty Blonde and Half-Cuban: A Novel. **New York: HarperCollins, 2005. ISBN 0-06-072174X. 246pp.**

On her death bed, Alysia's mother entreats her to find José Antonio, her birth father. Alysia spends a year in Havana on this quest. Stranded when her money is stolen and coldly cut off by the stepfather who raised her, Alysia finds herself obligated to join the ranks of the *jineteras*—people from Cuba's professional class who supplement their meager income by seducing international tourists.

> *He smiles. I pretend, despite the mounting evidence to the contrary, that I'm a First World girl in a First World city, being offered a friendly drink by an attractive man. That at the end of this exchange, we will trade business cards and a flirtatious smile, and in a few days I'll find a message on my cell phone and, who knows, there might be dinner and maybe a movie or a stroll and, you know, a date. (4)*

Key features: First person narration; sexual situations

Subjects: Cuba—Havana; Cubans; fathers and daughters; prostitutes

Similar titles: A birth parent and her daughter search for each other in *Highwire Moon* by Straight; immigrant children return to the home country for visits in *The Return of Felix Nogara* by Pablo Medina, *Mambo Peligroso* by Chao, and *When the Ground Turns in Its Sleep* by Sellers-Garcia.

Yglesias, Jose (Cuban American).

Tristan and the Hispanics. **New York: Simon & Schuster, 1989. ISBN 0671673351. 265pp.**

When uptight Northerner, Ivy-Leaguer, middle-child Tristan travels to Tampa, Florida, to arrange cremation for his famous Cuban writer grandfather, humorous situations ensue. What Tristan finds is an unexpected gaggle of cousins and other Cuban relatives, who drag him into an uncomfortable confrontation with his roots.

> *Tristan was too startled to catch his own name spoken in Spanish. Tristán. Tristán! The old woman spoke less to him than to the crowd behind her. She repeated Tristán! and then he got it. He smiled. (23)*

Subjects: coming-of-age; cremation; Cuban Americans; Cuban families; Florida—Miami; humor

Similar titles: *Holy Radishes!* by Fernández is another humorous novel about Cuban families in the United States.

Yglesias, Rafael (Cuban American).

Dr. Neruda's Cure for Evil. **New York: Warner Books, 1996. ISBN 0446520055. 694pp.**

Constructed as a case study written by Dr. Neruda, this novel tells his story in three parts. The first part focuses on his own childhood trauma; the second part is about a patient suffering from similar trauma and his ultimate failure to cure that person; and in the third part Dr. Neruda takes what he has learned and applies it to curing the evil in a malevolent father–daughter case.

> *His voice was too resonant, his head too large, his gray suit's fabric too thick, especially on that day, an unusually hot April day. (In fact while playing tennis with Daniel I took off my shirt. "You sweat like a spic," Daniel commented.) (14)*

Subjects: child abuse; Cuban Americans; evil; Jewish Americans; psychologists

Similar titles: Madness plays an important part in *Delirium* by Restrepo and *Blake's Therapy* by Dorfman; *In Perfect Light* by Sáenz looks at Latinos and therapy.

Anthologies and Collections

This selection includes collections by masters of the short story from Texas, California, New Mexico, and New Jersey. The stories are set in Mexico, Colombia, and Cuba. The subject matter ranges from the alienation of the new immigrant to everyone's need for love.

Casares, Oscar (Tejano).

Brownsville. **New York: Little, Brown, 2003. ISBN 0316146803. 192pp.**

Brownsville is right on the Texas–Mexico border, and these stories feature an array of eccentric working-class characters—from thirty-one-year-old slacker Bony, who keeps a monkey head he has found as a replacement for his dead friend, to sixty-eight-year-old Lola, champion bowler, whose favorite ball has been stolen.

> *Bony was walking back from the Jiffy-Mart when he found the monkey's head. There it was, under the small palm tree in the front yard, just staring up at him like an old friend who couldn't remember his name. It freaked him out bad. (41)*

Subjects: Texas—Brownsville; Mexican Americans; U.S.–Mexico border
Key features: First person narration

Díaz, Junot (Dominican American).

Drown. **(*Negocios,* 1997). Translated by Eduardo Lago. New York: Riverhead Books, 1996. ISBN 1573220418. 208pp.**

Teenage Dominican immigrant men in New York and New Jersey struggle to define themselves in adverse circumstances.

> *He stood out on the patio in his shorts and looked out over the mountains, at the mists that gathered like water, at the brucal trees that blazed like fires on the mountain. This, he said, is shit. (4)*

Subjects: Dominican Americans; Dominican Republic; New Jersey; New York; teenagers
Key features: First person narration; graphic language; sexual situations

🎗 García Márquez, Gabriel (Colombian).

Collected Stories. **Translated by Gregory Rabassa and J. S. Bernstein. New York: HarperCollins, 1999. ISBN 0060932686. 343pp.**

Twenty-six of García Márquez's best stories, presented in chronological order, are brimming with magic, humor, poverty, death, love, and that *ya conocido,* renowned lyricism.

> *The force of gravity seemed to attract him now with an irrevocable power. He was heavy, like a positive, undeniable corpse. But it was more restful that way. He didn't even have to breathe in order to live his death.* (8)

Subjects: classics; Colombia; magical realism

Awards: Nobel Prize for Literature, 1982

Gilb, Dagoberto (Tejano).

Woodcuts of Women. **New York: Grove Press, 2001. ISBN 0802116795. 167pp.**

Latino working-class men and women carry out the dance of love and desire.

> *I've got two sports coats, about six ties, three dressy pants, Florsheims I polish a la madre, and three weeks ago I bought a suit, with silk lining, Lemonde for Men. It came with a matching vest. That's what made it for me.* (3)

Key features: First person narration; sexual situations

Subjects: love stories; Mexican Americans; short stories; United States—Southwest

Lavín, Mónica, ed. (Mexican).

Points of Departure: New Stories from Mexico. **Translated by Gustavo V. Segade. San Francisco: City Lights, 2001. ISBN 9780870863811. 159pp.**

A new generation of Mexican authors born in the 1950s and 1960s writes stories that cover a wide range of topics and share a literary dexterity and mastery of the short story craft.

> *Then he saw himself coming back to the paper in the pouring rain, chain-smoking in a vain attempt to extirpate that stench of blood, sex, and alcohol that had clung to his body from the moment he entered the ruins of the movie theater.* (1)

Key features: First person narration; violence; sexual situations

Subjects: Mexico; short stories

Manrique, Jaime (Colombian American), with Jess Dorris, eds.

Bésame mucho. **New York: Painted Leaf Press, 1999. ISBN 1891305069. 253pp.**

This anthology of short fiction by gay Latino men explores the universal need for love and romantic passion, whatever the circumstance.

I wouldn't normally apologize for my well-developed sense of lust. It wouldn't be like me to belittle the one drive that has kept me yearning for another day, way in the future, when it would be fulfilled. Lust as hope, lust as the struggle for self-realization, lust as a zest for living. (7)

Key features: First person narration; sexual situations

Subjects: homosexuals; short stories

Mayo, C. M., ed. (Mexican American).

Mexico: A Traveler's Literary Companion. **Berkeley, CA: Whereabouts Press, 2006. ISBN 1883513154. 238pp.**

Renowned Mexican writers make the many regions of that country—each with its own distinct personality and cultural qualities—come alive.

From there it seemed one could see the volcanoes; the sun and moon shined more brightly; the taste of an ice cream lasted twice as long; one could buy more things for the same money. The people who had the privilege of living there were happier, more orderly, better educated, better dressed. (107–8)

Subjects: Mexicans; Mexico; travel

Obejas, Achy, ed. (Cuban American).

Havana Noir. **New York: Akashic Books, 2007. ISBN 9781933354385. 355pp.**

These short stories in the noir style by Cuban authors living both on and off the island are set in Havana. Each story takes place in a different neighborhood or barrio.

Back then, Havana still retained that halo of light and mystery. My bus came in on the old central highway, continued past Virgen del Camino, and straight through the disastrous streets of Luyanó. (21)

Key features: First person narration; violence; sexual situations

Subjects: crime; Cuba—Havana; short stories

Quintana, Leroy V. (New Mexican).

La Promesa and Other Stories. **Norman: University of Oklahoma Press, 2002. ISBN 0806134496. 151pp.**

Two veterans in San Miguel, New Mexico—Mosco, a World War II vet, and Johnny, a veteran of the Vietnam War—are featured in these stories.

It was on the last evening of Doña Matilda's novena to St. Jude, the patron saint of the impossible, that Mosco saw the burning rosary on the wall and ran out of the house, stark raving naked, all the way across San Miguel, and burst into church shouting "¡Milagro! ¡Milagro! ¡Milagro!" (3)

Key features: Glossary translating Spanish sayings and proverbs

Subjects: Chicanos; New Mexico; short stories; veterans—Vietnam War; veterans—World War II

Romero, Leo (New Mexican).

Rita & Los Angeles. **Tempe, AZ: Bilingual Press, 1995. ISBN 0927534444. 137pp.**

A witty, sensitive selection of strange, sad stories. This collection features eccentric characters and a young man coming of age in the West, an outsider in an alien, hostile world.

> *It wasn't until I was eleven years old that I realized that Las Vegas, New Mexico, and Las Vegas, Nevada, weren't one and the same town. . . . It was the week I waited for days outside the El Fidel hotel to see the couple arrive who had won an all-expense paid trip to Las Vegas. (72)*

Key features: First person narration; sexual situations

Subjects: California; Mexican Americans; New Mexico; short stories

Chapter 2

Historical Fiction

Ni tanto que queme el santo, ni tan poco que no lo alumbre.

Introduction

Historical fiction is story set in the past. For the purposes of this book, "the past" covers up through the 1960s, particularly when the historical setting plays a prominent role in the story.

The works in this chapter cover a broad spectrum of topics and themes. Many examine war and its painful legacies—from the Spanish Conquest of the Americas to the U.S.–Mexican War, to the revolutions and dirty wars of the twentieth century. These authors bring back to life colorful characters from the past—the famous lover Don Juan and the infamous crazy Queen of Castile, Juana La Loca, who perhaps wasn't so crazy. They introduce us to heroes and heroines who valiantly defended their culture and their *patria* and to unsavory dictators and torturers who greedily pillaged their *patria* and brutally mistreated their *compatriotas* and countrymen. The classic titles included here are contemporary to the epoch they portray but read like historical fiction to the twenty-first-century reader.

Appeal

Historical fiction puts a human face on historical happenings and brings history to life. Fans of this genre especially enjoy the rich detail of settings. People who enjoy books with high emotion, adventure, and passion also enjoy these stories.

Organization

Titles in this chapter are organized geo-chronologically into seven sections: "Spain and the Spanish Empire," "America *Conquistada*/Conquered," "New Nations in the Nineteenth Century/*Civilización y barbarie*," and three on the twentieth century— "Pre–World War II," "Post–World War II," and finally, "*Liberación*/Liberation."

Spain and the Spanish Empire

These novels are set in the dramatic Spain that ruled the world from the fifteenth to the seventeenth centuries. Legendary figures like the original Latin lover Don Juan Tenorio, the crazy queen Juana la Loca, and the mystic Sister Teresa come alive during the intrigues of their time. The ubiquitous and sinister Spanish Inquisition wields its power with fanaticism and is a force that most of the heroes in these books must reckon with.

Abrams, Douglas Carlton (U.S. American).

The Lost Diary of Don Juan. **New York: Atria Books, 2007. ISBN 1416532501. 307pp.**

Don Juan Tenorio's lost diary, now recovered, reveals the famous lover's life from his point of view—his sexual prowess, political intrigue, and philosophical musings on the nature of love, sex, and worship of women

> *It is this same pride that leads me to begin my account with the most daring seduction I have ever undertaken. My ambition was nothing less than to free the King's chaste and lonely daughter from her imprisonment in the royal palace of the Alcázar-for a night.* (2)

Key features: First person narration; sexual situations

Subjects: diaries; love affairs; Spain—17th century; spies; Tenorio, Don Juan

Similar titles: *Aztec Blood* by Gary Jennings, *Zorro* by Allende, and *Assault on Paradise* by Lobo all feature swashbuckling, Spanish conquistadors and melodrama.

Belli, Gioconda (Nicaraguan).

The Scroll of Seduction. **(*El pergamino de la seducción*, 2006). Translated by Lisa Dillman. New York: Rayo, 2006. ISBN 0060833122. 325pp.**

Lucía, an orphaned teenager living in a boarding school in modern-day Madrid, is befriended by Manual, a middle-aged art historian. Seeing a likeness to the notoriously crazy sixteenth-century Spanish queen, Juana la Loca, Manuel convinces Lucia to "channel" her at the house he shares with his maiden aunt, the house that was Juana's final home and prison. Her tragic tale of passion, betrayal, and court intrigues is juxtaposed with Lucía's strange coming-of-age.

> *As I watched him, standing in front of the portrait of Philippe the Handsome, in the shaft of light falling from the window, I had the disturbing sensation that there was a physical resemblance between the two.* (6)

Key features: First person narration; epistolary fiction

Subjects: art historians; Juana La Loca, Queen of Castile; love stories; men and women; Spain; spirits; teenagers

Similar titles: *Sor Juana's Second Dream* by Gaspar de Alba is another novel about strong women under Spanish rule facing the Inquisition.

Branston, Julian (U.S. American).

Tilting at Windmills. **New York: Shaye Areheart Books, 2003. ISBN 1-4000-4928-8. 314pp.**

While Miguel Cervantes was writing *Don Quixote*, he suffered unrequited love, a literary rival, and many challenges to the eventual success of the great novel.

> *This was a successful business venture, and Cervantes was writing with a joy and accomplishment hardly experienced before. But even with his hand so happily and firmly fixed on the enigmatic serpent of inspiration, the coils of his story were writhing free. He could not hold it; truth, action, speech were growing beyond the collusion of his hand and brain.* (17)

Subjects: Cervantes, Miguel; humor; knights; literary quarrels; Spain; writers—fiction

Similar titles: *Captain Alatriste* by Pérez-Reverte is also set in seventeenth-century Spain.

Espinosa, María (U.S. American).

Incognito: Journey of a Secret Jew. **San Antonio, TX: Wings Press, 2002. ISBN 0930324854. 190pp.**

Alfonso, a youth in the Spanish port city of Cádiz in 1492, confronts the truth that his ostensibly Catholic family are secretly Jews, who risk persecution during the brutal Spanish Inquisition.

> *He had been seven years old when the Jews left Spain. On a hot, dry day in late July, thousands of them began to swarm into the city of Cádiz, choking the dusty roads as they made their way towards the port.* (5)

Key features: Notes and glossary

Subjects: Jews; love stories; Spain; Spanish Inquisition

Similar titles: *Siguiriya* by López-Medina and *Spirits of the Ordinary* by Alcalá are other novels about Jews and the Spanish Inquisition.

López-Medina, Sylvia (Mexican American).

Siguiriya. **New York: HarperCollins, c1997. ISBN 0060172711. 309pp.**

Amahl Cozar, a Muslim, and Bianca de Lucena, a Jew, fall in love and suffer for it under the Spanish Inquisition. They and their children must survive violence and oppression as they find their own way to love and worship.

> *As he walked to the castle, purple shadows of twilight dotting the path before him, he wondered if the Donzella would find pleasure in his acceptance. He recalled her face, her evident resistance and her pride as strong as Lucifer's. Somehow, he did not believe she would be anything but indifferent to his presence.* (18)

Subjects: family histories; interracial relationships; Spain; Spanish Inquisition

Similar titles: *Incognito* by Espinosa is another novel about religious persecution during the Inquisition.

Mujica, Bárbara (U.S. American).

Sister Teresa: The Woman Who Became Saint Teresa of Avila. Woodstock, NY: Overlook Press, 2007. ISBN 9780715636725. 384pp.

Sister Teresa of Avila's story is narrated by her friend, companion, and fellow nun, Angelica de la Sagrada Corazón, who has been spurned by her suitor because she knows how to read. Sixteenth-century Spain is a world terrorized by the Spanish Inquisition, a place where these women find a rich life in the convent. Sister Teresa's otherworldly spirituality is balanced by Sister Angelica's earthy carnality.

> *It wasn't a formal trial, they said, just an interrogation. One by one they brought us into a murky, musty room lit by flickering candles placed at regular intervals along a table. A torch in the corner of the room cast an eerie light on the faces of the black-robed men, transforming them into ghouls.* (7)

Key features: First person narration

Subjects: Carmelite Order; Catholic Church; nuns; Saint Teresa of Avila; Spain—16th century; Spanish Inquisition

Similar titles: *Sor Juana's Second Dream* by Gaspar de Alba and *The Scroll of Seduction* by Belli are other novels set in sixteenth-century Spain with strong women as the main characters.

America *Conquistada*/Conquered

These novels tell the story of the Spanish Conquest and colonization from America's perspective. Exciting melodrama takes place among the great vanquished empires of the Aztec and the Inca during the *mestizaje*, the racial mixing of Spanish conquistador and Indian maiden.

Daniel, A. B. (French).

Inca Book Duo.

This duo tells the story of Inca maiden Anamaya and Conquistador Gabriel Montelucar y Flores—can their love transcend the Spanish Conquest?

Subjects: Incas; Peru—Atahualpa; Pizarro, Francisco; Spanish Conquest

Similar titles: The Aztec Series by Gary Jennings and *Malinche* by Esquivel are other melodramas that take place during the Spanish Conquest.

Incas: Book 1, The Puma's Shadow: A Novel of a Vanished Civilization. (*Inca: Princesse du Soleil,* 2002). Translated by Alex Gilley. New York: Simon & Schuster, 2001. ISBN 9780743432746. 369pp.

Blue-eyed Anamaya finds herself at the center of political intrigue during the Spanish Conquest of the Incas. Growing up as a captive destined for sacrifice, she is later entrusted with the dying emperor's secrets about the great civilization. One of Spanish Conquistador Pizarro's cohorts, Gabriel Montelucar y Flores, falls in love with Anamaya amid the chaos of the time.

> *Hers was a mineral stare, one that repulsed the gaze and invited derision but actually mostly inspired fear. Anamaya's eyes forbade affection and hindered*

friendship-during the last year spent in the acllahuasi *no girl had really dared to become her friend.* (13)

Incas: Book 2, The Gold of Cuzco: A Novel of a Vanished Civilization. (*Inca: L'Or de Cuzco,* 2002). Translated by Alex Gilley. New York: Simon & Schuster, 2002. ISBN 9780743432754. 373pp.

Anamaya and Gabriel's story continues. They are forced to confront their divided loyalties as the Spaniard's lust for gold and land confronts the Incas' defense of their civilization and culture.

> *Gabriel had no love of gold. Many times she had watched him stand by indifferent to, even irritated by, his companion's delirious rapture at the mere touch of a few gold leaves.* (16)

Key features: Glossary

Gaspar de Alba, Alicia (Mexican American).

Calligraphy of the Witch. New York: St. Martin's Press, 2007. ISBN 9780312366414. 373pp.

Concepción Benavidez, a *mestiza* love child, is indentured to the convent and trained to be a scribe to Sor Juana Inés de la Cruz. After escaping from the convent, she has many adventures, which include being captured by pirates, being sold as a slave, and finally being accused of witchcraft during the Salem witch trial hysteria by her own daughter.

> *With no pirates defiling her, no Aléndula to cradle and sing to and fight with, nothing but the stinking bilge water and the continual rocking of the ship to distract her, she was able to sleep and forget her floating purgatory.* (16)

Key features: Some first person narration

Subjects: mothers and daughters; New England—17th century; Salem witch trials; slaves

Similar titles: *Song of the Water Saints* by Rosario and *In the Name of Salomé* by Julia Alvarez are other novels about mothers and daughters; *Assault on Paradise* features adventures during colonial times.

Sor Juana's Second Dream. Albuquerque: University of New Mexico Press, 1999. ISBN 0826320910 (cloth); 0826320929 (pbk., alk. paper). 464pp.

Sor Juana Inés de la Cruz, the great intellectual of seventeenth-century Mexico, challenges the status quo of the stifling patriarchal society by confronting the Inquisition and finding a way to create and even love in her own way.

> *"Now I want her library expurgated and every single text she owns compared against the Index. As a censor for the Inquisition, Padre Antonio, you must weed out all her banned books. I shall take care of dispossessing her of all she values. Can I trust you to be our ally in this endeavor?"* (6)

Subjects: Catholic Church; convents; Mexico—17th century; Sor Juana Inés de la Cruz

Similar titles: *The Scroll of Seduction* by Belli is another novel about strong women versus Spanish royalty and the Inquisition.

Harrigan, Lana M. (U.S. American).

Ácoma: A Novel of Conquest. **New York: Tom Doherty Associates, 1997. ISBN 0312852576. 383pp.**

The story of the Spanish Conquest of what is now New Mexico is told through the experience of Rohona, a member of the Ácoma community, who suffered greatly for resisting the Spaniards from their fortress mesa. Rohona is rescued and nursed by Maria Angelica, the wife of one of the Spanish officers. What follows is a dramatic clash and mingling of two cultures embodied in the forbidden passions of two people.

> High on the summit, none of the Ácomas slept. Strident chanting and the accentuated beat of drums reverberated throughout the night, peopling with painted specters the dreams of those Spaniards who might have managed to fall into a restless sleep. (24)

Subjects: adultery; love affairs; *mestizaje;* mutilation; New Mexico—Acoma

Similar titles: The <u>Aztec Series</u> by Gary Jennings and the <u>Inca Book Duo</u> by A. B. Daniel also feature the struggle between the conquistadors and the native peoples.

Jennings, Gary (U.S. American).

Aztec Series.

This melodramatic version of the fall of the great Aztec empire begins with the Spanish Conquest and comes full circle, ending with the Mexican War of Independence from Spain.

Aztec. New York: Atheneum, 1980. ISBN 0689110456. 745pp.

"[A]n elderly male Indian" tells the story of the arrival of the Spaniards and the destruction of the great Aztec civilization, as a chronicle told to Bishop Zumárraga, full of sex, human sacrifice, decadence, and cruelty.

> "But Your Excellency wishes to hear of what I was. This has also been explained to me. Your Excellency desires to learn what my people, this land, our lives were like in the years, in the sheaves of years before it pleased Your Excellency's king and his crossbearers and crossbowmen to deliver us from our bondage of barbarism." (6)

Key features: First person narration; sexual situations

Subjects: Aztec Indians; Mexico—Spanish Conquest

Similar titles: *Malinche* by Esquivel also presents the Spanish Conquest from the Indians' point of view, whereas <u>Inca Book Duo</u> by A. B. Daniel presents the Spanish Conquest of the Incas.

Aztec Autumn. New York: Forge, "A Tom Doherty Associates Book," 1997. ISBN 0-312-86250-4. 380pp.

The <u>Aztec</u> saga continues after the Spanish Conquest. A young warrior, Tenamáxtli, plots a doomed insurrection, intending to exact revenge for his father's murder and ultimately to eliminate the Spaniards and restore the Aztecs to their former glory. Along the way, he has many adventures and fascinating encounters.

> But the sacrifices had always been done by means of the obsidian knife that tears out the heart. The executions had always been done with the maquáhuitl sword or with arrows or with the strangling "flower garland." (11)

Key features: First person narration; sexual situations

Subjects: Aztec Indians; Mexico—16th century; rebellion

Similar titles: <u>Inca Book Duo</u> by A. B. Daniel presents the Spanish Conquest of the Incas.

Aztec Blood. New York: Forge, 2001. ISBN 0312862512. 525pp.

Cristo, the *lépero*, is the new hero. No longer fully Aztec, he is the *mestizo* result of the union of Spanish and Indian, reviled by both, but destined to be the future of Mexico, *la raza cósmica*. He is a *pícaro* who survives by his wits. Educated by a renegade priest, Cristo enjoys many swashbuckling adventures and romance but also suffers torture at the hands of the Inquisition in sixteenth-century Mexico.

> The words of the capitán of the guard come to mind like hot embers from the torturer's pyre for the not-yet-dead. Of those treasures I will speak, but first there is the matter of my birth. My youth. Dangers surmounted and a love that conquers all. (22)

Key features: First person narration; sexual situations

Subjects: *mestizos*; Mexico—16th century; Spanish Inquisition

Similar titles: *Zorro* by Allende and *Assault on Paradise* by Lobo are also swashbuckling sixteenth-century sagas.

Aztec Rage. New York: Forge, 2006. ISBN-10: 0-765-31014-7; ISBN-13: 978-0-765-31014-7. 428pp.

Don Juan de Zavala is forced to flee when his uncle disinherits him because of his mixed blood. His subsequent adventures during the Mexican War of Independence feature historical figures such as Father Miguel Hidalgo and cover territory from Northern Mexico and Yucatán to Spain during the Napoleonic Wars. Zavala is obliged to see things from the perspective of the oppressed.

> My nightmare took life as invaders emerged from the fog like fantasmas, ghosts in the mist, dark figures on great beasts, menacing as shadow gods risen from Mictlán, the Dark Place. (13)

Key features: First person narration; sexual situations

Subjects: Aztec Indians; Mexico—War of Independence; Spain—Napoleonic Wars

Similar titles: *Call No Man Master* by Tina Juárez is also about the Mexican War of Independence.

Limón, Graciela (Mexican American).

Song of the Hummingbird. Houston, TX: Arte Público Press, 1996. ISBN 1558851577. 217pp.

Aztec princess Hummingbird, or Huitzitzilin in her native language, recounts her past to a young priest on her deathbed. A witness to the Spanish Conquest of Mexico, Huitzitzilin tells the story of those who were conquered so the priest may preserve the history and culture of her people.

> *Father Benito felt a tingle on the nape of his neck, as if he had been present at a disastrous event. He was feeling what he thought Huitzitzilin must have felt at the time. Like her and her people, he was experiencing the fear of the unknown, as if he had been a native himself. He forced himself to return to his writing because, he reminded himself, these were the captains from Spain, his people, and he should not be feeling such antagonism towards them.* (86)

Key features: First person narration

Subjects: ancestors; Aztecs; Mexico—Spanish Conquest

Similar titles: The <u>Aztec Series</u> by Gary Jennings is also set in pre-Hispanic times during the events of the Conquest; *The Hummingbird's Daughter* by Urrea presents another native woman called "hummingbird" as a protagonist.

Lobo, Tatiana (Chilean).

Assault on Paradise. (*Asalto al paraíso*, 1992). Translated by Asa Zatz. Willimantic, CT: Curbstone Press, c1998. ISBN 1880684462. 297pp.

In this swashbuckling, picaresque saga, Pedro Albarán, a Spaniard, takes part in the conquest of Central America.

> *First, because she was then going through a very difficult moment in her life and , secondly, because he bore the indecorous signs of dusty roads, his beard was matted, and the only thing noteworthy about his appearance was that there was water dripping on his frayed jacket.* (5)

Subjects: Catholic Church; Costa Rica—18th century; Mayan Indians; Spanish Conquest; Spanish Inquisition

Similar titles: The <u>Captain Alatriste Adventures</u> series by Pérez-Reverte and *Zorro* by Allende are also swashbuckling action adventures that take place during colonial times.

New Nations in the Nineteenth Century/*Civilización y barbarie*

These novels take place during the nineteenth century, beginning with the Mexican War of Independence from Spain and ending around the time of the Cuban War of Independence from Spain, the War of 1898. These are turbulent times in Latin America and the Southwestern United States as people seek to impose law and order in wild, lawless spaces. The great heroes in these books, Simón Bolívar and José Martí, were particularly dedicated to defining a Latin American vision of civilization. Several titles here explore and dramatize women's participation and experiences in that process.

Alcalá, Kathleen (Mexican American).

The Flower in the Skull. **San Francisco: Chronicle Books, 1998. ISBN 0811819167. 180pp.**

Three women tell their stories, which are bound up in rape, exile, and loneliness—Concha, who flees *federales* in Mexico after they've destroyed her Opata *pueblo* to work as a housekeeper in Tucson; her daughter, Rosa; and Shelly, their descendant, who mystically finds her way to these women through her own pain.

> *In the desert, deep inside the spiny center of the cactus, nests a bird no bigger than my finger. While the sharp thorns fend off animals that would eat the eggs, the parent birds come and go at will. And this was my mother's name, "living at the heart of the spiny cactus," Chiri, what others would call Hummingbird.* (3)

Key features: First person narration

Subjects: Arizona—Tucson; California—Los Angeles; mothers and daughters; Opata Indians; rape

Similar titles: *Let Their Spirits Dance* by Duarte is also about a pilgrimage; *Song of the Hummingbird* by Limón is another novel about the plight of pre-Hispanic women.

Spirits of the Ordinary. **San Francisco: Chronicle Books, 1997. ISBN 0811814475. 244pp.**

In nineteenth-century Mexico Estela, a Catholic, has married Zacarías, whose Jewish family practices their religion in secret. When her husband leaves her to prospect for gold and find his mystical calling, Estela seeks meaning in her own life.

> *Why can't you be like other men? He asked himself as he shaved by touch. Why can't you sell women's cotton goods and go to the symphony and give your wife yet another child?* (8)

Subjects: Jews; Mexico—Saltillo; spirituality

Similar titles: *Siriguaya* by López-Medina is another novel that explores the Jewish experience.

Treasures in Heaven. **San Francisco: Chronicle Books, 2000. ISBN 0811829537. 211pp.**

Estela—the abandoned wife from *Spirits of the Ordinary*—escapes the scandals and small minds of Saltillo, taking her infant son to Mexico City at the turn of the twentieth century. Once she is in the exciting and scary metropolis, her lover puts her in touch with the mysterious *La Señorita* for help finding a job. From this connection she is immersed in progressive prerevolutionary projects—a school for prostitutes and their children, an all-woman orchestra, and a subversive newspaper—that dangerously question the status quo of women and the poor at the time.

> *The city was vast with possibilities, voracious for new blood to spill on top of old, relentless in its consumption of power and labor. People jostled for a place near the top, and those in the know stayed at the Hotel Iturbide.* (7)

Subjects: feminism; historical fiction; Mexico—Mexico City; women's friendships

Similar titles: *Here's to You, Jesusa* by Poniatowska also presents women's experiences before, during, and after the Mexican Revolution.

Amado, Jorge (Brazilian).

Showdown. (*Tocaia Grande,* 1984). **Translated by Gregory Rabassa. New York: Bantam Books, 1988. ISBN 0-553-05174-1. 422pp.**

At the beginning of the twentieth century Tocaia Grande, a fictional town set in the Bahia region of Brazil, is a rough and tumble, lawless young settlement, similar to the American Old West. Natário da Fonseca is the patriarch of this town full of eccentric characters.

> *Before any houses existed, the cemetery was dug at the foot of the hill, on the left bank of the river. The first stone served as markers for the shallow ditches where, toward the end of the morning, at noontime, the corpses were buried when Colonel Elias Daltro finally appeared, riding at the head of a few gunmen.* (5)

Subjects: Brazil—Bahia; cacao plantations

Similar titles: *One Hundred Years of Solitude* by García Márquez, *The Hive* by Cela, and *A Place Where the Sea Remembers* by Benítez are other novels structured around the collective stories of *pueblos*; other Amado novels also take place in this setting.

Baroja, Pio (Spanish).

Zalacaín the Adventurer. (*Zalacaín, el aventurero,* 1909). **Translated by James Diendl. Fort Bragg, CA: Lost Coast Press, 1997. ISBN 1882897137. 188pp.**

Zalacaín is a young Basque soldier who has many humorous adventures during the Spanish Carlist Civil Wars of 1872.

> *He had among the other children the power of his boldness and temerity. There was no place in town that Martin did not know. For him, Urbia was the gathering place of all beautiful things, the compendium of all interests and splendors.* (8)

Subjects: Basques; picaresque; soldiers; Spain—19th century

Similar titles: *Captain Alatriste* by Pérez-Reverte and *Aztec Blood* by Gary Jennings also feature swashbuckling adventures.

Bauman, Jon R. (U.S. American).

Santa Fe Passage. **New York: Truman Talley Books, 2004. ISBN 031233348X. 323pp.**

Matthew Collins seeks his fortune in the part of nineteenth-century Mexico that will later become New Mexico. His adventures take him through many turbulent events, hobnobbing with the power brokers of the day. During and after the U.S.–Mexican War of 1848, he finds himself in a tricky and perilous situation, having married a Mexican woman and become a Mexican citizen.

> *The year before Matt became indentured to Banhofer, Mexico had thrown off Spanish colonial rule and had opened its doors to trade with the United States. At the store, Matt heard the stories that trickled back to Kaskaskia about William Becknell, a Franklin, Missouri man who had led a pack train loaded with*

merchandise through the Comanche country and into the newborn Mexican Republic." (18)

Subjects: Mexico—19th century; New Mexico—Santa Fe; U.S.–Mexican War

Similar titles: *Call No Man Master* by Tina Juárez also take place in nineteenth-century Mexico.

Boyd, Bill (U.S. American).

Bolivar: Liberator of a Continent. **New York: S.P.I. Books, 1998. ISBN 1561719443. 278pp.**

Simón Bolívar's life is recounted in this highly fictionalized and dramatized telling that concentrates on his exploits on the battlefield and in the bedroom.

> *Rodriguez was too astonished at the boy's audacity to stop him. The other two boys climbed onto the wall and stared in amazement as Simoncito walked toward the large bull.* (4)

Subjects: Bolívar, Simón; South America—Wars of Independence

Similar titles: *The General in His Labyrinth* by García Márquez is a masterful novel about the great Liberator, Simon Bolívar; *Our Lives Are the Rivers* by Manrique features Bolivar's lover as the protagonist.

Caparrós, Martín (Argentinian).

Valfierno: The Man Who Stole the **Mona Lisa.** (*Valfierno*, 2004). **Translated by Jasper Reid. ISBN 9780743297936. 342pp.**

Marqués de Valfierno, the mastermind behind the infamous heist of the *Mona Lisa* painting in 1911, tells his life story to an American journalist. It begins in illegitimacy and penury in nineteenth-century Argentina. Using his quick wit and an uncanny ability to forge paintings, will Valfierno be able to live life on his own terms?

> *I suppose that in the early days, while we were happy in the big house, it never occurred to me. Diego and Mariana were the ones with a father because they were the ones who had things; I had some things, too, and they also had a mother who was very pretty and had lighter hair than my mother and I never thought to ask.* (11)

Key features: First person narration in several voices

Subjects: Argentina; art forgery; con men; France; *Mona Lisa* (painting)

Similar titles: *The News from Paraguay* by Tuck and *The Way to Paradise* by Vargas Llosa are other novels that feature Latin Americans in nineteenth-century France.

🎋 Cela, Camilo José (Spanish).

Christ versus Arizona. (*Cristo versus Arizona*, 1988). **Translated by Martin Sokolinsky. Champaign, IL: Dalkey Archive Press, 2007. ISBN 9781564783417. 274pp.**

Wendell Liverpool Espana (the Spanish word for Spain, *casualmente*) narrates this novel in one longdrawn-out sentence, exposing the violence and racism typified by the infamous events at the OK Corral, when Wyatt Earp was sheriff in the North American Southwest.

> [I]t's all pretty hard to understand but it happened just the way I'm telling it, I swear I'm not lying, until I was twenty or twenty-two I just didn't know who I was, where I came from, in other words didn't know who my parents were, until I was told about my mother who worked as a whore in Tomistón. (3)

Key features: First person narration presented in one long, run-on sentence; afterword by Lucile C. Charelbois

Subjects: Arizona—Tombstone—1881; Earp, Wyatt; murder; OK Corral; racism

Similar titles: *The Color of Summer* by Arenas and *Palinuro of Mexico* by del Paso are other examples of innovative narrative styles.

Awards: Nobel Prize for Literature, 1989

Ephron, Amy (U.S. American).

White Rose: Una Rosa Blanca. **New York: W. Morrow, 1999. ISBN 0688163149. 259pp.**

A heroic figure to Americans, Evangelina Cisneros is imprisoned on the Isle of Pines for defending her revolutionary father and spurning the advances of an amorous general in 1890s colonial Cuba. Karl Decker, a reporter for the newspaper magnate William Randolph Hearst, is sent to interview and rescue Evangelina, a quest Hearst hopes will help push the United States into war with Spain. The married Decker finds himself forced to examine his own ideals and ethics when he falls for the beautiful Evangelina.

> And yet her spirit, visible in her eyes, in the way that she took everything in in a moment and her agility, evident even though she was seated, indicated something stronger and wild, if pushed. He wondered if he would be able to trust her. Trust was always fairly tricky with someone who believed in a cause more than in anything else. (6)

Subjects: adultery; Cuba—Havana; love stories; reporters; revolutionaries

Similar titles: *The News from Paraguay* by Tuck is another novel with a nineteenth-century Latin American female protagonist; *The Divine Husband* by Goldman is also set in nineteenth-century Latin America, amid the struggle for Cuban independence.

Fontes, Montserrat (Mexican American).

Dreams of the Centaur. **New York: W.W. Norton, 1996. ISBN 0-393-03847-5. 349pp.**

The saga of the Durcal family unfolds in the Northern Mexican state of Sonora during the dictatorial regime of Porfirio Diaz and his persecution of the Yaqui Indians. The Durcals are sympathetic to the Yaquis. Alejo, the oldest son, sets out to avenge his father's death, while his mother, Felipa, fights to protect him and their family.

> Determined to make his land yield, at first he had worked alone; when he had money, he hired Yaquis. Felipa had heard ranchers gossip of José Durcal and his Yaquis. "It's one thing to hire them, but to live with them? Never." (18–19)

Subjects: families; haciendas; Mexico—Sonora; mothers and sons; *Porfiriato*—Díaz regime; Yaqui Indians

Similar titles: *Book of Lamentations* by Castellanos is also about Indian struggles in Mexico; *The Hummingbird's Daughter* by Urrea, *The Flower in the Skull* by Alcalá, and *Wild Steps of Heaven* by Villaseñor are also set in prerevolutionary Northern Mexico.

García Márquez, Gabriel (Colombian).

The General in His Labyrinth. (*El general en su laberinto,* 1989). Translated by Edith Grossman. New York: Alfred A. Knopf, 1990. ISBN 0394582586. 285pp.

After leaving Bogotá and evading assassination attempts, on a final trip down the Magdalena River the great general Simón Bolívar recalls his momentous life and efforts to create a unified Latin America independent of Spain.

> He always considered death an unavoidable professional hazard. He had fought all his wars in the front lines, without suffering a scratch, and he had moved through enemy fire with such thoughtless serenity that even his officers accepted the easy explanation that he believed himself invulnerable. (8)

Key features: Chronology

Subjects: Bolívar, Simón; Latin America—independence; Magdalena River

Similar titles: *Our Lives Are the Rivers* by Manrique features Bolívar's lover as protagonist.

Goldman, Francisco (Guatemalan American).

The Divine Husband. New York: Atlantic Monthly Press, 2004. ISBN 0-87113-915-4. 465pp.

María de las Nieves, brought up in a cloister in nineteenth-century Central America, eventually makes her way to the salons of New York's Gilded Age. Here she encounters some of the famous celebrities of the time and takes part in intricate power struggles featuring José Martí, the poet and Cuban patriot.

> The story of how María de las Nieves had first come to live with Paquita and her family when both girls were six was a peculiar but fascinating one, and Juan Aparicio never tired of telling it. . . . How there had been a legend, or rumors, brought down by Indians to Quezaltenango, that far away in the mountains two women and a little girl were living on their own deep in the forest. The little girl had golden hair, one of the women had leathery black skin, and they spoke among themselves, the Indians claimed, in an unintelligible demon language. (17)

Subjects: Central America; Cuban independence; Martí, José; New York; nuns; poets; revolutionary struggles; single mothers; writers

Similar titles: *Silent Wing* by Bernardo is also about a Martí-type poet in love; *Our Lives Are the Rivers* by Manrique is also set in nineteenth-century Latin America.

Juárez, Tina (Mexican American; Tejana).

Call No Man Master. Houston, TX: Arte Público Press, 1995. ISBN 1558851240. 395pp.

Carmen Rangel is a child on the hacienda, a member of the Abrantes household and close companion to Don Esteban's son right before Mexico's War of Independence. When the rebellion against Spain begins, Carmen does not realize the republicans' cause is just until she suffers herself, as a half Indian *mestiza*. She later valiantly follows Father Miguel Hidalgo into battle, from Guanajuato to Mexico City to San Antonio de Bexar in Texas.

> *When we were children and played Cristóbal's games on the grounds of his father's estate near Guanajuato, I did not think it was a curse to be a woman. Some of the maids in Don Esteban's household said it was curse to be born a woman in the Viceroyalty of New Spain, a land the ancients had called Mexico.* (7)

Subjects: coming-of-age; Mexico—War of Independence; Texas; war

Similar titles: *Aztec Rage* by Gary Jennings is another novel about the Mexican War of Independence.

South Wind Come. Houston, TX: Arte Público Press, 1998. ISBN 1-55885-231-X. 286pp.

A sequel to *Call No Man Master*, this novel is told from the point of view of Carmen's young granddaughter, Teresa, a young girl who plays a part in the historic events happening in Mexico, Texas, and the United States during the second half of the nineteenth century.

> *Whatever my mother saw, or thought she saw, was a far different thing from what I imagined was happening, which was nothing less than a solemn and sacred ceremony that would make my brother and me forever unconquerable by mere mortal beings.* (8)

Subjects: Civil War—U.S.; love stories; Mexican Americans; Mexico—19th century; Texas

Similar titles: *The Hummingbird's Daughter* by Urrea and *Dreams of the Centaur* by Fontes are also set in prerevolutionary Mexico.

Moya, Ana Gloria (Argentinian).

Heaven of Drums. (*Cielo de tambores*, 2002). Translated by W. Nick Hill. Willimantic, CT: Curbstone Press, 2007. ISBN 9781931896252. 193pp.

Maria Kumba is a strong woman who actively participates in the Argentine war of independence. She falls in love with Manuel Belgrano, a *criollo* (considered to be a white Spanish immigrant) war hero who will not love her openly because she is a mulatto. Gregorio Rivas, a *mestizo*, is also active in the fight and in love with Maria Kumba.

> *What a pleasure to watch how she was transformed when the distant, nostalgic sounds of drums, mazacayas, and marimbas from some nighttime ceremony filtered through the silent house.* (7)

Key features: First person narration in multiple voices

Subjects: Argentina; Argentina—War of Independence; *mestizos*; mulattos; race relations

Similar titles: *In the Name of Salomé* by Julia Alvarez is another novel about race in a Latin American country.

Payno, Manuel (Mexican).

The Bandits from Río Frío: A Naturalistic and Humorous Novel of Customs, Crimes, and Horrors. (Los bandidos de Río Frío, 1891). **Translated by Alan Fluckley. ISBN 9781587368226. 456pp. (vol. 1); 9781587368233; 632pp. (vol. 2).**

The sweeping *costumbrista* novel portrays the social life and customs of the different classes in nineteenth century Mexico written in installments *a la* Charles Dickens. The story follows the life and destiny of the bastard son of a countess and a Colonel who hooks up with a notorious bandit after suffering injustice and indignity.

> *Their life for the most part was peaceful and monotonous. They got up at first light. The husband mounted his horse and rode off to his work: to the pastures, fields or town, and not a few times to Mexico City. He returned at the dinner hour and later sat on the little stone bench in the shade by the door and smoked aromatic cigars from the tobacconists in the city.* (11)

Key features: Dictionary of Spanish and Nahuatl terms

Subjects: bandits; illegitimate children; love stories; Mexico—19th century

Similar titles: *Santa Fe Passage* by Baumann, *Call No Man Master* by Tina Juárez, and *Aztec Rage* by Gary Jennings are also set in nineteenth-century Mexico; *Ramona* by Jackson is another classic novel written in the nineteenth century.

Tuck, Lily (U.S. American).

The News from Paraguay. **New York: HarperCollins, 2004. ISBN 0-06-620944-7. 248pp.**

In 1854 in Paris, Irishwoman Ella Lynch—already divorced and a mother at nineteen—is seduced by Francisco Solano Lopez, a dashing young Paraguayan. She becomes his mistress and returns with him to Paraguay. Francisco later inherits the presidency, ruling over the civilization and barbarity that was Paraguay in the second half of the nineteenth century.

> *For him it began with a feather. A bright blue parrot feather that fell out of Ella Lynch's hat while she was horseback riding one afternoon in the Bois de Boulogne.* (1)

Key features: Epistolary style; multiple points of view

Subjects: dictatorships—Solano Lopez; France—Paris; love stories; Paraguay; war

Similar titles: *In the Name of Salomé* by Julia Alvarez and *The Divine Husband* by Goldman are other novels set in nineteenth-century Latin America.

Urrea, Luis Alberto (Mexican American).

The Hummingbird's Daughter. **New York: Little, Brown, 2005. ISBN 0-316-74546-4. 499pp.**

Teresita Urrea is the illegitimate daughter of the local *cacique*. She grows up under the care of a midwife during the turbulent times before the Mexican Revolution. Teresita is a natural healer and survives hard times and mistreatment to become a famous *curandera*, a quasi-saint, in Northern Mexico.

> *The ranch workers set aside candied sweet potatoes, cactus and guayaba sweets, mango jam, goat jerky, dribbly white cheeses, all food they themselves would like to eat, but they knew the restless spirits were famished, and no family could assuage its own hunger and insult the dead. Jesús! Everybody knew that being dead could put you in a terrible mood.* (4)

Key features: Teresita Urrea was a real person and the author's great-grandmother.

Subjects: *curanderas*; family sagas; healers; Mexican Revolution; Mexico; Mexico—Sinaloa

Similar titles: *Dreams of the Centaur* by Fontes and *South Wind Come* by Tina Juárez are other novels set in nineteenth-century Mexico.

Vargas Llosa, Mario (Peruvian).

The Way to Paradise. (El paraíso en la otra esquina, 2003). **Translated by Natasha Wimmer. New York: Farrar, Straus & Giroux, 2003. ISBN 0-374-22803-5. 373pp.**

In alternating chapters, Vargas Llosa contrasts the lives of Flora Tristán (daughter of a Frenchwoman and a wealthy Peruvian), an activist in 1840s France for workers' rights and social justice, and Paul Gauguin, the famous painter in 1890s Tahiti, who happened to be Flora's grandson.

> *Most likely, Florita, your memory preserved only what your mother had told you of those early years. You were too little to remember the gardeners, the maids, the furniture upholstered in silk and velvet, the heavy draperies, the silver, gold, crystal, and painted china that adorned the salon and the dining room.* (5)

Key features: Second person narration

Subjects: feminists; France; Gaugin, Paul; painters; Peru; socialists; Tahiti; Tristán, Flora

Similar titles: *In the Name of Salomé* by Julia Alvarez is another novel structured around the intertwining stories of historical figures; *Our Lives Are the Rivers* by Manrique and *The Divine Husband* by Goldman are also set in nineteenth-century Latin America with historical protagonists.

The War of the End of the World. (La guerra del fin del mundo, 1981). **Translated by Helen R. Lane. New York: Penguin Books, 1981. ISBN 0374286515. 568pp.**

In turn-of-the-nineteenth-century Brazil, the town of Canudos is set up as a libertarian utopia by Counselor Antonio Vicente Mendes Maciel. More than 10,000 are killed when the government steps in to throttle this idealistic endeavor.

> *Perplexed, frightened, enraged, they nudged each other and communicated to each other their feelings of apprehension and wrath, in voices that mingled and blended into one, producing that belligerent music that was rising heavenward from Natuba as the Counselor and his shabby followers entered the town by way of the road from Cipó.* (21)

Subjects: Brazil—Conselheiro Insurrection, 1897; civil war; fanatical leaders; utopias

Similar titles: *Showdown* by Amado portrays a similar Brazilian utopia, and *Cellophane* by Arana presents utopia in Peru.

Villaseñor, Victor (Mexican American).

Wild Steps of Heaven. **New York: Dell Publishing, 1996. ISBN 0385315694. 296pp.**

This fictionalized account of the author's paternal grandfather, Don Juan Jesus Villaseñor, portrays the times leading up to the Mexican Revolution. Don Juan Jesus, descended from Spaniards, has married Doña Margarita, of indigenous extraction, and fathers a dynasty that confronts the chaos and violence of the revolution with heroism and magic.

> *But Juan had already dallied his* reata *about his saddle horn, and the wooden horn was smoking fire as he dragged and fished and pulled and jerked the mighty snake through the brush and boulders.* (12)

Subjects: families; Mexican Revolution

Similar titles: *The Book of Lamentations* by Castellanos is another novel about Indian struggles in Mexico; *The Hummingbird's Daughter* by Urrea, *Dreams of the Centaur* by Fontes, and *The Flower in the Skull* by Alcalá are also set in prerevolutionary Northern Mexico. *Rain of Gold*, also by Villaseñor, is another novel about his family.

Twentieth Century: Pre–World War II

These novels bring to life the hard times following the Mexican Revolution and the War of 1898, including the penury of the Great Depression, the heroism of the Spanish Civil War, and the horror of Trujillo's massacre of the Haitians in the Dominican Republic. They also portray the artistic creativity and the rich bohemian life that flowered during that period in Mexico City and Havana.

Baca, Ana (New Mexican American).

Mama Fela's Girls. **Albuquerque: University of New Mexico Press, 2006. ISBN 0826340239. 318pp.**

In northeastern New Mexico, Mama Fela lives surrounded by her "girls"—her daughter Cita, her doting six-year-old granddaughter Cipriana, and Cipriana's mother, Graciela. Together these women sacrifice themselves, their dreams, and their time with their children to keep their families alive and thriving during the height of the Great Depression.

> *Cita felt like slapping her brother. She didn't want him to dredge up old memories, especially here, especially now. She wished he would just go away like he had so many years ago when she needed him. She and Mama Fela could take care of Sara, Rebecca and Benny. They had already been doing just that.* (198)

Subjects: families; Great Depression—1929; Mexican Americans; New Mexico

Similar titles: *The Chin Kiss King* by Veciana-Suarez is another novel about several generations of women; *The Wise Women of Havana* by Bernardo is also about family struggles during the Depression.

Bernardo, José Raúl.

The Wise Women of Havana. **New York: HarperCollins, 2002. ISBN 0066211239. 323pp.**

Newlyweds Lorenzo and Marguita agree to move into his parents' house to help out the family as the Great Depression rolls on. Once there, Marguita and Lorenzo's spinster sister, Loló, have a difficult time as they struggle with jealousy, loneliness, and hard times. After a chance encounter with a young priest at a party, Loló soon discovers she is pregnant and must keep it hidden. Marguita too finds herself pregnant, with a second child the young couple can't afford. Both women are faced with the most difficult decision a mother ever has to make.

> *None of this was meant to happen, Loló tells herself as she falls on her bed. None of this was meant to happen, she keeps telling herself hours later, as she lies sleepless in the middle of the night, looking up at the heavily carved plaster ceiling that seems to be hovering oppressively above her. (211–12)*

Subjects: Cuba—Havana; Cubans; family relationships; Great Depression—1929; pregnancy; women's friendships

Similar titles: *Mama Fela's Girls* by Baca is another novel about family struggles during the Depression; *The Chin Kiss King* by Veciana-Suarez also deals with the difficulties of pregnancy and having children.

Carlson, Lori Marie (U.S. American).

The Flamboyant. **New York: HarperCollins, 2002. ISBN 0066210682. 241pp.**

The story of Lenora Demarest is set in the 1920s and 1930s. Lenora is an ingénue whose father decides after the death of Lenora's mother to move from their home in Western New York to the relatively new U.S. possession of Puerto Rico to start a new life. As Lenora adapts to life on their new plantation, will she choose to follow her dream to become an aviatrix with the dashing George, or settle down with the debonair Ignacio, or perhaps do both?

> *On those evenings, an array of nocturnal creatures held Lenora's attention. At dusk, standing beneath her mother's clematis-covered pergola, she was amused by the hummingbirds. She would peer at them from behind a pine tree intrigued by their fluttered dance, amazed at their tiny magnificence. (7)*

Subjects: aviation; love triangles; New York; Puerto Rico

Similar titles: *Captain of the Sleepers* by Montero also features aviation and is set in Puerto Rico; *The Last Masquerade* by Rodríguez is also set in the Caribbean in the 1920s.

Castellanos, Rosario (Mexican).

The Book of Lamentations. (*Oficio de tinieblas,* **1962). Translated by Esther Allen. New York: Marsilio Publishing, 1996. ISBN 1-56886-038-2. 400pp.**

The Tzotzil Indians' way of life, daily struggles, and suffering in Chamula, Chiapas, are portrayed against the backdrop of their rebellion against the Spanish *ladinos* in Mexico in the 1930s.

> *Morning comes late to Chamula. The cock crows to chase away the darkness. As the men grope toward wakefulness, the women find their way to the ashes where they bend and blow to reveal the embers. (3)*

Subjects: 1930s; Mexico—Chamula; Tzotzil Indians

Similar titles: *Deep Rivers* by Arguedas is another classic about Indian uprisings in Latin America. *The Hive* by Cela also presents daily life under repression; *A Place Where the Sea Remembers* by Benítez portrays repression of Indians in the present day.

Danticat, Edwidge (Haitian American).

The Farming of Bones: A Novel. **New York: Soho Press, 1998. ISBN 1-56947-126-6. 312pp.**

Amabelle, a Haitian servant living in the Dominican Republic during the dictatorship, tells her story of Trujillo's slaughter of Haitians in 1937. She is companion, maid, and midwife to Señora Valencia and lover to the field hand Sebastien. With fragile hope for a future together, Amabelle and Sebastien are haunted by the memory of their parents' violent deaths.

> *He is lavishly handsome by the dim light of my castor oil lamp, even though the cane stalks have ripped apart most of the skin on his shiny black face, leaving him with crisscrossed trails of furrowed scars.* (1)

Subjects: dictatorships—Trujillo; Dominican Republic; dreams; Haitians; *kout/ kouto*

Similar titles: *In the Time of the Butterflies* by Junot Alvarez presents the Trujillo regime from the Dominican perspective, as does *The Brief Wondrous Life of Oscar Wao* by Junot Díaz.

🏆 Delahunt, Meaghan (Australian).

In the Casa Azul: A Novel of Revolution and Betrayal. **New York: St. Martin's Press, 2001. ISBN 0-312-29106-X. 308pp.**

Leon Trotsky hid from Stalin's assassins in Mexico City in a fortresslike household. The radical artists Frida Kahlo and Diego Rivera befriended Trotsky and included him in their bohemian milieu. Trotsky's diary entries, Stalin's suicidal wife, several Mexican artists, as well as Trotsky's bodyguard, and Kahlo's cook give testimony to the rich and intriguing stew present in Mexico City at that time. The story of Trotsky and Kahlo's love affair is set against the larger backdrop of the story of the Russian Revolution—the hopes and final doom of both the revolution and Trotsky himself.

> *At the last moment, a gust from the furnace blasted the body upright, fiery strands of hair across her face, the eyes in the centre of the blazing hair. Like the face of a flower. Like something from her own hand. As if she had painted herself, one last time, a still life that was never still, to sit upright like that, with eyes that saw through fire.* (3)

Key features: First person narration in the form of diaries and fictional testimony

Subjects: artists; Kahlo, Frida; love affairs; Mexico—Mexico City; revolutionaries; Russian Revolution; Soviet Union; Trotsky, Leon

Similar titles: *Tinisima* by Poniatowska is another vision of postrevolutionary, bohemian Mexico City; *Treasures in Heaven* by Alcalá presents women in revolutionary Mexico City.

Awards: Saltire Society First Book Award, 2001; Commonwealth Writers Prize for Best First Book—regional winner (Southeast Asia and South Pacific), 2002

Estrada, Alfredo José (Cuban American).

Welcome to Havana, Sr. Hemingway. **Miami, FL: Planeta Publishing, 2005. ISBN 1-933169-01-X 380pp.**

Javier López Angulo's grandson travels to Cuba to find out about his grandfather's friendship with Ernest Hemingway and why it ended. Most of the action takes place in Havana in the 1930s amid coups, revolution, and Prohibition.

> *In those days, it was a dilapidated village of wooden houses whose sloping roofs funneled rainwater intro cisterns. But the wrought-iron balconies were draped with allamanda blossoms, and the pale nights smelled of rum and cigar smoke. (28)*

Key features: Some first person narration

Subjects: Cuba—Havana—1930s; Hemingway, Ernest; love affairs; revolution

Similar titles: *Adiós Hemingway* by Padura also features Ernest Hemingway in Cuba.

Forbes, Charlotte (U.S. American).

The Good Works of Ayela Linde. **New York: Arcade Publishing, 2006. ISBN 1559708077. 227pp.**

Told through stories from those who knew her, the enigmatic life of Ayela is captured in this novel. Born during the Great Depression to a Mexican dressmaker, Ayela is raised by her mother and grandmother, who some suspect is a witch. The gem of her small town, Ayela marries a Bostonian who is too besotted with her to ever leave Santa Rosalita. Married, the couple has numerous children, and Aleya grows into an intriguing, complex woman who mystifies even those who know her well.

> *He was afraid of her; I had inherited his fear but mine was different and because of her beauty. If only she hadn't been beautiful. Beauty was the truth of her, but there was another truth beyond the first, and not even he could have prepared me. (107)*

Subjects: biographies—fiction; marriage; Mexicans; motherhood; mothers and sons

Similar titles: Titles by Julia Alvarez also feature multiple narrators and a similar tone.

Lagasse, Mary Helen (U.S. American).

❦ *The Fifth Sun: A Novel.* **Willimantic, CT: Curbstone Press, 2004. ISBN 1-931896-0504. 339pp.**

In 1926 Mercedes Vasconcelos leaves Tabasco and her father's family, where she has lived as an *arrimada*—illegitimate daughter/servant—to seek her fortune in New Orleans. There she meets her future husband, Chucho (Jesse) Ibáñez, a mining engineer from Hidalgo, Mexico, and they struggle to raise a family.

> *Unmottled by the fevered anguish that had tethered soul to body, Nicolasa's face was as fine-grained and even-colored as a clay urn. The bridge of her nose was keener, the nostrils fixed in their natural audacious flair. (1)*

Subjects: immigrants—Mexican; Louisiana—New Orleans; Mexicans; Mexico—Hidalgo; Mexico—Tabasco

Similar titles: *Music of the Mill* by Luis J. Rodriguez and *Dark Side of the Dream* by Grattan-Domínguez are other novels about Mexican American families in the United States.

Awards: Mármol Prize, 2004

Massey, Cynthia Leal (Tejana).

Fire Lilies. **Helotes, TX: Rocking M Press, 2001. ISBN 1-59109-250-7. 367pp.**

Dolores and Alicia Guzman, sisters belonging to the rich *hacendado* class, follow separate paths seeking love throughout the travails of the Mexican Revolution of 1910 where they cross paths with the likes of Pancho Villa and Francisco I. Madero. The dialectics of the Revolution play themselves out within the Guzman family as it struggles to maintain its social status and come to grips with the new society.

> *Arango looked into Dolores' green eyes. "Señora, I will never forget what you have done. Adiós." He picked up the guard's rifle and under the cloak of darkness, Doroteo Arango and his* compañero *stole into the night.* (5)

Subjects: *hacendados*; historical fiction; love stories; Mexican Revolution; Mexicans; Nuevo León—Monterrey

Similar titles: *The Underdogs* by Azuela is the classic novel of the Mexican Revolution; *Tear This Heart Out* by Mastretta also presents the feminine perspective.

Medina, Pablo (Cuban American).

The Cigar Roller: A Novel. **New York: Grove Press, 2005. ISBN 0802117929. 178 pp.**

El viejo, Amadeo Terra, is in a nursing home in Tampa after a massive stroke. When the nurse feeds him a spoonful of mango from a baby food jar, Amadeo's memory takes a journey back through his long life as a *cabrón*, a Cuban immigrant, and a refugee fleeing the Spaniards before the War of 1898.

> *He avoids her eyes and voice, gentle and cheery, riding a crest of impatience, and concentrates on the taste that has filled his mouth, spread up his nostrils, and taken over his whole being. He can smell the past, smell his childhood, pungent and silky, see the sun through the branches of the tree he hid behind until his father tired of looking for him and headed home with anger swelling his forehead.* (5)

Subjects: cigar industry; Cuba—Havana; families; Florida—Tampa; immigrants—Cuban; stroke patients

Similar titles: *The Death of Artemio Cruz* by Carlos Fuentes also features an old man and his memories; *The Second Death of Única Aveyano* by Mestre-Reed features an old woman and her memories as a Cuban immigrant to the United States.

Montero, Mayra (Caribbean: Cuban, Puerto Rican).

The Messenger: A Novel. (Como un mensajero tuyo, 1998). **Translated by Edith Grossman. New York: HarperCollins, 1998. 21pp.**

Caruso's daughter tells of the love affair between the mythic tenor and a Chinese Cuban mulata woman, which occurred during the time he disappeared after fleeing a bomb attack on the theater where he was singing in 1920s Havana—a thrilling story of music, magic, and love.

> *While I drank I looked into his eyes and remembered what he had said, and that was like remembering what was going to happen: first the noise and then the wreckage, and the face of a man, his whole body, coming out of the smoke.* (11)

Key features: First person narration

Subjects: Caruso, Enrico; Cuba—Havana; historical fiction; love stories; opera; revolutionary struggles; Santería

Similar titles: *A Simple Habana Melody* by Hijuelos is also about music, Cuba, and love, although not necessarily in that order.

Philoctete, René (Haitian).

Massacre River. (Peuple des terres melées, 1989). **Translated by Linda Coverdale. New York: New Directions, 2005. ISBN 0811215857. 238pp.**

When Dominican dictator Trujillo orders death to all Haitian "devils," Pedro Brito seeks to protect his Haitian wife, Adele, by enlisting the support of the community. As an ominous bird of prey glides over the *pueblo,* evil and magic are unleashed with the hateful dictates that force good people to confront demons in many forms.

> *So it goes while the contraption, hovering between the fields and the stars, continues to brood a nightmare, and piled-up machetes lie resting, recuperating for the next onslaught on Haitian heads. The bells are quiet now.* (26)

Key features: Preface and introduction

Subjects: Dominican Republic; Haiti; love stories; massacres; racism

Similar titles: Danticat's, Junot Díaz's, and Belli's novels deal with similar subject matter —cruelty and magic in the Caribbean.

Poniatowska, Elena (Polish Mexican).

Tinisima. (Tinísima, 1992). **Translated by Katherine Silver. New York: Farrar, Straus & Giroux, 1996. ISBN 0374277850. 357pp.**

This is Tina Modotti's tumultuous and tragic story. An Italian actress, model, and photographer, Modotti embodied the free, sensuous spirit and revolutionary fervor of that generation of artists living in postrevolutionary Mexico City, where anything seemed possible. Tragically, Julio Antonio Mella, her Cuban communist lover, was assassinated, which resulted in a sensational trial that titillated the whole world when Tina was unjustly accused of the deed.

> *The combination of cold and fear makes Tina tremble uncontrollably. Enea Sormenti pats her reassuringly on the arm and speaks to her in the language of her*

childhood. Now, now. More soft caresses, until Tina gives up and lets her head fall on his shoulder. (3)

Subjects: Mella, Julio Antonio; Modotti, Tina; photographers; revolutionaries; Mexico; Soviet Union; Spain

Similar titles: *In the Casa Azul* by Delahunt, *Treasures in Heaven* by Alcalá, and *Frida* by Mujica are also set among the bohemian milieu in postrevolutionary Mexico City.

Ramos, Luis Arturo (Mexican).

Within These Walls. (*Intramuros*, **1983**). **Translated by Samuel A. Zimmerman. Pittsburgh, PA: Latin American Literary Review Press, 1997. ISBN 0935480897. 221pp.**

Uncle Gabriel Santibañez leaves Spain for Mexico in 1915 and meets his nephew, Esteban Niño, at the Port of Veracruz, after he flees the Spanish Civil War in the 1930s. The two must reconcile their very different dreams of freedom and prosperity in the New World with hard reality.

> *The port was becoming familiar to them. The streets, plazas, statues were taking on meaning. Everything became less hostile, and that first odor that had invaded their noses, was defining itself, taking on a name.* (17)

Subjects: immigrants—Spanish; Mexico—Veracruz

Similar titles: *Monkey Hunting* by Cristina García is another novel about immigrants to Latin America. An interesting look at emigration from Spain can be found in *The Disinherited: Exile and the Making of Spanish Culture, 1492–1975* by Kamen.

Rivera-Garza, Cristina (Mexican).

🖋 *No One Will See Me Cry.* (*Nadie me verá llorar*, **1999**). **Translated by Andrew Hurley. Willimantic, CT: Curbstone Press, 2003. ISBN 1880684918. 229pp.**

In a Mexican insane asylum in the 1920s, photographer Joaquin Buitrago encounters Matilda, a woman he believes is a prostitute he knew back in the day. He becomes obsessed with investigating her past. They tell each other their stories—how does one come to be a photographer of crazy people, and how does one become crazy, and what is crazy anyway in the crazy times of postrevolutionary Mexico?

> *His hair is too long for the time; the wide lapels of his jacket are out of fashion now and his gaunt face makes one think of sleeplessness, illness. If it were not for the whiteness of his skin and a certain fineness of his features, people would surely give him a wide berth on the sidewalks.* (12)

Subjects: insane asylums; Mexico—Mexico City—1920s; photographers; prostitutes

Similar titles: *In the Casa Azul* by Delahunt and *Treasures in Heaven* by Alcalá are other novels set in postrevolutionary Mexico.

Awards: Winner, Sor Juana Inés de la Cruz Prize, 2002

Rodríguez, Antonio Orlando (Cuban).

The Last Masquerade. (*Aprendices de brujo*, 2005). **Translated by Ernesto Mestre-Reed. New York: Rayo, 2005. ISBN 0-06-058632-X. 464pp.**

In the 1920s, a pair of Cuban gay blades has many outrageous and decadent adventures while on the trail of grand dame actress, *a la Sarah Bernhardt*, Eleonora Duse. Famous characters of the time, such as Gloria Swanson and Thomas Edison, join in the fun.

> *Pointing at each image, my lover specified the date and place where it had been taken, and added any pertinent details about the important fights, along with glowing remarks about the Chilean's fierce demeanor, about his pointy nipples, which would make even the most serene observer lose his mind, and about the manly stance with which he faced the photojournalists at Madison Square Garden.* (5)

Subjects: Caribbean—1920s; séances; theater; upper classes

Similar titles: A *Simple Habana Melody* by Hijuelos and *The Messenger* by Montero are also set in the Caribbean in the 1920s.

Taibo, Paco Ignacio, II (Mexican).

The Shadow of the Shadow. (*Sombra de la sombra*, 1986). **Translated by William I. Neuman. El Paso, TX: Cinco Puntos Press, 1991. ISBN 9781933693002. 233pp.**

Four *amigos*—a poet, a crime reporter, a lawyer whose principal clients are prostitutes, and a Chinese Mexican union organizer—in postrevolutionary Mexico City meet every evening to play dominoes. They find themselves in the middle of a conspiracy that puts them through some hard-boiled adventures.

> *It was hard to know what to think about that face, sometimes peaceful as a child's, sometimes convulsed with an inner fury. It was hard to tell the difference between wit and bile, hard to distinguish the amiable youth from the tortured razor-sharp man. There was something broken somewhere inside the poet.* (3)

Subjects: conspiracies; Mexico—1920s; murder

Similar titles: *Treasures in Heaven* by Alcalá, *In the Casa Azul* by Delahunt, and *Here's to You, Jesusa* by Poniatowska are other novels set in Mexico City after the Mexican Revolution.

Tejera, Nivaria (Spanish).

The Ravine. (*El barranco*, 1959). **Translated by Carol Maier. New York: State University of New York Press, 2008. ISBN 9780791472927. 165pp.**

A seven-year-old girl tells the terrible story of the Spanish fascists coming for her father, who is in hiding as a defender of the Republic. When they find him, they take him to a concentration camp. How can the family live with the fear that he may be placed in front of a firing squad?

> *When I woke up this morning it was Sunday.*
>
> *I found out because Grandpa came into Auntie's room and he was wearing his suit with a waistcoat. I've been sleeping here since "the coup," because it's where they came to search for Papa and this way I can feel close to him.* (15)

Key features: First person narration; afterword and notes

Subjects: child narrators; Civil War—Spain; concentration camps

Similar titles: *Balún Canán* by Castellanos is another novel narrated by a child.

Twentieth Century: Post–World War II

After World War II Latin America, Spain, and Portugal suffered oppressive regimes under despots like Franco, Pinochet, Trujillo, and Salazar. The power elite were beginning to rot, while Latinos in the United States were grappling with the Vietnam War and racial tensions.

Antunes, António Lobo (Portuguese).

🏆 *The Inquisitors' Manual. (O Manual dos Inquisidores, 1996)*. **Translated by Richard Zenith. New York: Grove Press, 2003. ISBN 0802117325. 435pp.**

During the close of the twentieth century, the family of one of dictator Salazar's advisors languishes and decays. Senhor Francisco is confined to a nursing home. João, his son, and João's illegitimate and resentful half-sister Paula must get used to life after their fall from grace. Many other voices from Portugal and its African colonies under the Fascist dictator's thumb come to life through the inquisitor's reports.

> [T]he house and farm from my father's day with the staircase flanked by granite angels, with hyacinths growing all along the walls, and with a bustle of maids in the hallways like the people bustling in the lobby outside the courtroom. (4)

Key features: Stream-of-consciousness narration

Subjects: dictators; fascism; Portugal; Salazar, Antonio de Oliveira

Similar titles: *The Autumn of the Patriarch* by García Márquez and *The Feast of the Goat* by Vargas Llosa are other novels about aging patriarchs; Saramago's novels are also set in Portugal and are written in a postmodern style.

Awards: ALA (2004) and New York Times (2003) Notable Book

Baulenas, Lluís-Anton (Spanish).

For a Sack of Bones. (Per un Sac d'Ossos, 2005). **Translated by Cheryl Leah Morgan. Orlando, FL: Houghton Mifflin, 2008. ISBN 9780151012558. 359pp.**

Genis Aleu is from Barcelona in Catalonia, an area particularly targeted by Generalísimo Franco during his dictatorship. Genis becomes a member of the Foreign Legion in a quest to fulfill a promise to his dying father: recover his friend's bones from the POW camp, now a military base, and give them a decent burial in Barcelona. Along the way, he learns the price of loyalty and revenge.

> My mother asked me if I wanted to kiss my father goodbye. I said yes, but I couldn't face up to it. I simply dropped down into a chair as the apartment began to fill up with strangers. My mind kept turning over the promise I'd made. I meant to keep that pledge, no matter what and no matter when. (22)

Key features: First person narration

Subjects: POWs; quests; Spain—Barcelona

Similar titles: *The Shadow of the Wind* by Ruiz Zafón is set in Barcelona and also deals with the sinister legacy of the Spanish Civil War.

Bolaño, Roberto (Chilean).

Amulet. (*Amuleto*, 1999). Translated by Chris Andrews. New York: New Directions Books, 2006. ISBN 9780811216640. 184pp.

A Uruguayan woman named Auxilio Lacouture has settled in Mexico City and keeps house for a revolutionary couple who are poets. Caught up in the Mexican army's occupation of the Universidad Nacional Autónoma de México in 1968, she refuses to surrender; after her ordeal, she is revered as a muse for poets and artists. One of these is Arturo Belano, a writer she has inspired, who is later imprisoned in Chile by Pinochet's regime.

> With the benefit of hindsight I could say I felt it coming. I could say I had a wild hunch and it didn't catch me unawares. I foresaw, intuited or suspected it; I sniffed it on the wind from the very first minute of January; I anticipated and envisaged it even as the first (and last) piñata of that innocently festive January was smashed open. (21)

Key features: First person narration

Subjects: Chile; Mexico—Mexico City—1968; political repression; Universidad Nacional Autónoma de México

Similar titles: *My Tender Matador* by Lemebel is another novel set in Pinochet's Chile, and *Final Exam* by Cortázar has a similar sinister tone and is also set at a university.

By Night in Chile. (*Nocturno de Chile*, 2000). Translated by Chris Andrews. New York: New Directions Books, 2000. ISBN 0-8112-1547-4. 130pp.

During a long night on the cusp of the twenty-first century, Father Urrutia makes his deathbed confession—a tale of corruption centering on the decadence of the Catholic Church, compromised by Opus Dei's collusion with Pinochet's rotten regime.

> So, propped up on one elbow, I will lift my noble, trembling head, and rummage through my memories to turn up the deeds that shall vindicate me and belie the slanderous rumours the wizened youth spread in a single storm-lit night to sully my name. (1)

Key features: First person, stream-of-consciousness narration

Subjects: Catholic Church; Chile; dictatorships—Pinochet; Opus Dei

Similar titles: *The Dew Breaker* by Danticat is another novel whose protagonist was a collaborator in a totalitarian regime; *The Art of Political Murder* by Goldman and *The Inquisitors' Manual* by Antunes are also about totalitarian regimes and corruption. *The Cigar Roller* by Pablo Medina and *The Death of Artemio Cruz* by Carlos Fuentes are other novels that center on the memories of dying old men.

Distant Star. (*Estrella distante*, 1996). Translated by Chris Andrews. New York: New Directions Books, 2004. ISBN 0-8112-1586-5. 149pp.

The elusive and sinister Alberto Ruiz-Tagle, aka Carlos Weider, is suspiciously present at a prison camp during Pinochet's cruel reign of terror. Has Weider had a hand in undertakings much more sinister than inflicting his terrible poetry and skywriting on an innocent public?

> *Right then, probably the only thing he knew was that he wanted to get out of there, away from Ruiz-Tagle and never return to that naked, bleeding flat. Those are his words. Although, to judge from his description, the flat could not have looked more antiseptic.* (8)

Key features: First person narration

Subjects: airplane pilots; Chile; dictatorships—Pinochet; murder; prison camps; writers—fiction

Similar titles: *The Shadow of the Wind* by Ruiz Zafón, *Captain of the Sleepers* by Montero, and *Of Forgotten Times* by Rizik all feature dictatorships and conspiracies; *Swallowing Stones* by St. Aubin de Terán also presents one man's participation in the low points of Latin American history.

Bryce Echenique, Alfredo (Peruvian).

A World for Julius. (Un mundo para Julius, 1970). **Translated by Dick Gerdes. Austin: University of Texas Press, 1992. ISBN 0292790465. 430pp.**
Young Julius is born into Lima, Peru's, social elite, which is falling into decadence and decay during the 1940s and 1950s.

> *There was even a carriage that your great-grandfather used, Julius, when he was President of the Republic, be careful, don't touch! It's covered with cobwebs, and turning away from his mother, who was lovely, Julius tried to reach the door handle.* (1)

Key features: Multiple narrative perspectives

Subjects: aristocracy; decadence; Peru—Lima

Similar titles: *Empress of the Splendid Season* by Hijuelos tells another story of an aristocrat brought down; *The Sleeping Sisters* by Yañez Cossio, *Balún Canán* by Castellanos, and *Captain of the Sleepers* by Montero are other novels told from a child's perspective.

🏃 Cela, Camilo José (Spanish).

The Hive. (La Colmena, 1951). **Translated by J. M. Cohen and Arturo Barea. Normal, IL: Dalkey Archive Press, 2001. ISBN 1-56478-268-9 (pbk.). 250pp.**
The stories of many lower middle-class inhabitants of Madrid's Outer Belt villages are woven together in this novel, which takes place during the oppressive regime of Generalísimo Francisco Franco.

> *When she is in a good mood, she sits on a stool in the kitchen and reads novels or serials, the bloodier the better: it's all grist for her mill.* (1)

Subjects: classics; dictatorships—Franco; *pueblos*; Spain

Similar titles: *Distant Star* by Bolaño and *The President* by Asturias are other novels that portray life under repressive regimes from multiple points of view.

Awards: Nobel Prize for Literature, 1989

Cercas, Javier (Spanish).

🌺 *Soldiers of Salamís.* (*Soldados de Salamina,* **2001**). **Translated by Anne McLean. New York; Bloomsbury: Distributed to the trade by Holtzbrinck Publishers, 2003. ISBN 1582343845. 210pp.**

The narrator, Javier Cercas (which also happens to be the author's name), is looking into an old tale about the founder of the Spanish Falange movement, Rafael Sánchez Matas. He supposedly miraculously escaped execution by firing squad during the Civil War to later become a national Fascist hero during Franco's regime. The investigation centers on the search for the soldier who famously spared Sánchez Matas's life.

> *My father always kept the trousers and sheepskin jacket he was wearing when they shot him, he showed them to me many times, they're probably still around; the trousers had holes in them, because the bullets only grazed him and he took advantage of the confusion of the moment to run and hide in the woods.* (6)

Subjects: journalists; Sánchez Matas, Rafael; soldiers; civil war—Spain

Similar titles: *Dancing to "Almendra"* by Montero and *Any Wednesday I'm Yours* by Santos-Febres are other novels that feature journalists as narrators.

Awards: Premi Libreter, 2001, Premi Ciutat de Barcelona, Premio de la Critica de Chile, Premio Salambó, Premio Qué Leer, Premio Extremadura, and Premio Grinzane-Cavour, all for *Soldados de Salamina;* Independent Foreign Fiction Prize, 2004, for *Soldiers of Salamis.*

Cruz, Angie (Dominican American).

Let It Rain Coffee. **New York: Simon & Schuster, 2005. ISBN 0-7432-1203-7. 292pp.**

This novel dances among three generations of the Colón family in the Dominican Republic in the 1960s: freedom fighters (Don Chan, the patriarch), refugees fleeing from strife in the homeland toward the mirage of prosperity in the United States(Esperanza, Don Chan's resented daughter-in-law), and immigrants in the *barrios* of present-day New York City.

> *She scrubbed the chicken, chopped its limbs, gutted its belly, and damned those men who were too content spending all their hours talking* políticas. *Just like they did in Los Llanos, sitting in the backyard with friends, carrying out Don Chan's every whim, because among the campesinos, Don Chan was the only one who had traveled as far as China.* (19)

Subjects: Dominican Americans; Dominican Republic; immigrants—Dominican; New York—New York City

Similar titles: *In the Time of the Butterflies* by Julia Alvarez is another novel that features the tragic history of the Dominican Republic; *Caramelo* by Cisneros is another multigenerational epic; and *The Brief Wondrous Life of Oscar Wao* by Junot Díaz is a multigenerational epic that features Dominican immigrants in the United States.

García, Cristina (Cuban American).

A Handbook to Luck. **New York: Alfred A. Knopf, 2007. ISBN 9780307264367. 259pp.**

The lives of three people from very different backgrounds become intermingled in strange ways as they take chances with the cards fate has dealt them in Las Vegas,

Nevada, from the late 1960s through the mid-1980s. Enrique's magician father fled Cuba after his wife died in a tragic accident during one of his magic shows; Marta fled El Salvador's brutal civil war, hoping to send for her little brother someday; and Leila has left postrevolutionary Iran with her wayward mother en route to an arranged marriage.

> *The roses looked perfect, delicate and darkly veined. Yet to her the garden seemed decorous and static, like a roomful of her mother's friends. There was no comfortable place to sit anymore, nowhere to think or watch the clouds. She missed the date palms and the stubborn pomegranate tree and the old poplars and plane trees, too.* (30)

Subjects: Cuba; El Salvador; immigrants; Iran; love stories; Nevada—Las Vegas

Similar titles: *The Cigar Roller* by Pablo Medina is also about Cuban fathers and sons; *The Weight of All Things* by Benitez is also about the brutal war in El Salvador.

Goldman, Francisco (Guatemalan American).

The Ordinary Seaman. **New York: Atlantic Monthly Press, 1997. ISBN 0871136716. 387pp.**

Esteban is a nineteen-year-old veteran of the Sandinista wars in Nicaragua who signs up for a job on a ship in New York harbor, looking forward to taking the first step toward prosperity and the American dream. Instead, he and his fourteen companions find themselves dumped on *Urus*, a wreck of a ship, abandoned to their fate, until Esteban takes matters into his own hands.

> *Esteban was the tallest of the five. His brown skin had a smooth, saddle-soaped luster, and his build was so slender and bony that his jeans and white, short-sleeved shirt seemed tenuously hung from his hip and collar bones.* (6)

Key features: Based on a true story

Subjects: Central Americans; immigrants; New York—New York City—Brooklyn; refugees; sailors

Similar titles: *Paradise Travel* by Franco features other immigrants alone and desperate in New York City.

González, Genaro (Tejano).

The Quixote Cult. **Houston, TX: Arte Público Press, 1998. ISBN 1558852549. 260pp.**

As De la O takes to the road on his way to a new college in 1960s Texas, he tries to figure out his place in the world as a Chicano honor student.

> *But when you learn a language at school without using it at home, you tend to approach it analytically. You learn to take it apart and put it back together as though it were a weapon.* (24)

Subjects: Chicanos; college students; drugs; Texas

Similar titles: *Unsettling* by Sandoval is another novel about a road trip with friends; *The Best Thing That Can Happen to a Croissant* by Tusset features another slacker philosopher protagonist; and *Amnesia in a Republican County* by Gary Soto also takes place on campus, with mind-altering substances along for the ride.

Hijuelos, Oscar (Cuban American).

A Simple Habana Melody (from When the World Was Good). **New York: HarperCollins, 2005. ISBN 0-06-017569-9. 342pp.**

Israel Levis is a composer who has created a new sensation—*Rosas puras*, a rumba that catches on around the world. He dedicates this rumba to his one true love, Rita Valladares. After creating an international sensation, he is persecuted during World War II in Europe because of his name, even though he is not Jewish. Now he looks back at his early life and success from the perspective of his later years in post–World War II, prerevolutionary Havana.

> *He was not yet sixty, but his hair had turned white and he had grown an unruly beard, so that he resembled a forlorn* guajiro *of the countryside, or the painter Matisse in his later years.* (5)

Subjects: composers; Cuba—Havana; France—Paris; love stories; music—rumba

Similar titles: *The Wake* by Glantz is another novel about music, regrets, and lost love; *The Messenger* by Montero is also set in prerevolutionary Havana.

Lamazares, Ivonne (Cuban American).

The Sugar Island. **Boston: Houghton Mifflin, 2000. ISBN 0395860407. 205pp.**

When Fidel Castro overthrows Batista's government in Cuba, Tanya balks at her mother's decision to move the family to Miami. Tanya does not trust her mother, who has spent years in jail because of her involvement in revolutionary activities. Can they find a better life in Miami, or is Tanya's mother merely trading one set of problems for another?

> *My stomach shut like a fist. Mamá was running again, and this time she'd drag us with her in a flimsy boat across the black water. Finally the thing I'd feared had come. I hated Mamá harder than the Storm Captain hated enemy pirates from the North.* (11)

Key features: First person narration

Subjects: Cubans; Florida—Miami; mothers and daughters; refugees; revolutionary struggles

Similar titles: *Broken Paradise* by Samartin, *Days of Awe* by Obejas, and *Havana Split* by Bevin are other novels about Cuban refugees in the United States.

Latour, José (Cuban).

Havana World Series: A Novel. **New York: Grove Press, 2003. ISBN 0-8021-1754-6. 320pp.**

An unlikely group of criminals plot to rob the winnings of a Havana mob boss, aided by his rival in New York, during the 1958 baseball playoffs.

> *Lansky smoked placidly, sipped his drink, or drummed his fingers on the arm of the couch. Shaifer, shirt cuffs folded up under the elbows, had the inscrutability of a Siamese cat. Angelo Dick methodically reviewed figures in his mind, waiting for a new round of questions.* (13)

Subjects: baseball; Cuba—Havana; gambling; mob; singers; World Series, 1958; World War II—concentration camps

Similar titles: *Dancing to "Almendra"* by Montero is another novel about the mob in prerevolutionary Havana.

Lemebel, Pedro (Chilean).

My Tender Matador. (*Tengo miedo torero*, 2001). **Translated by Katherine Silver. New York: Grove Press, 2003. ISBN 0-8021-1768-6. 170pp.**

In 1986 Santiago, Chile, the Queen of the Corner, a transvestite who embroiders for a living, falls in love with the revolutionary Carlos and unwittingly lets him use her apartment and contacts to plan an assassination attempt on dictator Pinochet.

> Boarded up for so many years, so full of rats and ghosts and bats the Queen implacably evicted, feather duster in hand, broom in hand, sweeping out the cobwebs with her fairy energy as she sang Lucho Gatica songs in that faggot falsetto. (2)

Subjects: Chile—Santiago; homosexuals; love stories; Pinochet, Augusto; revolutionaries

Similar titles: *Kiss of the Spider Woman* by Puig is another novel about homosexual and straight men in a relationship under a dictatorship.

Martín Gaite, Carmen (Spanish).

Behind the Curtains. (*Entre Visillos*, 1958). **Translated by Frances M. Lopez-Morillas. New York: Columbia University Press, 1990. ISBN 0231068883. 279pp.**

The lives of several young women in Spain during General Franco's rule are brought to life through their simple conversations in the novel. Stifled by the constraints of the time, many of the young girls succumb to the pressures to marry, while a few succeed in gaining their independence.

> "But father, I don't influence him at all; why, he keeps on thinking the same things as before. He doesn't value anything that I do for him, he laughs at me, he says I'm silly." (85)

Subjects: feminists; men and women; small towns; Spain; women's friendships

Similar titles: *Dirty Girls Social Club* by Valdes-Rodriguez is another novel about women's friendships enduring through adversity.

Martínez, Tomás Eloy (Argentinian).

Santa Evita. (*Santa Evita*, 1995). **Translated by Helen Lane. New York: Alfred A. Knopf, 1996. ISBN 0-679-44704-0. 371pp.**

In this macabre novel, after her death Eva Peron's corpse is manipulated for political purposes, and those who come into contact with it are doomed.

> Little by little Evita began to turn into a story that, before it ended, kindled another. She ceased to be what she said and what she did to become what people say she said and what people say she did. (13)

Subjects: Argentina; black humor; corpses; Peron, Eva; politics

Similar titles: *The General in His Labyrinth* by García Márquez is another novel that presents a strong personality's influence after death.

Menendez, Ana (Cuban American).

Loving Che. **New York: Atlantic Monthly Press, 2003. ISBN 0-87113-908-1. 228pp.**

A young, unnamed Cuban woman narrates the search for her mother in Havana, after receiving a mysterious package of letters and notes postmarked from Spain. The bulk of the novel is the "transcript" of these notes framed at the beginning and end by the narrator's story of her search. The notes/diary tells the story of Teresa's experience of the Cuban Revolution seen through the perspective of an illicit love affair with Che Guevara.

> *I hoped, at first, that by arranging the notes and recollections in some sort of order, I might be able to make sense of them. But on each rereading I found myself drawn deeper and deeper, until I feared I might lose myself among the pages, might drown in a drop of my own blood.* (12)

Key features: Epistolary fiction

Subjects: Cuba—Havana; Cuban Revolution; diaries; Florida—Miami; Guevara, Ernesto "Che"; historical fiction; love affairs; mothers and daughters

Similar titles: *When the Ground Turns in Its Sleep* by Sellers-García and *The Lady, the Chef and the Courtesan* are other novels about the descendents of Latino immigrants' quests in their parents' home country.

Montero, Mayra (Caribbean: Cuban; Puerto Rican).

Captain of the Sleepers. (*Capitán de los dormidos*, **2002). Translated by Edith Grossman. New York: Farrar, Straus & Giroux, 2002. ISBN 0-374-11882-5. 181pp.**

Andrés Yasín tells of his return to St. Croix to confront the man who traumatized him as a child and whom he had once promised to kill—J.T., the Captain of the Sleepers. They are both now old men as J.T. tells Andrés his version of passionate happenings involving Andrés's mother in Puerto Rico in 1949–1950, weaving together the personal and the political.

> *I'm in the last place on earth I'd like to be. Waiting for the last person in this life I thought I'd ever see again. It's almost six. I'm sipping beer at the bar of the Pink Fancy, a hotel on St. Croix where I arrived just a few minutes ago, carrying a small weekend bag.* (3)

Key features: First person narration; sexual situations

Subjects: airplane pilots; coming-of-age; love affairs; Puerto Rico; Puerto Rico—Independence Movement; revolutionary struggles

Similar titles: *The Cigar Roller* by Pablo Medina and *The Second Death of Única Aveyano* by Mestre-Reed are other novels structured around memories and flashbacks.

Dancing to "Almendra". (*Son de Almendra*, **2005). New York: Farrar, Straus & Giroux, 2007. ISBN-10: 0-374-10277-5; ISBN-13: 978-0-374- 10277-5. 272pp.**

Joaquín Porrata, cub reporter for a Havana newspaper, is hungry to write real news instead of the nightclub reporting he has been doing. While covering the death of the hippopotamus at the zoo, he is put on the trail of the murder of

Anastasia, a Mafia capo murdered in New York City. The story of Joaquín's investigation intertwines with the story of his one-armed lover, Yolanda. Both tales delve into the dark, twisted Havana of the early 1950s.

> Among all these people seeing me for the first time, who could have known that less than two hours earlier I'd tried to write a story about Umberto Anastasia, shot to death in a chair in the barbershop of the Park Sheraton in New York? (11)

Key features: First person narration

Subjects: Cuba—Havana—1950s; gangsters; journalists; love stories; nightclubs

Similar titles: *Havana World Series* by Latour is also set in 1950s Havana among the mob.

Pfarrer, Chuck (U.S. American).

Killing Che: A Novel. **New York: Random House, 2007. ISBN 9781400063932. 470pp.**

Paul Hoyle is a former CIA agent hired by the agency to bring down the revolutionary movement in Bolivia, feared to be another Vietnam. He is pitted against Che Guevara as they play out an intense game that includes women, government secrets, machinations, corrupt officials, and armed encounters in the Bolivian jungle.

> Guevara knew that from the valley the smoke could be seen for miles. As he crossed the road, he looked back at the burning hulk; inside the cab he could see the steering wheel ablaze in a perfect circle of flames. He was certain now that the army would come, and he was confident that at this distance, the Bolivian soldiers would not see him, his men, or the ambush put down on the last of the tight hairpin turns carved into the mountainside. (4)

Subjects: Bolivia; CIA; guerrilla warfare; Guevara, Ernesto "Che"

Similar titles: *Loving Che* by Menendez is another novel featuring Che Guevara; *A Good Day to Die* by Coltrane is a novel about the CIA in Cuba.

Romano-Lax, Andromeda (U.S. American).

The Spanish Bow. **New York: Harcourt, 2007. ISBN 9780151015429. 554pp.**

Feliu Largo inherits his father's bow and is destined to become a master cellist. He and his accompanist, Justo Al-Carraz, embark on a career that takes them through the Spanish Civil War and, World War II, in contact with the great historical figures of the twentieth century while they vie for the affections of Aviva, the beautiful violinist who is their accompanist.

> When the cellist reached a crescendo on one of the lower strings, I felt a strange sensation, both pleasurable and disturbing. It reminded me of holding a cat, feeling its purrs resonate with me. Listening, I felt the sensation strengthen, as if the cello's quivering vibrato were actually boring into me, opening a small hole in my chest, creating a physical pain as real as any wound. (33)

Key features: First person narration

Subjects: cellists; Civil War—Spain; music; World War II

Similar titles: *A Simple Habana Melody* by Hijuelos is another novel about musicians during World War II; *The Wake* by Glantz and *Inez* by Carlos Fuentes are other novels that revolve around music and life.

Sáenz, Benjamín (New Mexican).

Names on a Map. New York: HarperCollins, 2008. ISBN 9780061285691. 426pp.

The year is 1967 and the place is El Paso, Texas, on the eve of the Vietnam War. Each Espejo family member—Octavio and Lourdes, the immigrant parents; their children Gustavo, Xochil and Charlie; their friends and *compañeros*—tells his or her story in his or her own voice as they all live through this difficult period of U.S. history.

> *Octavio—husband, father, son—is asleep. He is lost in an unwelcome dream, a gust of wind kicking up the loose fragments of memory, grains of sand in the eye. He is struggling to see. He is struggling to understand what his father is saying to him, his father who has been dead for more than three years.* (3)

Key features: First person narration; multiple narrative voices; interviews and other extras (this edition)

Subjects: families; immigrants; Mexican Americans; Vietnam War

Similar titles: *Monkey Hunting* by Cristina García also explores Latinos and the Vietnam War.

Valdés, Zoé (Cuban).

🏃 *I Gave You All I Had.* (*Te di la vida entera,* 1996). Translated by Nadia Benabid. New York: Arcade Publishing, 1999. ISBN 1-55970-477-2. 238pp.

Cuca Martinez flees the countryside to seek her fortune in prerevolutionary Havana in the 1950s and ends up as a housemaid, rooming with prostitutes in a squalid tenement. The love of her life, Juan "Uan" Perez, a nightclub singer with mob ties, flees, leaving Cuca to fend for herself during the revolution and the post-revolutionary hard times. She raises Juan's daughter, pining for his return and barely surviving while Juan lives it up in Miami.

> *Cuquita breathed out a deep and loud sigh, already in love with the proprietor of that diabolically melodic voice. It only took La Puchunguita, who had guessed her sentiments, a couple of pokes to bring her sand castle crashing down.* (13)

Key features: First person narration

Subjects: Cuba—Havana; Cuban Revolution; historical fiction; humor; love stories; mob

Similar titles: *A Simple Habana Melody* by Hijuelos and *The Messenger* and *Dancing to "Almendra"* by Montero are other novels set in prerevolutionary Havana with a strong musical theme.

Awards: Finalist, Planeta Prize, Spain, 1996

Vargas Llosa, Mario (Peruvian).

The Feast of the Goat. (*Fiesta del chivo,* 2000). Translated by Edith Grossman. New York: Farrar, Straus & Giroux, 2000. ISBN 0-374-15476-7. 404pp.

Urania Cabral, daughter of one of Trujillo's ministers, returns to Santo Domingo, Dominican Republic, as an adult to visit her estranged, ailing father. Chapters that tell her story are interspersed with the narrative of the end of Trujillo's decadent and brutal regime, a time and place rife with betrayal and intrigue.

> You wouldn't have come back if the rancor were still sizzling, the wound still bleeding, the deception still crushing her, poisoning her, the way it did in your youth, when studying and working became an obsessive defense against remembering. Back then you did hate him. (6)

Key features: Second person narration

Subjects: dictators; Dominican Republic; Trujillo Molina, Rafael Leónidas

Similar titles: *In the Name of Salomé* and *In the Time of the Butterflies* by Julia Alvarez, *The Brief Wondrous Life of Oscar Wao* by Junot Díaz, and *The Farming of Bones* by Danticat are other novels about Dominican history and struggles.

Liberación/Liberation

These novels encompass the sweep of movements against oppression throughout the twentieth century, beginning with the Mexican Revolution of 1910 and including struggles in Cuba, the Dominican Republic, Puerto Rico, and the Portuguese colonies, as well as the Chicano movement in the United States.

Alvarez, Julia (Dominican American).

In the Name of Salomé. (*En el nombre de Salomé*, 2002). Chapel Hill, NC: Algonquin Books of Chapel Hill, 2000. ISBN 1-565-12276-3. 353pp.

Salomé Ureña de Henriquez was the national poetess of the Dominican Republic, whose story is ineluctably bound to the history of the United States. Her extraordinary life as the Dominican Republic's national poetess is juxtaposed with her daughter Camila's life as an exile in the United States and Cuba during the turbulent times of the twentieth century.

> She herself is worried about the emptiness that lies ahead. Childless and motherless, she is a bead unstrung from the necklace of the generations. All she leaves behind here are a few close colleagues, also about to retire, and her students, those young immortals with, she hopes, the Spanish subjunctive filed away in their heads. (2)

Subjects: biographies—fiction; Cuba; de Henríquez, Salomé Ureña; Dominican Americans; Dominican Republic; Henríquez Ureña, Camila; mothers and daughters; poets; revolutionary struggles

Similar titles: *Frida* by Mujica and *Tinisima* by Poniatowska are other biographical novels about women artists; *The Brief Wondrous Life of Oscar Wao* by Junot Díaz also vividly portrays life in the Dominican Republic under Trujillo and Dominican immigrants in the United States.

In the Time of the Butterflies. (*En el tiempo de las mariposas*, 1995). New York: Plume, 1994. ISBN 0-452-27442-7. 325pp.

Raised in a conservative and pious household, the three Mirabal sisters find themselves becoming leaders of a revolution in the Dominican Republic against the thirty-year, terrifying regime of *El Jefe*—the dictator Rafael Trujillo. Each sister finds her own way to live, love, and raise her family while fighting for the rights of all Dominicans. But how long will Trujillo allow them to do so?

> *A chill goes through her, for she feels it in her bones, the future is now beginning. By the time it is over, it will be the past, and she doesn't want to be the only one left to tell their story.* (10)

Subjects: corruption; Dominican Republic; Mirabal, Maria Teresa; Mirabal, Minerva; Mirabal, Patria; revolutionary struggles; Trujillo Molina, Rafael Leonidas

Similar titles: In *The Feast of the Goat* by Vargas Llosa, Trujillo is the protagonist; *The Farming of Bones* by Danticat portrays the same period from the Haitian perspective.

Antunes, António Lobo (Portuguese).

The Natural Order of Things. (A Ordem Natural das Coisas, 1992). **Translated by Richard Zenith. New York: Grove Press, c2000. ISBN 0802116582. 298pp.**

The history of twentieth-century Portugal plays out through the lives of two families—the history of Portugal as family history. The brutality and torture that affected society come out through dreams, hypnosis, and madness.

> *And today, my love, lying in my bed waiting for the Valium to kick in, the same thing happens as when I used to lie down, on hot summer afternoons, in the coolness of the dilapidated graves: I feel a tombstone decoration pressing against my leg, I hear the grass of the graves in my sheets, I see the plaster Jesuses and angels threatening me with their broken hands.* (3)

Key features: First person narration; multiple narrators

Subjects: dictatorships; family relationships; Portugal; secrets

Similar titles: *The Obscene Bird of Night* by Donoso is another dark novel about families and madness; *A World for Julius* by Bryce Echenique also presents a family's history as national story.

Azuela, Mariano (Mexican).

The Underdogs. (Los de abajo, 1915). **Translated by E. Munguía Jr. New York: Modern Library, 2002. ISBN 0-375-75942-5. 160pp.**

In this classic novel Demetrio Macías, *campesino* cum general, and Luis Campos, medical student cum revolutionary profiteer, find their lives and fortunes changed by the Mexican Revolution. Men must put their lofty ideals to the test and don't always find themselves up to the task.

> *The moon peopled the mountain with vague shadows. In every crag and in every scrub oak tree, Demetrio could see the poignant silhouette of a woman with a child in her arms.* (6)

Subjects: dictatorships; Mexican Revolution; Mexico

Similar titles: *The Death of Artemio Cruz* by Carlos Fuentes and *Tear This Heart Out* by Mastretta are also novels about the Mexican Revolution; *Chicano* by Vasquez follows refugees from that revolution to the United States.

Carrillo, H. G. (Cuban American).

Loosing My Espanish. **New York: Pantheon Books, 2006. ISBN 0-375-42319-2. 325pp.**

Oscar Delossantos has been fired from his job as history teacher at a parochial school. He uses his last days on the job to teach the class his version of Latin American history and growing up as a Cuban immigrant in Chicago.

> *Well, you know sometimes you no know you no going to like something until you right in the middle of no liking, Amá will say whether things are good or bad. She'll say it at the start of something, or in the middle, or long after it's finished, which makes it difficult to tell when you've gotten to the moral of the story.* (3)

Key features: First person, stream-of-consciousness narration, with Cuban Spanglish syntax and spelling

Subjects: Illinois—Chicago; immigrants—Cuban; mothers and sons

Similar titles: *Yo-Yo Boing!* by Braschi also plays with Spanglish, and *The Color of Summer* by Arenas presents Cuba and the Cuban immigrant experience using stream-of-consciousness narration.

Ferré, Rosario (Puerto Rican).

Eccentric Neighborhoods. **New York: Farrar, Straus & Giroux, 1998. ISBN 0374146381. 340pp.**

Elvira Vernet traces her family's history through two lines of Puerto Rico's most influential families. Her mother, Clarissa Rivas de Santillanas's, side of the family made a fortune from a sugar plantation that ultimately failed them as Puerto Rico progressed. Her father, Santiago Vernet, on the other hand, came from a family dedicated to industrializing Puerto Rico that met with success. Close to her father, Elvira revisits her history for a deeper connection to the mother who died so many years before.

> *He carried a picture of me standing in a field of blue agapanthus in his wallet; he didn't carry photographs of any of his other grandchildren. He told me that when I was born he insisted I be named Elvira. That had been his mother's name, and he felt bad because she had died in Cuba without his ever having seen her again. But after I grew up, I hardly ever went to visit Changuito. It must have broken his heart, but he never complained. He was my first abandoned lover.* (234)

Subjects: ancestors; family relationships; mothers and daughters; Puerto Ricans; Puerto Rico

Similar titles: *The Day of the Moon* by Limón and *The Pearl of the Antilles* by Andrea Herrera are other family sagas.

Fuentes, Carlos (Mexican).

The Death of Artemio Cruz. **(*La muerte de Artemio Cruz*, 1962). Translated by Alfred MacAdam. New York: Farrar, Straus & Giroux, 1991. 307pp.**

From his deathbed, Artemio Cruz relives many key episodes from a misspent life that spans the twentieth century in Mexico, from his humble idealistic beginnings as a soldier in the 1910 Revolution to his ultimately corrupt existence as a landowner *hacendado* and newspaper owner.

> *Yesterday you did what you do every day. You don't know if it's worthwhile remembering it. You only want to remember, lying back there in the twilight of your bedroom, what's going to happen: you don't want to foresee what has already happened. In your twilight, your eyes see ahead; they don't know how to guess the past. (7)*

Key features: Second person narration; structure is not linear or chronological

Subjects: death; Mexican Revolution; Mexico

Similar titles: *By Night in Chile* by Bolaño, *The Cigar Roller* by Pablo Medina, and *The Second Death of Única Aveyano* by Mestre-Reed are similarly structured as end-of-life narratives that take the reader through transcendent moments of the twentieth century; *Tear This Heart Out* by Mastretta gives a feminine perspective on the Mexican Revolution.

The Years with Laura Díaz. (*Años con Laura Díaz,* 1999). **Translated by Alfred MacAdam. New York: Farrar, Straus & Giroux, 2000. ISBN 0374293414. 518pp.**

These years follow Laura Diaz, a mother, wife, lover, and nationally renowned artist who endures great tragedy along with great passion as she navigates the turbulent history of Mexico in the twentieth century. Her story is presented in the voice of her Chicano great-grandson, from his vantage point in Detroit and Los Angeles.

> *I was staring at the face of that strange beautiful woman dressed as a worker, and as I did, all the forms of recollection, memory of whatever you call those privileged instants of life, poured into my head like an ocean whose unleashed waves are always yet never the same: it's the face of Laura Díaz I've just seen; the face revealed in the hurly-burly of the mural is that of one woman and one woman only, and her name is Laura Díaz. (9–10)*

Subjects: artists; family histories; love affairs; Mexico—20th century

Similar titles: *The Death of Artemio Cruz* is Fuentes's original classic novel about twentieth-century Mexico; *Caramelo* by Cisneros is another novel that has Mexican/Chicano family history at its core; and *Peregrina* by Reed is the true story of a woman journalist participant in the culture of postrevolutionary Mexico.

García, Cristina (Cuban American).

Monkey Hunting. **New York: Alfred A. Knopf, 2003. ISBN 0375410562. 251pp.**

Chen Pan immigrates to Cuba from China in 1857. His granddaughter, Chen Fang, is born in China and raised as a boy. His great-great-grandson Domingo is sent to fight in the Vietnam War. Each generation faces the struggles inherent to their time and place.

> *It was a hot, sunny morning, and the city looked like a fancy seashell in the distance, smooth pink and white. A brisk wind stirred the fronds of the palms. The water shone so blue it hurt his eyes to stare at it. (20)*

Subjects: China; Chinese; Cuba; Cuban Americans; slavery; Vietnam War

Similar titles: *Mambo Peligroso* by Chao and *The Island of Eternal Love* by Chaviano are other novels about Asians and Cuba.

Grattan-Domínguez, Alejandro (Mexican American).

The Dark Side of the Dream. Houston, TX: Arte Público Press, 1995. ISBN 1-55885-140-2. 434pp.

The Salazar family emigrates to the United States when the patriarch's deathbed request sends the brothers there to improve their family's lot. Miguel enlists and is sent to Italy, becoming a hero during World War II, only to be faced with exploitation in the fields on his return. Francisco stays in Texas to organize the Mexican migrant workers in those same fields.

> *In the first fragile light of that cold December morning, Miguel Salazar stood at the foot of his grandfather's bed and watched as the old man struggled for breath in his tortured sleep. Miguel waited, hoping each gasp would be the last one.* (13)

Subjects: family histories; labor struggles; Mexican Americans; migrant farmworkers; Texas—El Paso; World War II—Mexican American units

Similar titles: *Chicano* by Vasquez and *Music of the Mill* by Luis J. Rodriguez are other novels about Chicano families' perseverance in the twentieth century.

Houston-Davila, Daniel (Mexican American).

Malinche's Children. Jackson: University Press of Mississippi, 2003. ISBN 1-57806-521-6. 354pp.

Interlocking stories tell of life in the Mexican farmworkers' community of Carmelas, California, throughout the twentieth century. From the aging starlet to the victim of domestic abuse to the caring schoolteacher, each character contributes his or her little piece to the richly textured quilt that is Carmelas.

> *His eyes fixed on the moon, and for a moment he wondered if it were a bad omen, if bringing Gloria and their children here would mean their lives would always be like this sliver of moon, only a piece of the whole their lives might have been had fortune blessed them and allowed them to stay in Mazatlán, washed by the salty whispers of the sea.* (19)

Subjects: California; family histories; Mexican Americans; migrant farmworkers; *pueblos*

Similar titles: *Music of the Mill* by Luis J. Rodriguez is another novel about Mexicans in twentieth-century California, *The Dark Side of the Dream* by Grattan-Dominguez also features the farmworkers' plight, and *The Hive* by Cela is another story about a community.

Chapter 3

Women's Fiction

Jessica Reed

Mujer que sabe latín . . . ¡claro que tiene buen fin!

Titles in this category are typically books about women, by women, that are intended primarily for a female audience. But this is a somewhat loose association. Male authors—for example, Allan Gurganus, author of *Oldest Living Confederate Widow Tells All*, and for our purposes, José Raúl Bernardo, author of *The Wise Women of Havana*—are also known to write popular titles in this genre. So how does one determine whether a book fits into "women's lives" or another genre?

Diana Tixier Herald's standard readers' advisory work, *Genreflecting,* labeled women's lives, also known as women's fiction, as an "emerging genre" in 2006 (494). Suffice it to say, the genre has not been unequivocally defined. For the purpose of this chapter, materials selected for this category were written by Latino women (and some men) and adhere to the definition set forth by readers' advisory specialist Joyce Saricks:

> These are books that explore the reaches of women's lives; that deal with the dynamics of relationships with family, friends, and lovers; that may or may not end happily (although they do end with issues resolved or the resolution suggested); that examine the issues women confront in their lives (at home and at work) and the distinctive way in which women deal with these concerns. (2001, 371)

Although not always thought of as a separate genre from literary fiction or romance genres, these titles contributed greatly to the publishing of women authors for women readers. In fact, according to one industry study, "one can easily conclude that Women's Fiction comprises at least 40% of adult popular fiction sold in the United States and approximately 60% of adult popular fiction paperbacks. According to a Gallup Poll, we're talking a $24 billion dollar industry" (Craig 2000).

The women in these novels experience the difficulties of being daughters, wives and mothers, sisters and friends—roles that most women take on at some time in their lives. Although not always guaranteed a happy ending as in romantic titles, most readers enjoy the overall tone of these novels, in which the women protagonists learn and grow from even the most difficult of situations and emerge triumphant or at least battered but still standing, on the verge of conquering their world (Saricks 2001, 371–73).

Appeal

Women readers find this genre appealing because it gives them the opportunity to see their own lives depicted in a story. They may get some insight into their own daily routines and relationships through the variety of women featured—weak and strong, emotional and apathetic. The reader can also identify with the emotional charge of the characters, whether a single protagonist or a circle of friends, and the situations they find themselves in.

Multicultural literature, including titles from Latina authors, was accepted more readily in this genre than in others. Within this particular genre readers "appreciate learning how issues that affect women are played out in different parts of the world" (Saricks 2001, 384). Thus many Latina authors have found success and avid readers in the industry.

Latina women's lives are similar to those of women in other cultures, a fact that is evident in today's literature. Latinas experience love, loss, single parenthood, domestic violence, rape, and other social issues along with other women around the world. These are universal themes in women's fiction.

More unique to Latinas are the themes of immigration, political upheaval, the refugee experience, and the search for cultural identity. Family sagas or multigenerational tales also flourish in this genre. Many Latina authors focus on generations of women and the lessons they pass on to one another.

Readers may find titles they consider romance, suspense, and literary or mainstream fiction in this chapter. However, because these elements were not considered the central theme of the novel, the title has been included in this chapter. Readers interested in similar titles by and about women in chapters on other genres can find them by searching the subject index under "*chica* lit," "chicanas," "*chiquita* lit," "*curanderas*," "feminists," "grandmothers and granddaughters," "Latinas," "lesbian detectives," "lesbians," "mothers and daughters," "pregnant women," "prostitutes," "*quinceañeras*," "sisters," "violence against women," "widows," "women detectives," "women—Latin America," "women's friendships," "women's lives."

Organization

This chapter contains two sections—one for novels and the other for anthologies and collections. Novels classified as the Latino equivalent of Chick Lit—*chica* lit—are integrated with others, but *chica* lit is used as a subject term. More *chica* lit titles can be found in Chapter 4, "Latina Romance and Love Stories,", in which *chica* lit is also used as a subject term, and in Chapter 7, "Young Adult Fiction."

Novels

Acevedo, Chantel (Cuban American).

🌲 *Love and Ghost Letters*. **New York: St. Martin's Press, 2005. ISBN 9780312340469. 312pp.**

Raised by Antonio, a father who is both secretive and stern, Josefina longs for a different life . . . an exciting one. Rejecting her father and the privileged Cuban upbringing he provides, she runs away with Lorenzo. But instead of the life she envisioned, she finds abject poverty and a philandering husband who is gone for months at a time. Injured in an uprising, Antonio escapes to the United States, leaving Josefina to believe he is dead. Soon Josefina begins receiving mysterious letters from her "dead" father, which guide her to a better understanding of his life and therefore her own.

> *During the months that followed, the sergeant stepped up the pace of his letter writing. Nearly every day he sent a letter to Abel to be delivered to Josefina. He never wrote about Miami, about the United States or Mona. How would he explain his failure at her doorstep?* (170)

Subjects: Cuba; exile; family secrets; fathers and daughters

Similar titles: *The Agüero Sisters* by Cristina García, *The Day of the Moon* by Limón, and *Havana Split* by Bevin all reveal family secrets.

Awards: Latino Literacy Now Award, 2006

Alvarez, Julia (Dominican American).

Saving the World. **Chapel Hill, NC: Algonquin Books of Chapel Hill, 2006. ISBN 156512510X. 368pp.**

Alma Huebner's husband, a member of a humanitarian organization dedicated to eradicating AIDS in developing countries, invites her to travel with him to the Dominican Republic. Alma declines, convincing him that she must work on her latest novel. Secretly, she is busy researching another humanitarian figure. In 1803 Francisco Xavier Balmis undertook the mission of eradicating smallpox in Spain's colonies. To do so, he needed live vaccine carriers. Twenty-two orphans were chosen for this experiment. Alma becomes fascinated with Isabel Sendales y Gómez, the orphanage director, who agreed to this arrangement as long as she could journey with the boys across the ocean as they tried to save the New World.

> *It worked. I did not know if it was the story or the way I held their attention with my eyes. I am here with you, my look said. You are not alone. By the end of an hour, I felt black and blue all over my arms as if I, too, had been pricked a dozen times.* (210)

Key features: First person narration

Subjects: AIDS; smallpox; vaccinations; writers—fiction

Similar titles: *Coachella* by Taylor similarly tackles the difficulties of life with AIDS.

Ambert, Alba (Puerto Rican American).

A Perfect Silence. Houston, TX: Arte Público Press, 1995. ISBN 1558851259. 234pp.

Blanca tells her story from the mental hospital after a suicide attempt. It is a woman's story of survival under the worst circumstances of abuse and poverty in Puerto Rico and as a child, brought to the United States to grow up between two worlds.

> *Blanca reconstructed her mother's life like a puzzle, from overheard conversations, things people told her. Her mother's name was Isabel. She was a shantytown-dwelling seamstress. Another* arrabalera. *Blanca's father, Ramón, was a milkman and a skirt chaser.* (19)

Subjects: New York—New York City—South Bronx; poverty; Puerto Rican women; suicide

Similar titles: *America's Dream* by Esmeralda Santiago also focuses on Puerto Rican women in difficult situations. *Delirium* by Restrepo similarly deals with mental illness in women.

Argueta, Manlio (Salvadoran).

A Place Called Milagro de la Paz. (*Milagro de la Paz,* 2000). Translated by Michael B. Miller. Willimantic, CT: Curbstone Press, 2000. ISBN 1880684683. 206pp.

Latina lives in Milagro de la Paz with her daughters. Life is a daily struggle and sleep impossible amid the constant fear of soldiers and unknown assassins. A mysterious young girl befriends the family and brings magic and love to their home.

> *The words speak of yellow flowers that brighten the paths leading up to the volcano. Her thoughts about the dogs interrupt the melody. It is night and she wonders if they're howling out of fear, or at the soldiers who patrol the barrio, or at* los seres desconocidos *as they are called, faceless assassins who in recent days have been dumping dead bodies into Calle de las Angustias—the Street of Anguish.* (1)

Key features: Glossary

Subjects: civil war; El Salvador; magic; mothers and daughters

Similar titles: *The Inhabited Woman* by Belli also uses magic realism to detail life under a repressive regime. Both *Bitter Grounds* by Benitez and *The Heiress of Water* by Barron also concentrate on the civil war in El Salvador.

Barrientos, Tanya Maria (Guatemalan American).

Family Resemblance. New York: New American Library, 2003. ISBN 0451208722. 250pp.

Twenty-five years after the death of her mother, Nita DeLeon is forced to place her father in a nursing home after he has a disabling stroke. Sorting through her parents' things, Nita discovers a cryptic letter from her Aunt Pancha in Guatemala, whom she believed had died years before. Intrigued, Nita sets out to discover her family history, with the help of old friends and new love.

> *After years of trying to imagine the possible stories behind each of those faces, I have the opportunity to find out exactly who they are. I could sit down right now and ask my aunt whether The Martinis were my mother's artsy friends, as I imagined they were. Or whether they were university chums of my father. She*

could tell me how the tall, thin man with the horn-rimmed glasses and narrow bow tie, who is pictured dancing with the bride, fit into my mother's life. (173)

Key features: First person narration

Subjects: fathers and daughters; Guatemalans; identity

Similar titles: Characters in *The Mixquiahuala Letters* by Ana Castillo and *The Lady, the Chef and the Courtesan* by Marisol also use letters left by loved ones to search for their cultural identity.

Frontera Street. New York: NAL Accent, 2002. ISBN 0451206355. 243pp.

Recently widowed and pregnant, Dee Paxton applies for a job at a fabric shop on Frontera Street in her West Texas town. Her new coworker, Alma Cruz, dislikes Dee's secretiveness but soon realizes Dee needs a friend. Herself a single mother, Alma understands the difficulties Dee now faces and takes her under her wing. The two women, from vastly different cultures and classes, develop a deep friendship, and Dee finds a new home.

> But then I'd remember how Alma took me in because she was convinced I had nothing, and how she would have never done that if she'd known I grew up on the Westside. I had convinced myself that even though things were getting tough, it was best for me to stay quiet. Because if I lost Alma and Socorro now, if I lost the trust of everyone on Frontera Street, then I really would have nothing, and the thought of being that lonely again terrified me. (141)

Key features: First person narration

Subjects: single mothers; Texas; upper classes; women's friendships

Similar titles: Unique friendships between women can also be found in *Havana Thursdays* by Suárez, *The Mixquiahuala Letters* by Ana Castillo, and *Playing with Boys* by Valdes-Rodriguez. *Streets of Fire* by Soledad Santiago similarly deals with the trials and tribulations of single motherhood.

Barron, Sandra Rodriguez (Puerto Rican American).

❦ *The Heiress of Water.* New York: HarperCollins, 2006. ISBN 0061142816. 299pp.

Massage therapist Monica Winters was brought up by her father in Connecticut after her mother, marine biologist and socialite Alma Borrero Winters, died during the civil war in El Salvador. Now Will Lucero seeks Monica's help for his wife, who is in a coma. Monica and Will return to El Salvador to find a possible remedy through Alma's research on a venomous type of cone sea snail. The trip also results in Monica finding out many secrets about her mother and her family.

> As Monica looked out to the vast field of dancing silver light, she caught the first glimpse of where this was headed, and how deep and sharp the fall ahead. Years later, she would pinpoint the shock wave of consequences that followed back to this moment, to this casual conversation that sent her whole family, and life forever after, into a sick and dizzying spin. (13)

Subjects: civil war; coma patients; El Salvador; love stories; marine biologists; mothers and daughters; sea

Similar titles: *Bitter Grounds* by Benitez and *A Place Called Milagro de la Paz* by Argueta also dramatize the civil war in El Salvador; *The Scorpion's Tail* by Torti also features a female biologist.

Awards: Best First Book Award, International Latino Book Awards, 2007

Benitez, Sandra (Puerto Rican American).

🌹 *Bitter Grounds.* **New York: Hyperion, 1997. ISBN 0786861576. 445pp.**

Set amid the political unrest and bloody civil wars of El Salvador, *Bitter Grounds* tells the story of three generations of women. Elena de Contreras, a wealthy socialite, and her daughter Magda revel in the good life of European adventures and parties. On the other side, Jacinta Prieto, the Contreras' maid, struggles to forget her past and the loss of all her loved ones to the war.

> *For all her life, there had been a war of some kind. Her girlhood was blighted by the interminable bloody warfare that wrenched all loved ones from her. Although the years she had spent with Elena and then Magda placed some distance between her and the horror of her past, she still lived in a world that held plenty of reminders.* (148)

Subjects: civil war; El Salvador; mothers and daughters; plantations

Similar titles: *The Heiress of Water* by Barron and *A Place Called Milagro de la Paz* by Argueta also take place during the civil war in El Salvador.

Awards: American Book Award, 1998

Night of the Radishes. **New York: Hyperion, 2003. ISBN 0786864001. 276pp.**

Annie Rush is a Minnesota mom caring for her mother, who is dying of emphysema, and carrying the guilt and baggage from a tragedy that happened when she was a child. She finds letters from her estranged brother Hub and, after her mother's passing, decides to search for him. The search takes her to Oaxaca, where a new friend, Joe, urges her to give in to the magic of Mexico.

> *Early March in Minneapolis. A cold, raw time, colder and rawer for being the dead of night. Ma is downstairs, dying, and I'm up here, curled like a wounded cat on Hub's bed. Despite the weather, I'm not cold. We've cranked the thermometer up high to keep Ma warm. Besides, there's that hot coal of anger burning in my brain.* (3)

Key features: First person narration

Subjects: Americans; expatriates; Mexico—Oaxaca; Minnesota

Similar titles: Characters in *Sofia's Saints* by Diana Lopez also struggle with the loss of a parent; *Breathing Lessons* and *The Accidental Tourist* by Tyler also address how a tragic past can affect current relationships. *Lies* by De Hériz similarly highlights mothers taking a break from the family routine.

Bevin, Teresa (Cuban).

Havana Split. **Houston, TX: Arte Público Press, 1998. ISBN 1558852298. 232pp.**

At her mother's insistence, Lara Canedo fled Cuba as a teenager like many other refugees in the 1960s. Now an adult, Lara returns home to visit her family and the beautiful city she left behind. Upon her arrival, Lara discovers the city is dilapidated, and both she and her family are keeping secrets.

> *As a child, I would share a bed with an adult when the family got together in San Venancio, Camagüey, or in Cojímar. I felt safe then from all the strange shadows that lurked in the night. That comforting feeling had taken me by surprise and put me to sleep in less than two minutes.* (127)

Key features: First person narration

Subjects: Cuba; Cuban Americans; families; lesbians; refugees

Similar titles: Similar titles featuring Cuban refugees include *Broken Paradise* by Samartin, *Days of Awe* by Obejas, and *The Sugar Island* by Lamazares. *Faults* by Peña and *Coachella* by Taylor prominently feature lesbian characters and their dysfunctional families.

Cañón, James (Colombian).

Tales from the Town of Widows. **New York: HarperCollins, 2007. ISBN 0061140384. 340pp.**

A small Colombian town is besieged by a band of guerrillas, who demand that all men join them in the fight against the ruling government. They leave behind only a few men, and the town comes to a standstill as the women of Mariquita mourn the loss of their husbands, sons, and brothers. Problems abound for the women, until the wife of the former police sergeant, Rosalba viuda de Patiño, declares herself in charge and takes the town beyond its former glory, with the widows' help.

> *So much had happened recently that she wasn't certain of how many days or nights had passed, and so dressing for a Sunday just felt right. She had chosen to remain faithful to the conventional system of reckoning day and night, because she felt it was her responsibility to record events at least by the color of the sky. A white dog scratching at its fleas in the middle of main street seemed to confirm the magistrate's conviction that everything in Mariquita was just fine.* (204)

Subjects: Colombia; grief; guerrilla warfare; kidnapping; *pueblos*; small towns

Similar titles: *Erased Faces* by Limón and *The Scorpion's Tail* by Torti also focus on women's involvement in guerrilla warfare.

Carlson, Lori Marie (U.S. American).

The Sunday Tertulia. **New York: HarperCollins, 2000. ISBN 0060195363. 208pp.**

Claire, a young non-Latina Hispanophile, is befriended by a diverse group of Latin American women in New York City, where she, like so many before her, has come to find her future. She is included in their monthly Sunday *tertulia* gatherings, an occasion to gossip, philosophize, learn each other's stories, and, ultimately, connect.

> *I've always thought stereotypes about what looks Latin or American or European are wildly inaccurate. This goes for temperaments, too. When I studied Romance languages in college, most of my classmates were much like me, distinctly North American but possessed by more Latin fire than Yankee coolness. We couldn't wait to connect with others just like us, wherever they happened to be in the world.* (9)

Subjects: Latinas; New York—New York City; women's friendships

Similar titles: *Tertulias* are also prominent in *Playing with Light* by Beatriz Rivera.

Castillo, Ana (Mexican American).

🌹 *The Mixquiahuala Letters*. **Binghamton, NY: Bilingual Press, 1986. ISBN 0916950670. 132pp.**

Two young women, one Mexican, one Anglo, meet while in Mexico and strike up a friendship strong enough to last a lifetime. Although both go their own ways, they continue to correspond and travel together throughout the years. Through their personal letters to each other these completely opposite women expose their lives and loves.

> *In that country, the term "liberated woman" meant something other than what we had strived for back in the United States. In this case it simply meant a woman who would sleep nondiscriminately with any man who came along. I inhaled deeply from the strong cigarette he had given me and released the smoke in the direction of his face which diminished the sarcastic expression.* (73)

Key features: Epistolary style

Subjects: epistolary fiction; identity; letters; women's friendships

Similar titles: *Tarzan's Tonsillitis* by Bryce Echenique and *The Eagle's Throne* by Carlos Fuentes are also written in epistolary form. The unique friendships between women can also be found in *Havana Thursdays* by Suarez, *Playing with Boys* by Valdes-Rodriguez, and *Frontera Street* by Barrientos.

Awards: American Book Award, 1987

Peel My Love Like an Onion. (*Carmen la Coja*, **2000). Translated by Dolores Prida. New York: Doubleday, 1999. ISBN 0385496761. 213pp.**

Carmen contemplates her days as a famous flamenco dancer and all the passion and excitement of those times, which contrast starkly with her tedious present situation. Now, abandoned by her lovers, Carmen lives with her mother, and even worse, her polio returns. All is not lost, however, and Carmen will survive! There is humor, there is passion, there is dancing.

> *She looked like a one-woman float in an ethnic parade.* (40)

Key features: First person narration

Subjects: Chicanos; flamenco dancers; Illinois—Chicago; men and women; mothers and daughters; polio

Similar titles: Women also triumph in *Loving Pedro Infante* by Denise Chavez; *Mambo Peligroso* by Chao also features the passion of dance. *Le Affaire* by Diane Johnson also takes a humorous look at love affairs and cultural clashes.

Castillo, Mary (Mexican American).

Switchcraft. **New York: HarperCollins, 2007. ISBN 9780060876081. 282pp.**

Aggie Portrero is a single girl who owns a failing boutique in San Diego and envies her friend Nely Mendoza's life as a married mom. They switch bodies through the meddling of a "grumpy guru," and each has to contend with the realities of the other's situation, with humorous results.

> *She never found the time to get all the things she'd wanted to do done, like fold and put away all of Audrey's laundry, shop for clothes to wear to Ventana de Oro, much less have hot, grinding sex with her husband, who had been working insane hours on a case.* (8)

Key features: Sexual situations

Subjects: body-switching; *chica* lit; ; Latinas; women's friendships

Similar titles: Other *chica* lit novels about friends getting reacquainted are *Unsettling* by Sandoval and *Dirty Girls on Top* by Valdes-Rodriguez.

Chao, Patricia (U.S. American).

Mambo Peligroso. **New York: HarperCollins, 2005. ISBN 0060734175. 300pp.**

Half-Cuban, half-Japanese Catalina Ortiz Midori is immersed in her Cuban roots when she enters the dance studio of the fascinating, seductive, yet *cabrón*, one-eyed instructor, El Tuerto.

> *After dinner they'd roll up the rugs and practice: an ice-dance lift he'd seen on TV, a hip-hop shine the Puerto Domingo kids had made all the rage, or they'd just improvise to the latest Grupo Gale or Gran Combo single. Then they'd sprawl on his black satin sheets swigging passion fruit juice mixed with seltzer and watch old dance videos—everything from Fred and Ginger to bootleg tapes of Eddie Torres in his heyday—commenting and analyzing and comparing.* (106)

Key features: Strong language; sexual situations

Subjects: Cuban Americans; dancing; love affairs; New York

Similar titles: *Peel My Love Like an Onion* by Ana Castillo also focuses on the passion of dance.

Chavez, Denise (New Mexican American).

Loving Pedro Infante. **(*Por el Amor de Pedro Infante*, 2002). Farrar, Straus & Giroux, 2001. ISBN 0374194114. 325pp.**

Tere Avila, a divorcee and secretary of the Pedro Infante Fan Club in small town Cabritovillo, New Mexico, is stuck in a dead-end relationship with a married man. As she and her best friend Irma dream about Pedro (a handsome move star killed in an airplane crash), they search for meaning, cope with the dreary reality of small town life, and keep Cabritoville titillated with their antics.

> *[F]or any woman who has the misfortune to be single and dating, Cabritoville is twenty years behind the times. . . . A night out on the town is going to La Tempestad or the Diary Queen to get a Dilly Bar.* (26)

Subjects: adultery; Chicanas; divorced women; fan clubs; Infante, Pedro; New Mexico; small towns

Similar titles: *Midnight Sandwiches at the Mariposa Express* by Beatriz Rivera, *¡Caramba!* by Nina Marie Martínez, and *Face of an Angel* by Denise Chavez humorously detail life in a small town; *The Love You Promised Me* by Molina examines the effects love affairs and cultural clashes have on such an environment.

De Hériz, Enrique (Spanish).

Lies. (Mentira, 2004). Translated by John Cullen. New York: Doubleday, 2007. ISBN 9780385517942. 415pp.

Isabel is an anthropologist studying death rituals in the Peten in Guatemala. She has been declared dead after an accident, but is actually recuperating and is not sure she wants to return to her previous life. In Barcelona, her daughter Serena researches and writes the family history, investigating the truth behind certain family legends.

> *I think about my children crying. How they must have wept for me, how they must be weeping for me still. I don't count the quantity of their tears as a measure of their grief; weeping is a learned skill, and everyone cries the way he knows how, the way he can.* (10)

Subjects: anthropologists; Guatemala; historians; mothers and daughters; Spain—Barcelona

Similar titles: *The Queen Jade* by Murray also features an archaeology adventure in Central America; *Night of the Radishes* by Benitez similarly highlights mothers taking a break from the family routine. *The House on the Lagoon* by Ferré also traces the family histories of its characters.

Ferré, Rosario (Puerto Rican).

Flight of the Swan. (Vuelo del cisne, 2002). New York: Farrar, Straus & Giroux, 2001. ISBN 0374156484. 262pp.

While touring, Madame, a world-famous Russian prima ballerina, is forced to remain in Puerto Rico while her country suffers political turmoil. While on the island, Madame falls in love with Diamantino, a local revolutionary half her age. Will Madame choose to give up her art for the man she loves?

> *Before, when I looked into it, I thought love simply wasn't in the cards for me. God had given me talent, professional success, beauty, and good health. To complain would have been ungrateful. Today I look into the shimmering black stone and Diamantino's face emerges from its depths: dark and dangerous and fascinating; powerful as a magnet.* (168–69)

Key features: First person narration

Subjects: dancing; love affairs; Puerto Rico; revolutionary struggles

Similar titles: The life-altering choice between love and art is also the theme of *The Messenger* by Montero.

The House on the Lagoon. New York: Farrar, Straus & Giroux, 1995. ISBN 0374173117. 407pp.

Wealthy housewife Isabel Monfort, decides to fulfill her dream to write a novel about her ancestors and her husband's in Puerto Rico. When her husband, Quinton, sneaks a look at her manuscript, he is appalled by her version of history.

So he makes his own notes in the margins, revealing the true history of their families.

> *It was then that we made our pledge. We promised we would examine carefully the origins of anger in each of our families as if it were a disease, and in this way avoid, during the life we were to share together, the mistakes our forebears had made.* (6)

Key features: First person narration

Subjects: families; Puerto Ricans; writers—fiction

Similar titles: *Lies* by De Hériz also traces the family histories of its characters.

García, Cristina (Cuban American).

The Agüero Sisters. **New York: Knopf: Distributed by Random House, 1997. ISBN 0679450904. 299pp.**

Sisters Constancia and Reina Agüero grew up in Cuba with their scientist parents. But the death of their parents and Constancia's decision to move to the United States create a rift between the two. Estranged for thirty years, the women live separate and completely different lives. The story of their lives, their feelings about their mother's unexpected death, and the background of their estrangement from each other unfolds in alternating chapters. As time passes, each sister gets closer to the other and to learning the truth about their mother's death.

> *Reina couldn't mourn her father's death. By the time he put the twelve-gauge shotgun to his heart, Reina was gangly with anguish from her mother's untimely death. She had spurted nearly a foot in two years. Reina remembers the cottony smell of Sundays, the stagnant contractions of weekly routines. She wished her sister could have given her something vital then, something to ease her grief. But all that was essential collapsed between them in those years, collapsed but did not die.* (238)

Subjects: Cuban Americans; family relationships; family secrets; Florida—Miami; sibling rivalry; sisters

Similar titles: Unique relationships between women can also be found in *Playing with Boys* by Valdes-Rodriguez, *The Mixquiahala Letters* by Ana Castillo, and *Frontera Street* by Barrientos.

Gershten, Donna (U.S. American).

❦ *Kissing the Virgin's Mouth.* **New York: HarperCollins, 2001. ISBN 0060185678. 228pp.**

Guadalupe Magdalena Molina Vásquez narrates her story, from her beginnings on the poverty-stricken Mexican coast to her affluent rise in the United States. Born in a patriarchal society, Magda learns to follow their rules, but also makes many of her own. Forced out of town by the wives of her admirers, Magda ends up in the United States and marries. But in this new world the same rules don't apply, so Magda returns to her homeland. There she revisits her life, finding wisdom to pass on to her daughter.

> *When I was old enough, I attended every Saturday dance, and people commented on my dancing. Some said I was without shame. Some said I could be a professional.* (118)

Key features: First person narration; sexual situations

Subjects: Mexicans; Mexico; mothers and daughters; saints

Similar titles: *Empress of the Splendid Season* by Hijuelos also features a determined matriarch.

Awards: Bellwether Prize for Fiction, 2000

Grande, Reyna (Mexican American).

🌻 *Across a Hundred Mountains.* **New York: Atria Books, 2006. ISBN 0743269578. 259pp.**

When her father travels to the United States to earn more money for his family and ends up leaving the family high and dry, Juana Garcia begins her own journey to find him. A chance encounter at the Tijuana jail leads Juana to a new friend, prostitute Adelina Vasquez, who takes her in after she runs out of money to cross the border. Adelina is a runaway from the United States who followed her low-life boyfriend to Mexico and ended up in a tough situation. Together the two women gather the courage to cross the border to find what they are ultimately after—a missing father and a chance for a new beginning.

> *From the rock at the very top of the hill, Juana could see the town below, the towers of the church sticking out like two fingers pointing at the sky, the fields, the river that divided them in half, the mountains encircling the town. But it was the mountains to the west that most held her attention. Those were the mountains Apá had pointed at and said he would be on the other side of.* (78)

Subjects: family relationships; immigration; Mexico; prostitutes; women's friendships

Similar titles: Other experiences of immigrants crossing the border may be found in *Crossing the Wire* by Hobbs and *La Línea* by Jaramillo.

Awards: American Book Award, 2007

Herrera, Andrea O'Reilly (Cuban American).

The Pearl of the Antilles. **Tempe, AZ: Bilingual Press/Editorial Bilingue, 2001. ISBN 0927534959. 353pp.**

Recounting the history of a Cuban family through its generations of women, this story centers on Margarita as she struggles with her two identities as a Cuban and an American, and the shame she feels for not passing on her Cuban heritage to her children.

> *"I'd die in the city, mi cielo," the old woman said, as she snapped shut the clasps on Rosa's steamer trunk. "Besides, everyone knows that you can't pull a stubborn old weed like me out by its roots. But you know that I will never abandon you. I will always be waiting for you and the girls when you return to Tres Flores. Siempre, m'ija."* (10)

Subjects: ancestors; Cuba; Cuban Americans; immigrants—Cuban; mothers and daughters

Similar titles: *The Day of the Moon* by Limón and *Eccentric Neighborhoods* by Ferré are also family sagas.

Hijuelos, Oscar (Cuban American).

Empress of the Splendid Season. **New York: HarperCollins, 1999. ISBN 0060175702. 342pp.**

Lydia, the empress of the title, was exiled to New York from Cuba before the revolution, as punishment for her sexual peccadilloes. The novel tells the story of her life in the United States as a member of the working class, after having been raised as a pampered *burguesa*. The people around her, her children, friends, and employers interact with her in the New York City of the second half of the twentieth century.

> *[S]he had never given the idea of work or the suffering of others much thought; but that was before her family, turning unfairly against her with a nearly Biblical wrath, had banished her, unprepared to contend with an indifferent world.* (4)

Subjects: Cubans; immigrants—Cubans; love stories; New York—New York City

Similar titles: *In the Name of Salomé* by Julia Alvarez also highlights an immigrant woman's life, and *Esperanza Rising* by Ryan features an aristocrat in her home country who is reduced to physical labor in the United States. A woman is also the head of a New York City household in *Streets of Fire* by Soledad Santiago. *Kissing the Virgin's Mouth* by Gershten also features a determined matriarch.

Limón, Graciela (Mexican American; Californiana).

The Day of the Moon. **Houston, TX: Arte Público Press, 1999. ISBN 1558852743. 228pp.**

Don Flavio, a rough man who has won money by playing cards, denies his past as a poor half-Indian and begins a new life as part of the upper class. Angry that his new wife, Velia, has developed an intimate relationship with his sister, Don Flavio leaves his family. Upon his wife's death, Don Flavio returns to his home, to find his sister crazy and his beautiful daughter, Isadora, headstrong and passionately opposed to his racism. Isadora's love for an Indian, Jeronimo Santiago, fuels Don Flavio to do the unthinkable. Family secrets remain buried until Don Flavio's death. Finally, the family can finally be at peace with their identities.

> *There were other similar lessons later on, lessons in which he was careful to emphasize the difference between races: A white person, especially a white woman, should never mix her blood with a man of another race. When Isadora asked why not, he told her of the deformed child, half-animal, half-human that resulted from such a union, and how it was doomed to travel in a circus as a living example of what happens when men and women fall into such depravity.* (44)

Key features: Sexual situations

Subjects: family relationships; Mexico; race relations; secrets

Similar titles: *The Pearl of the Antilles* by Andrea Herrera and *Eccentric Neighborhoods* by Ferré are also family sagas.

🌱 *Erased Faces.* **Houston, TX: Arte Público Press, 2001. ISBN 1558853421. 258pp.**

Photojournalist Adriana Mora travels to Chiapas, Mexico, to record images of the Mayan civilization. In Chiapas Adriana meets Chan K'in, a shaman, who gives her clues to what lies behind her repeated nightmares. In a small village Adriana also encounters Juana Galván, a woman heavily involved in the tumultuous Zapatista uprising. Juana invites Adriana to join her and see beyond the camera lens to embrace the real women whose images she captures.

> *The thought of violence shocked Adriana, forcing her to wonder if she had the courage. On the one hand, she found it easy to identify with the suffering of the natives; she had recognized it each time she focused her lens on a woman; she saw it stamped on her face. She was convinced that she understood their misery because it reminded her of something inside of her.* (39–40)

Subjects: dreams; guerrilla warfare; Mexico; reincarnation; revolutionary struggles; women's friendships

Similar titles: Women's involvement in guerrilla warfare can also be found in *Tales from the Town of Widows* by Cañon and *The Scorpion's Tail* by Torti.

Awards: Gustavus Myers Outstanding Book Award, 2002

Lopez, Diana.

Sofia's Saints. **Tempe, AZ: Bilingual Press/Editorial Bilingüe, 2002. ISBN 1931010072. 147pp.**

Thirty-year-old waitress and part-time artist Sofia struggles to save the childhood home in Corpus Christi, where she has lived since her mother's death twelve years earlier.

> *I can't convince him that my woodburning gives this house character. If I stare long enough, the lines undulate and quiver against the wall like guitar strings. What else do I have here? What's mine besides memories so fragile they crumble beneath time?* (119)

Key features: First person narration; strong language

Subjects: artists; home ownership; Mexican Americans; single women; waitresses

Similar titles: *Night of the Radishes* by Benitez also deals with the loss of a parent.

Martínez, Nina Marie (Mexican American; Californiana).

¡Caramba! **New York: Alfred A. Knopf, 2004. ISBN 0375413758. 360pp.**

This lively tale is peppered with *dichos*, Mexican sayings and proverbs. The chapters unfold according to the Mexican pack of cards called *Lotería*, which features images such as *El Borracho*/The Drunk, *El Diablo*/The Devil, and *La Dama*/The Lady. All the action takes place in the fictional town of Lava Landing, California, featuring good friends Consuelo, Natalie, and Lulabelle.

> *[Consuelo] and Natalie would have liked to have gone to the rodeo. But they were otherwise occupied. They were going to have a yard sale where they intended to sell anything and everything they could in order to raise enough money to send Natalie on the trip south to try to free Don Pancho's soul.* (117)

Subjects: apparitions; Mexican Americans; road trips; United States—Southwest; women's friendships

Similar titles: *Loving Pedro Infante* by Denise Chavez also takes a humorous look at friendship between women. *Esperanza's Box of Saints* by Escandón similarly uses magic realism.

Molina, Silvia (Mexican).

🖈 *The Love You Promised Me.* (*El amor que me juraste,* 1998). **Translated by David Unger. Willimantic, CT: Curbstone Press, 1999. ISBN 1880684624. 152pp.**

Stuck in an unsatisfying marriage, Marcela turns to another man for love and attention. The affair between Marcela and her mother's doctor is intense. Unfortunately the affair is also short-lived, as the good doctor soon declares he no longer cares for Marcela. Devastated, she returns to San Lázaro, the *pueblo* of her childhood, to search for her self and her history.

> *Yes, I suppose it was that, to know one another, which was the source of nervousness for us both. It was as if we were reading the same novel and wanted to reach the end very slowly, or we were listening to the same music and were dying to have the score in hand so we could follow it at our leisure. Desire increased within both of us with each passing word.*
> (50)

Key features: First person narration

Subjects: adultery; families; Mexicans; Mexico

Similar titles: *Loving Pedro Infante* by Denise Chavez also details adulterous affairs and cultural clashes.

Awards: Sor Juana Inés de la Cruz Prize, 1998

Obejas, Achy (Cuban American).

🖈 *Days of Awe.* **New York: Ballantine Books, 2001. ISBN 034543921X. 371pp.**

Like many fellow Cubans, Alejandra San Jose and her family immigrated to the United States after the rise of Fidel Castro. Too young to remember life in Cuba, Ale only knows about her home country through stories. Captivated by the Spanish language, Ale grows up to be a translator. This job puts her in a position to return to her homeland; once there she discovers her family secret: they are Jews. This opens Ale's eyes to a whole new version of the family history.

> *The problem is that when I stand alone before the mirror—that's me there, the one with the blue-gray eyes just like my great-grandfather, my mother's pouty pillows for lips—I know everything and nothing at all, and I am overwhelmed, unable to look myself in the eye, struggling to swallow and to breathe, thinking always: Like the emperor, I have no clothes, no clothes. (193)*

Subjects: ancestors; Catholic Church; Cuba; family relationships; Jews and Judaism; refugees

Similar titles: Cuban refugees are also main characters in *Broken Paradise* by Samartin, *Havana Split* by Bevin, and *The Sugar Island* by Lamazares.

Awards: Lambda Literary Award for Lesbian Fiction, 2001

Peña, Terri de la (Mexican American).

Faults: A Novel. Los Angeles: Alyson Publications, 1999. ISBN 1-55583-478-7. 286pp.

Toni Dorado, a former librarian, returns to LA, leaving her Anglo lover in the Pacific Northwest, to return home to her first love and a dysfunctional family. Five women narrate the story—Toni, her antagonistic sister Sylvia, their mother Adela, Sylvia's daughter Gabriela, and Toni's lover Pat. In addition to an abusive brother-in-law and sibling rivalry, a violent earthquake comes to town and settles some issues.

> *Around the corner of the cabin, I found the birds silent and still, the chickadee surely dead, a flurry of tiny feathers surrounding it. The merlin lay on its side, talons curved, beak slightly open, its unblinking eyes gazing into nothingness.* (20)

Subjects: Chicanos (Mexican Americans); earthquakes; lesbians

Similar titles: *Havana Split* by Bevin and *Coachella* by Taylor also prominently feature lesbian characters and their dysfunctional families.

Pineda, Cecile (Mexican American).

The Love Queen of the Amazon. Boston: Little, Brown, 1992. ISBN 0316708127. 255pp.

Expelled from the convent school for stripping naked to save a drowning classmate, Ana Magdalena becomes intrigued by her body and newfound sexuality. Shortly thereafter Ana is married off to a dreary, much older writer, who pays little attention to her. Tired of a loveless marriage and seeking adventure, Ana decides to turn her home into a bordello, right under her husband's nose.

> *It was past nine, and still there was no sign of Ana Magdalena. When he heard the sound of footsteps on the stair, he threw open the door. But what he saw there made him abandon all thought of his night demons. Here was a heavenly vision with a breakfast tray. He rubbed his stomach in anticipation, though not so much of the scones, or the boiled egg, or the steaming pot of tea.* (180)

Key features: Strong language; sexual situations

Subjects: adultery; brothels; magic; Peru

Similar titles: Brothels are also found in *Esperanza's Box of Saints* by Escandón.

Puig, Manuel (Argentinian).

Pubis Angelical. (*Pubis Angelical,* 1979). Translated by Elena Brunet. Minneapolis: University of Minnesota Press, 2000. ISBN 0816636818. 236pp.

Three women's lives are strangely connected: Ana, a woman from Argentina confined to a psychiatric institution in Mexico; the Mistress, a young movie star/actress involved in intrigue in the period before the Second World War; and W218, a sex worker cyborg from the future.

> *Four in the afternoon + bare trees + dying light + trek toward work + pleasurable sensation of bundled up clothes + sensation of day that will depart never to return again + fear of finding patient disagreeable + sensation that something either very good or very bad will happen.* (127)

Subjects: Austria—Vienna; Mexico—Mexico City; science fiction

Similar titles: *Secret Weavers* by Agosín contains stories about women with a fantastical flavor.

Quintero, Sofía (Nuyorican). *See also* Black Artemis.

Divas Don't Yield: Four Chicas, One Car, Tons of Baggage . . . : A Novel. New York: One World Ballantine Books, 2006. ISBN 0-345-482838-7. 354pp.

Four New York *chicas* take a two-week, life-changing road trip to attend a conference in San Francisco. Jackie is a strong Afro-Latina who has issues with her boyfriend Eric and his baby's mama; Lourdes is a radical, devout Catholic premed student from Denver; Hazel is a gorgeous lesbian in love with Jackie; and Irena is the *güera* of the group, a blonde, sensitive New Age vegetarian.

> As I walk up the street, I pull off my sling bag and search the crowd, wondering which ones are the bullies and what nasty things they called Li'l Bit. Did they call her Brillo Pad? Bembe Face? Or the one I really hate . . . cocola. The little snots I grew up with used to call me that because they were too ignorant to realize that being black didn't make me not Latina. (13)

Key features: First person narration; glossary and reader's guide

Subjects: Afro-Latinas; *chica* lit; Cuban Americans; feminists; lesbians; Nuyoricans; women's friendships

Similar titles: *Unsettling* by Sandoval and *¡Caramba!* by Nina Marie Martínez are other novels about Latina girlfriends on a road trip.

Restrepo, Laura (Colombian).

The Angel of Galilea. (Dulce compañía, 1995). Translated by Dolores M. Koch. New York: Crown, 1995. ISBN 0609603264. 193pp.

Journalist Mona is sent to the poor barrio of Galilea on the outskirts of Bogotá, Colombia, to investigate reported sightings of an angel. There she finds the town in conflict over one man. Is he an angel or an impostor? Soon Mona finds herself not only reporting about this mysterious man but also falling under his spell.

> The pilgrims had assembled at the holy place, waiting for the angel to appear. They had brought him their sick to be healed and their newly born to be baptized. The old came seeking consolation, the young for novelty, the sad ones in search of hope, the women love, the homeless shelter, the unfortunate a blessing. (48)

Key features: First person narration

Subjects: angels; Colombia—Bogotá; miracles; poverty; reporters; superstition

Similar titles: *In a Town Called Mundomuerto* by Silvis similarly features a town shrouded in mystery and superstitions.

Rivera, Beatriz (Cuban American).

Midnight Sandwiches at the Mariposa Express. **Houston, TX: Arte Público Press, 1997. ISBN 1558852166. 182pp.**

Trish Izquierdo lives in the town of West Echevarria, New Jersey, home to a large Cuban community. She knows its history well, and as she and others begin to plan the annual celebration of the town's founding, Trish decides to give her lackluster town a whole new history, to satisfy her need for fun and adventure.

> *But the day of the parade was so different! Even the middle class was there! Yes! There were quite a few by-standers from Riverview Avenue who absolutely hate the street and are scared to death of what they call the people—"el pueblo." Some of them were just there by accident, but what a great coincidence! (56)*

Subjects: Cuban Americans; event planners; small towns

Similar titles: *Loving Pedro Infante* by Denise Chavez is similar in its humorous portrayal of small town life and culture.

Playing with Light. **Houston, TX: Arte Público Press, 2000. ISBN 1558853103. 245pp.**

Rich housewife Rebecca Barrios decides to lead a *tertulia*—an old Cuban tradition to bring women together weekly for conversation—at her house. She convinces her friends to join a book club, and the women select the novel *Playing with Light* as their first read. As the women read, they long for the passions found in the historical saga and soon find themselves intertwined with the story of the Santa Cruz family.

> *Conchita grinned and held onto a thought for a little while, then she said that since Rebecca had been reading this novel out loud to her in the car for the past two weeks, the pages of the novel seemed to be scattered all over Miami. Pages one through five, for example, were on Alton Road, six through fifteen on the Julia Tuttle Causeway, the rest of that chapter on the expressway with Miami on the left. (97)*

Subjects: Cuban Americans; books; Florida—Miami; upper classes; women's friendships

Similar titles: *Tertulias* are also prominent in *The Sunday Tertulia* by Carlson.

Romo-Carmona, Mariana (Chilean American).

Living at Night. **Duluth, MN: Spinsters Ink, 1997. ISBN 1883523222. 257pp.**

Distraught when her mother has a stroke, twenty-one year old Erica Garcia decides to drop out of college and take a job as a nurse's aide at an institution for the developmentally disabled in upscale Connecticut. The only Puerto Rican in a mostly white community, Erica struggles to find her place and discovers there is a lot to be learned from those she cares for, such as compassion and dignity.

> *I didn't know what I was supposed to do at the ward. How I could help, how I could make things better for the residents? Then again, I wasn't even sure how to make things better for myself, other than to keep things under control. (42)*

Key features: First person narration; sexual situations

Subjects: disabled people; lesbians; Puerto Rican Americans

Similar titles: *Frontera Street* by Barrientos also features a lonely woman looking for friendship in a new place

Samartin, Cecilia (Cuban American).

🏆 *Broken Paradise.* **New York: Atria Books, 2007. ISBN 0743287797. 340pp.**

Happily living a pampered lifestyle, cousins Nora and Alicia enjoy all the comforts of prerevolutionary Cuba, until Castro's rise to power. Forced apart, Nora flees to the United States with her family, while Alicia remains behind. The friendship between the two continues through lengthy letters over the years. In her new home Nora tries to retain her Cuban heritage and adjust to American ways. Alicia experiences hardship under Castro's rule. Nora soon learns that Alicia can no longer care for herself or her child and has resorted to prostitution to survive. This knowledge sends Nora back to Cuba to help her beloved cousin.

> *We took pictures with our hearts and minds, and the little time we had expanded into an eternity of tomorrows we would never have. I found myself gazing at the Caribbean in the distance for hours at a time trying to make up for a lifetime of lost memories.* (86)

Key features: First person narration

Subjects: cousins; Cuba; Cuban Americans; letters; prostitutes; refugees; revolutionary struggles

Similar titles: The plight of Cuban refugees can also be found in *Days of Awe* by Obejas, *Havana Split* by Bevin, and *The Sugar Island* by Lamazares.

Awards: International Latino Book Award, 2008

Tarnished Beauty. **New York: Atria Books, 2008. ISBN 9781416549505. 339pp.**

Jamilet is the tarnished beauty of the title, a smart and lively young lady with an ugly birthmark that has doomed her to ostracism in her native village in Mexico. She follows her tía Carmen to seek her fortune in the United States, where she meets Señor Peregrino. He is an old gentleman at the mental hospital where Jamilet has found employment, who coerces her into listening to his story.

> *A child who was the perfection of human form in face, but hid a hideous swirl of blood and disfigurement that few had ever seen, but all had heard about. It was said by some to resemble a freshly gutted cow, by others to writhe like many snakes in a pit of blood.* (6)

Subjects: California—Los Angeles; friendship; love stories; mental hospitals; patients; undocumented workers

Similar titles: *Living at Night* by Romo-Carmona similarly portrays a young woman learning from older patients.

Santiago, Eduardo (Cuban American).

Tomorrow They Will Kiss. **New York: Little, Brown, 2006. ISBN 0316014125. 282pp.**

Graciela has immigrated to New Jersey from a small village in Cuba to work in a doll factory. She and her two friends (who also narrate their own chapters) from Palmagria keep up with the nightly *telenovelas* and try to guess when the protagonists will kiss, while hoping for their own prince charming to sweep them off their feet and away from the daily grind.

> *I liked the telenovelas for their predictability. It was comforting to know something was going to work out, that the dark-haired girl was always going to be good, the blonde was always going to be bad. But most important, if the love of your life was engaged to marry someone else, he would be yours in the end.* (77)

Key features: First person narration; reading group guide

Subjects: Cuba; factories; immigrants; New Jersey; women's friendships

Similar titles: *Frontera Street* by Barrientos also focuses on friendship between working Latinas.

Santiago, Esmeralda (Puerto Rican American; Nuyorican).

America's Dream. **New York: HarperCollins, 1996. ISBN 0060172797. 325pp.**

Housekeeper América Gonzalez works in a hotel off the coast of Puerto Rico, serving the wealthy tourists who visit her small island. Surrounded by a family that both resents and abuses her, América jumps at the chance to be a live-in maid and nanny for an affluent family in Westchester, New York. After her arrival, América realizes that the life of the wealthy suburbanites is all a façade, much like her feeling of safety.

> *Adela is the first Spanish-speaking housekeeper she's met since she came here, and she's both excited and apprehensive about getting to know her. She's so . . . América struggles to find the right word. Familiar. That's it. Even though they addressed each other formally, used usted, América still feels as if Adela assumes they can be friends just because they're both maids.* (211)

Subjects: abuse; housekeepers; mothers and daughters; Puerto Rican women

Similar titles: *A Perfect Silence* by Ambert also focuses on Puerto Rican women in difficult situations.

Santiago, Soledad (Nuyorican).

Streets of Fire. **New York: Dutton/Penguin Group, 1996. ISBN 0-525-94078-2. 342pp.**

Officer Francesca Colon has just been promoted to NYPD's Public Information Department, where she faces many challenges as the first Latina woman in the department. New York City is facing the threat of race riots provoked by police brutality, and Francesca must walk a fine line between defending her "people" and supporting her fellow officers. At the same time, she's dealing with family issues involving her two rebellious teenagers and her sickly mother.

> *I felt a flash of panic that quickly turned to anger. Talk about a kick in the gut. So this was the setup. They had scheduled my public promotion as a diversion from the autopsy report.* (209)

Subjects: interracial relationships; love stories; New York—New York City; police officers; Puerto Rican women; single mothers; teenagers; women's friendships

Similar titles: The main character of *Unsettling* by Sandoval is also a female police officer; *Frontera Street* by Barrientos similarly concentrates on the trials and tribulations of single motherhood.

Serrano, Marcela (Chilean).

Antigua and My Life Before. (*Antigua vida mía*, 1995). **Translated by Margaret Sayers Peden. New York: Doubleday, 2000. ISBN 0385498012. 352pp.**

Famous Chilean singer Josefa Ferrér awakens one morning to find her best friend since third grade, Violeta Dasinski, entangled in a horrific tragedy. Josefa knows she must get her friend's journals at once to tell her story. As Josefa begins to tell Violeta's story, she finds that, like so many relationships among women, their stories of joy, sorrow, regret, and forgiveness are similar.

> *I think of Cayetana and about how much Violeta is like her. No, I can't accuse Violeta of putting convenience first. She gave up everything she knew, all that was comfortable; the easy way was never an option for her. Just like Cayetana.* (213)

Key features: First person narration

Subjects: Chile; grief; singers—fiction; women's friendships

Similar titles: *Havana Thursdays* by Suárez also explores death and grief; *The Mixquiahala Letters* by Ana Castillo, *Playing with Boys* by Valdes-Rodriguez, and *Frontera Street* by Barrientos also focus on the friendships between women. *Inez* by Carlos Fuentes features musical elements.

Silvis, Randall.

In a Town Called Mundomuerto. **Richmond, CA: Omnidawn Publishing, 2007. ISBN 9781890650193. 155pp.**

Alberto regales his grandson with tales of his lifelong love, Lucia Luna. The most beautiful woman in the village at the age of seventeen, Lucia had her choice of any man she wanted. Now she is a withered old woman, and the superstitious townspeople have turned against her because of the man she chose to love.

> *In the meantime, Lucia Luna turned on her heels. She spun once, a slow pirouette, causing her dress to billow around her thighs. Women gasped, and men laid scarred hands upon their hearts. Down the center of the street she began to stroll then, her eyes focused straight ahead, a wry smile on her lips.* (95)

Subjects: death; grandfathers and grandsons; memories; small towns; storytelling; superstition; widows

Similar titles: *The Angel of Galilea* by Restrepo similarly features a town shrouded in mystery and superstition.

Suárez, Virgil (Cuban American).

Havana Thursdays. Houston, TX: Arte Público Press, 1995. ISBN 1558851437. 250pp.

While on a business trip in Brazil, Zacarías Torres dies of a heart attack. Back home in Miami, his wife is living a perfectly normal boring day until the phone call about his death comes. Family members descend on their home to grieve his passing. Upon returning home, personal secrets come to light for many as they try to cope with the crisis.

> *At her age (she'd lost track of the years), she'd buried all her friends, her husband, and now a son. She never intended to outlive her loved ones. Never intended to live this long. She was like an American car, not the ones being made now, but from the forties and fifties. She'd been built to last, but for how long Jesús . . . how long?* (167–68)

Subjects: alcoholism; Cuban Americans; family relationships; grief

Similar titles: *Antigua and My Life Before* by Serrano similarly deals with grief.

Taylor, Sheila Ortiz (Mexican American).

Coachella. Albuquerque: University of New Mexico Press, 1998. ISBN 0826318436. 187pp.

Yolanda Ramírez, a phlebotomist in California's Coachella Valley in the early 1980s, sees the effects AIDS has on the people around her on a daily basis. Yolanda is sure that people are contracting AIDS through a virus in the blood, but no one will listen to her. Meanwhile Marina, a woman who has escaped her abusive past, moves into the trailer next door. Marina and Yolanda begin an intimate relationship; Yolanda's father says good-bye to his lover, who is dying from what is most likely AIDS.

> *Curiosity was being smart. Otherwise you were dead in the water. Little people, the ones pushed back, not seen, the silenced—those were the people who needed to stay curious no matter what it cost them. To ask questions, the questions inside themselves, to keep on asking them. How come, how come, how come?* (23)

Subjects: AIDS; California; lesbians; Mexican Americans

Similar titles: *Saving the World* by Julia Alvarez similarly tackles the difficulties of life with AIDS. *Havana Split* by Bevin and *Faults* by Peña prominently feature lesbian characters and their dysfunctional families.

Torti, Sylvia (U.S. American).

🌺 *The Scorpion's Tail.* Willimantic, CT: Curbstone Press, 2005. ISBN 97819-31896177. 268pp.

Mexico's Zapatista Rebellion is told through the eyes of two women: U.S. biologist Amy, who arrives in Mexico unprepared for the revolution, and Chan Nah K'in from the indigenous Hach Winik tribe, who fights alongside the rebels.

> *Through the night we cut and hacked at the tall pine. It fell slowly at first, but then hit the road hard. I can still hear the sound. Death makes a violent tone. Afterwards, there is a thick silence. I never imagined war would be so quiet.* (119)

Key features: First person narration

Subjects: biologists; guerrilla warfare; Mexico—Chiapas; rebellion; rebels; young women

Similar titles: Barron's *The Heiress of Water* also features a female biologist; women's involvement in guerrilla warfare can be found in *Erased Faces* by Limón and *Tales from the Town of Widows* by Cañon.

Awards: Mármol Prize for Latina/o First Fiction, 2005

Valdés, Zoé (Cuban).

Dear First Love: A Novel. (*Querido Primer Novio*, 1999). Translated by Andrew Hurley. New York: HarperCollins, 2002. ISBN 0060199725. 291pp.

Middle-aged Danae leaves Havana and returns to the *campo* to find her first love, Fortuna, whom she met during the difficult time when she was assigned to work in the sugar cane fields as a teenager, in the same situation as others obligated to perform extreme physical labor under a cruel overseer. Bringing Fortuna back to Havana with her creates another set of problems for Danae and her family.

> *She needed to look once again upon the greenness of those* mogotes *in the Valle de Viñales, the huge pillars of limestone, covered with trees and bushes, that made the most haunting and beautiful landscape in the world, in a certain person's opinion. She told herself that although it was very lovely, if you compared it with other landscapes she had seen as she leafed through books, it was nothing out of this world. She thought about her past and gave an ironic little smile-a pretty stupid little life.* (13)

Key features: Anthropomorphic and inanimate narrators, such as a suitcase or a ceiba tree

Subjects: Cuba; lesbians; love stories; midlife crisis

Similar titles: Anthropomorphic narrators can also be found in *Two Brothers* by Atxaga; *The Cutter* by Suárez also details the experiences of Cuban cane-field workers.

Valdes-Rodriguez, Alisa (Cuban American).

Dirty Girls Social Club. (*El Club Social de las Chicas Temerarias*, 2003). Translated by Mercedes Lamamié de Clairac. New York: St. Martin's Press, 2003. ISBN 0312313810. 308pp.

The original *chica* lit novel. Lauren, Sara, Amber, Elizabeth, Rebecca, and Usnavys are Latina girlfriends who have been meeting regularly since their days at Boston University. They are now in their late twenties and facing challenges in their professional and personal lives—from abusive husbands to cheating boyfriends to racism and homophobia. The girlfriends support each other in their quest for professional fulfillment, love, and happiness.

> *Twice a year, every year, the* sucias *show up. Me, Elizabeth, Sara, Rebecca, Usnavys, and Amber. We can be anywhere in the world—and, being* sucias, *we travel a lot—but we get on a plane, train, whatever, and get back to Boston for a night of food, drink (my specialty), chisme y charla. (That's gossip and chat, y'all.)* (1)

Key features: First person narration—each *sucia* narrates her sections

Subjects: *chica* lit; columnists; domestic violence; lesbians; love stories; magazine editors; Massachusetts—Boston; musicians; television personalities; women's friendships

Similar titles: *A Little Love* by C. C. Medina and *Sex and the South Beach Chicas* by Piñeiro are other novels about Latina girlfriends and love. *Dirty Girls on Top* by Valdes-Rodriguez catches up with the *sucias* five years down the road.

Dirty Girls on Top. **New York: St. Martin's Press, 2008. ISBN 9780312349677. 324pp.**

The Dirty Girls are back—five years older, although not necessarily wiser. This time around they help each other face alcoholism, promiscuity, infertility, domestic abuse, homophobia, and other challenges when they reunite at a resort in beautiful New Mexico, the land of enchantment.

> *"I could have taken him right then, okay,* nena*? I coulda had him this morning, that's how bad he wanted me. But I had lunch to attend to in the resort café. Some things are better if you have to wait for them—including me."* (6)

Key features: First person narration—each *chica* narrates her sections

Subjects: *chica* lit; columnists; domestic violence; lesbians; love stories; magazine editors; Massachusetts—Boston; musicians; television personalities; women's friendships

Similar titles: *A Little Love* by C. C. Medina and *Sex and the South Beach Chicas* by Piñeiro are other novels about Latina girlfriends and love. *Dirty Girls Social Club* by Valdes-Rodriguez introduces the *sucias.*

Playing with Boys. **(***Jugando con chicos,* **2004). Translated by Daina Chaviano. New York: St. Martin's Press, 2004. ISBN 0312332343. 325pp.**

Alexis is a publicist, a Texan transplanted to Los Angeles and working with a *rudo norteño* band. She befriends Marcella and Olivia, who come from very different circumstances. Alexis is a high-maintenance Tejana; Olivia came to the United States as a child refugee from El Salvador; and Marcella is a Mexican soap opera star fallen on hard times. Their interlocking lives help them find that they have a lot in common. And, *de pilón*, they may all find true love!

> *I was a Dallas girl, born and raised, armed with an arsenal of acronyms, BA and MBA from SMU, darlin'—but I was trying to become a California girl, with mixed results. I came to Hell-eh because I thought it was shameful that in a city where the top-three FM radio stations now played Mexican music, the big PR companies were oblivious to the talent and riches in Spanish-speaking America.* (4)

Key features: First person narration—each protagonist tells her story

Subjects: California; *chica* lit; El Salvadorans; humor; Latinas; Mexican Americans; music industry; refugees; Tejanos; women's friendships

Similar titles: *A Little Love* by C. C. Medina and *Unsettling* by Sandoval are other novels about Latina girlfriends.

Veciana-Suarez, Ana (Cuban American).

The Chin Kiss King. **New York: Farrar, Straus & Giroux, 1997. ISBN 0374121303. 311pp.**

Cuca, a spiritual woman who can talk to ghosts, heads a household comprised of three generations of women. Adela, Cuca's daughter, is a promiscuous gambler, and the granddaughter, Maribel, is a hardworking, cautious person. The premature birth of Maribel's son, Victor, brings these very different women together as they struggle to deal with the severe birth defect that may take Victor's life.

> *His heart, there was something wrong with his heart. It was too big, and even with its generous size, it could not hold everything. It could not contain all the love and pain of the world, this huge heart, so big and so full that it had arrived already broken.* (91)

Subjects: Cuban Americans; family relationships; Florida—Miami; grief

Similar titles: The difficulties of family and home for generations of women can also be found in *Mama Fela's Girls* by Baca and *The Wise Women of Havana* by Bernardo. Another family confronting the challenge of a child with disabling health problems can be found in *The Fragrance of Roses* by Arana.

Anthologies and Collections

Agosín, Marjorie (Argentinian).

Women in Disguise. (*Alfareras*, 1994). Translated by Diane Russell-Pineda. Falls Church, VA: Azul Editions, c1996. ISBN 1885214014. 164pp.

These short, almost poem-like, stories about women are dreamlike, with a fantastical flavor, written in a beautiful and melancholy style.

> *I liked to pretend I was a widow from the time I was a little girl. But now that I am thirty-six and slowly falling into the details of life, now that it is getting difficult to hear the beating of my heart, being alone makes me happy.* (110)

Subjects: dreams; love stories; potters; widows

Báez, Annecy (Dominican American).

🐦 *My Daughter's Eyes and Other Stories.* Willimantic, CT: Curbstone Press, 2007. ISBN 9781931896382. 176pp.

This bold collection of fourteen interrelated stories focuses on Dominican women immigrants assimilating to their new country's values and dealing with their emerging sexuality.

> *Mia listened to those words and knew that no matter what happened, they were words that would remain in her heart forever—words that would echo around her mind and soul for a long time to come. He did not love her anymore.* (47)

Subjects: Dominican Americans; family relationships; immigrants; New York—New York City—Bronx

Similar titles: *Drown* by Junot Díaz is another collection about Dominican Americans in the United States.

Awards: Mármol Prize for Latina/o First Fiction, 2007

Cisneros, Sandra (Midwestern Mexican American).

🔖 *Woman Hollering Creek.* New York: Random House, 1991. ISBN 0394576543. 165pp.

This collection of short stories provides readers with a window into the lives of Latina women who have lived both the Mexican and the American life. Young and old, their lives are full of suffering and joy, as well as an unmatched capacity to love and survive.

> *But when the moment came, and he slapped her once, and then again, and again, until the lip split and bled an orchid of blood, she didn't fight back, she didn't break into tears, she didn't run away as she imagined she might when she saw such things in the telenovelas. (47)*

Subjects: family relationships; Latinas; short stories

Similar titles: *The Truth About Alicia* by Matiella is another short story collection highlighting women's suffering.

Awards: PEN USA Literary Award for Best Fiction 1991; Anisfield-Wolf Book Award, 1991

Erro-Peralta, Nora, and Caridad Silva, eds.

Beyond the Border: A New Age in Latin American Women's Fiction. Gainesville: University Press of Florida, 2000. ISBN 0813017858. 254pp.

This collection is comprised of stories from some of Latin America's top female authors, along with new voices from the region. Each entry has a short literary biography before the story, which is followed by a bibliography.

> *In the course of the morning Teresa would abandon the bed; she would sweep, or "dustmot," as she called it, and do the ironing. Around two in the afternoon she would lie down next to him again, still dressed, to be within reach of his desire when he woke up. (163)*

Key features: Strong language; sexual situations

Subjects: short stories; women's lives

Similar titles: Short stories featuring the voices of multiple Latina authors can also be found in *Cubana* by Yañez and *Out of the Mirrored Garden* edited by Posey.

Mastretta, Angeles (Mexican).

Women with Big Eyes. (*Mujeres de ojos grandes,* 1990). Translated by Amy Schildhouse Greenberg. New York: Riverhead Books, 2003, c1990. ISBN 1573223468. 372pp.

In this collection of short stories, each chapter is headed with the name of the aunt whose story is told within it. Thirty-nine women's lives are recounted, and the message is a resounding one: women are loving, mysterious, charming, stubborn, and more when they embrace life. This edition features both English and Spanish texts.

> *They were teenagers when Aunt Isabel fell off a horse. Nobody wanted to know why or where or with whom she had gotten on. They found her flung down by the military field, repeating a great deal of nonsense that her husband decided not to listen to. He devoted himself to kissing her as though she were a medal and staying near to her all the time, when in the past he had been so busy.* (42)

Subjects: family life; Mexico; short stories

Similar titles: Carlson's stories about multiple women in *The Sunday Tertulia* are similarly arranged.

Matiella, Ana Consuelo (New Mexican American).

The Truth About Alicia and Other Stories. **Tucson: University of Arizona Press, 2002. ISBN 0816521638. 141pp.**
Women face the heartbreak of adultery, divorce, murder, and loss in this riveting short story collection.

> *Between keeping the house, cooking elaborate meals in unusual combinations, working on her Ph.D., taking care of Tomás, and teaching and reading, she hadn't needed anything else. She had been comfortable and her life serene. But now it was different. She felt discarded and alone, often like she was not really touching the ground when she walked.* (54–55)

Subjects: family relationships; Mexican American families; Mexican American women

Similar titles: *Woman Hollering Creek* by Cisneros is another short story collection highlighting women's suffering.

Posey, Delia, ed.

Out of the Mirrored Garden. **New York: Doubleday, 1996. ISBN 0385475942. 222pp.**
This anthology features the work of seventeen Latin American women writers in English translation. They belong to a variety of narrative styles and literary generations.

> *I like to drink coffee alone, very slowly, lock myself in my room, look out at the terrace and see nothing on the horizon, nothing but sky (some sky, preferably a tiny fragment of sky, preferably gray) and forget about the damn racket that always, always, always makes it way through the wall the same way flies get around obstacles so that they always reach the light.* (4)

Subjects: Latin America; short stories; women

Similar titles: *Beyond the Border* and *Cubana* are anthologies of short stories by Latina authors.

Yañez, Mirta (Cuban).

Cubana. **Boston: Beacon Press, 1998. ISBN 0807083364. 213pp.**

Sixteen Cuban women authors share their voices and reflect on their cultures and country in this collection of stories from the often marginalized feminine point of view.

> *In a way, that was her: she used to say that chance took only the lazy and the stupid by surprise. She said her life was a script she wrote, and, of course, it was a good script in which nothing was missing and nothing was in excess.* (72)

Subjects: Cubans; short stories

Similar titles: Short stories featuring Latina women's voices can also be found in *Beyond the Border* and *Out of the Mirrored Garden.*

References

Craig, Lisa. 2000. "Women's Fiction vs. Romance: A Tale of Two Genres." *Writing World.* Available at www.writing-world.com/romance/craig.shtml (accessed November 1, 2007).

Herald, Diana Tixier. 2006. *Genreflecting: A Guide to Popular Reading Interests.* 6th ed. Westport, CT: Libraries Unlimited.

Saricks, Joyce G. 2001. *The Readers' Advisory Guide to Genre Fiction.* Chicago: American Library Association.

Chapter 4

Latina Romance and Love Stories

Amor con amor se paga

Amor y pasión: Mexican spitfires, Latin lovers, tempestuous relationships full of shouting, histrionics, broken crockery, and tears. Beyond these admittedly thrilling stereotypes lies the contemporary Latina version of the romance.

Introduction

A romance is a novel whose main focus is the felicitous resolution of the emotional relationship between the two protagonists. It consists of two basic elements—"a central love story [*amor*] and an emotionally satisfying and optimistic ending or *final feliz*" (Charles and Linz 2005, 43). Today, romance novels enjoy unabashed popularity in a variety of formats and subgenres.

Romance novels featuring ethnic heroines and heroes are a part of this positive trend. Kristin Ramsdell defines ethnic romance as

> a love story in which one or both of the protagonists are African-American, Latino, Native American, Asian, Pacific Islander, or have a heritage other than European. Additionally, in these romances, the ethnicity of the characters is both important and acknowledged, lending a culturally authentic flavor to the book and providing a realistic setting for the story. (1999, 289)

Appeal

In an article in *Public Libraries*, Cathie Linz, a romance novelist herself, points out some of the reasons people enjoy reading romances: They identify with the characters and their emotions; they can count on finding a place where "things end happily and people do find exactly what they are seeking"; they find a place to escape, to "live in another world for a few hours" (Charles and Linz 2005, 43–44).

This appeal applies to Latina readers also, according to author Mary Castillo:

> [I]n this crazy world we live in, our romances allow us to vicariously experience the conflicts and emotional turmoil through the heroine; but also the victory when she captures the prize, which when you really think about it isn't the man, but a sense of self and deeper wisdom. (2005)

Latinas enjoy heroines who share their struggles and "do find exactly what they are seeking," which in this case ends up being success AND a sensitive partner who overcomes his macho tendencies. Non-Latinas will appreciate situations like this *tambien*!

Discussion on the RRA-L listserv archives in 1998 expressed frustration at the lack of heroes from nonwhite cultures, and the indignant feeling brought on by the idea that white people would not be interested in reading such novels: "People like to read about heroes that are like them, but also like to read about people who are *not* like them at times." The participants in the discussion lamented the fact that novels published with Hispanic heroines could be counted on the fingers of one hand (1998).

Evolution of the Genre

The sentiments appearing on the RRA-L listserv presaged the creation of the Encanto "line" by the Kensington Publishing Company in 1999. In fact, readers commenting on the listserv were enthusiastic about the promised new line. Kensington had already published a line of romances featuring African American heroines. Encanto, featuring Latinas, was a logical next step as the country started to feel the effects of a new wave of Latino immigration. Encanto performed a real service for the Latino community by finding and nurturing Latina writers. One of the Encanto authors, Sylvia Mendoza, said, "I'm idealistic thinking that a romance written in English and Spanish in one volume can help teach readers a second language" (quoted in Saenger 2002, 27).

But not many people read romances to learn another language, and those who speak both languages usually feel comfortable reading only in one or the other. Although idealistic, Encanto suffered without a clear strategy for marketing to the Latino reader. Author Caridad Scordato talks about the problems Kensington authors faced with the Encanto titles: "If I did a signing, the books would sometimes be in the romance section, sometimes in the Spanish section (which were not that common in 1999) and even more often, the books would be placed next to the Spanish–English dictionaries" (2005).

After the demise of Encanto, some of these authors found mainstream venues for their work; others are publishing with Harlequin and Silhouette. Harlequin, St. Martin's Press, and HarperCollins are finally publishing Latino romances by Latinas such as Caridad Scordato, Lynda Sandoval, and Tracy Montoya, all Encanto authors.

Although Hispanics make up 11 percent of romance readers (RWA 2004), it is still a challenge to find romance novels dedicated to this audience. I couldn't find any Latino titles on the Romantic Times Web page, for example (2008). Non-Latino authors use Latino protagonists, the Latin lover always being a great favorite, and exotic, tropical settings in Spanish-speaking countries, but Latino authors are uniquely able to provide more than just authentic "flavor" to these novels, drawing on their own experiences as American Latinos.

Current Themes and Trends

Latino romance writing today is vibrant and hip. Most Latina love stories are contemporary romances. Latina romance heroines are professional women seeking to build a life with their unique gifts. They struggle with issues related to integrating their Latino cultural upbringing with their professional American women's lifestyle choices. They struggle against family and societal expectations of domesticity. They are entrepreneurs, nurses, movie stars, principals, building contractors, lawyers, and everything in between. They respect their parents but yearn to be independent. Most of the heroines are twenty- and thirtysomethings, often carrying baggage from previous struggles. The *compañerismo* inherent in female friendships is a key element to plot development. These networks of friends and family also lend themselves to sequels.

Settings are generally urban, cosmopolitan cities that enjoy large Latino populations, especially Miami, New York City, or Los Angeles, with some taking place in the Southwest or on the border with Mexico. There is a road novel *corriente* featuring a search, or a trip toward self-knowledge and growth, for example, *Unsettling* or *¡Caramba!* Some romance authors are expanding into the paranormal (Scordato) and suspense (Bicos, Montoya) genres as well. Another trend is anthologies and books centered on multiple protagonists, following the lead of the trailblazing *Dirty Girls Social Club,* which in turn copied the trend begun by Candace Bushnell in *Four Blondes.* Books like *Unsettling* by Lynda Sandoval or *A Little Love* by C. C. Medina mix up the stories of three or four friends who all end up with a *final feliz.*

These independent heroines still yearn for the love of a strong man who can accept his sensitive side and his own need for a soul mate. This man must be intelligent and look studly and macho, but also be supportive of the heroine's desire for a professional life (or able to be won over to her way of thinking!).

Family is *always* important to Latinos. These novels usually feature protagonists with large families who sometimes provide the plot complication. They pressure the protagonists to either follow tradition or stay faithful to their class. Either of the protagonists may also have children from a previous relationship to further complicate matters.

Scope and Selection Criteria

This selection relies heavily on Encanto romances published by Kensington. Unfortunately, Encanto is now defunct. These titles are available via WorldCat. The novels are written primarily by Latina writers. Most of the books date from 1999, with a few earlier exceptions.

Organization

The love stories in this chapter fall into the following categories: contemporary, historical, paranormal, and collections and anthologies. Readers who enjoy more sensual stories should check the subject terms. Stories that feature sexual situations are integrated and are tagged with the subject term "sexual situations." *Chica* lit titles are identified in the subject terms. More *chica* lit can be found in Chapter 3, "Women's Fiction," and in Chapter 7, "Young Adult Fiction."

Contemporary Romance

The most plentiful subgenre of Latina romance tells love stories set in current times. Readers identify with characters like themselves, whose lives reflect their own. Some of the titles in this category contain more explicit sexual situations; others are "innocent." The former can be identified by checking the key features for the designation "sexual situations."

Aguilar, Rebeca.

Cristina's Secret. (*El secreto de Cristina*, 1999). **Translated by Asa Zatz. New York: Kensington Publishing, 1999. ISBN 0786010355. 360pp.**

Refugee Cristina Ortiz has left secrets behind in El Salvador. She meets Eric Gomez, an injured policeman, while working in a Washington, D.C., hospital; but her secrets threaten to destroy their newfound love.

> *She was tortured by a repetitive nightmare every time she went to sleep. She would see the clinic at San Cristóbal clearly and hear slow, faraway steps as though somebody dragging an artificial leg were approaching. Cristina saw a big man stabbing Juan Gabriel there in the clinic. She tried to run away but the man caught her and tore out her insides. (10)*

Key features: Bilingual format

Subjects: El Salvador; love stories; nurses; police officers; Puerto Ricans; Washington, D.C.

Similar titles: *Miracle of Love* by Gloria Alvarez and *In Hot Pursuit* by Marquez also feature love with policemen; *Rio Grande Wedding* by Wind is about another softhearted nurse in love.

Alberro, Elaine (Cuban American).

Forever True. (*Solo Tuya*, 1999). **Translated by Daniel Santacruz. New York: Kensington Publishing, 1999. ISBN 0-7860-0669-2. 336pp.**

Elena Garcia and Antonio del Valle fell in love at her *quinceañera*, but were kept apart by Elena's snobbish Cuban family because Antonio was the cleaning woman's illegitimate son. When they meet again eight years later, the sparks are still there but may not be enough to overcome past disappointments.

> *"A part of me is happy to see him again. A very small part, though. It would just never work."*
>
> *"Because of your family?"*

"Right."

Sandra shook her head in disapproval. "Girl, you need to remind your family they're in the United States. Things are different here. Women make their own decisions." (190)

Key features: Bilingual format

Subjects: Cuban Americans; Florida—Miami; lawyers; love stories; models; old flames

Similar titles: *Better Than Ever* by Scordato is also about Cubans and their old flames.

Heart of Gold. (Corazon de Oro, 2000). New York: Kensington Publishing, 2000. ISBN 0786010606. 352pp.

TV morning show host Natalia Perez finds true love with Cuban refugee Alejandro Sandoval after he rescues her from a would-be mugger, but snobbery and circumstances threaten to keep them apart.

There was understanding in her eyes, and power in her voice. He especially liked the way she closed the show with, "Sean felices y hagan de éste un buen día." (27)

Key features: Bilingual format

Subjects: Cuban Americans; Florida—Miami; love stories; refugees; television personalities

Similar titles: *To Catch a Star* by Ivette Gonzalez and *Dreaming of You* by Sandoval are other novels structured around reverse Cinderella scenarios.

Alonso-Cruz, Elaine (Cuban American).

Dance with Me. New York: Kensington Publishing, 2001. ISBN 0-7860-1213-7. 256pp.

Iliana Castellanos, a flamenco dancer, leaves her parents' home for South Beach, Florida, to get away from an ex-boyfriend who has stalker tendencies, and she swears off men until she meets Marco De Cordova.

"Iliana, you never listen to advice. El que no oye consejo . . . ."

" . . . no llega a viejo," Iliana finished for her. "I know, Mami, you've said it a hundred times."

"If Arturo ever finds out you have a new boyfriend—"

"I won't have a new boyfriend, Mami," Iliana said defiantly. "I'm through with men." (7)

Subjects: Cuban Americans; flamenco dancers; Florida—Miami; love stories; stalkers

Similar titles: *Wild for You* by Marquez is another novel that features a stalker.

Alvarez, Gloria.

Miracle of Love. (*Milagro de amor,* 2000). Translated by Eva García. New York: Kensington Publishing, 2000. ISBN 0-7860-1167x. 208pp.

> Elena Santiago, a widow, has gone back to work as an elementary school principal in New Orleans. She reconnects with her old flame, policeman David Mendoza, after a violent incident at her school.

> > *He tucked the gun in his hand, still aimed right at her. Slowly she walked toward the main entrance, ¡Cálmate! she told herself. Don't lose your head. Get him away from the kids first.* (10)

> **Subjects:** Louisiana—New Orleans; love stories; Mexican Americans; police officers; principals; widows

> **Similar titles:** *Canyon of Remembering* by Poling-Kempes is another novel whose protagonist is a Mexican American widow

Winning Isabel. (*Isabel, Mi Amor,* 2000). Translated by Nancy Hedges. New York: Kensington Publishing, 2000. ISBN 0786010592. 360pp.

> Isabel Sanchez arrives at a small South Texas town to manage the clinic as the new physician. This does not sit well with the old-fashioned, but sexy, mayor, Javier Montoya. His teenaged daughter makes common cause with Isabel against his domineering ways.

> > *"Ayúdame," he said softly, and though she didn't understand the actual words, she instinctively knew what he meant. Shyly, as if she hadn't seen thousands of male bodies in her medical career, she turned to face him and began unbuttoning his shirt.* (71)

> **Key features:** Bilingual format

> **Subjects:** love stories; mayors; Mexican Americans; Mexicans; physicians; single fathers; teenagers; Texas

> **Similar titles:** *Destination: Love* by Reyna Rios and *Border Heat* by Roman are other romances that feature antagonism and family complications that challenge the couple.

Arana, Nikki (Mexican American).

Regalo Grande Series.

> Angelica Perez, née Amante, navigates the difficult path of a lawyer in love with an illegal immigrant. Her faith helps her to persevere through adversity and difficult times.

> 🎗 *The Winds of Sonoma.* Grand Rapids, MI: Revell, 2005. ISBN 0-8007-3048-8. 367pp.

> > Angelica leaves her job in a high-powered New York law firm when she is asked to take on a case that will exploit undocumented Mexican workers. She returns home to face the displeasure of her parents and falls in love with an undocumented Mexican worker.

> > > *If she signed the paper, it would move on through the system and result in legalizing the exploitation of hundreds of illegal Mexicans. If she didn't, her job and career would be in jeopardy.* (11)

Subjects: Christian faith; lawyers; love stories; Mexican Americans; undocumented workers

Similar titles: Other romance novels that feature lawyers in love are *Forever True* by Alberro and *Feliz Navidad* by Scordato.

Awards: Women's Fiction Book of the Year, 2006 (American Christian Fiction Writers)

In the Shade of the Jacaranda. Grand Rapids, MI: Revell, 2006. ISBN 0-8007-3049-6. 335pp.

Angelica and Antonio face the struggles of their life together, working through the difficult choices they've made with the help of God—an unexpected pregnancy, problems with her parents, and the challenges of his struggling business and her career as a defense attorney.

Subjects: Christian faith; families; Mexican Americans; pregnancy

🌢 *The Fragrance of Roses.* Grand Rapids, MI: Revell, 2006. ISBN 0-8007-3050-X. 336pp.

The Perez family now faces the dire illness of their child, whose survival depends on finding a compatible organ donor from Antonio's family in Mexico.

Subjects: cancer; Christian faith; families; Mexicans

Awards: Women's Fiction Book of the Year, 2007 (American Christian Fiction Writers)

Borges, Luz.

Debt of Love. **(*Deuda de Amor*, 2000). Translated by Asa Zatz. New York: Kensington Publishing, 2000. ISBN 0-7860-1119X. 384pp.**

Ex-lovers Soledad Cabañas, newspaper editor, and Alvaro de la Daga, construction company magnate, are thrown together many years after a bitter breakup, when Alvaro purchases *El Semanal*.

> He wondered if Soledad already knew who she would be working for. If she did, she was probably shaking in her boots. And with good reason. For a few moments, Alvaro savored the idea of meeting her face-to-face under these new circumstances. Soledad Cabañas would pay dearly for all her dirty tricks, one by one, with interest. (26)

Key features: Bilingual format

Subjects: businessmen; construction companies; Illinois—Chicago; love stories; Mexican Americans; newspapers; reporters

Similar titles: *Florida-Miami Heat* by Platas Fuller and *The Perfect Mix* by Scordato are other romances that take place in a construction company setting.

Bryce Echenique, Alfredo (Peruvian).

Tarzan's Tonsillitis. **(*Amigdalitis de Tarzan*, 1998). Translated by Alfred MacAdam. New York: Pantheon Books, 2001. ISBN 0375421432. 262pp.**

Juan Manuel Carpio, middle-class *mestizo* singer-songwriter from Peru, and Fernanda de la María Trinidad del Monte Montes, upper-class

Salvadoran, maintain their friendship and love through an epistolary relationship that endures thirty years.

> *It's also true that our loyalty was always honest and absolute, although here we've got to recognize (why not?) that we often acted like two players on the same court playing different games with the same ball. (4)*

Subjects: California—Oakland; El Salvador; England—London; epistolary fiction; friendship; love stories; men and women; Peru; singers—fiction

Similar titles: *A Simple Habana Melody* by Hijuelos is also about long-distance love and music.

Carvajal, Lourdes.

Only a Kiss Away. **New York: Kensington Publishing, 2001. ISBN 0786012447. 203pp.**

Mercedes Garcia is a journalist whose Cuban mother keeps trying to set her up with Hispanic men. Mercedes is resistant, but finally agrees to a date with sexy Joaquin Muriel. He is about to be deported unless he can marry a U.S. citizen. Joaquin doesn't think much of American career women. Will the chemistry and culture they share help them get past the stereotypes?

> *My life is fine the way it is. I don't need any complications and dating alone is a complication, not to mention dating a Hispanic man. They make great relatives, fun friends, but as mates they leave a lot to be desired. I don't want to get involved with them. (11)*

Subjects: Costa Ricans; Cuban Americans; deportation; divorced women; love stories; Maryland—Baltimore; reporters

Similar titles: *Debt of Love* by Borges is also about reporters in love.

Castillo, Mary (Mexican American).

In Between Men. **New York: Avon Trade, 2006. ISBN 0-06-076682-4.**

Shy, single mom and ESL high school teacher Isa Avellan is going through a rough patch when she becomes acquainted with sexy Alex Lujon. An imaginary Joan Collins gives Isa advice—much like Bogart in Woody Allen's movie *Play It Again, Sam*—encouraging her to take chances and live dangerously.

> *The last thing she expected to learn that Tuesday afternoon at the emergency staff meeting was that the student body of Isa's alma mater and current employer had voted her the unsexiest teacher alive. (1)*

Subjects: California; *chica* lit; coaches; humor; love stories; Mexican Americans; teachers

Similar titles: *Thief of Hearts* by Sandoval features another teacher in love.

Hot Tamara. **New York: Avon Trade, 2005. ISBN 0060739894. 246pp.**

Tamara is ready for a change. She leaves home to attend graduate school and escape the stifling expectations of her family and stodgy boyfriend. When she runs into and falls in love with erstwhile bad boy Will Benavides from her hometown, she is afraid Will may also ask her to give up her dreams.

Free. She was free like she'd just been behind the wheel of a spinning car with screaming tires throwing up smoke, the unstoppable centripetal force gluing her to the seat until suddenly it jarred to a stop, inches from the center divide.

For five horrifying days Tamara sat in the spinning car, seeing all of her plans to hack off the apron strings flash before her eyes. (1)

Subjects: artists; California—Los Angeles; *chica* lit; firefighters; love stories; Mexican Americans

Similar titles: *Becoming Latina in 10 Easy Steps* by Lara Rios is another novel about a Latina's journey to independence.

Delgado, Anjanette (Puerto Rican).

The Heart Break Pill. **New York: Atria Books, 2008. ISBN 9780743297530. 277pp.**

Erika Luna works for a pharmaceutical company. Her husband leaves her for his pregnant mistress, whom he plans to marry. Erika's heart is broken, so she sets out to develop an antidote, using herself as the guinea pig. Her friends, family, and handsome neighbor all pitch in to help in more traditional ways. Will she survive her experiments to find the true antidote to a broken heart?

Alex doesn't love you? Just flip off the love switch and presto: you don't love him either. Charlie needs his space? Pull a small lever and he'll be on a reverse-less rocket ship en route to the stratosphere where he can have all the space he wants. (2)

Key features: First person narration

Subjects: Florida—Miami; Latinas; scientists—women

Similar titles: *Look of Love* by Sandoval also features a female scientist as the protagonist; Scordato's <u>CellTech Series</u> takes place in a pharmaceutical company.

Fuentes, Erica.

First Love. **New York: Kensington Publishing, 2000. ISBN 0-7860-1156-4. 208pp.**

Gina Ramon and Miguel Lopez Garza meet again, two decades after a failed romance. Gina lives in Mexico and is in Washington for a visit when they are reunited. Multiple complications to the rekindled romance ensue, as Gina is deported and must confront her fiancé, and Miguel faces cultural issues after he pursues her to Mexico.

"Of course I remember Miguel." She hesitated, then continued as if talking about the weather. 'Whatever happened to him?' she asked casually, sure that every patron in the restaurant could see her heart thumping in her chest. (24)

Subjects: deportation; international romance; love stories; Mexican Americans; Mexicans; Mexico—Mexico City; playboys; teachers; Washington, D.C.

Similar titles: *Thief of Hearts* by Sandoval also features playboys brought down by love.

Island Dreams. (*Sueños isleños*, 2000). **Translated by Nancy Hedges. New York: Kensington Publishing, 2000. ISBN 0786010703. 256pp.**

Mickey Campos de Vasco is a widowed, high-powered diplomat for the Mexican government whose parents are divorced. Her mother lives in the United States, and her father lives in Mexico City. She had decided to dedicate her life to career and children when she meets Dr. Mauricio García on a flight to Cuba.

> *"You love your life? What life? You haven't had a date with anybody interesting in over a year, and the last man you thought was interesting turned out to be married!" Laura had raised her voice without even realizing it.*
>
> *"I don't measure my life by dates! I don't have time for dates!" Mickey answered.* (7–8)

Key features: Bilingual format

Subjects: Cuba; Cubans; diplomats; love stories; Mexicans; physicians; teenagers; widows

Similar titles: *Better Than Ever* by Scordato is another romance about a career woman in love.

Window to Paradise. **New York: Kensington Publishing, 2001. ISBN 0786011815. 256pp.**

Valentina Valladares of Mexico City travels to Hawaii to visit her godmother and try to get over the death of her husband. In Hawaii she encounters Pablo, the little boy who promised he would marry her when they were five, now all grown up. They have a hard time hitting it off—Vali brings her neurasthenic, suspicious, big city ways, and Pablo can't find the right tone to strike with her. They are attracted to each other, but can they find the way to love? The book contains lots of Hawaiian cultural references and lore.

> *"Madre Santísima! he thought, three months of this prune-faced witch? Maybe it's time to take an extended vacation to Fiji."* (32)

Subjects: Hawaii; love stories; Mexicans; ranchers; single mothers; widows

Similar titles: *Canyon of Remembering* by Poling-Kempes is another novel about a widow finding love again, with a similar melancholy tone.

Gabriel, Kristin.

Night after Night. **New York: Harlequin, 2004. ISBN 0-373-69196-3. 224pp.**

Mia Maldonado takes her roommate's place in a sleep study to earn some quick money and save her roommate's romance at the same time. Mia falls in love with the other subject in the study, who happens to be a detective investigating the roommate, in a humorous case of mistaken identity.

> *Mia Maldonado knew there was trouble the moment she heard "Blue Suede Shoes" blaring from the stereo speakers. Elvis always meant a crisis was brewing, so she proceeded warily through the front hall of the house, ready for anything.* (5)

Key features: Sexual situations

Subjects: businesswomen; experiments; humor; interior decorating; love stories; Mexican Americans; Pennsylvania—Philadelphia; private investigators—men

Similar titles: *Love's Destiny* by Quezada is also about interior decorators in love.

Garcia, Diana.

Help Wanted. (*Aviso oportuno*, 2000). Translated by Nancy Hedges. New York: Kensington Publishing, 2000. ISBN 0-786-01138-6. 368pp.

Rosa Osario, a professional woman needing household help during her two boys' summer vacation, runs an ad that Brian Torres, a sexy freelance writer, answers. He gets the job and brings his little girl along.

> *Rosa felt a sympathetic communion she hadn't experienced in a long time—and something she had insisted to herself that she didn't need. Her closest friends had no children. They could sympathize with Rosa's parenting problems, but they couldn't empathize. It made all the difference in the world. Then Rosa cleared her throat. She wasn't looking for a friend, what she needed was a housekeeper.* (http://members.aol.com/dianagar1)

Key features: Bilingual format

Subjects: Arizona; blended families; businesswomen; love stories; Mexican Americans; single parents; writers

Similar titles: *Waves of Passion* by Sylvia Mendoza is also about a career woman in love.

Love Lessons. (*Lecciones amorosas*, 1999). Translated by Rafael Marcos. New York: Kensington Publishing, 1999. ISBN 0786010207. 173pp.

Uptight urbanite Susana Diaz is roped into chaperoning a camping excursion with easygoing, nature-loving photographer Daniel Stephens. Unbeknownst to the couple, their daughters are matchmaking.

> *He was very handsome in an Anglo, blond, blue-eyed way—if you liked that sort of thing. But Susanna wasn't fooled. As her grandmother used to say, "Te conozco bacalao aunque vengas disfrazado." She knew his type—brash and cocky, and certain that he was the first item on any woman's Christmas list.* (12)

Subjects: businesswomen; camping; Colorado; love stories; Mexican Americans; single parents; teenagers

Similar titles: *Now and Always* by Scordato is another romance about a mismatched couple.

Stardust. New York: Kensington Publishing, 2001. ISBN 0-786-01214-5. 204pp.

Returning from a remote clinic, Dr. Julia Huerta must make an emergency landing of her plane on Antonio (Tony) Carrera's isolated ranch. Tony, a reclusive country and western singer, is leery of strangers. His priority is to protect his two teenaged kids from the prying eyes of the voracious public. Can Dr. Huerta break through his protective shell?

> *Julia didn't wait for Tony's answer before urging her horse faster; Tony didn't seem the type to walk away from a contest and she wanted all the advantage she could get.* (http://members.aol.com/dianagar1)

Subjects: Arizona; love stories; Mexican Americans; physicians; ranchers; singers—fiction; single fathers

Similar titles: Similarly, in *Island Dreams* by Erica Fuentes, the protagonist must decide between her career and romance.

Gomez, Leticia.

Sweet Destiny. **New York: Kensington Publishing, 2000. ISBN 0786012218. 203pp.**

Independent country girl Amparo Reyes, owner of a bed and breakfast in rural New Mexico, must play hostess to burned out Miami executive Enrique Aleman.

> *Sensing the outsider was watching her every move, Amparo walked briskly to the kitchen and sheltered herself behind the counter. Enrique followed close behind, studying her slender but curvaceous figure.* (42–43)

Subjects: Argentinians; bed and breakfast proprietors; businessmen; Mexican Americans; New Mexico

Similar titles: Opposites also attract in *On Fire* by Sylvia Mendoza.

Gonzalez, Ivette.

Love's Song. **(*Canto de amor*, 2000). Translated by Mercedes Lamamie. New York: Kensington Publishing, 2000. ISBN 07-8601-116-5. 384pp.**

Manny Becker wants to sign lovely Violet Sandoval to his record label after watching her sing karaoke at a bar. But Violet is leery of men and suspicious of success.

> *Manny Becker was stunned. What timing! He had found himself his new star for his record company's new label, Downtown Records. She was hip, retro, yet fresh.* (19)

Key features: Bilingual format.

Subjects: Florida—Miami; Latinos; love stories; Mexicans; music industry—fiction; singers—fiction

Similar titles: *Leading Lady* by Vazquez also features singers in love.

To Catch a Star. **(*Alcanzar una estrella*, 1999). Translated by Mercedes Lamamie. New York: Kensington Publishing, 1999. ISBN 0-7860-1019-3. 190pp.**

Latina actress Marta Alvarez (a poor little rich girl) finds that her attractive chauffeur, Mario Santana, has hidden depths.

> *"OK, now look." Marta looked at him, waving her salad fork . . . . "This is going to have to stop. This flirting. You are my driver."* (25)

Key features: Bilingual format

Subjects: actresses; chauffeurs; Cuban Americans; Florida—Miami; love stories

Similar titles: *Heart of Gold* by Alberro and *Dreaming of You* by Sandoval are other novels structured as reverse Cinderella scenarios.

Griffey, Jackie. (U.S. American).

Spanish Eyes. **New York: Thomson-Gale, 2007. ISBN 9781594146145. 233pp.**

Eleana, a Mexican immigrant, is searching for her missing brother. Oliver, an artist, falls in love with Eleana at first sight. An intrigue involving Eleana's brother and other missing immigrant workers ensues. Things become more complicated when Eleana's sister-in-law shows up pregnant and undocumented.

> Her Spanish eyes had reason to be troubled. None of the faces Eleana peered down on looked even a little like Carlos. She pictured her brother's handsome face, excited and smiling at her as they'd talked of both of them working in Las Flores. Her heart ached for her big brother, sure now there must be something wrong. (11)

Subjects: love stories; undocumented workers

Similar titles: *Rio Grande Wedding* by Wind and *The Winds of Sonoma* by Arana also present the challenges of falling in love with an undocumented worker.

Marisol (Venezuelan American).

The Lady, the Chef and the Courtesan. (La dama, la cocinera & la cortesana: una novela, 2004). **Translated by José Lucas Badué. New York: Rayo, 2003. ISBN 0-06-053042-1. 239pp.**

Pilar Castillo returns to Caracas for her grandmother's funeral and receives her grandmother's diaries as an inheritance. As she reads them, she looks at her own life. The diaries help Pilar choose between true but inappropriate love in Chicago and the suitor chosen for her by her mother in Venezuela. They also contain sexy lessons about being a woman—a lady in the living room, a chef in the kitchen, and a courtesan in the bedroom, according to the proverb.

> With his usual grace and polish, Rafael Uslar Mancera greeted both women and then turned to the younger, whose eyes tried hard to avoid his. He kissed her gently on the cheek and whispered to her, "Lo siento mucho cariño—I know how much she meant to you." (3)

Key features: Sexual situations

Subjects: family secrets; grandmothers and granddaughters; Illinois—Chicago; love stories; men and women; Venezuela—Caracas

Similar titles: In *When the Ground Turns in Its Sleep* by Sellers-García, another American searches for his Latin roots in the mother country, in this case Guatemala.

Marquez, Victoria.

Holiday Heaven. **New York: Kensington Publishing, 2001. ISBN 0786012781. 256pp.**

Social worker Gabriela Morales, after agreeing to participate in an auction to raise funds for her favorite charity, is thrown for a loop when Dr. Marcos Calderon bids $10,000 for a date with her. Dr. Calderon gets more than he bargained for when he convinces Gabriela to act as his phony fiancée so that his meddling *abuelita* won't nag him about settling down during her visit. (Dr. Calderon is Marisol's brother from *Wild for You.*)

> This hip-swaying bombshell couldn't be the same Gabriela who hid behind demure, oversize suits. The same woman who always seemed to be on opposing sides from him at hospital board meetings.
>
> Damn. ¡Qué guapa! (9)

Subjects: Florida; hospitals; love stories; physicians; social workers; Venezuelan Americans

Similar titles: Another hospital romance takes place in *Cristina's Secret* by Aguilar; in *On Fire* by Sylvia Mendoza, opposites also attract.

In Hot Pursuit. (Cortejo Cálido, 2000). Translated by Ramona Sola. New York: Kensington Publishing, 2000. ISBN 078601136X. 368pp.

Isabel Garcia was burned by her late ex-husband's violent death and his involvement in illicit drug activities. She tries to fight her attraction to police detective Linc Heller as she has her hands full managing the family's nursery business. But Linc is willing to take the time to woo her and her small daughter.

> *His eyes crinkled appealingly as the corners of his mouth lifted. Isabel got a funny feeling in her stomach as she suddenly saw him with new eyes. He was ruggedly handsome, with a charming smile. She must have been too terrified out of her wits during Frank's investigation not to notice Linc's good looks earlier.* (11)

Key features: Bilingual format

Subjects: businesswomen; Cuban Americans; drug trafficking; Florida—Miami; love stories; police detectives—men; single mothers; tropical nurseries

Similar titles: In *All of Me* and *Florida-Miami Heat* by Platas Fuller, carrying on the family business is also an important theme.

Wild for You. New York: Kensington Publishing, 2001. ISBN 0786012196. 208pp.

Marisol, an immigrant from Venezuela who owns a beauty salon, is being stalked. Marisol's brother (Dr. Calderon from *Holiday Heaven*) has asked his friend Che (Clay), a police detective, to keep an eye on Marisol. Che and Marisol marry for her protection, but their romance is put in jeopardy when Marisol finds out she's been set up.

> *There was nothing demure about Marisol Calderon. She wore dangling hoop earrings and a knit tangerine minidress that hugged her petite, curvaceous frame. On her feet were matching high-heeled sandals. Clay watched Marisol laugh delightedly on the telephone and tap her long, lacquered nails against the reception counter.*
>
> *This little piece of fluff was going to be a handful.* (10)

Subjects: Argentine Americans; beauticians; Florida—Miami; love stories; police detectives—men; stalkers; Venezuelan Americans

Similar titles: A marriage of convenience is also central to the plot of *Rio Grande Wedding* by Wind.

Medina, C. C. (Cuban American; Floridian).

A Little Love: A Novel. New York: Warner Books, Inc., 2000. ISBN 0446524484. 357pp.

Four privileged Latina friends (Cuban, Dominican, and Mexican American) support each other through their search for "a little love," each wrestling with a different stumbling block. Mercy, the high-powered, promiscuous realtor, can't find a man to suit her reactionary mother; Julia can't commit to the seemingly perfect Felipe while being attracted to Beatriz; and Isabel and Mercy tell their stories in the first person—Isabel, burned after her failed marriage, finds it hard to trust her feelings for any man, and Lucinda struggles to forgive her husband's infidelity to her and to their dreams.

> And now, they were all naked. Mami was draping each one with a blanket. She left one for me on the sofa and went into the kitchen. I got the message. I poured everyone a brandy snifter of Cointreau and settled on the floor, wrapped in a blanket too. We stared at the monstrous flames; they looked like naked nymphs dancing a hot merengue at a Dominican nightclub.

> "Do you remember any of the chants, Mercy?" I asked. (65)

Key features: Some first person narration

Subjects: artists; *chica* lit; college professors; Cuban Americans; Dominican Americans; family relationships; Florida—Miami; love stories; men and women; Mexican Americans; photographers; realtors; women's friendships

Similar titles: *Dirty Girls Social Club* by Valdes-Rodriguez and *Unsettling* by Sandoval are other *chica* lit novels about Latina girlfriends and love.

Mendoza, Sylvia (Californiana).

On Fire. (Al rojo vivo, 2000). **Translated by Nancy Hedges. New York: Kensington Publishing, 2000. ISBN 0-786-01175-0. 203pp.**

Movie star Rubina Flores needs a handyman at her San Diego home. When gorgeous firefighter Marco Carrillo shows up, he meets her needs in more ways than one. Can their love survive when he finds out the truth about Rubina?

> He leaned nearer, forgetting proper respect for space, reveling in the way the scent of her flowery perfume and perspiration emanated from her body. "Am I at risk right now if I ask the wrong question or make the wrong move?" (8)

Key features: Bilingual format

Subjects: actresses—fiction; California—San Diego; firefighters; love stories; Mexican Americans

Similar titles: Opposites also attract in *Holiday Heaven* by Marquez.

Waves of Passion. **New York: Kensington Publishing, 1999. ISBN 0-786-01029-0. 208pp.**

Alex Rivera, a Navy officer, would like to "settle down" with Marissa Buenaventura, but after growing up in a military family, she is skittish about getting involved with a military man. She wants stability and a career.

> Alex sputtered. "This meeting is over." Marissa whirled on him. "Don't give me any orders, Alex. I do NOT report to you." (35)

Key features: Bilingual format

Subjects: California—San Diego; love stories; Mexican Americans; naval officers; tourism

Similar titles: *Feliz Navidad* by Scordato is another novel about a traditional love interest for a modern Latina.

Nieves-Powell, Linda (Nuyorican).

Free Style. New York: Atria Books, 2008. ISBN 9781416542810. 262pp.

Idalis and Selenis are old friends who take a walk down memory lane as their marriages go south. Can they find the old sparkle and energy, or is it time to move on and embrace the future?

> *I couldn't imagine what I would do if I actually found him. I wondered if he was married. I wondered if he looked the same. Some guys get better with time. I wondered what he'd think of me now. Then again, Trisco was one of those guys who, no matter how much time went by, was always happy to see me.* (4)

Key features: First person narration

Subjects: *chica* lit; Latinas; New York—New York City; women's friendships

Similar titles: *Switchcraft* by Mary Castillo is another look at two Latina friends at a crucial moment in their friendship; *Dirty Girls Social Club* by Valdes-Rodriguez is the ultimate novel about Latina girlfriends and love.

Piñeiro, Caridad (Cuban American). *See also* Scordato, Caridad.

Sex and the South Beach Chicas. New York: Downtown Press, 2006. ISBN 1-4165-1488-0; ISBN-13: 978-1-4165-1488-6. 285pp.

Four Latina girlfriends—a journalist, a chef, a restaurant owner, and a lawyer—seek love, sex, and career fulfillment in Miami.

> *She clapped her hands together as if in prayer and rolled her eyes upward.* "Dios mio. Que desgracia! Mi'jita, que eastabas pensando?" (7)

Subjects: *chica* lit; love stories; women's friendships

Similar titles: *A Little Love* by C. C. Medina and *Dirty Girls Social Club* by Valdes-Rodriguez are other novels about Latina girlfriends and love.

Platas Fuller, Berta (Cuban American).

All of Me. (*Todo de mi*, 2000). Translated by Omar Amador. New York: Kensington Publishing, 2000. 368pp. ISBN 0-7860-1118-1. 375pp.

Alina Marquez has resuscitated her uncle's defunct vineyard and is preparing for an evaluation crucial to its success. When Felipe, a handsome Spaniard with a secret, shows up early to review the vineyard in preparation for the judges' visit, Alina tries to resist his sexy charm. Will she save the vineyard but lose her heart?

> *Steps sounded behind.* "Lourdes, I told you not to wash my robe so much. I had to come out here in a towel, and you know I hate wet towels." "But you look charming in one." *The very masculine voice was certainly not Lourdes's.* (7)

Subjects: Cuban Americans; Georgia; love stories; Spaniards; vineyards; vintners

Similar titles: *The Perfect Mix* by Scordato and *Debt of Love* by Borges also present romance that involves the family business.

Cinderella Lopez. New York: St. Martin's Griffin, 2006. ISBN 0-312-34172-5. 277pp.

Cyn Lopez is stuck as *cuidandera*, babysitting the stepsisters from hell, *Las Diablas*, because of a promise she made to her dying father. They are the veejays of the moment on an MTV-like channel, with all the diva, spoiled brat behavior that implies. These little devils are set to ruin Cyn's chances with her Prince Charming—Eric, the station's new owner.

> Cynthia Lopez knew it was going to be a bad day when a shouting mob slammed her against the studio wall and thundered down the perforated metal stairs toward Times Square. (3)

Subjects: *chica* lit; Cuban Americans; humor; New York—New York City; Puerto Ricans; television industry; veejays

Similar titles: *Heart of Gold* by Alberro is another Cinderella story featuring a Latina TV personality.

Florida-Miami Heat. (*Pasión en Florida-Miami*, 1999). **Translated by Ramon Soto. New York: Kensington Publishing, 1999. ISBN 0-7860-1022-3. 375pp.**

Miri is a hardworking construction contractor carrying on the family business, when she meets Peter Crane, a subcontractor. A career woman in a traditionally male occupation, Miri struggles to hold her own against a loving family who want her to get married and settle down.

> His chiseled profile reminded her of a 1920s Arrow shirt ad. What was she doing in the car with this guy? They both came from the same Caribbean island, but their backgrounds were so different they might as well be from different planets. (37)

Key features: Bilingual format

Subjects: construction companies; Cuban Americans; engineers; Florida—Miami; love stories

Similar titles: *In Hot Pursuit* by Marquez is another novel that features a Latina's dedication to the family business.

Poling-Kempes, Lesley (U.S. American; New Mexican).

Canyon of Remembering. **Lubbock: Texas Tech University Press, 1996. ISBN 0-8967-2363-1. 278pp.**

Dominga De Jesús, a widow with three stepsons and her own son, Atencio, a Vietnam vet with mental problems, has a house to rent in the little town of Mi Ojo. She rents it to Whitney Slope, a successful artist who feels the need to get away from Santa Fe and fame or notoriety. The story follows this couple, their story, and that of the town of Mi Ojo.

> Whitney declined to stare at Dominga, although after staring at sand hills and sky, rusting pumps and crumbling adobe, a woman as beautiful as Dominga de Jesús was difficult to look away from. (50)

Subjects: artists; love stories; Mexican Americans; New Mexico; *pueblos*; veterans—Vietnam War

Similar titles: *Hearts Remembered* by Quezada is another novel about artists in love; *Miracle of Love* by Gloria Alvarez has a similar melancholy tone, also with a widow as protagonist.

Rios, Lara (Californiana).

Becoming Latina in 10 Easy Steps. **New York: Berkley Publishing, 2006. ISBN 0-425-20755-2. 372pp.**

When successful animator Marcela Alvarez finds out her real father is not Mexican, she decides to put together a ten-step plan to get in touch with her Latino-Mexican side—part of which entails dating Latino men. Unfortunately George Ramirez, the one she is most attracted to, can't even speak Spanish.

> *If my family and everyone else even could finally accept that, then maybe I'd finally stop feeling Mexican in the Anglo world, and like a sell-out, a* pocha, *in my own family.* (3)

Subjects: animators; California; *chica* lit; love stories; Mexican Americans

Similar titles: *A Little Love* by C. C. Medina contains a similar search for identity and love.

The Conquest. **(***La Conquista,* **2000). Translated by Raquel Albornoz. New York: Kensington Publishing, 2000. ISBN 0-786-01157-2. 208pp.**

Tess Romero and Logan Wilde are rivals in the fashion industry, competing for a contract with an important Argentinian client, when they get distracted by their mutual attraction. Can Tess keep Logan at arm's length long enough to win the deal, without losing him forever?

> *Logan turned on his side, leaning his hip on the rail so he could get a better look at Teresa, She had gorgeous lips. He returned her smile, wanting to hold her again, to kiss her. "Well, although you're not a billionaire CEO yet, you do get to work with me. That's a benefit, isn't it?"* (www.amazon.com)

Subjects: Argentina—Patagonia; businessmen; businesswomen; fashion designers; love stories; Mexican Americans

Similar titles: *Border Heat* by Roman, *Pearl* by Romero Cooper, and *Sweet Destiny* by Gomez are other romances that mix business, Latinas, and love.

Rios, Reyna (Tejana).

Destination: Love. **(***Destino: Amor,* **2000). Translated by Nancy Hedges. New York: Kensington Publishing, 2000. ISBN 0-7860-1159-9. 208pp.**

Single mother Josie Hernandez is on the road toward a new life, when she and her small son walk into the middle of an armed robbery in a small town in West Texas. Although Sheriff Rafael is attracted to Josie, she and her son remind him of painful memories he desperately wants to forget.

> *Last night, when he'd carried her in his arms, their eyes had held, and Rafael sensed a sweet vulnerability about her, a sadness. For a heartbeat, he had felt a connection with her.* (28)

Subjects: grief; love stories; Mexican Americans; mothers and sons; sheriffs; single mothers; Texas

Similar titles: *Window to Paradise* by Erica Fuentes and *Love Lessons* by Diana Garcia are other titles about single mothers in love.

Rivera, Jeff.

Forever My Lady. Orlando, FL: JoAnne/Horatio Books, 2005. ISBN 9780976283805. 192pp.

Dio and Jennifer find each other and become friends and later lovers amid their struggles to survive violently dysfunctional families and the perils of urban street life in Las Vegas. Will Dio's stint in boot camp make him into the man Jennifer needs before it's too late?

> *It wasn't just some puppy love for the two of them. No, it was true love, real love that only comes around once in a lifetime and Dio felt lucky just to hold her in his arms. He felt alive kissing her soft lips, or smelling the scent of her hair when she would hug him and bury her head in his chest.* (10)

Subjects: love stories; Nevada—Las Vegas; street lit

Similar titles: Black Artemis's novels *Burn, Explicit Content,* and *Picture Me Rollin'* have a similar urban tone.

Roman, Hebby.

Border Heat. (Pasión en la Frontera, 2000). **Translated by Nancy Hedges. New York: Kensington Publishing, 2000. ISBN 0786010584. 172pp.**

Leticia Rodriguez and Ramon Villarreal find love on the border. He's an attorney she has asked to help with a crusade to find deadbeat dads in Mexico. She also owns a furniture store that is in financial trouble, and he's on a crusade for vengeance against the father who abandoned him.

> *She took the glass from his hand. Their fingers touched. This time, she didn't jerk her hand away. Their fingers lingered, hers curled over his. Electricity sizzled between them, leaping from fingertip to fingertip.* (13)

Key features: Bilingual format

Subjects: businesswomen; lawyers; love stories; Mexican Americans; U.S.–Mexico border

Similar titles: *Forever True* by Alberro is another novel about lawyers in love.

Romero Cooper, Cecilia.

Pearl. (La Perla, 2000). **Translated by Ramón Soto. New York: Kensington Publishing, 2000. ISBN 0-786-01036-3. 172pp.**

Julia Fuentes must contend with sexy and infuriating competitor Dan Powers as she struggles to build a charter business with the dilapidated boat she inherited from her *abuelito* (grandpa).

> *"That's not the only thing you're going to be sorry about," Julia mumbled as she crossed to the galley sink, assessing the damages. No man was going to tell her what was best for her. Not now, and not ever. No matter how sexy he looked as the muscles in his forearms and legs rippled while he climbed the companionway's ladder.* (10)

Key features: Bilingual format

Subjects: businessmen; businesswomen; love stories; Puerto Ricans; Texas

Similar titles: *The Conquest* by Lara Rios is another novel about mixing business and love.

Rose, Elizabeth.

Eden's Garden. **Columbus, MS: Genesis Press, 2000. ISBN 1-58571-018-0. 253pp.**

Jack Talon needs to make a success of his father's restaurant before his father returns from vacation. He had loaned money to Eden Ramirez's father, who lost it on an expedition to Peru searching for Incan treasures. Jack intends to make Eden pay after her father dies, but the seemingly simple, beautiful young woman may prove to be more than a match for him.

> *Eden bit her lip, wanting to curse at him in his native language. She understood him perfectly. It was all coming back to her after being here and hearing the English language for a few days now. . . . Well, she wasn't going to give him the benefit of knowing she understood him. Not after he called her father a swindling souse and her a child. Let him stew in whatever it was that was eating him. She'd tell him in due time she knew what he was saying, but for now she'd let him suffer a bit.* (17)

Key features: Sexual situations

Subjects: Illinois—Chicago; Incas; love stories; Peru; Peruvians; restaurant business; suspense; treasure

Similar titles: *The Perfect Mix* by Scordato is another novel about love and intrigue in restaurants.

Salcedo, Daniela.

Intrigue. **(*Intriga*, 2000). Translated by Ramón Soto. New York: Kensington Publishing, 2000. ISBN 0786011173.192pp.**

Antonio Colón and Isabela Santiago's apartment windows face each other, giving Antonio a clear view into Isabela's bedroom through his Venetian blinds. He is unable to resist peeking every once in a while. Antonio's sister, Carmen, and Isabela have both been victims of sexual assault. Isabela falls for Antonio when they meet at a club, but can they have a relationship when she finds out about his peeping tom ways?

> *"ATRÉVETE." Antonio's overwhelming stature intimidated the jerk immediately. Antonio's words were uttered firmly, with no strain. And the slimeball heard and understood. Antonio turned to Isabela, wanting to soothe her.* (25)

Key features: Bilingual format

Subjects: dancing; Latinos; love stories; New York—New York City; rape; voyeurs

Similar titles: *Dance with Me* by Alonso-Cruz is another novel about love and dancing.

Sandoval, Lynda (Colorado Latina).

One Perfect Man. **New York: Silhouette Special Edition, 2004. ISBN 0-373-24620-X. 256pp.**

When Tomas Garza hires Erica Goncalves to plan a fabulous *quinceañera* party to celebrate his daughter's fifteenth birthday, these two independent, self-sufficient professionals might find out they need love in their lives after all.

So, she wouldn't experience marital love in her life, but that didn't matter to her. She'd find companionship and sex along the way, with men who wouldn't compromise her goals, men with their own goals, and she'd have her independence. Not a whole lot sounded better than that. (http://lyndalynda.com/books/perfect.htm)

Subjects: *chica* lit; event planners; fathers and daughters; love stories; New Mexicans; New Mexico; *quinceañeras*; teenagers

Similar titles: *Winning Isabel* by Gloria Alvarez is also about a single father finding love with an independent woman.

Three Amigas Series.

Featuring three best friends—Esme, Lilly, and Pilar—and how they find their soul mates.

Look of Love. (*Miradas de amor*, 2000). New York: Kensington Publishing, 2000. ISBN 0786010347. 384pp.

Sweet, bookish scientist Esme Jaramillo is tricked into appearing on a makeover show, believing she will be discussing human cloning. Fascinating Gavino Mendez is a make-up artist, who falls in love with her before the show and later wants to take steps to heal the blow to her self-esteem. Can he earn her trust?

That sweet woman with the heart-shaped face and trusting eyes didn't deserve this. He'd expected a renowned young scientist to be arrogant and aloof. . . . Instead Esme Jaramillo had turned out to be one of the most down-to-earth, reachable women he'd met in a long time. (12)

Key features: Bilingual format

Subjects: artists; cloning; Colorado—Denver; love stories; Mexican Americans; reality television; scientists

Similar titles: *Love Lessons* by Diana Garcia and *Love's Destiny* by Quezada are other romances set in Colorado.

Dreaming of You. (*Soñando contigo*, 2000). Translated by Nancy Hedges. New York: Kensington Publishing, 2000. ISBN 0786010975. 352pp.

Supermodel Lilly Lujan and Mexican gardener Enrique Pacias find love in spite of their unequal status.

Antoine, Schmantoine. She'd rather shave her head shiny bald than spend the evening in the brain-melting company of Ego Boy. So what if he was the modeling world's newest designer underwear sensation. Every time she'd been around him, he'd acted like a brainless, conceited, Generation-X twit. (http://lyndalynda.com/books/dreaming.htm)

Key features: Bilingual format

Subjects: Colorado; fashion models; gardeners; immigrants—Mexican; love stories; Mexican Americans

Similar titles: *Help Wanted* by Diana Garcia and *To Catch a Star* by Ivette Gonzalez are also about finding love with sexy working-class Latinos.

One and Only. (*Solo Tú*, out of print). New York: Encanto/Kensington Publishing, 2001. ISBN 0-786-01212-9. 208 pp.

Pilar Valenzuela has decided to give up on her husband, Danny, and start a new life. He is a dedicated police officer who just can't seem to make space in his life for their family. Can Danny change his ways enough to convince Pilar of his sincerity?

> *"Daddy has to . . . go on a trip," she finished, clearing her throat. A trip to Get-A-Clue Land, where absentee fathers and husbands realized they couldn't continually put their families last, or they'd find themselves alone.* (9)

Subjects: Colorado; love stories; makeovers; Mexican Americans; police officers; separated couples

Similar titles: *Cristina's Secret* by Aguilar and *A Miracle of Love* by Gloria Alvarez are also about police officers in love.

Thief of Hearts. New York: Encanto/Kensington Publishing, 2001. ISBN 0786012358. 256pp.

Erstwhile wild child Graciela Obregon is on the road to a new "respectable" life when she slams into a semi and is rescued by bad boy Iso Pacias. Her attraction to him threatens to pull her back into the old patterns she is struggling to leave behind.

> *"It's not a sign," she muttered. "It's not." For good measure, she hastily crossed herself. Her life had changed so much over the past four years. For God's sake, she had a brand new teaching degree. It's not like someone rolled up that diploma and slipped it into her G-string as a reward for a particularly energetic table dance.* (www.kensingtonbooks. com/kensington/catalog)

Subjects: automobile accidents; Colorado; love stories; Mexican Americans; playboys; teachers

Similar titles: *First Love* by Erica Fuentes is also about playboys in love.

Unsettling. New York: HarperCollins, 2004. ISBN 0060546875. 326pp.

At the altar, Lucy panics and runs off with her girlfriends for a soul-searching road trip, on which they bond and have adventures while searching for a famous *curandero* who can cure what ails them. But will Lucy's jilted groom, Raul, take her back?

> *Lucy fought very hard not to cover her ears and smiled stiffly as she was sucked into the smothering vortex that was her* familia. (11)

Subjects: *chica* lit; *curanderos*; road trips; weddings; women's friendships

Similar titles: *¡Caramba!* by Nina Marie Martínez and *Divas Don't Yield* by Quintero are other novels that feature road trips with a carful of *amigas*.

Scordato, Caridad (Cuban American). *See also* Piñeiro, Caridad.

CellTech Series.

All this *pasión* at a biotech company! *¡Increíble!* Each one of these stories involves CellTech's founders and their families.

Better Than Ever. (*Mejor que Nunca*, 2000). Translated by Ramón Soto. New York: Kensington Publishing, 2000. ISBN 0-786-01137-8. 368pp.

At a conference in Miami, Florida, Maya Alfonso runs into her old flame, Alex Martinez. Maya heads an up-and-coming biotech company; Alex is a successful pediatrician and single parent. That old flame is hotter than ever, but can Alex handle Maya's dedication to her career this time?

> *"Carajo," Maya hissed beneath her breath and put on her best smile even as Alex came to stand before them. An Alex seven years had treated quite well, she thought, examining him.* (12)

Key features: Sexual situations; bilingual format

Subjects: biotech companies; Cuban Americans; Florida—Miami; love stories; physicians

Similar titles: The protagonists in *Ties That Bind* by Suzanne and *Blue Moon* by Vargas also rekindle romance with their old flames.

All My Love. (*Con todo mi Corazon*, out of print). New York: Kensington Publishing, 2001. ISBN 0-786-01280-3. 208pp.

Daisy Ramos and Brad Evans are partners at CellTech and have known each other for seven years, but they have been antagonists for most of that time. Brad is a confirmed bachelor, and Daisy is a beautiful, intelligent businesswoman. Can they meet on common ground?

> *Brad had never felt anything sweeter, anything more desirable than the gentle sweep of Daisy's hand across his lips. For so long he had wanted her, but had been afraid. After all, Daisy was the kind of woman every man wanted and yet every man ran away from. Beautiful enough to bring you to your knees and sharp enough mentally to cut you down to size when necessary.* (8)

Key features: Sexual situations

Subjects: biotech companies; Cuban Americans; Florida—Miami; geniuses; love stories

Similar titles: *Florida-Miami Heat* by Platas Fuller is another romance set in Miami.

The Perfect Mix. New York: Kensington Publishing, 2001. ISBN 0-786-01276-5. 256pp.

Blanca and her partners hire Rey as a contractor to build her new restaurant. Rey thinks Blanca's a high-maintenance princess, and Blanca feels in her bones that Rey is trouble AND he's hiding something—but he's just so sexy!

> *"We want quality work, Rey," she jumped in, her voice hard and her grey-green eyes turbulent.*
>
> *Rey wondered what those eyes would look like during passion and tamped down the thought with all the strength he could muster.* (13)

Key features: Sexual situations

Subjects: chefs; construction companies; Cuban Americans; love stories; restaurants

Similar titles: *Debt of Love* by Borges and *All of Me* by Platas Fuller are romances that also take place in the construction industry.

Feliz Navidad. New York: Kensington Publishing, 2001. ISBN 0786012528. 256pp.

Rebecca García, a corporate attorney from Miami, travels to New York on a high pressure business trip right before the holidays. There she meets Raul Santos, her adversary in law and in love.

> *"Mi'ja. Noche Buena is less than a week away. I don't understand why this couldn't wait until the New Year," her mother complained, and quite frankly, Rebecca didn't know how to counter that grievance.* (7)

Subjects: Cubans; lawyers; love stories; New York—New York City

Similar titles: *Forever True* by Alberro and *The Winds of Sonoma* are other romances about lawyers in love.

Gonzalez Sisters Series.

These two stories are about the Gonzalez sisters, two *marielitas* who came to the United States on the Mariel boatlift of Cuban refugees.

Now and Always. (*Para siempre*, 1999). Translated by Omar Amador. New York: Kensington Publishing, 1999. ISBN 0-786-00666-8. 380pp.

FBI agent Connie Gonzalez meets Dr. Victor Cienfuegos ("100 fires" in English) when her sister Carmen gets a job in his clinic. Connie is scrappy and streetwise; Victor is a conservative member of Miami's privileged class.

> *She tried to tell herself she didn't like his attention, but it would have been a lie. Here was a handsome, gorgeous man who wasn't looking at her as competition or some asexual Braniac.* (25)

Key features: Bilingual format

Subjects: Cuban Americans; FBI agents; Florida—Miami; love stories; physicians

Similar titles: *Florida-Miami Heat* by Platas Fuller is another romance set in Miami.

Faith in You. (*Tengo Fe en Ti*, 2000). New York: Kensington Publishing, 2000. ISBN 0-786-01057-6. 384pp.

Latina spitfire Carmen Gonzalez falls in love with conservative, blueblood Anglo FBI agent Paul Stone, her sister's nemesis from *Now and Always.*

> *This very handsome, seemingly polite man could not be the same Paul Stone who had broken her sister's arm and been the bane of Connie's existence throughout the Academy. That Paul Stone would have been staring down his nose at her and her family's very simple home.* (8)

Key features: Bilingual format

Subjects: Cuban Americans; FBI agents; Florida—Miami; love stories; nurses

Similar titles: *Florida-Miami Heat* by Platas Fuller is another romance set in Miami.

Skármeta, Antonio (Chilean).

The Dancer and the Thief. (Baile de la victoria, 2003). **Translated by Katherine Silver. New York: W.W. Norton, 2008. ISBN 9780393064940. 300pp.**

Angel Santiago is back on the streets after the Chilean president issues a pardon for nonviolent prisoners. He wants revenge and needs money. He meets Victoria Ponce, who has a grudge of her own. The two fall in love and join forces with legendary safecracker Nicolás Vergara Gray, who longs to woo back his wife and reconstruct his life after the pardon. Meanwhile, Angel's nemesis, the warden, has given a lifer thirty days' freedom in order to get rid of Angel.

> *She followed his gaze, then ran her fingers through her hair. As they both looked down, their eyes locked for a brief, intimate moment. She smiled at him; he thought it would be attractive and virile to do nothing, so he held her stare and brushed his hair off his forehead.* (24)

Subjects: Chile—Santiago; criminals—pardoned; dancers; love stories; revenge

Similar titles: *Dance with Me* by Alonso-Cruz features another dancer in love; *Mambo Peligroso* also has a protagonist who dances and a similar tone of danger.

Suzanne, Kathleen.

Ties That Bind. **Columbus, MS: Genesis Press, 2000. ISBN 1-58571-010-5. 272pp.**

Paloma Ortega, contractor, and her old flame, builder Raul Fernandez, meet again over a job. They were torn apart many years before by a lie his ex-girlfriend told; she then married Raul and nearly destroyed him. Raul is unaware that he has a child by Paloma, whom she gave up for adoption and is now searching for.

> *Thoughts of her had haunted him on and off, ever since she'd disappeared from his life. Was she married with a husband and children? The thought shook him even after twelve years. She had been the one woman he'd have given his life for, the one he had wanted to grow old with. Why had she left like that?* (10–11)

Subjects: adoption; construction companies; love stories; Mexican Americans; Michigan

Similar titles: *Debt of Love* by Borges is another romance in which love happens in a construction company.

Valdes-Rodriguez, Alisa (Cuban American; Floridian).

Make Him Look Good. **New York: St. Martin's Press, 2006. ISBN 0-312-34966-1. 376pp.**

This novel is narrated by the voices of many females whose lives are affected by Latino singing sensation Ricky Biscayne, including the publicist who has a huge crush on him, his wife, former lovers, potential lovers, and his estranged daughter.

> *I would be pretty by normal standards, but because I live in Florida—Miami, a city where pretty must be nipped, tucked, and*

liposuctioned into uniformity and submission to qualify, I am plain by association. (11)

Key features: First person narration; sexual situations

Subjects: *chica* lit; Cuban Americans; Florida—Miami; humor; love stories; music industry

Similar titles: *Sex and the South Beach Chicas* by Piñeiro is also about Latinas, the music business, and love.

Vargas, Dalia.

Blue Moon. **New York: Kensington Publishing, 2001. ISBN 0-7860-1209-9. 204pp.**

Silvia Martinez encounters her ex-fiancé, Miguel Escudero, working on the boat she will use for her study of sharks, and falls in love with him again. When they were engaged, he wanted her to abandon her studies and settle down. Now she's on the verge of success as an oceanographer. Will he be able to support her dedication to her chosen profession this time around?

> *Miguel went to the bar. Silvia watched him. Yes, Miguel was still the same lovely man who had driven her crazy years ago. His strong shoulders, his masculine profile, his dark, deep eyes and those dimples that formed in his cheeks when he laughed, where she had planted so many kisses.* (13)

Key features: First person narration; sexual situations

Subjects: California—San Diego; love stories; marine biologists; Mexican Americans; oceanographers

Similar titles: *Better Than Ever* by Scordato is another novel in which old flames are rekindled.

Vazquez, Consuelo.

Leading Lady. **(*Estrella*, 2000). Translated by Lia Burgueño. New York: Kensington Publishing, 2000. ISBN 0-7860-1139-4. 173pp.**

Mercedes Romero is a star on the way up when she meets Quinn Scarborough, who hires her as a backup singer and then falls hard for her. Will she trade love for a chance at the big time?

> *He became a cowboy climbing into his saddle, a young military man putting the final touches on his uniform; a good-looking guy, something of a quiet rebel, with his hands all over a guitar-tuning it, preparing it, listening to it murmur in response to his touch. The effect was as exciting as those other romantic images.* (43)

Key features: Bilingual format

Subjects: Dominican Americans; love stories; music industry; singers—fiction

Similar titles: *Love's Song* by Ivette Gonzalez is another novel about love in the music business.

Wind, Ruth.

Rio Grande Wedding. **New York: Silhouette Books, 1999. ISBN 0-373- 07964-8. 248pp.**

Molly Sheffield is a widow and nurse living near the Mexican border in New Mexico. She finds Alejandro Sosa, an undocumented worker who has been injured in a border crossing melee with the border patrol and was separated from his niece. Molly nurses Alejandro and helps him search for his niece; then marries him in a "marriage of convenience"—but for whom is it convenient?

> It was that face, manifesting right out of her most private imaginings, that halted her. He moved her. Physically, as in hormonal, as in she had forgotten what that sudden, pleasurable swoop of sexual attraction could feel like. He had the long-limbed body she most liked on a man, and the healthy, lean strength that came from working the land. His hair, black as licorice and slightly curly, was a bit too long and a little untamed. Sexy. (18)

Subjects: love stories; marriage; Mexicans; New Mexico; undocumented workers; U.S.–Mexico border; widows

Similar titles: *Cristina's Secret* by Aguilar is also about nurses in love; *Wild for You* by Marquez uses a marriage of convenience as a plot device.

Historical Romance

Historical romances offer readers double pleasure—all the trappings of rich historical settings, including details about costumes, locations, events, and people of the past—in addition to engaging love stories.

Allende, Isabel (Chilean).

Daughter of Fortune. (*Hija de Fortuna*, 1999). Translated by Margaret Sayers Peden. New York: HarperCollins, 1999. ISBN 0-06-019491-X. 399pp.
Eliza Sommers, raised by an English family in Chile, falls in love and follows Joaquín Anieta to California during the Gold Rush. She helps and is helped by her loyal friend, the doctor Tao Chi'en, during exciting times.

> Rose was only twenty, but she was already a woman with a past, and her chances for making a good marriage were minimal. In addition, she had totted up her possibilities and had decided that marriage, even in the best of cases, was a dreary business. (7)

Subjects: California Gold Rush; Chile; historical fiction; love stories; physicians

Similar titles: *Ramona* by Jackson is another romance set in nineteenth-century California.

Bernardo, José Raúl (Cuban American).

Silent Wing. New York: Simon & Schuster, 1998. ISBN 0-684-84389-7. 236pp.
In Mexico City, Cuban poet Julián had promised to marry fellow exile Lucía, but he then meets Sol in Guatemala. Realizing that Sol is the true soul mate who shares his passion for the liberation of Cuba from Spain, will Julián honor his promise to Lucia?

> A week ago, after one more such confrontation, Xenufla lowered her voice and confidentially told Sol, "A man can be a lot of fun, niña. Believe me.

You may think I am just an old Indian woman now, but, niña," she said, raising her voice just a little bit as she touched her ample breasts, "I am still a woman." (14)

Subjects: Cuban independence; Guatemala; historical fiction; love stories; Martí, José; Mexico—Mexico City; poets—fiction

Similar titles: *The Divine Husband* by Goldman is another novel that takes place during the Cuban independence movement, featuring José Martí in Guatemala.

Esquivel, Laura (Mexican).

The Law of Love. (*La ley del amor,* 1995). **Translated by Margaret Sayers Peden. New York: Crown, 1996. ISBN 0-517-70681-4. 266pp.**

This is the story of a love 14,000 years in the future, between Azucena, an astroanalyst, and Rodrigo, her true soul mate. Unfortunately, right after they find each other they are separated, and to reunite with Rodrigo means saving the universe by rescuing the Law of Love. And so Azucena, searches for Rodrigo through many epochs of the past.

> *If she did not deactivate the alarm immediately, the apparatus would process him as a unknown body and his cells would be prevented from correctly reintegrating inside the aerophone booth. After waiting all this time, how could she end up doing something so stupid! At best, Rodrigo would run the risk of disintegrating for twenty-four hours.* (21)

Subjects: future worlds; karma; love stories; Mexicans; reincarnation

Similar titles: *Inez* by Carlos Fuentes is another novel that follows one love throughout the ages.

Malinche. **New York: Atria Books, 2006. ISBN-10: 0-7432-9033X; ISBN-13: 978-0-7432-9033-3. 191pp.**

The infamous Malinche was Hernan Cortés's interpreter during the Spanish Conquest and thus became the symbol of treachery for Mexico. The *conquista* transforms her from an Indian slave into a powerful consort and ally of the Spanish conquerors. Along the way she finds a true love, and their union will bring a new era to the Americas.

> *Thus the newborn, daughter of the Tlatoani of Painala, was welcomed into her paternal grandmother's arms. The grandmother sensed that the girl was destined to lose everything so that she might gain everything.* (5)

Key features: Bibliography

Subjects: Cortés, Hernán; historical fiction; love stories; Malinche; Mexico—Conquest

Similar titles: *Aztec* by Gary Jennings also takes place during the Spanish Conquest of the Aztecs; *Song of the Hummingbird* by Graciela Limón also presents the Spanish Conquest from an Indian woman's perspective.

Gonzalez, Béa (Spanish Canadian).

The Mapmaker's Opera. **New York: St. Martin's Press, 2005. ISBN 9780312364663. 277pp.**

Spaniard Diego travels to the Yucatan to work with a famous naturalist. He falls in love with Sofia, another aristocratic bird lover. Alas, the Mexican Revolution is about to turn everything on its head. The last pair of carrier pigeons the lovers hope to save are endangered, as are they.

> *In her accented English, with Spanish peppering the narrative—"because Spanish," our Abuela would insist, "is not only the language of love, oigan bien, but the language of life itself"—our grandmother would transport us to a world where we would easily lose all sense of time.* (4)

Subjects: bird lovers; historical fiction; love stories; Mexican Revolution; Mexico —Yucatán; naturalists; Spain—Seville

Similar titles: *Wild Steps of Heaven* by Villaseñor and *The Hummingbird's Daughter* by Urrea also take place during the Mexican Revolution.

Manrique, Jaime (Colombian).

Our Lives Are the Rivers. (Nuestras vidas son los ríos, 2006). **New York: HarperCollins, 2006. ISBN 0-06-082070-5; ISBN-13: 978-0-06-082070-1. 349pp.**

The story of Manuela Sáenz, told by herself and her slaves, Natán and Jonotás. Manuela becomes the lover of General Simón Bolívar (the Liberator) and is fiercely devoted to the cause of independence for South America.

> *But the story I want to tell you, the story of my love for the liberator, Simón Bolívar, began long before I met him. It began when I was a young girl in the school of the Concepta nuns in Quito, where my mother's family kept me imprisoned until I eloped with the first man who said he loved me.* (3)

Subjects: adultery; Bolívar, Simón; love stories; slavery; South America—Wars of Independence

Similar titles: *The General in His Labyrinth* by García Márquez and *Bolivar: Liberator of a Continent* by Boyd are other historical novels based on Simón Bolívar's life.

Mastretta, Ángeles (Mexican).

Lovesick. (Mal de amores, 1996). **Translated by Margaret Sayers Peden. New York: Riverhead Books, 1997.**

Set in Puebla, Mexico, during the time of the Mexican Revolution, the beginning of the twentieth century. Dr. Emilia Sauri is the daughter of a Mayan healer/doctor and a maternal society woman and niece of a nonconformist, heartbreaker aunt. Emilia is torn between her love for her childhood friend, Daniel, who is always off following the Revolution, and a more stable, tranquil love for her colleague, Dr. Antonio Zavalza. In this magical novel, she might be able to have both!

> *Diego had spent too much time in pursuit of his destiny not to know it when he saw it. He had wandered all those years, all over the world, only to have life turn around and hand him his future at the same meridian where the past has taken it from him, and as he approached the woman's table he never broke stride.* (7)

Subjects: *curanderos*; families; historical fiction; love stories; Mexican Revolution; Mexico—Puebla; physicians; revolutionaries

Similar titles: *The House of Spirits* by Allende and *Like Water for Chocolate* by Esquivel also mix magic and romance.

Wulf, Jessica.

The Wild Rose. **New York: Kensington Publishing, 1995. ISBN 0-8217-5103-4. 471pp.**

Philadelphian Jennifer Mainwaring is Preston Cantrell's goddaughter; she is visiting him at his California ranch. During her visit John Cantrell, Preston's illegitimate first son by his first and one true love, Ana María Novales of Mexico, shows up to *rendir cuentas* and take his revenge on Preston. Jennifer and John fall in love, but must overcome the underhanded machinations of old lovers and family to keep them apart.

> *The flare of rage in John's eyes made Jennifer want to step back, but she would not, nor would she lower her own gaze. She watched as he struggled to control himself, almost wishing he would make a move toward her. She would love to hit him again.* (30)

Subjects: California—Mexicans; California—19th century; godfathers; historical fiction; illegitimate children; love stories; ranchers

Similar titles: *Daughter of Fortune* by Allende and *Ramona* by Jackson are other romances set in nineteenth-century California.

Paranormal Romance and Romantic Suspense

In paranormal romance and romantic suspense, stories contain magical or mysterious elements. A suspenseful atmosphere and the unpredictability in these stories accentuate the romance and increase their emotional appeal.

Acosta, Marta (Mexican American).

Casa Dracula Series.

This is the comical odyssey of would-be writer Milagro de los Santos's romance with the sexy vampire Oswald, who happens to be a plastic surgeon.

Key features: Sexual situations

Subjects: humor; love stories; vampires

Similar titles: The Calling series by Scordato is a more serious take on Latinas, vampires, lust, and love; another humorous fantasy novel is *A Nameless Witch* by A. Lee Martínez.

Happy Hour at Casa Dracula. New York: Simon & Schuster, 2006. ISBN 9781416520382. 314pp.

Milagro de los Santos meets Oswald, who, apart from being a vampire, is just plain inappropriate for her because she is, after all, an Ivy League grad on her way up in the world. Can love grow from their magnetic attraction, and can they survive the dark forces working against them, including Milagro's snotty ex-*novio*?

> *Kathleen had a magpie's fascination with all things shiny, so the room gleamed with polished floors, glittering mirrors, and lustrous furniture. I was afraid that if I moved too quickly, I'd skitter and crash down on my sincere and serious* colita. *(6)*

Midnight Brunch at Casa Dracula. New York: Simon & Schuster, 2007. ISBN 9781416520399. 328pp.

Milagro has moved into Oswald's ranch home in California, but while she's waiting for a proposal, he takes off on a humanitarian mission, leaving her vulnerable and suspicious. She finds out she's the sacrificial *chica* needed for the vampires' plot to take over the world. Will Oswald make it back in time to save her? Will he finally propose?

> *Oswald had to wear sunblock every day because he had a genetic autosomal recessive disorder that made him highly sensitive to sunlight and subject to unusual food cravings. On the plus side, he never got sick and healed rapidly from injuries. (1)*

The Bride of Casa Dracula. New York: Simon & Schuster, 2008. ISBN 9781416559634. 286pp.

Milagro and Oswald are finally to wed—IF they can get past extravagant wedding planners, shape-shifters, conniving in-laws, the sinister Vampire Council, and attractive distractions.

> *Best of all, I could bake in the sunlight until I got as toasty brown as a* buñuelo, *to no ill effect. I was a new, improved version of myself, Milagro 2.0. (3)*

Key features: Sexual situations; reading group guide

Escalera, Diane.

Dangerous Heat. (*Jugando con Candela,* 2001). New York: Kensington Publishing, 2001. ISBN 0786011696. 208pp.

Private investigator Mia Hartmann goes undercover as sexy banker Emilio De Leon's new secretary. Emilio is the prime suspect in a high-tech embezzlement scheme, and Mia has secrets of her own.

> *Not that she had a problem handling herself. She was better than most of the men he'd worked with. Mia never left a stone unturned, going over every detail with a keen eye. (10)*

Key features: Sexual situations

Subjects: bankers; Cuban Americans; embezzlers; Florida—Miami; love stories; private investigators—women

Similar titles: *In Hot Pursuit* by Marquez is another novel about Cubans and their secrets.

Montoya, Tracy.

Finding His Child. **New York: Harlequin, 2007. ISBN 0373691536. 256pp.**

Detective Aaron Donovan's daughter has been kidnapped. Sexy tracker extraordinaire Sabrina Adelante is assigned to the case and almost loses her life to the insane killer. Can Donovan risk falling in love with her?

> *Even though he probably looked like a madman to her, she looked like refuge to him. All he wanted to do was sink into her, inhale the fresh scent of her hair that he remembered so well, and forget about everything.* (www.tracymontoya.com/ html/fhcexcerpt.html)

Subjects: police detectives; trackers; Washington, D.C.

I'll Be Watching You. **New York: Harlequin, 2008. ISBN 9780373693245. 224pp.**

Beautiful Addy Torres is being stalked by a ruthless murderer whom the police had thought was dead. It could be the same maniac who killed her fiancé. Daniel Cardenas, one of Monterrey's finest, is assigned the difficult task of protecting her.

> *But something in her normally no-nonsense voice had sent his cop sense into overdrive, and he knew it was shut-up-and-go time. So he shut up, hung up, and went.* (www.tracymontoya.com/html/watchingexcerpt.html)

Key features: Graphic violence

Subjects: California—Monterey; Mexican Americans; police detectives; serial killers; yoga instructors

Similar titles: *White Rabbit* by David Daniel is another novel about a serial killer committing gruesome murders in California.

Maximum Security. **New York: Harlequin, 2004. ISBN 0-373-22750-7. 251pp.**

Maggie Reyes, a true crime writer, is being stalked by a serial killer, the Surgeon, from whom she had escaped before, but not without scars on her body and mind. She has hidden herself away on the coast of California near Monterrey, becoming a hermit and going a little crazy. Billy Corrigan needs Maggie's help to find the Surgeon, who also counts Billy's sister as one of his victims.

> *With that, Maggie pulled her hand out of the canister and swung around. She switched off the safety of her Firestar M43 and aimed the small gun right for his mojo-covered heart. "But if you're James Brentwood, then I really am Sheena, Queen of the Jungle."* (19–20)

Key features: Violence

Subjects: California—Monterey; FBI agents; love stories; Mexican Americans; serial killers; writers—fiction

Similar titles: *White Rabbit* by David Daniel is another novel about a serial killer committing gruesome murders in California.

Mission: Family.

This series of suspenseful novels is set in the same neighborhood near St. Xavier University in Los Angeles, featuring the Rodriguez family of law enforcement officers and their friends.

Similar titles: *Brotherhood of Dolphins* by Ybarra is a police procedural that also takes place in Los Angeles in the Mexican American community.

House of Secrets. New York: Harlequin, 2005. ISBN 0373228775. 248pp.

Private eye Joe Lopez's mother was a cop; she was murdered in the house Emma Jensen Reese lived in twenty years earlier. Now the house is the center of another investigation involving Emma, as strange events take place that put her in danger.

> *The so-called Mystery man was staring at her front door. And in the daylight, he was what her students would call a hottie.* (32)

Subjects: California—Los Angeles; college professors; corruption; Mexican Americans; murder; police officers

Next of Kin. New York: Harlequin, 2005. ISBN 037322883X. 251pp.

Daniel Rodriguez is a former gangbanger turned LA cop. His old flame, Celia Viramontes, is the university librarian at St. Xavier's. She is being threatened by a rival who has just been released from prison and is bent on revenge for old grievances. It's been eleven years, but Daniel needs to protect Celia, even if she wants him to keep away once those uncomfortable old feelings start resurfacing.

> *Because even though a long time had passed since Celia had last spoken to him without using the words "jerk" and "flying leap off my universe," as well as a few choice Spanish phrases his mother used to wash his mouth out with soap for uttering, he still found himself wanting to tear apart the person who'd put that look of fear on her face.* (12)

Subjects: arson; California; gangs; librarians; love stories; Mexican Americans; murder; police officers

Shadow Guardian. New York: Harlequin, 2005. ISBN 0373228899. 248pp.

Stalked by a crazy fan, Sadie Locke needs a bodyguard. Patricio Rodriguez is the best one around (Daniel's brother from *Next of Kin*). Can he avoid mixing business with pleasure while protecting the beautiful actress?

> *He looked the way she expected Lucifer had just before he fell—dark, dangerous, beautiful. Not that she didn't see a whole lot of beautiful people in her line of work, but there was something there, some blend of intelligence and fearlessness and confidence in his striking light brown eyes that just took her breath away.* (52)

Subjects: actresses; bodyguards; California; Mexican Americans; stalkers

Piñeiro, Caridad (Cuban American). *See also* Scordato, Caridad.

South Beach Chicas Catch Their Man. **New York: Downtown Press, 2007. ISBN 9781416514893. 285pp.**

Sylvia Amenabar, the journalist from *Sex and the South Beach Chicas*, confronts her attraction to Carlos Ramírez, who has taken a bullet for her. While wrestling with her commitment issues, Sylvia takes on a case that is uncomfortable for her friends and family, seeking to prove herself a serious journalist.

> She had thought there was very little that could scare her big, brave cop. Sneaking a glance at the source of that terror—his mami and hermanita—it occurred to her that they didn't seem all that fear inspiring. (5)

Key features: Sexual situations; author interview

Subjects: *chica* lit; journalists; love stories; mothers and daughters; police officers

Similar titles: *Only a Kiss Away* by Carvajal is another novel about a Latina reporter and love.

The Calling.

The books in this series are police procedural sensual romances that feature vampire protagonists in New York City.

> Powerful, dangerous and the key to catching a psychotic killer, Ryder Latimer was everything she couldn't have—and everything she wanted. He haunted her nights, shattered her reserve and made her feel . . . more than she ever had before. But once she learned his secret, would his sensual promises of eternal love be enough to garner her forgiveness? For Ryder was more than a lover of the night . . . he was a vampire. (www.thecallingvampirenovels.com/darkness-calls/)

Key features: Graphic sexual situations

Subjects: Cuban Americans; FBI agents; love stories; New York—New York City; serial killers; vampires

Similar titles: The <u>Casa Dracula Series</u> books by Acosta are humorous romances about vampires and love.

Darkness Calls. New York: Silhouette, 2004. ISBN 0373273533. 256pp.

FBI agent Diana Reyes is no stranger to life on the mean streets, but she has never encountered anyone like club owner Ryder Latimer, who happens to be a vampire. While on the job searching for a serial killer, Diana encounters Ryder and fears he may be that killer.

Danger Calls. New York: Silhouette, 2005. ISBN 0373274416. 256pp.

Dr. Melissa Danvers inherits the role of personal physician to Ryder, the vampire, after her parents are killed in a suspicious car accident. She falls in love with Sebastian Reyes, but is leery of involving him in the unnatural situation. Their relationship may have a chance to mature as they work with Ryder and Diana to learn the truth behind the car accident and keep Melissa safe. That is, if carefree, unreliable rule breaker Sebastian can prove he's up to the challenge.

Temptation Calls. New York: Silhouette, 2005. ISBN 0373274602. 256pp.

Samantha Turner is an undercover vampire who runs the Artemis shelter for battered women in Spanish Harlem. When she helps victims of a drive-by shooting, she comes under the scrutiny of Detective Peter Daly. Is her secret safe?

Death Calls. New York: Silhouette, 2006. ISBN 0373617534. 288pp.

> Diana Reyes and Ryder are back. Diana is having second thoughts about spending her life with a vampire. While she is taking some breathing space, her job takes her on a dangerous mission. Ryder struggles to give her the space she asked for, keep an eye on her safety, and fight off the powerful Stacia.

Devotion Calls. New York: Silhouette, 2007. ISBN 0373617550. 304pp.

> Vampire healer Ricardo Fernandez falls in love with the reluctant and suspicious nurse Sara Martinez, while fighting off danger from the horrible Chupacabras.

Blood Calls. New York: Silhouette, 2007. ISBN 0373617631. 288pp.

> Art gallery owner, patron of the arts, and vampire Diego Rivera (!) is fascinated by a young artist who is also terminally ill—Ramona Escobar. Ramona is going through a rough patch, caring for her mother, being accused of forging paintings, AND being threatened by a psychotic millionaire.

"Fate Calls." in *Holiday with a Vampire: Christmas Cravings/Fate Calls.* By Maureen Child and Caridad Piñeiro. New York: Silhouette, 2007. ISBN 0373617763. 288pp.

> Vampire Hadrian abducts Connie Morales to make her quit the annoying bell-ringing, but finds she affects him in a deeper way.

Platas Fuller, Berta.

Livewire. **New York: Kensington Publishing, 2001. ISBN 0786012897. 256pp.**

> Candela Escovedo, private eye, and Alfonso Rivera, recalcitrant macho man, are doomed to clash, but in the interest of saving Alfonso's kidnapped daughter, they must collaborate and try to resist their mutual attraction.

> > *He looked like a model for an Italian couture house: dark eyes, strong nose, well-formed sensuous lips, and fabulous clothes. All she could think was* wow. *You never saw guys like this in real life.* (15)

Subjects: Cuban Americans; fathers and daughters; Florida—Miami; love stories; private investigators—women

Similar titles: Opposites also attract in *Sweet Destiny* by Gomez; *Finding His Child* by Montoya also features a woman helping a man find his kidnapped child.

Quezada, M. Louise.

Love's Destiny. **Columbus, MS: Genesis Press, 1999. ISBN 1-885478-682. 163pp.**

> Marisa Gallegos has put off marriage and family to dedicate her life to building a respectable career as an interior decorator, when she runs into Steve Duran, whom she knew as a child. Steve is on a mission to find his brother's murderer, an obsession that may tear their newfound love apart.

> *He watched as she tucked her shiny black hair behind both ears. Her face appeared smooth and free of any makeup. Thick, long eyelashes framed her deep brown eyes. Marisa Gallegos had turned into a beautiful woman.* (12)

Subjects: Colorado—Denver; interior decorating; love stories; marketing; Mexican Americans; murder; suspense

Similar titles: Old flames are also reignited in *Better Than Ever* by Scordato while *Ties that Bind* by Suzanne features old flames involved in a suspenseful situation.

Hearts Remembered. **Columbus, MS: Genesis Press, 1998. ISBN 1-885478-38-0. 183pp.**

Isabel Medina's romance with cowboy Alex McCormick was ruined long ago by his unscrupulous landowner father. Her settled life as an artist and teacher is disrupted when she is threatened by a killer for hire. Will Alex return in time to save her and rescue their lost love?

> *Moving backwards with Ray, her unwavering glance masked the fear burgeoning from within. Isabel's eyes locked momentarily with the man from her past. Alex McCormick. The only man she ever loved-and hated.* (5)

Subjects: artists; Colorado; cowboys; love stories; Mexican Americans; murder; suspense

Similar titles: *Intrigue* by Salcedo and *Dangerous Heat* by Escalera are other romances involving secrets, sex, and suspense.

Zamora, Genaro Lucio (Tejano).

Pretty Brown. **Miami, FL: Urbano Publishing, 2008. ISBN 978-0976283836. 125pp.**

In an unidentified southeast Texas town, Alex is working for the local drug running operation, leaning on buyers to pay up. He is getting tired of the business and starting to look for a way out when he meets his crush from high school, Sandra. Can Alex find the strength to get out with his life and find happiness with the pretty brown lady?

> *He always wondered what happened to her and now standing in front of him, he was starting to feel his ears grow red all over again.* (25)

Subjects: drugs; love stories; street lit; Texas

Similar titles: *Forever, My Lady* by Rivera is another title with a similar urban tone.

Anthologies and Collections

Blair, J. H., ed. (U.S. American).

¡Caliente! The Best Erotic Writing in Latin American Fiction. **New York: Berkley Books, 2002. ISBN 0-425-18466-8. 203pp.**

This anthology contains excerpts, the "good parts" from Latin American and U.S. Latino fiction writing, organized alphabetically by author. The earliest piece is from Brazilian Jorge Amado's *Doña Flor and Her Two Husbands*, but the majority of the pieces were published in the 1990s and 2000s. Many are translated from the Spanish; the rest were written originally in English.

> *No one does food, nature, music, or sex better than Latins . . . for Latin/South American fiction writers, the pleasures of reading are the pleasures of the body and the questions they raise are answered with instincts of survival—not the if questions but hows. (x)*

Key features: Graphic sexual situations

Subjects: love stories; sensual fiction

Castillo, Mary, et al.

Friday Night Chicas. **New York. St. Martin's Griffin, 2005. ISBN 0312335040. 352pp.**

An eventful and sexy Friday night in the lives of four Latinas in four different cities.

Key features: Sexual situations; some first person narration

Subjects: chefs; *chica* lit; cruise ships; fashion; high school reunions; Latinas; lawyers; love stories; parties; writers—fiction

Castillo, Mary.

"My Favorite Mistake."

Isela is looking to save her Hollywood career when she crashes an industry party, with surprising results.

> *The first time I ever broke all of my rules to be with this incredible guy, this is what happens. God was punishing me for this. Unlike Lydia, my one-night stand wouldn't end up as my husband or as the father of my child. Mine would be a catastrophy. (51)*

Piñeiro, Caridad.

"Hearts Are Wild."

Tori's girlfriends thwart her plans for a quiet birthday celebration at home with family and whisk her off to a gambling cruise ship off Miami's South Beach.

> *The last thing she needed was for most of Little Havana to think that Victoria Dolores de la Caridad Rodriguez needed to get laid. (89)*

Platas, Berta.

"Revenge of the Fashion Goddess."

Cali attends her high school reunion in Chicago determined to settle an old score, but she may get more than she bargained for.

> *If a stiff drink is Dutch courage, then a double* mojito *is liquid Cuban backbone. (163)*

Sofia Quintero.

"The More Things Change."

In New York City, Gladys's raunchy bachelorette party stars a stripper who may embolden her to change her wedding plans.

> *How we resented that there were few if any Latinos represented in the core curriculum, but you could always find a goddamn Margarita Night somewhere on campus.* (262)

Mulligan, Michelle Herrera, ed.

Juicy Mangos. **New York: Atria Books, 2007. ISBN 9780743294447. 302pp.**

These erotic short stories by Latina authors feature strong Latina protagonists and all take place around a holiday. The women take the opportunity to break from their daily routine and try on new personas, with surprising results. The settings range from New York, Los Angeles, and Chicago to exotic locales in Spain, Puerto Rico, and Brazil. The love interests may be former gangbangers, scientists, or even other women. Language plays an important part in these stories, and some contain magical or fantastical elements.

> *With my* boca sucia, *you'd think I got more* acción, *she wondered. As she stretched out on the stiff new mattress, she pondered how long it had been since someone had shared a bed with her.* Podría yo dormir con otro? (11)

Key features: Sexual situations; some first person narration

Subjects: Latinas; love stories; sensual fiction

Rivera, Beatriz (Cuban American).

African Passions and Other Stories. **Houston, TX: 1995. ISBN 1558851356. 168pp.**

These stories all explore Latina women's dedication to passion, sometimes at the expense of their own good judgment and self-interest. All the Latinas in these stories live in the same New Jersey barrio, and several characters appear throughout the book. Ages are from recent college graduate to middle-aged mother, from professional women to women who don't need to work. There is magic; there is humor.

> *And since Teresa did summon the African Powers, they came.*
>
> *Babalú Ayé was the first. He emerged from the corn, in a foul mood because Teresa had summoned him last. And besides, he didn't like her tone of voice; it was too arrogant.* (10)

Subjects: Latinas; love stories; New Jersey

Rivera-Valdés, Sonia (Cuban American).

The Forbidden Stories of Marta Veneranda. (*Las historias prohibidas de Marta Veneranda,* **1997). Translated by Dick Cluster et al. New York: Seven Stories Press, 2001. ISBN 158322047X. 158pp.**

These nine stories are presented as research collected by Marta Veneranda for her doctoral thesis; they are stories about what people consider forbidden in their lives. All the stories feature Cuban and other Latino immigrants in the modern-day United States, with kinky and erotic entanglements, who are all related in some way.

> You'll judge my story according to your own criteria, but for me this whole matter is very disturbing. Not just that I had a sexual relationship with a woman, but the series of circumstances that surrounded the episode and the impact it had on me. It changed my life. (9)

Key features: Sexual situations

Subjects: Cuban Americans; Cubans; sensual fiction; short stories

References

Castillo, Mary. 2005. Correspondence with the author, April 13.

Charles, John, and Cathie Linz. 2005. "Romancing Your Readers. How Public Libraries Can Become More Romance Reader Friendly." *Public Libraries* 44, no. 1 (January/February): 43.

Ramsdell, Kristen. 1999. *Romance Fiction. A Guide to the Genre.* Englewood, CO: Libraries Unlimited.

Romance Readers Anonymous (RRA-L). 1998. Listserv Archives. May 5 Thread: Multi-cultural Ramblings (posted by Joyce French). At http://listserv.kent.edu/cgi-bin/wa.exe?A2=ind9805A&L=RRA-L&P =R3394&I=-3 (accessed July 7, 2005).

Romantic Times Web page. 2008. www.romantictimes.com (accessed November 22, 2008).

Romance Writers of America (RWA). 2004. *2004 Romance-Fiction Sales Statistics, Reader Demographics and Book-Buying Habits.* Available at www.rwanational.org (accessed July 11, 2005).

Saenger, Diana. 2002."USC Grad Courts Success as Romance Novelist: Uses Rediscovered Latino Culture as Backdrop." *Hispanic Outlook in Higher Education* 12, no. 22 (August 12): 27.

Scordato, Caridad. 2005. Correspondence with the author, November 29.

Chapter 5

Mysteries and Suspense

Brandi Blankenship and Sara Martínez

Más sabe el Diablo por Viejo que por Diablo

Introduction

Bringing order to chaos is often part of the classic definition of the mystery genre, but the Latino take on this genre is often just fine with chaos. Latino authors love to break rules and explore the boundaries between genres, and these mysteries feature homosexual lawyers, dinosaur private investigators, tough female bounty hunters, and everything in between. Magic and mysticism are elements that many of these detectives have to grapple with or, *en el caso contrario*, they may depend on these elements to assist them in a pinch. Latino mysteries are often used as vehicles to bring home the reality of social inequalities and injustice.

Appeal

Readers of this genre enjoy identifying with heroes and heroines in difficult situations who find the resources, strength, and smarts to triumph over hardship, injustice, and evil. They also often enjoy the exotic locales, unexpected magic, and humor. As readers are taken out of their comfort zone, they may get the satisfaction of figuring out the answer to the puzzle before the detective does.

Organization

Titles in this chapter are organized into four sections: "Private Investigators," "Police Procedurals," "Amateur Sleuths," and "Thrillers and Suspense." There are not many cozy mysteries to be found in this chapter, most feature some level of violence and strong language Titles often classified as street lit(erature) or urban fiction have the subject tag "street lit."

Private Investigators

The private investigators in this section are hard as nails idealists cut from the same cloth as Sam Spade. They talk tough and fight when they need to, but will put themselves in danger to see that justice is done. Their tools are similar to those of other PIs—trusty sidekicks; family, friends, and community; an intimate knowledge of the martial arts; and the Colt .45 and its descendants. Unlike other PIs, they may rely on the *más allá*—the spirit world and the magical realm of intuition and dreams. They solve murders and robberies and seek to right old wrongs, from the gritty urban landscapes of Los Angeles, Mexico City, or Miami to the ethereal desert land of the Southwest. They are single moms, sexy studs, one-eyed engineers, poets, and . . . dinosaurs!

Allyn, Doug (U.S. American).

Welcome to Wolf Country. **Waterville, ME: Five Star, 2001. ISBN 0786234210. 216pp.**

> Roberto "Bobby" Cruz, Detroit PI, is hired by a shady law firm to look into the mysterious disappearance of Roland Costa and Rol Junior. Traveling north to Algoma, Michigan, Bobby soon finds out that someone wants him off the case, and this means dead. If he can dodge the hunters, Cruz just might live long enough to solve the case.
>
> > *Beer? You've got to be kidding. You think that when I'm a famous mob hit man I'll still be drinking beer? Somehow I don't think Lester Bradleigh hauls around a kegger of Blatz in the back of his Benz.* (23)
>
> **Key features:** First person narration; strong language
>
> **Subjects:** Latinos; Michigan—Detroit; missing persons; private investigators
>
> **Similar titles:** *Convenient Disposal: A Posadas County Mystery* by Havill deals with missing persons, and the <u>Amos Walker</u> series by Estleman has a private eye as the main character and is also set in Michigan.

Anaya, Rudolfo (New Mexican American).

<u>Sonny Baca Mysteries.</u>

> Sexy Chicano private investigator Sonny Baca matches wits with Raven, a nefarious genius who uses any weapon—including magic and murder—to carry out his will to power. Sonny is descended from the great lawman Elfego Baca and still carries his *bisabuelo's* Colt .45. He finds strength and wisdom from his own contacts with the spiritual realm. Most of the titles address environmental concerns such as water usage or nuclear power.
>
> **Subjects:** ancestors; *brujos;* Chicanos; dreams; environment; *naguales;* New Mexico—Albuquerque; private investigators; shamans
>
> **Similar titles:** Hillerman's <u>Joe Leaphorn</u> series mirrors the <u>Sonny Baca Mysteries</u> in that the stories occur in New Mexico and the author uses mystical plot devices. Alcalá's *The Flower in the Skull* also features dreams and communication with ancestors.

Zia Summer. New York: Warner Books, 1995. ISBN 0446518433. 386pp.

In this first encounter with Raven, Sonny investigates the gruesome murder of his cousin, Gloria Dominic, who was also his first love. Gloria was married to the power-hungry mayoral candidate Frank Dominic, and her murder takes place in a poisonous swirl of politics, environmental battles and cult religious practices. Can small-time PI Sonny Baca get to the bottom of this and see that justice is done?

> *He didn't like it. A dream like that meant no good. His mother believed dreams predicted the future. There was the grim flash of death in the woman's eyes as she swung the saw at him.* (2)

Subjects: Chicanos; dreams; environment; New Mexico—Albuquerque; private investigators; shamans

Rio Grande Fall. New York: Warner Books, 1996. ISBN 0446518441. 359pp.

Raven is back with a vengeance as he leads Sonny on a merry chase, beginning at the Balloon Festival, where Raven is seen pushing the lead witness against him out of a balloon to her death. The chase leads Sonny through the twisted evil of drug smuggling and murder and into the realm of magic, where he and Raven face off using *naguales*—their animal alter egos—and *brujos.*

> *I studied with curanderas in Río Arriba, learned their prayers and ceremonies. I also listened to their cuentos, the stories they told about men and women who could turn into animals. Some could turn into owls and fly at night. Those brujos, some good and some evil, knew the world of the nagual.* (7)

Subjects: *brujos;* Chicanos; drug trafficking; *naguales;* New Mexico—Albuquerque; private investigators

Shaman Winter. New York: Warner Books, 1999. ISBN 0446523747. 374pp.

Sonny and Raven battle it out in the field of dreams, where Raven attempts to wipe out Sonny's existence by eliminating his female forebears. Wheelchair bound, Sonny's only hope is that old-timer Don Eliseo can teach him to navigate the world of spirits and dreams before it's too late.

> *In the dream I was a Spanish soldier named Andres Vaca. I was with Oñate on the banks of the Río Grande just before he started his march into New Mexico in 1598.* (4)

Subjects: ancestors; Chicanos; dreams; environment; New Mexico—Albuquerque; private investigators; shamans

Jemez Spring. Albuquerque: University of New Mexico Press, 2005. ISBN 0-8263-3684-1. 298pp.

As Sonny investigates the murder of New Mexico's governor, he confronts his old nemesis Raven and uncovers a conspiracy that could have dire environmental consequences. Sorcerers, ghosts, dreams, and mirages confound Sonny's quest.

> *Cupping his hands he held the light, let it shine as deep into his soul as possible. Then he felt what he hadn't felt since the winter solstice.*

> *Something palpable in the light rays, the Lords and Ladies of the Light entering his soul.* (12)

Subjects: Chicanos; dreams; environment; New Mexico—Albuquerque; private investigators; shamans

Braithwaite, Kent (U.S. American, California).

The Wonderland Murders. **Titusville, FL: Four Seasons Publishers, 1999. ISBN 189192933X. 324pp.**

Poet Jesse Ascencio has worn many hats—former FBI agent, ex-congressman, and now he's a private detective. When a woman is murdered at the Wonderland amusement park, Jesse is called into action. But the murders don't stop, and soon Ascencio and his family are in danger too!

> *Disneyland's never come close to such a homicide record. Disneyland's "The Happiest Place on Earth," I quipped. Wonderland merely claims to be "A Park Filled with Thrills."* (63)

Key features: First person narration; strong language

Subjects: amusement parks; Latinos; private investigators; serial murders; Southern California

Similar titles: Both *Shame: A Novel* by Russell and Frost's *Never Fear* take place in California and have the detectives going up against serial murderers.

Corpi, Lucha (Mexican American, Californiana).

Brown Angel Series.

The titles in this series follow Chicana detective Gloria Damasco and her detective agency as they investigate disturbing crimes of murder and rape that often have their beginnings in the chaotic and violent times of the civil rights struggles of the 1970s. Their investigations usually contend with magical and mystical elements in the form of dreams and apparitions.

Eulogy for a Brown Angel. **Houston, TX: Arte Público Press, 1992. ISBN 1558850503. 189pp.**

When she was a young, idealistic activist back in 1970, Gloria Damasco was involved in the Chicano civil rights march. She discovered the defiled body of a child in the chaotic aftermath of that terrible day. Since then this crime has haunted her, bringing her terrible visions until she almost gives up hope—will she ever bring the culprit to justice?

> *As I put the receiver on the hook, I realized that somewhere in that city named after Our Lady of the Angels of Porciúncula, a killer roamed the streets or waited at home for news, the knowledge of his crime still fresh in his consciousness.* (22)

Key features: First person narration; strong language in English and Spanish

Subjects: California—Los Angeles; Chicanas; murder; private investigators; women detectives

Similar titles: *The Ballad of Rocky Ruiz* by Manuel Ramos and White's <u>Ronnie Ventana</u> mystery series feature California, murder, and aspects of the Chicano movement.

Cactus Blood. Houston, Texas; Arte Público Press, 1995. ISBN 1558851-348. 249pp.

> When Gloria Damasco investigates a rape that occurred sixteen years before, she discovers that of the seven people who helped the young woman who was assaulted, one is dead and two are missing. Has their past come back to haunt them? Only Gloria can find out.
>
> > *A minute later, I forced myself to overcome my fear. I got out of the van and started towards my house. Whatever had caused my unwillingness to go in was dispelled by the time I unlocked the front door.* (66)
>
> **Key features:** First person narration; sexual situations; strong language in English and Spanish
>
> **Subjects:** California; Chicanas; murder; private investigators; women detectives
>
> **Similar titles:** The <u>Ronnie Ventana</u> series by White has a Chicana detective investigating a murder in California. Manuel Ramos's *The Ballad of Rocky Ruiz* also includes murder in California.

Black Widow's Wardrobe. Houston, TX: Arte Público Press, 1999. ISBN 1558852883. 193pp.

> After a Day of the Dead procession in San Francisco, Gloria Damasco and her family witness an altercation between the infamous Black Widow and two ghostly *conquistadores* on horseback. During the melee, a woman is kidnapped and the Black Widow is stabbed. Investigating this crime will take Gloria out of the Bay Area to the Sierra de Tepoztlán in Mexico.
>
> > *What previous sins we were all paying for, I wondered. Something was terribly wrong when our future lay lifeless on cold November ground, drowned in a fluid meant only to preserve the dead.* (67)
>
> **Key features:** First person narration; strong language in English and Spanish
>
> **Subjects:** California; espionage; private investigators; reincarnation; women detectives
>
> **Similar titles:** Fowler's <u>Benni Harper Mysteries</u> and Long's *Weave Her Thread with Bones: A Magda Santos Mystery* showcase the skills of women detectives hunting down criminals in California.

Crimson Moon: A Brown Angel Mystery. Houston, TX: Arte Público Press, 2004. ISBN 1558854215. 177pp.

> Justin Escobar, a partner in Brown Angel Investigations, and Dora Saldaña are working on seemingly unrelated cases that hearken back to shady happenings during the Chicano civil rights movement. These past events may bring deadly consequences for friends and family in the twenty-first century.
>
> > *Her breathing quickened and her hands began to shake. She wanted to take her eyes away from the scene, but she could not. All sorts of memories she had managed to bury underneath thirty years of living raged in, unexpectedly and uncontrollably.* (12–13)
>
> **Key features:** Strong language in English and Spanish

Subjects: California; Chicanas; missing persons; private investigators; women detectives

Similar titles: Chicana detectives investigating crimes in California play prominent parts in the <u>Whitney Logan</u> series by Lambert and the <u>Elena Oliverez</u> series by Muller.

Douglas, Laramee.

Dancing at the Shoulder of the Bull. Victoria, TX: Alligator Tree Press, 2002. ISBN 0971343047. 281pp.

John Suarez has quit the police force after a devastating shootout that left an innocent victim. When his former girlfriend's father asks him to investigate a murder that took place in her backyard, he reluctantly agrees to help out. Suarez ventures back to Houston to protect Ranita and her family from a stalker and murderer, who might just be her abusive husband.

> *Getting out of bed, she slid into her robe tying the belt tightly about her waist. The robe gave her a feeling of security, as if it were made of chain mail rather than satin. She stared at the phone for a few moments.* (5)

Subjects: domestic violence; murder; private investigators; Texas—Houston

Similar titles: The <u>Tres Navarre Series</u> by Riordan is also set in Texas.

Garcia, Eric (Cuban American).

<u>Vincent Rubio Series.</u>

The genre-bending premise for this series is that the dinosaurs faked their extinction and are now living among the human population with the help of elaborate disguises. Vincent is a Velociraptor and a private investigator in Los Angeles who must grapple with some dangerous, mystifying cases and his basil addiction, with wise-cracking tongue firmly in cheek and the help of his partner, Watson—a Cranotaur.

Anonymous Rex: A Detective Story. New York: Villard Books, 2000. ISBN 0375503269. 276pp.

Private investigator Vincent Rubio (Velociraptor) has some problems. He never found out who killed his Cranotaur partner. He can't find work or keep it, and he also has a heavy basil-use problem. Vincent finally gets a job to investigate a fire at a dinosaur nightclub that eventually leads him back to New York City and his partner's murderer. If he can stay off the basil, he just might survive.

> *I don't know what died on this bus, but from the tidal wave of scents streaming toward me from the back three rows, I imagine that it was large, that it was ugly, and that it had eaten a good deal of curry in its waning moments of life.* (24)

Key features: First person narration; strong language

Subjects: alternate realities; California—Los Angeles; dinosaurs; humor; New York—New York City; private investigators

Similar titles: *Bone Polisher* by Hallinan features another private investigator in Los Angeles; *The Automatic Detective* by A. Lee Martínez is a similarly humorous genre-bending mystery.

Casual Rex. New York: Villard Books, 2001. ISBN 0679463070. 337pp.

Vincent Rubio's partner, Ernie Watson, was missing in the first <u>Rubio</u> mystery, but he's back in the second. A member of a dinosaur cult is found dead, and now Rubio and Watson are on the case. While investigating this death, they also take on the case of the missing Mussolini.

I turn to find a small, green tail—still wiggling, mind you—poking out from between my partner's lips. I had to hold back my strong desire to cringe.

"That a snake?" I ask.

"Newt," he mumbles, and finishes it off with a hearty swallow. (59)

Subjects: alternate realities; California—Los Angeles; cults; dinosaurs; humor; private investigators

Hot and Sweaty Rex: A Dinosaur Mafia Mystery. New York: Villard Books, 2004. ISBN 0375505237. 336pp.

The crime boss of the Raptor mafia has a job for PI Velociraptor Vincent Rubio. Rubio travels to Miami to find out why a group of Hadrosaurs are moving in on Raptor turf. Rubio will have to hold his tail close, if he wants to keep it.

But what I do know about the dinosaur mafia is enough to make me hope this afternoon's meeting is a quick one: they make all the human mob coalitions—the Italians, the Asians, the Latinos—look like suburban book clubs. (43)

Subjects: alternate realities; dinosaurs; humor; organized crime; private investigators

García-Aguilera, Carolina (Cuban American).

Lupe Solano Mysteries.

Lupe Solano can boast a special connection to Miami's Cuban community as the daughter of wealthy Cuban exiles. Her father keeps a boat ready to return to Cuba in the case of Castro's demise or destitution; other family members include her sister, a nun who embodies the exact opposite of Lupe's hedonistic lifestyle, and a muscleman cousin who shares her office space. The Miami Cuban community's unique culture and problematic situations are usually at the heart of Lupe's cases.

Bloody Waters. New York: G.P. Putnam, 1996. ISBN 039914157X. 274pp.

A baby obtained by illegal means needs a bone marrow transplant. When the seedy lawyer who arranged the adoption refuses to help, private eye Lupe Solano is hired to find the child's real mother. With the clock ticking, Lupe must try to save the child's life, which could also mean saving her own.

> *Alone with the child, I reached out and caressed her cheek. Her eyelids seemed to flutter, just for an instant. I guess I should introduce myself. I felt ridiculous. My name is Lupe Solano. I'm a private investigator. (56)*

Key features: First person narration; strong language in English and Spanish

Subjects: Cuban Americans; Florida—Miami; private investigators; women detectives

Similar titles: *Died Blonde* by Cohen is another novel about women detectives in Florida; the Little Havana Mystery Series by Lantigua also takes place in Miami and features the Cuban American community.

Bloody Shame. New York: G.P. Putnam, 1997. ISBN 0399142568. 275pp.

Lupe is called in to investigate a case of apparent self-defense. At the same time, her best friend dies in a suspicious car accident. Lupe is determined to understand how these two incidents are related.

> *I had no idea how much time had passed before I woke up. I was on my side on a cold concrete floor, and I felt a bit bruised, but I was basically unhurt. This is not to say that I was comfortable. (247)*

Key features: First person narration; strong language in English and Spanish

Subjects: Cuban Americans; Florida—Miami; private investigators; women detectives

Similar titles: The Britt Montero Mysteries by Buchanan are set in Miami and feature Cuban American women with a female detective protagonist; the Little Havana Mystery Series by Lantigua is also set in Miami among the Cuban American community.

Bloody Secrets. New York: G.P. Putnam, 1998. ISBN 0399143866. 274pp.

Cuba's past makes its way to present-day Miami when Lupe Solano takes on the case of a Cuban refugee. This attractive man believes a prominent Cuban couple stole his family's share of their cigar fortune and now wants him dead so they won't have to pony up.

> *Investigations have a lot in common with other important aspects of life-love, war, and sex, for instance. In all of these, timing and preparation are essential for success. (256)*

Key features: First person narration; strong language

Subjects: Cuban Americans; Florida—Miami; private investigators; women detectives

Similar titles: The Britt Montero Mysteries by Buchanan are also set in Miami and feature Cuban American women and women detectives; the Little Havana Mystery Series by Lantigua also takes place in Miami among the Cuban American community.

A Miracle in Paradise. New York: Avon Twilight, 1999. ISBN 0380977796. 277pp.

A sister of the Order of the Illumination of the Sacred Virgin goes missing, and a body is found floating in Buscayne Bay. Private eye Lupe Solano is on the case, but it might take a miracle to solve this one.

> *"Well, this is Catholic business," Lourdes said. "I think in this instance the end justifies the means. If there was an Olympic competition for rationalization, my sisters and I would have been perennial medal contenders." (41)*

Key features: First person narration; strong language in English and Spanish

Subjects: Cuban Americans; nuns; private investigators; women detectives

Similar titles: The <u>Britt Montero Mysteries</u> by Buchanan are also set in Miami and feature Cuban American women and women detectives; the <u>Little Havana Mystery Series</u> by Lantigua also takes place in Miami among the Cuban American community.

Havana Heat: A Lupe Solano Mystery. New York: William Morrow, 2000. ISBN 038097780X. 358pp.

Private eye Lupe Solano figures attending the wedding of her niece is just a good excuse to get dressed up; she's not expecting to run into her next case. At the wedding she meets Aunt Luchi and her missing tapestry. A couple of murders, a trip to Havana . . . all in a day's work for Lupe.

> *Maybe we did need the ass-reduction machine, I thought I was seeing more of his ass than anyone should, except maybe after dinner and drinks. I was just about convinced we needed a lavado.* (144)

Key features: First person narration; strong language

Subjects: Cuba—Havana; Cuban Americans; private investigators; women detectives

Similar titles: The <u>Little Havana Mystery Series</u> by Lantigua is also set in Miami among the Cuban American community.

Bitter Sugar. New York: William Morrow, 2001. ISBN 0380977818. 315pp.

It's a first for Lupe Solano: her father needs her services as a private investigator. When a shady character, Alexander Suarez, is murdered, his uncle, one of Papi's best friends, is accused. Lupe dodges bullets to prove Tío Ramón's innocence.

> *And then the world turned all red. I felt my knees buckle, and my head exploding. Just before I blacked out, instinct compelled me to throw my mug of scorching coffee at whoever or whatever had just attacked me.* (175)

Key features: First person narration; strong language

Subjects: Cuban Americans; Florida; murder; private investigators; women detectives

Similar titles: The <u>Little Havana Mystery Series</u> by Lantigua is also set in Miami among the Cuban American community.

Grady, P. J. (New Mexican).

Momento Mori Series.

Matty Madrid, a true daughter of the desert, does her sleuthing in Santa Fe, New Mexico. A tough *mujer*, she fearlessly investigates corruption and murder, from the state pen to the state capital.

Maximum Insecurity: A Matty Madrid Mystery. New York: Memento Mori Mystery, 1999. ISBN 0966107241. 189pp.

While visiting Mingo, her ex, in prison, Matty finds out that a suspicious death has taken place there. Mingo compels Matty to investigate the death. Even though Mingo walked out on her, how can Matty say no?

> *Mingo frowned. Most killers kill for love or money. That he could understand. He could see himself wasting somebody for a million bucks. He wasn't so sure he'd do it for a woman.* (58)

Key features: First person narration; strong language in English and Spanish

Subjects: murder; New Mexico—Santa Fe; prison; private investigators; single mothers; women detectives

Similar titles: The <u>Ella Clah</u> series by Thurlo and Thurlo is also about women detectives investigating murder in New Mexico.

Awards: Nominated for a Shamus Award, 2000

Deadly Sin. New York: Memento Mori Mystery, 2001. ISBN 097050490X. 223pp.

Private investigator Matty Madrid takes on the case of the missing San Miguel statue. This investigation is put on hold when a murdered woman is found in that same church.

> *"You know what's in those letters, father. ¿Que no?"*
>
> *He nodded, but he didn't answer.*
>
> *"Father, there's not a damn thing I can do—?"*
>
> *"Marta!"*
>
> *"¡On chite! I'm sorry, but you gotta tell me if it's true. You and Dionne—you lovers?"* (46)

Key features: First person narration; strong language and sexual situations

Subjects: murder; New Mexico—Santa Fe; private investigators; single mothers; women detectives

Similar titles: *Digging Up Mama: A Samantha Adams Mystery* by Shankman is also set in Santa Fe, New Mexico, and deals with a woman detective investigating a murder.

Lantigua, John (Cubano Riqueño; Nuyorican).

Little Havana Mystery Series.

Cuban American private eye Willie Cuesta lives and works (and drinks) in Miami's Little Havana neighborhood, where his cases originate. These cases take him from the seedy alleys and the glitzy nightclubs to the dark corners and desperation of the human soul.

Player's Vendetta. New York: Signet, 1999. ISBN 0451198468. 261pp.

Willie is recruited by a beautiful woman to find her missing boyfriend. When he agrees, he soon finds out there is more to this case than meets the eye. The *novio* is also looking for someone, and not necessarily to give him an *abrazo*, unless it's the embrace of death.

> *Willie was six feet tall and thin, so that the sides of the hammock curled over him like a cocoon. At the moment, he was dressed in cream-colored linen pants and a long green shirt imprinted with large crimson palm trees. His skin was olive,*

gone a golden brown, because of the Miami sun. (www.amazon.com/gp/reader/0451198468/ref= sib_dp_pt#reader-link)

Subjects: Cuban Americans; Florida—Miami; missing persons; private investigators

Similar titles: The <u>Lupe Solano Mysteries</u> by García-Aguilera are also set in Miami among the Cuban community.

The Ultimate Havana. New York: Signet, 2001. ISBN 0451202783. 312pp.

Willie Cuesta is asked by an old friend to find Carlos Espada, a famous Cuban cigar maker's son. During his investigation, he uncovers a counterfeit Cuban cigar network and becomes embroiled in a dangerous rivalry between two tobacco companies. As Willie tries to rescue Espada, ensuing events lead all the players to the Dominican Republic.

> *Rui was a big, round-bellied Cuban man who wore his chestnut hair in a pompadour, so that it resembled the red coxcombs of his fighting birds. He was also renowned for his expertise with a straight razor, which he kept as keen as the blades that he tied to the claws of his roosters.* (5)

Subjects: cigar industry; Cuban Americans; Dominican Republic; Florida—Miami; private investigators

Similar titles: The <u>Lupe Solano Mysteries</u> by García-Aguilera are also set in Miami among the Cuban community. See especially *Bloody Secrets*, which is also about lethal rivalry in the cigar business.

The Lady from Buenos Aires: A Willie Cuesta Mystery. Houston, TX: Arte Público Press, 2007. ISBN 3234503322808. 214pp.

Willie Cuesta is hired by Fiona Bonaventura, who is certain her niece is in Miami, adopted by the Argentine torturer who murdered her sister. It's been twenty years, though, and her niece doesn't have a clue about her true family's fate.

> *In Miami, given the history of Latin America over the past fifty years and all the people who had come running for their lives, you never knew who you were looking at. Was the old guy with the lunch pail a former general, now working as a janitor?* (16)

Subjects: Argentina—Dirty War; Cuban Americans; Florida—Miami; kidnapping; private investigators; torture

Similar titles: *When Darkness Falls* by Grippando is another novel about Argentina's Dirty War resonating in Miami; the <u>Lupe Solana Mysteries</u> by García-Aguilera are also set in Miami among the Cuban community.

Riordan, Rick (U.S. American, Texas).

<u>Tres Navarre Series.</u>

Tres Navarre holds a PhD in English literature. He makes his living, however, by working as a private investigator in San Antonio, Texas, with a special talent for tai chi and tending bar.

🎋 *Big Red Tequila.* New York: Bantam Books, 1997. ISBN 0553576445. 372pp.

Tres Navarre returns to San Antonio after a ten-year absence to confront the unsolved murder of his father. The mafia, an old girlfriend, and a Thunderbird are all in Tres's way as he tries to find his father's killer.

> *If John Lennon had been born Hispanic and then overfed on buttered gorditas, he would've looked like Ralph. His hair was long and tangled, parted in the middle and his eyes were invisible behind the sheen of his thick round glasses.* (78)

Key features: First person narration; strong language in English and Spanish.

Subjects: murder; private investigators; Texas—San Antonio

Similar titles: *Home Is Where the Murder Is* by Rogers is another novel about murder in San Antonio, Texas.

Awards: Shamus Award, 1998

🎋 *The Widower's Two-Step.* New York: Bantam Books, 1998. ISBN 0553576453. 383pp.

The closer Tres Navarre is to getting his PI license, the more trouble he seems to find. This time a fiddle player is shot while Tres is supposed to be on the lookout for a thief. Add an up-and-coming singer and her two wannabe managers, and Tres has the perfect recipe for trouble.

> *I grabbed Cam Compton by his frizzy blond hair, yanked him back from Miranda, and slammed his head into a beer keg. I'm not sure whether the lovely metallic sound came from the keg or Cam's skull, but it stopped him from pestering Miranda pretty effectively.* (100)

Key features: First person narration; strong language

Subjects: country musicians; murder; private investigators; Texas

Similar titles: *Sound of Murder* by Matthews and *Music to Die For* by Nehring are other novels about murder and country musicians.

Awards: Winner of the Edgar Allan Poe Award for Best Paperback Original, 1998

The Last King of Texas. New York: Bantam Books, 2000. ISBN 0553801562. 320pp.

A murder puts PI/PhD Tres Navarre in a teaching position at the University of Texas at San Antonio. It should be a piece of cake for Tres to teach the dead professor's class and move on, but nothing is very easy for Tres as more murders ensue, putting him in mortal danger.

> *It was a tai chi upper cut, only slightly less forceful than a pile driver. By the time I required the feeling in my hand, Kelsey was doubled over, contemplating the pool his lunch had made in the dirt.* (45)

Key features: First person narration; strong language

Subjects: murder; private investigators; Texas—San Antonio; University of Texas

Similar titles: *Death on the Riverwalk: A Henrie O Mystery* by Carolyn Hart is another murder mystery set in San Antonio, Texas.

The Devil Went Down to Austin. New York: Bantam Books, 2001. ISBN 0553110977. 319pp.

Accepting a teaching job at the University of Texas at Austin means English professor/private investigator Tres Navarre has to stay with his Jimmy Buffet–loving older brother Garrett. All is relatively well until Garrett's business partner is shot, and Garrett is suspect number 1.

> *The scary thing was that despite everything I suspected about her collaborating with Peña, despite the fact that she was quite possibly the worst thing that ever happened to my brother with the exception of the northbound train— I found myself wanting to help her.* (178)

Key features: First person narration; strong language

Subjects: college professors; murder; private investigators; Texas—Austin

Similar titles: *Lost in Austin: A Tony Kozol Mystery* by Ripley and the <u>Tony Boudreaux</u> series by Conwell are also about murder in Austin, Texas.

Southtown: A Novel of Suspense. New York: Bantam Books, 2004. ISBN 0553801848. 260pp.

Tres Navarre is following convicted killer Will "the Ghost" Stirman after the Ghost escapes from prison. Tracking the Ghost means Navarre has to step over a lot of bodies Stirman has left behind. Ultimately, Tres will have to travel to San Antonio's Southtown to find the answers he needs.

> *I didn't mind bounty-hunting Dimebox Ortiz. What I minded were his cousins Lalu and Kiko, who weighed three-fifty a piece, smoked angel dust to improve their IQ, and kept handgrenades in a Fiestaware bowl on their coffee table the way some people kept wax apples.* (18)

Key features: First person narration; strong language

Subjects: college professors; fugitives; private investigators; Texas—San Antonio

Similar titles: The <u>Homer Kelly</u> series by Langton and the <u>Professor Simon Shaw</u> series by Shaber also feature college teachers as private investigators.

Mission Road. New York: Bantam Books, 2005. ISBN 0553801856. 293pp.

Things can't get much worse for PI Tres Navarre when his old friend Ralph Arguello shows up at his home covered in blood. Ralph is wanted for the murder of his wife, who happens to have been a SAPD detective about to arrest her husband on a murder charge. Tres and Ralph go on the lam, trying to stay alive long enough to prove Ralph's innocence.

> *Monday morning I got a paying client. Wednesday afternoon I killed him. Friday evening I buried him. The Tres Navarre Detective Agency is a full-service operation. Did I mention that?* (13)

Key features: First person narration; strong language

Subjects: fugitives; murder; policewomen; private investigators; Texas—San Antonio

Similar titles: The <u>Hair-Raising Series</u> by Bradley is also set in San Antonio, Texas.

Rebel Island. New York: Bantam Books, 2007. ISBN 0553804235. 339pp.

Tres swears off the private eye business and takes his new bride to Rebel Island for a nostalgic trip to pleasant childhood memories and a vacation before their baby arrives. Unfortunately, dead bodies start piling up, and Tres finds it's not so easy to escape the business or the secrets from his past. Can he solve the mystery before the hurricane hits Rebel Island?

> He found the graves with no effort: one large, two small, lined up cozily on a knoll, enjoying the million-dollar view. Like they come to watch fireworks, he thought. (7)

Key features: First person narration; strong language

Subjects: honeymoons; murder; private investigators; Texas—San Antonio

Similar titles: The <u>Hair-Raising Series</u> by Bradley is also set in San Antonio, Texas.

Rodriguez, Abraham (Nuyorican).

South by South Bronx. **New York: Akashic Books, 2008. ISBN 9781933354569. 292pp.**

Detective Sanchez must find Spook for the CIA. The drug dealer has agreed to launder money for a terrorist group and has disappeared with it. How did the CIA agent's blonde assistant end up in Alex, an artist's, apartment? And what does poet Anne Sexton have to do with it all?

> She was in a strange bathroom doing her laundry. It made her laugh, not laugh, some sort of spasm. Like choking. She squeezed her burning eyes shut. The wave of nausea almost keeled her over. She heard shattering glass, the thud of bullets. (21)

Key features: Multiple narrative perspectives; sexual situations; strong language

Subjects: detectives; drug trafficking; New York—New York City—Bronx; terrorists

Similar titles: Michele Martinez's <u>Melanie Vargas Series</u> also features the Nuyorican community and drug trafficking.

Sanchez, Thomas (Californiano).

King Bongo: A Novel of Havana. **New York: Alfred A. Knopf, 2003. ISBN 0679406964. 309pp.**

Cuban American private eye King Bongo is present when a bomb goes off at the Tropicana Club in Havana in 1957. After the explosion King Bongo finds his sister has vanished. He will see all that Havana has to offer as he searches for the bombers and his sister.

> It was Bongo's job to be skeptical. He was an insurance investigator, and for the right price, a private dick. Stenciled in bold black letters on the frosted glass of his office door was KBII, which stood for "King Bong Insurance and Investigations. (52–53)

Key features: Sexual situations

Subjects: Cuba—Havana; historical fiction; murder; private investigators

Similar titles: *Havana: An Earl Swagger Novel* by Hunter and *Havana World Series* by Latour are other historical mysteries set in Havana.

Satterthwait, Walter (New Mexican).

Joshua Croft Series.

Enchanting Santa Fe, New Mexico, is home to illustrious families, hippies, culture vultures, and criminals. Rita Mondragon's private investigation agency assigns the toughest cases to her best detective and main squeeze, Joshua Croft.

Key features: First person narration; some sexual situations

Subjects: New Mexico—Santa Fe; private investigators

Similar titles: The Sonny Baca Mysteries by Anaya are also set in New Mexico.

Wall of Glass. New York: St. Martin's Press, 1987. ISBN 0312015305. 246pp.

> Joshua and Rita are on the trail of a missing diamond necklace, which takes them from the homes of the wealthy to the hovels of the desperate.

At Ease with the Dead. New York: St. Martin's Press, 1990. ISBN 0312042604. 237pp.

> This case takes Joshua to remote areas of the Navajo reservation and out to El Paso as he searches for the lost remains of a Navajo leader to return to their proper burial site.

A Flower in the Desert. New York: St. Martin's Press, 1992 ISBN 0312077513. 248pp.

> TV star Roy Alonzo hires Joshua to clear his name after his ex-wife Melissa accuses him of sexually abusing their daughter.

The Hanged Man. New York: St. Martin's Press, 1993. ISBN 0312098278. 258pp.

> Croft is surrounded by eccentrics as he investigates murder at a psychic convention.

Accustomed to the Dark. New York: St. Martin's Press, 1996. ISBN 0312145357. 245pp.

> Joshua Croft is spurred into action when his business partner and lover, Rita Mondragon, is shot by a stalker. His pursuit of this lunatic takes him far from home in New Mexico to Florida, to Colorado, and to Kansas. Joshua finds himself collaborating with some quirky characters before he can confront his, and Rita's, nemesis.

> > *Striding toward me between the cars was Hector Ramirez, a friend, a sergeant in the Santa Fe police department. He was a body builder, thick and powerful, but he always moved as lightly on his feet as a ballerina.* (6)

Taibo, Paco Ignacio, II (Mexican).

Hector Belascoarán Shayne Mystery Series.

Hector has given up his career as an engineer to devote himself to independent sleuthing in Mexico City. He loves Coca-Cola and cigarettes. These mysteries are intricate, tightly plotted, and literary. (This list begins with number 2 in the series; number 1, *Días de combate* [1970], has not been translated into English.) On a side note, Taibo organizes the *Semana Negra* (Noir Week) in Gijón, Spain every year.

Subjects: ghosts; human trafficking; Mexicans; Mexico—Mexico City; missing persons; murder; private investigators

Similar titles: *Blood Sacrifice: A Mystery of the Yucatan* by Alexander also features a Mexican detective.

An Easy Thing. (*Cosa fácil*, 1977). Translated by William I. Neuman. New York: Viking, 1990. ISBN 0670824623. 230pp.

> Hector has taken on three difficult cases—to search for the mythical hero Emiliano Zapata, to find the kidnapped daughter of a porn star, and to investigate murder at a steel plant.

> > *It was a high-class dive located inside the old feudal city of Azcapotzalco, in what had once been the outskirts of Mexico City, but was now just another link in an endless chain of industrial zones, where the picturesque remains of haciendas, graveyards, and village churches stood in the shadow of a monstrous oil refinery, the pride of fifties technology. (3)*

Some Clouds. (*Algunas nubes*, 1980). Translated by William I. Neuman. New York: Viking, 1992. ISBN 067083825X. 163pp.

> Hector agrees to help out his sister's friend Anita, who has been brutally beaten and raped after inheriting a large sum of money from her murdered husband.

> > *So why get involved? To protect Anita, to get her out of the mess she was in, to get her the hell away from all that trash. For the first time in a long time his curiosity wasn't there to push him along. He didn't feel that thirst for vengeance either, for vengeance in the name of the dead, in the name of the living, for the sake of what he thought this country ought to be. (52)*

No Happy Ending. (*No habrá final feliz*, 1989). Translated by William I. Neuman. New York: Mysterious Press, 1993. ISBN 0892965177. 175pp.

> This time Hector becomes a target when he refuses to be frightened off the case of a dead man. He finds the corpse dressed as a Roman soldier and placed in his bathroom as a warning along with the photo of another dead man and an airplane ticket to New York City.

Frontera Dreams. (*Sueños de frontera*, 1990). Translated by Bill Verner. El Paso, TX: Cinco Puntos Press, 2002. ISBN 093831758X. 120pp.

> The love of Héctor Belascoarán Shayne's childhood has disappeared. Hector searches for her along the U.S.–Mexican border, where he wrestles with *narcotraficantes* and Pancho Villa's ghost.

> > *Hector didn't think himself a good judge in the area of nations and nationalism. A guy who frequently failed to recognize himself when he saw his image in the mirror wasn't a good judge of anything. (30)*

Return to the Same City. (*Regreso a la misma ciudad y bajo la lluvia*, 1992). Translated by Laura Dail. New York: Warner Books, 1996. ISBN 0892965908. 178pp.

> Héctor is on the case of a killer in white patent leather shoes who murdered a woman, but discovers he isn't the only one looking for the killer. The tables soon turn, and Héctor, the hunter, finds himself being hunted.

> > *"Hello, I am Dick," he stammered, in English. "I'm not," said Héctor, who had always wanted to start a dialogue that way, with the absolute worst timing, as in every crime movie he'd ever seen.* (57)

Taibo, Paco Ignacio, II, and Subcomandante Marcos.

The Uncomfortable Dead: What's Missing Is Missing. (***Muertos incómodos: falta lo que falta***, 2005). **Translated by Carlos Lopez. New York: Akashic Books, 2006. ISBN 1933354070. 268pp.**

> In this innovative novel, Héctor partners with a private investigator from Chiapas, Elias Contreras, to find a man murdered in the midst of the Zapatista Revolution. They follow the trail of cryptic messages the murdered man left on answering machines that lead them on a merry chase all over Mexico and through the political intrigue of the day.

> > *Hell, I'd be sixty-one now, but I ain't, cause I'm dead, which means I'm deceased. I first met Sup Marcos back in 1992, when we voted to go to war.* (16)

> **Key features:** First person narration, by two narrators, one of whom is deceased

> **Subjects:** allegory; Chiapas; Mexico—Mexico City; murder; politics; Zapatistas

> **Similar titles:** *Death in the Andes* by Vargas Llosa has a similarly unconventional structure and employs political allegory.

Wishnia, K. J. A. (U.S. American, East Coast).

Filomena Buscarsela Series.

> These novels are written in a noir style, with a tough female cop born in Ecuador but raised on the streets of New York City. Filomena's sense of justice forces her to leave the force to pursue her own brand of fighting crime, as she struggles to raise her daughter. These are gritty novels spiced with cynical humor.

> 🌳 ***23 Shades of Black.*** New York: Signet, 1998. ISBN 0451197488. 304pp.

> > Filomena is still on the police force, aspiring to be a detective, when she and her partner are sent to investigate a leak of toxic chemicals that ultimately and suspiciously kills a pesky environmentalist.

> > > *I was riding around with my partner, Bernie, a Cabeza de chorlito so cerebrally-challenged he couldn't see a hole in a forty-foot ladder without the aid of a telescope and a detailed map, when we both spot what looks like a typical Saturday night street fight.* (www.kjawishnia.com/23_Shades.htm)

> > **Awards:** Edgar Award finalist, 1998

Soft Money. New York: Dutton Books, 1999. ISBN 0525945016. 226pp.

Even though she has left the New York police department, Filomena Buscarsela cannot sit idly by when the owner of a local bodega is killed. She teams up with a rookie cop to find those responsible, but making her way through the city's underbelly might prove more than she can handle.

> *The EPA is hidden in the monolithic labyrinth of 26 Federal Plaza. There's a large, featureless object that somebody apparently thinks is a sculpture blocking half the open space out front. I'm not sure, but I think it's that big slab of concrete The Who were pissing on for the cover of Who's Next.* (57)

Key features: First person narration; strong language in English and Spanish; sexual situations

Subjects: Ecuadorian Americans; murder; New York—New York City; single mothers; women detectives

Similar titles: *It's Raining Men* by Rand also features a single mother working as a detective investigating murder in New York; Michele Martinez's <u>Melanie Vargas Series</u> features a single mom who is also a prosecutor in New York City and constantly finds herself investigating murders.

The Glass Factory. New York: Dutton Books, 2000. ISBN 0525945458. 215pp.

Although busy taking care of her daughter and enjoying a new romance, Filomena does find time to investigate reports that a glass factory in a shady area of Long Island is dumping toxic materials into the local water supply. As usual, murder must make an appearance.

> *Wai-Wai says she knows the way. It is tempting to hope this is true, because right now it's like a scene from a grade-C horror-slasher movie: Ooh, we're lost. Look there's a house. Yes. Even the dialogue is trite. So I'll skip it and get to the good part.* (143)

Key features: First person narration; strong language in English and Spanish; sexual situations

Subjects: corruption; Ecuadorian Americans; environmentalism; murder; politicians; pollution; women detectives

Similar titles: *Red Sky in Mourning* by Rushford also features a woman detective investigating murder and pollution.

Red House. New York: St. Martin's Minotaur, 2001. ISBN 031228182X. 261pp.

Filomena has worked many jobs to support her young daughter, and now she is trying her hand at PI work. Will balancing the case of a missing illegal immigrant with her responsibilities to the neighborhood be more than Filomena can handle?

> *Tuesday morning, 9 a.m. Eastern Standard time, finds me waiting in a police cage that still smells of the cigars the detectives used to smoke here until the late 1980s. Ah yes, the days when you could smoke in the interrogation room. That takes me back to the late Ice Age.* (105)

Key features: First person narration; strong language in English and Spanish; sexual situations

Subjects: Ecuadorian Americans; New York—New York City; private investigators; single mothers; undocumented workers

Similar titles: *Stealing for a Living: An Emma Price Mystery* by Rand also has a single mother detective working and living in New York.

Blood Lake. New York: St. Martin's Minotaur, 2002. ISBN 0312281862. 324pp.

New York City PI Filomena Buscarsela and her daughter return to Filomena's home country of Ecuador. The homecoming is bitter-sweet when a priest who helped Fil find refuge in America is murdered. Finding the killer won't even-up her debt to the priest, but it will help her feel better.

> *The censer swings. The smoke rises. Voices rise, chanting the requiem in Latin, the words drifting upwards like sparks from a funeral pyre. I sit in the shadow of St. Anthony, praying for help finding my padre's killers.* (149)

Key features: First person narration; strong language in English and Spanish; sexual situations

Subjects: Ecuador; Ecuadorian Americans; murder; private investigators; single mothers; women detectives

Similar titles: *Dead Letter* by Waterhouse also features a single mother working as a detective investigating a murder.

Police Procedurals

The novels in this section feature police detectives at work. These men and women, working alone or in teams, strive to see justice done within the confines of departmental regulations. Locales range from exotic Rio de Janeiro in Brazil to the Bay Area in California, and from the unique cultural duality of the U.S.–Mexico border region to the urbane sophistication of Barcelona in Spain, with side trips to the different Caribbean experiences in Havana and Puerto Rico. The crime scenes range from high-level conspiracy at the Vatican to the ugly world of dog fighting. Most of the novels are graphic and violent; some delve into the mystical realm of Santería.

Correa, Arnaldo (Cuban).

Cold Havana Ground. New York: Akashic Books, 2003. ISBN 1-888451-52-1. 317pp.

The seemingly innocuous case of a corpse stolen from the Chinese cemetery in Havana takes on unexpected significance, leading to a baffling case involving Santería.

> *He raised his cup to drink, then visibly repressed an urge to retch, repelled by the sweet, pungent aroma of the* aguardiente *mixed with all the other odors of the place: the rancid stench emerging from the* nganga *recently sprinkled with blood from two roosters and a black goat.* (6)

Key features: Glossary

Subjects: Chinese Cubans; Cuba—Havana; Santería; suspense

Similar titles: *Dead of Night* by Abella, *Shangó* by Curtis, and *Tropic of Night* by Gruber are other novels about Santería, magic, and murder.

Curtis, James Roberto (Cuban American; Floridian).

Shangó. **Houston, TX: Arte Público Press, 1996. ISBN 1-55885-096-1. 197pp.**
Lieutenant Gutierrez investigates murders that seem related to Santería rituals with the help of Miguel, a Cuban American college student estranged from the culture of his native Cuba, and Professor Krajewski, professor of anthropology and specialist in Santería.

> *Supine at the base of the altar was the body of a man, naked from the waist up, a garland of red carnations and white chrysanthemums around his neck, a double-bladed ax buried in his chest.* (9)

Subjects: college professors; college students; Cuban Americans; murder; Santería

Similar titles: *Dead of Night* by Abella, *Cold Havana Ground* by Correa, and *Tropic of Night* by Gruber are other novels that feature Santería, magic, and murder.

Daniel, David (U.S. American).

White Rabbit. **New York: St. Martin's Minotaur, 2003. ISBN 0312304293. 320pp.**
Detective John Sparrow, still grieving the death of his wife, and handsome inspector Pete Sandoval join forces with flower girl alternative journalist Amy Cole, to find a ruthless killer who preys on the free spirits hanging around 1960s San Francisco and disfigures their corpses in a gruesome way.

> *Later, resuscitated with night and neon (and drugs, Sparrow had little doubt) the district would spark to life again. At the moment he didn't have to remind himself there was death to deal with.* (22)

Subjects: California—San Francisco—Haight Ashbury; hippies; police; reporters; serial killers

Similar titles: *The Investigation* by Saer is also about serial killers; *I'll Be Watching You* and *Maximum Security* by Montoya also find their sleuths investigating serial killers in California.

Diez, Rolo (Argentinian).

Tequila Blue. **Translated by Nick Caistor. London: Bitter Lemon Press, 2004. ISBN 1904738044. 168pp.**
Carlos "Carlito" Hernandez, a cop with a plan, is on the take. While conducting his illicit activities, he also has to find the time to investigate the murder of a man found in a seedy motel. This murder is definitely putting a cramp in Carlito's lifestyle.

> *I've no idea how many glasses the barman served me, but I know he must have been a magician because all of a sudden he made Madonna appear at my table.* (102)

Key features: First person narration; strong language; sexual situations

Subjects: Mexico—Mexico City; murder; police corruption; police procedural

Similar titles: *Hidden River* by McKinty is another novel about police corruption and murder; *Juarez Justice* by Trolley deals with a similar theme set in Mexico.

Garcia-Roza, Luiz Alfredo (Brazilian).

Inspector Espinosa Series.

Inspector Espinosa loves literature and the ladies. He stands out from the other cops on the corrupt police force in Rio de Janeiro for being a classy guy who won't take a bribe.

The Silence of the Rain. (*O silêncio da chuva*, 1997). Translated by Benjamin Moser. New York: Henry Holt, 2002. ISBN 0805068899. 261pp.

An executive is found dead in his car, shot in the head. It looks like a robbery/murder, and Inspector Espinosa is brought in on the case. One million dollars, a missing secretary, and corrupt fellow police officers are just a few of the things Espinosa must contend with.

> *The professor told me that on Thursday he was with you until six o'clock and that at nine you went to a Japanese restaurant. Chinese. Sure Chinese. I don't care about the restaurant's nationality, I'm just looking for times and a few subjective details.* (59)

Key features: Strong language; sexual situations

Subjects: Brazil—Rio de Janeiro; detectives; murder; police procedural

Similar titles: *Done for a Dime* by Corbett is a similar police procedural in which the detective investigates a robbery/murder.

December Heat. (*Achado e perdidos*, 1998). Translated by Benjamin Moser. New York: Henry Holt, 2003. ISBN 0805068902. 273pp.

Investigating the murder of an old friend's girlfriend looks like an easy assignment at first glance, but when other people turn up dead, Inspector Espinosa realizes there is more at stake here . . . maybe even his heart.

> *Until seconds earlier, Espinosa had thought of the boy like a cloud of uncertain density but clear form, while Kika looked like a strike of lightning in the middle of the night, fascinating and disturbing.* (69)

Key features: Strong language; sexual situations

Subjects: Brazil—Rio de Janeiro; murder; police detectives

Similar titles: *Mission Road* by Riordan shares a similar plot about the murder of the detective's friend's spouse.

Southwesterly Wind. (*Vento sudoeste*, 1999). Translated by Benjamin Moser. New York: Henry Holt, 2004. ISBN 0805068910. 242pp.

The blowing of the southwesterly wind brings unwelcome change to Inspector Espinosa. A young man confronts Espinosa, saying a psychic told him he would commit murder, and the man is convinced this prediction has come true. Coupled with more violent murders, Espinosa makes his way down a dark and treacherous path.

> *He felt like a lone wolf, walking with his eyes to the ground, his body hunched over, his shoulders rounded. He was threatened from every side, but he himself was also a threat. (78)*

Key features: Strong language; sexual situations

Subjects: Brazil—Rio de Janeiro; mental illness; murder; police detectives; psychics

Similar titles: *Whisper of Evil* by Hooper is another novel about psychics and murder.

A Window in Copacabana. (*Uma janela em Copacabana*, 2001). Translated by Benjamin Moser. New York: Henry Holt, 2005. ISBN 0805074384. ISBN13: 978080507438. 243pp.

Even though they weren't good cops, three dead policemen are three too many for the inspector. Add one dead woman and one obsessed woman, and that equals big trouble for Espinosa.

> *The light from the building lit him from behind, and the lamp lit him from above. For someone who felt that he was being followed and watched, he thought that the only thing missing was a sign around his neck with his name written in fluorescent ink. (144)*

Key features: Strong language; sexual situations

Subjects: Brazil—Rio de Janeiro; murder; police detectives

Pursuit. (*Perseguido*, 2003). Translated by Benjamin Moser. New York: Henry Holt, 2006. ISBN 9780805074390. 244pp.

A psychiatrist is worried that a patient is stalking him. Soon after, the patient and the psychiatrist's daughter go missing. Espinosa is called in to investigate, but when the patient is found dead, he must wade through a web of lies.

> *I'm not a warrior, I'm a cop; I'm not a hero, I'm a public employee; and I'm no philosopher, despite my name. (168)*

Key features: Strong language; sexual situations

Subjects: Brazil—Rio de Janeiro; missing persons; police detectives; psychiatrists; stalkers

Similar titles: *The Interview Room* by Anscombe also features psychiatrists and stalkers.

Giménez-Bartlett, Alicia (Spanish).

Petra Delicado Mysteries.

When Barcelona's finest run into a staffing shortage, they ask police librarian and former lawyer Petra Delicado to work with veteran Fermín Garzón. Against all expectations, they create a formidable team. Petra is full of vim and vigor and wrestling with a chaotic personal life; Fermín is cynical, stodgy, and often discomfited by Petra's willingness to bend the rules, but his instincts are razor sharp.

Death Rites. (*Ritos de muerte*, 1996). Translated by Jonathan Dunne. New York: Europa Editions, 2008. ISBN 9781933372549. 300pp.

Barcelona inspectors Petra and Fermín are paired for the first time, thanks to a staff shortage, to investigate a serial rapist who brands his victims with a strange symbol. Petra is coming off a long period of being relegated to desk duty and is hungry to prove herself. This will be difficult because she must deal with this challenging case and her pesky ex-husbands at the same time, while her superiors, the press, and the victim's relatives are pressuring to have her taken off the case. (This title is number 1 in the series, although it was the last one translated into English.)

> *Though they may well have been able to solve the mystery of the ten little Indians, they were forgetting that certain rules, certain forms, had to be respected. I'd never caught a male inspector phoning home out of concern for his children's gastronomy.* (14)

Key features: First person narration

Subjects: rape; Spain—Barcelona; women detectives

Similar titles: *White Rabbit* by David Daniel features a similar serial criminal.

Dog Day. (*Día de perros,* 1997). Translated by Nicholas Caistor. New York: Europa Editions, 2006. ISBN 1933372141. 311pp.

Police inspector Petra Delicado and partner Fermín Garzón go deep into the unsavory world of dog fighting when an unidentified man is found beaten to death.

> *Every time I come across one of those flat stone slabs of Charles the Fifth, the lovers of Teruel, or the Duke of Alba, a shudder of awe sends a shiver down my spine. But this prone figure had neither a sense of nobility nor the charisma of a national hero about him. He looked more like a small, mangled bird or a run-over cat.* (14)

Key features: First person narration

Subjects: dog fighting; murder; Spain—Barcelona; women detectives

Similar titles: *Death of a Saint Maker* by Allana Martin also deals with a mystery ostensibly about a dog attack.

Prime Time Suspect. (*Muertos de papel,* 2000). Translated by Nicholas Caistor. New York: Europa Editions, 2007. ISBN 9781933372310. 299pp.

When a corrupt, gossip-mongering TV personality with many enemies is murdered, Petra and Fermín are assigned to the case. It starts looking grim for more than one guilty party as the bodies continue piling up.

> *A case in which image, appearance, and influence on other people, as well as the reputation of a celebrity, were at the heart of the affair. A murder that raised more dust than a Touareg in the desert.* (12)

Key features: First person narration

Subjects: murder; Spain—Barcelona; television personalities; women detectives

Similar titles: *Cover-up* by Michele Martinez is another mystery featuring a female sleuth investigating a TV personality's murder.

Gómez-Jurado, Juan (Spanish).

God's Spy. (*El espía de Dios,* 2006). Translated by James Graham. New York: Dutton, 2007. ISBN 9780525949947. 358pp.

Around the time following Pope John Paul II's death, Paola Dicanti is called in to the Vatican to investigate a cardinal's brutal murder. She joins forces with Father Anthony Fowler, an American priest who has been investigating priests accused of sex abuse. They find themselves in the middle of a disturbing conspiracy and they are in danger of encountering the same fate as previous victims—tortured, mutilated, and murdered.

> *Paola looked worriedly out over the scene. The people had spent all night in line, but those who might have seen something were already far away. The pilgrims glanced in passing at the discreet pair of carabinieri standing at the entrance to the church.* (13)

Subjects: Catholic Church; conspiracies; murder; sexual abuse; Vatican City

Similar titles: *The Secret Supper* by Sierra and *Valley of Bones* by Gruber are other mysteries that feature the Catholic Church, mysticism, and murder.

Gruber, Michael (U.S. American).

Jimmy Paz Series.

Unlike Sonny Baca, who embraces the spiritualism and mysticism inherent to his heritage, Jimmy Paz, a hard-nosed police detective, is uncomfortable with the mystical African side of his Cuban heritage. But these cases force him to open up that side of himself and work with the strange forces of Santería.

Tropic of Night. New York: HarperCollins, 2003. ISBN 0060509546. 419pp.

A gruesome murder takes police detective Jimmy Paz into a terrifying world of African magic. Anthropologist Jane Doe is hiding out in Miami after faking her own suicide to escape from her husband, who is dangerously possessed by a powerful African god. When she hears of the ritual style murder, she knows he is on to her. She searches through her past and present to find the spiritual allies, including Jimmy, she will need to beat her husband at a game that could have the future of the world at stake.

> *There was even a little shoot-out, although the mope had only been wounded and nobody got on Paz's case because he, too, was black and so, under the peculiar rules of American police practice, he had a license to shoot down citizens of whatever color with only nonhysterical investigation to follow. Even more so, in his case, because he was also of Cuban extraction, which accounted for the wit of the bystanders here, shouting, "Yo, spigger!"* (23)

Key features: Some first person narration; sexual situations; glossary

Subjects: Africa; anthropologists; Cuban Americans; Florida—Miami; magical realism; serial murders; suspense

Similar titles: *Cold Havana Ground* by Correa and *Shangó* by Curtis are other novels about African magic and murder.

Valley of Bones. New York: HarperCollins, 2005. ISBN 0060577665. 436pp.

Emmylou Dideroff is found muttering and communing with long dead saints in the hotel room of an oil millionaire who was recently impaled ten stories below. Policeman Tito Morales joins forces with fellow Cuban American celebrity detective Jimmy Paz in trying to get to the bottom of this bizarre case.

> *He stood and looked over the wrought iron railing. He could see the impaled victim, ten stories below, with the CSU swarming around him, photographing and taking samples. Paz wished them well but thought that most of the relevant evidence would be found right up here in 10D.* (8)

Key features: Some first person narration; sexual situations

Subjects: Catholic Church; Cuban Americans; Florida—Miami; murder; saints; suspense

Similar titles: *The Secret Supper* by Sierra and *God's Spy* by Gómez-Jurado are other mysteries featuring the Catholic Church, murder, and mysticism.

Night of the Jaguar. New York: HarperCollins, 2006. ISBN 0060577681. 372pp.

Jimmy Paz comes out of retirement to investigate the grisly deaths of several Miami businessmen. A jaguar seems to be on the loose, or maybe it's a shaman who takes on the shape of a jaguar. Once again, Jimmy comes up against it in the spirit world, but this time his daughter's life is on the line.

> *After drinking some water from his water skin, he made himself as comfortable as he could amid the pallets of lumber and ate the herbs and started the ritual that would slow his body's functions down to a level near to death, although he know his spirit would keep lively enough in a different world.* (20)

Key features: Glossary

Subjects: Cuban Americans; Florida—Miami; serial murders; shamans; suspense

Similar titles: The <u>Sonny Baca Mysteries</u> by Anaya also feature murder, shamans, and shape-shifting.

Hinojosa, Rolando (Tejano).

Rafe Buenrostro Series.

Lieutenant Rafe Buenrostro of the Belken County Homicide Squad and Captain Lisandro Gomez Solís, Cuerpo de Policía Estatal, Sección de Orden Público de Barrones, Tamaulipas, work together to solve cases along the Texas–Mexico border. Hinojosa relates these tales in a chatty, downhome style born of the border region's quirky culture.

Partners in Crime. Houston, TX: Arte Público Press, 1985. ISBN 0934770379. 248pp.

Buenrostro and Gómez Solís investigate murder and drug running on the border. (This book is also part of Hinojosa's <u>Klail City Death Trip Series</u>.)

> *It had begun as one of those harmless domestic disputes, so called. Husband I had a girlfriend who also had a husband. Husband I also*

> *had a wife, of course, and it was she who accosted the girlfriend, before two witnesses, in the laundry room of the apartment building. A regular punch-up.* (9)

Subjects: murder; police procedural; Texas; U.S.–Mexico border

Similar titles: The novels by Allana Martin are mysteries that are also set in the U.S.–Mexico border region.

Ask a Policeman. Houston, TX. Arte Público Press, 1998. ISBN 1558852263. 196pp.

A convicted murderer, Lee Gomez, escapes from jail. Inspector Rafe Buenrostro thinks this is all he has to handle, and so it is until the Gomez twins decide to go into the family business. Now Buenrostro is investigating crimes on both sides of the border.

> *Buenrostro replied that money was still the biggest player across the river, and that Lu Cetina could still have a devil of a time. Still, the Belken County police would help.* (97)

Key features: Strong language; sexual situations

Subjects: drugs; Mexican Americans; murder; police procedural; Texas; U.S.–Mexico border

Similar titles: *California Girl: A Novel* by T. Jefferson Parker is another police procedural about murder in Mexico.

La Pierre, Janet (U.S. American, California).

Baby Mine. Santa Barbara, CA: John Daniel, 1999. ISBN 1-880284-32-4. 255pp.

The small town of Port Silva is being terrorized by a band of thugs; and the local fertility clinic is the target of protestors. Just another day at the office for Chief Gutierrez who must also contend with a short-sighted mayor who has a tendency to be swayed by public fervor. Vince is supported by wife Meg and his step-daughter Katy, but his family is threatened by the pall hanging over the town.

> *"Officer Grebs believes they were Mexicans," she said in a rush. Last night she'd kept the mean edge of the police-station exchange to herself. Now she reverted to adulthood and told the chief of police what he needed to know about his subordinate's behavior and attitude. Vince surprised her with a grin. "Singe the old bastard's fur a bit did you?"* (23)

Subjects: California; family relationships; fertility clinics; Mexican Americans; Mexicans; police chiefs; teachers

Similar titles: The Precinct Puerto Rico Series by Steven Torres also features a Latino police chief of a small town dealing with big crimes.

Lopez, Steve (U.S. American, California).

In the Clear. New York: Harcourt, 2002. ISBN 0151002843. 344pp.

Sheriff Albert LaRosa is offered a job as head of security at a New Jersey casino. The position comes with threats against his life, bombs, and a dead body. He can deal with these, but not with the possibility of arresting one of his friends for murder.

Albert was deep in boozy hibernation, sleeping the sleep of burrowing animals, when the smoke curled into the room, clocked straight up his nose, and penetrated his brain. (166)

Subjects: casinos; New Jersey; police detectives; small towns

Similar titles: The <u>Mary Hopkins</u> series by Carlson and the <u>Walt Longmire</u> series by Craig Johnson are other police procedurals that feature sheriffs investigating murders in small towns.

Padura, Leonardo (Cuban).

Mario Conde Series.

Police detective Mario Conde does his job with cynical dexterity, frustrated because he cannot make a living as a writer. He must consistently tangle with the bureaucracy and desperation of postrevolutionary Cuba. (The series is listed here in the order in which it was originally published, although it was not translated in that order.)

Havana Blue. (*Pasado perfecto*, 1991). London: Bitter Lemon, 2007. ISBN 1904738222. 286pp.

Forced to wake up from a mongo hangover, Lieutenant Mario Conde of the Havana police force is put to work investigating the murder of a high-level bureaucrat. Rafael Morín Rodríguez was a schoolmate of Conde's and married the girl Conde has long idolized from afar, which only complicates the case further.

He found the packet of cigarettes on the floor. The packet was grimy and had been trampled on, but he gazed at it optimistically. Slid off the edge of the mattress and sat on the floor. Put two fingers in the packet and the saddest of cigarettes seemed like a reward for his titanic effort. (4)

Key features: Strong language; sexual situations; violence

Subjects: Cuba—Havana; murder; police procedural

Similar titles: Novels by Burke are written with a similar hard-boiled, world-weary tone; *Tango for a Torturer* by Chavarría and *Cold Havana Ground* by Correa are also set in contemporary Havana.

Havana Gold. (*Vientos de cuaresma*, 1994). Translated by Peter Bush. London: Bitter Lemon Press, 2008. ISBN 9781904738282. 286pp.

Conde visits his alma mater, wrestling with nostalgia, bureaucracy, and state interests as he investigates twenty-four-year-old Lissette Delgado's vicious rape and murder. Ms. Delgado was an attractive teacher obviously living beyond her means.

By the side of the outline chalked on the floor he spotted another silhouette, a smaller patch that had almost disappeared, staining the bright shiny tiles. Why did they kill you? he wondered as he imagined the girl raped, beaten, tortured and strangled, lying in her own blood. (37)

Key features: Strong language; sexual situations; violence

Subjects: Cuba—Havana; murder; police procedural; teachers

Similar titles: *White Shadow* by Atkins is another police procedural about murder in Cuba.

🌱 ***Havana Red.*** *(Máscaras,* 1997). Translated by Peter Bush. London: Bitter Lemon Press, 2005. ISBN 1904738095. 233pp.

Lieutenant Conde is working on the case of a murdered transvestite, which takes him through parts of Havana he is loath to visit.

> *If God exists, I hope he's listening to you. . . . What a self-interested bugger you are. . . . And what are you into now, Conde? I'm after whoever killed a transvestite. . . . But it's not easy I can tell you.* (128)

Key features: Strong language; sexual situations; violence

Subjects: Cuba; murder; police procedural; transvestites

Similar titles: *White Shadow* by Atkins is another police procedural about murder in Cuba.

Awards: Café De Gijón Prize, 1995

🌱 ***Havana Black.*** *(Paisaje de otoño,* 1998). Translated by Peter Bush. London: Bitter Lemon Press, 2006. ISBN 190473815X. 261pp.

The body of a man once in charge of removing art from the possession of those fleeing the revolution washes up on shore. Lieutenant Mario Conde must look into the backgrounds of some of Cuba's oldest and most influential families to bring the guilty to justice.

> *He boldly opened his eyes, in the certain knowledge that he had reached the horrendous age of thirty-six and that it would indeed be his last day as a policeman, and what he saw no longer shocked him.* (156)

Key features: Strong language; sexual situations

Subjects: Cuba; murder; police procedural

Similar titles: *Hard Currency* by Kaminsky is another police procedural about murder in Cuba.

Awards: Hammett Prize, 1998 (International Association of Crime Writers)

Adiós Hemingway. *(Adiós Hemingway,* 2001). Translated by John King. New York: Canongate, 2005. ISBN 184195795X; ISBN-13: 9781841957951. 229pp.

Two stories converge into one, and both involve Hemingway and Hemingway's Cuba. In the present time, Conde is retired but is called in to investigate a body found on Hemingway's old estate. The parallel story from the past focuses on Hemingway's life in Cuba around the time of the murder.

> *What I've got is something I owe myself. I worshipped that man and now I can't stand him. But the fact is I don't know him.* (80)

Key features: First person narration; strong language

Subjects: Cuba—Havana; Hemingway, Ernest; murder

Similar titles: *Dancing to "Almendra"* by Montero is another historical novel about murder in Cuba.

Saer, Juan José (Argentinian).

The Investigation. (*La pesquisa,* **1994**). **Translated by Helen Lane. London: Serpent's Tail, 1999. ISBN 1852422971. 182pp.**

Elderly women in Paris are being wined and dined . . . then killed. The killer leaves no trace. Chief Inspector Morvan must hurry to catch this murderer before he can kill again.

> *To tell the truth, everything that Morvan saw in his dreams, though not particularly horrible, caused him not so much anxiety as a vague and persistent revulsion.* (20)

Subjects: Argentina; France—Paris; police procedural; serial murders

Similar titles: The Aimee Leduc series is also about serial murders set in Paris, France; *Borges and the Eternal Orangutans* by Verissimo is about murder in Argentina.

Sanderson, Jim (U.S. American).

Dolph Martinez Series.

Seasoned Border Patrol agent and amateur historian Dolph Martinez can find his way around both sides of the border to get to the bottom of some mystifying and dangerous cases.

Key features: First person narration; graphic violence

Subjects: Border Patrol agents; human trafficking; U.S.–Mexico border

Similar titles: *Frontera Dreams* by Taibo and *Desert Blood* by Gaspar de Alba are other novels about murder on the U.S.–Mexico border.

🌸 *El Camino del Rio.* Albuquerque: University of New Mexico Press, 2000. ISBN 978-0826321916. 230pp.

Sister Quinn may be a nun and *curandera,* but Dolph suspects things are not what they seem when a murdered smuggler is found with a vial that may link him to the revered sister.

> *Some said that during the night, Sister Quinn could turn into an owl, just like the souls of the dead could, and perch on tombstones. They said she was probably flying overhead, returning from a tombstone, when she saw me dying.* (3–4)

Awards: Frank Waters Southwest Writing Contest winner, 2000

La Mordida. Albuquerque: University of New Mexico Press, 2002. ISBN 0826328156. 254pp.

Something's up with the suspicious papers Dolph Martinez finds in a suspect's backpack, something that could spell death and disaster for Martinez.

> *Now I woke some nights with a dream that was a replay of memory-the image of blood and brains spraying out of the side of Vincent Fuentes's head, and then the movement of the Paso Lujitas boys dipping their white handkerchiefs in the pool of his blood draining from the exit wound., and then the sound of Sister Quinn's voice as she begged me and the world for forgiveness, mercy, and grace.* (9)

Somoza, José Carlos (Cuban).

The Art of Murder. (Clara y la penumbra, **2001). Translated by Nick Caistor. London: Abacus, 2001. ISBN 0349118833. 470pp.**

Annek Hollech is painted and posed to perform as a piece of art placed in a gallery for all to see. When she is murdered, detectives April Wood and Lothar Bosch are sent to investigate the crime. They will have to traverse the world of modern art to find the killer before another model is murdered.

> *"I don't believe it!" Talia crowed when she saw how surprised Clara was. "Haven't you ever heard of HD art? Of course it's made of flesh and blood, just like you and I! It's a hyper . . . work."* (45)

Key features: Strong language; sexual situations

Subjects: modern art; murder; police detectives

Similar titles: *The Mosaic Crimes* by Leoni and *Pale as the Dead* by Mountain are other police procedurals featuring murder and art.

Torres, Steven (Puerto Rican American).

Precinct Puerto Rico Series.

Luis Gonzalo has been in law enforcement a long time before serious violence comes to his little corner of the world, a small seaside town called Angustias (which translates as "anguish" in English) in Puerto Rico. He must face new challenges like drug smuggling and human trafficking, train new officers with quirky personalities, and defend his family from sinister threats.

🌺 *Precinct Puerto Rico: Book One.* New York: Thomas Dunne Books, 2002. ISBN 0312285809. 245pp.

On a trip to visit his wife's family in Rincón, Sheriff Gonzalo finds himself investigating a shipwreck. No one wants Gonzalo looking into the crime, which puts his life and those of his family in jeopardy.

> *He rose and took a step back and turned to the sea again. By the time Viña returned, Gonzalo was exhausted and had lined more than a dozen bodies on the beach.* (57)

Subjects: corruption; human trafficking; murder; police detectives; undocumented workers

Similar titles: *Strawman's Hammock* by Wimberley also has a police detective investigating a murder having to do with undocumented workers.

Awards: *Library Journal's* Best Mystery Books, 2002

Death in Precinct Puerto Rico: Book Two. New York: Thomas Dunne Books, 2003. ISBN 0312289898. 274pp.

Elena Maldonado, a woman Gonzalo has known since she was a child, has been murdered. He immediately suspects her abusive husband. Unfortunately, more suspects appear by the minute to complicate the seemingly straightforward case.

> *Let me make this easy, Jose. There was a murder. Elena Maldonado was stabbed seven times. Young woman, very pretty. She had a hard life and somebody ended it for her just one day after she became a mother.* (182)

Subjects: domestic violence; murder; police detectives

Similar titles: *The Long Falling* by Ridgway and *The Star: A Tarot Card Mystery* by Skibbins have police detectives investigating domestic violence and murder.

Burning Precinct Puerto Rico: Book Three. New York: Thomas Dunne Books, 2004. ISBN 13: 9780312321093. 242pp.

The people of Angustias throw Luis a party to celebrate his twenty-five years as sheriff. The party is interrupted by fire and the discovery of dead bodies. The perpetrators of the crime return to town, and Gonzalo must fight to stay alive and see justice done.

> *"What's the plan, Chief? The house is almost ready to collapse."*

> "What do you mean, what's the plan? We don't give up, that's the plan." (19)

Subjects: arson; corruption; drug trafficking; murder; police detectives

Similar titles: *St. Alban's Fire* by Mayor has a police detective investigating murder and arson.

Missing in Precinct Puerto Rico: Book Four. New York: Thomas Dunne Books, 2006. ISBN13: 9780312321116. 246pp.

Luis Gonzalo believes the disappearance of an Angustias child to be routine. He probably wandered off and got lost. That theory goes south when another child is reported missing. Now the town fears a darker reason for the disappearances, and Gonzalo is charged with making it right.

> *The boy crossed his arms and gave the sheriff an insufferable grin that made him want to scare humility into the child by slapping cuffs on his girlish wrists or by simply slapping him.* (75)

Subjects: child pornography; missing children; police procedural

Similar titles: *Every Secret Thing* by Lippman is another police procedural about missing children.

Villatoro, Marcos (Salvadoran American).

Romilia Chacón Series.

The Nashville, Tennessee Police Department, in need of bilingual support, has hired an unexpectedly formidable detective in Romilia Chacón, originally from El Salvador. Romilia uses her language skills, familiarity with Nashville's Latino community, and passion to avenge her sister's death and combat crime. She is good enough to graduate from the force to the homicide unit and, ultimately, to the FBI. Tekún Uman is Romilia's relentless, elusive, and lethal nemesis. Romilia has a challenging home life as a single mom who shares the house with her own strong-willed *mamá*.

🌶 *Home Killings.* Houston, TX: Arte Público Press, 2001. ISBN 1558853367. 248pp.

Romilia Chacón's first case has her challenging her partner over arresting the wrong man. She encounters Guatemalan death squads, drug running, and a deadly love interest.

> *I was a homicide detective not a damned debutante who waited on her fifteenth birthday at the church doors for the perfect man to come by and sweep her away. I'm Latina, but damned if I'll be that Latina.* (3)

Key features: First person narration; strong language in English and Spanish

Subjects: detectives; drug trafficking; Latinas; serial murders; Tennessee—Nashville

Similar titles: The protagonists in the Filomena Buscarsela Series by Wishnia and in the *Bone Factory* by Sidor are also Latina detectives investigating murders.

Awards: First prize, Latino Literary Hall of Fame, 2001

Minos. Boston: Justin, Charles, 2003. ISBN 1932112138. 300pp.

Romilia Chacón is now a member of the Nashville Homicide Unit. Tracking her sister's killer, Minos, Romilia will also have to watch out for Tekún Uman, a drug lord, and the heartless agents that do his bidding.

> *The paralysis was strange. I thought it began in my head, then I confused it with the sting in the nape of my neck, under my hairline. Then I wasn't sure where the numbness began, for it was everywhere. My voice froze. I dropped.* (182)

Key features: First person narration; strong language in English and Spanish

Subjects: detectives; Latinas; Salvadorans; serial murders; Tennessee—Nashville

Similar titles: The protagonists in the Filomena Buscarsela Series by Wishnia and in the *Bone Factory* by Sidor are also Latina detectives investigating murders.

A Venom Beneath the Skin. Boston: Justin, Charles, 2005. ISBN 1932112375. 230pp.

FBI agent Romilia Chacón's lover is murdered, and all signs point to Tekún Uman, a man wanted by the FBI who is also obsessed with Romilia.

> *There's nothing like the narrow-mindedness of a person who speaks only one language. And Nancy was beyond provincial; she was über-cracker. I had to explain everything to her about my Latino world, which was starting to piss me off.* (105)

Key features: First person narration; strong language in English and Spanish

Subjects: California—Los Angeles; FBI agents; Latinas; serial murders

Similar titles: *The Narrows* by Connelly features another female FBI agent investigating serial murders in Los Angeles, California.

Ybarra, Ricardo Means (Mexican American).

Brotherhood of Dolphins. Houston, TX: Arte Público Press, 1997. ISBN 1558852158. 288pp.

After an arsonist sets fire to the Los Angeles Public Library, Detective Pete Escobedo follows the criminal into the barrios of his childhood. From his investigation, Escobedo deduces the arsonist has committed murder in conjunction with previously set fires. As Pete closes in on the killer, the killer closes in on Escobedo, his firefighter friend Sylvia, and Carmen, the woman he loves.

> *He was a man in his barrio and he couldn't calm down, and the longer he stood there and watched the student, the more he thought of Carmen having to walk through their neighborhood alone at night, their barrio.* (137)

Key features: Strong language; sexual situations

Subjects: arson; California—Los Angeles; libraries; police detectives

Similar titles: *Dream House* by Krich is another procedural dealing with arson and set in Los Angeles, California.

Amateur Sleuths

The sleuths in these novels are not professional detectives, but they engage in detection for altruistic purposes or because circumstances put them in the right place at the right time (or the wrong place at the wrong time). They are uniquely qualified to unravel the mystery and, hopefully, see that justice is done. Mysticism and social issues play an important part in many of these novels. The protagonists may work with the legal system—lawyer, prosecutors, public defenders, and bond agents—or just be regular *gente*—writers, shop owners, priests, and teachers.

Novels with urban settings are set in New York City, Denver, Miami and Tampa in Florida, Los Angeles and San Francisco in California, and international cities like Mexico City, Barcelona, Madrid, the Vatican, and ancient Athens. The Texas–Mexico border provides rural settings, in the El Paso–Juarez and Big Bend areas.

Abella, Alex (Cuban American).

Dead of Night. **New York: Simon & Schuster, 1998. ISBN 0684814269. 300pp.**

A man is missing, and lawyer Charlie Morell is drawn into the world of Santería as he searches for him. The murder of a friend pulls Charlie even deeper into danger and closer to the killer.

> *The old black crone in sheriff's uniform nodded, her face so gaunt you could make out the death's head beneath her shiny skin. She lifted a bony hand, pointed a crooked index at the door. "She's waiting for you."* (43)

Key features: First person narration; strong language

Subjects: California; Cuban Americans; Florida—Miami; missing persons; murder; occult; Santería

Similar titles: Abella's novel *Final Acts* also features Cuban Americans, the occult, and Santería; *Player's Vendetta* by Lantigua is a mystery about finding a missing person that takes place in the Cuban American community.

Bertematti, Richard (Cuban American).

Project Death: A Tito Rico Mystery. Houston, TX: Arte Público Press, 1997. ISBN 1558851933. 189pp.

When Tito Rico's childhood friend, Pepito, is brutally murdered, the cops aren't investigating the case; so Rico and his ex-con friend Alonzo set out to find Pepito's killer. Their investigation sparks a chain reaction of trouble for Rico that could send him to jail, or worse—to the graveyard.

> *Whoever killed Pepito is dead. He stuck out his hand. I should have thought about it some more, but I grabbed his hand and we shook the way we used to do it when we were young.* (26)

Key features: First person narration; strong language

Subjects: Cuban Americans; murder; New York

Similar titles: *Shangó* by Curtis and *Night of the Jaguar* by Gruber are other novels about Cuban Americans and murder.

Black Artemis (Nuyorican). *See also* Quintero, Sofia.

Burn: A Novel. New York: Penguin Group, 2006. ISBN 0451218574. 318pp.

Bail bond agent and ex-hooker Jasmine Reyes takes a chance on Malcolm "Macho" Booker, a gifted graffiti artist. When Booker jumps bail she pursues him, only to find herself in a world of dark secrets that threaten to expose her own and put her in mortal danger.

> *The minute she'd met him, Jasmine had suspected the flake would skip his court date. But she posted his bail anyway, knowing that the big baby would run straight to his auntie's store.* (17)

Key features: Reader's guide

Subjects: artists; bond agents; brothers and sisters; graffiti; HIV/AIDS; transgendered people; women's lives

Similar titles: Leto's <u>Naughty Girls Series</u> features another Latina bounty hunter.

Dos Santos, José Rodriguez (Portuguese).

Codex 632: The Secret Identity of Christopher Columbus. (O Codex 632, 2005). Translated by Alison Entrekin. ISBN 9780061173189. 319pp.

Thomas Noronha is a professor and cryptologist hired to continue the work of a professor who has been murdered while in the middle of a project ostensibly about Brazil's colonial past. Thomas reluctantly takes on the job while battling challenges on the home front and an overenthusiastic and available foreign exchange student. Will he be successful at uncovering Columbus's secret without losing his life or his family?

> *Had someone told Thomas Noronha, that morning, that the next few months would take him all over the world and into the unraveling of a five-hundred-year-old conspiracy, complete with stories of seafaring adventures during the Age of Discovery, royal espionage between the first two global superpowers, and the esoteric world of Kabbalah and the Knights Templar, he wouldn't have believed it.* (3)

Subjects: college professors; Columbus, Christopher; conspiracies; Portugal—Lisbon; Spain—15th century

Similar titles: *The Scroll of Seduction* by Belli is another novel that juxtaposes Golden Age and contemporary Spain.

García-Aguilera, Carolina (Cuban American).

Luck of the Draw. **New York: HarperCollins, 2003. ISBN 0-06-053633-0. 368pp.**

When the family is ready to inaugurate their new casino business in Miami, Esmeralda is charged with finding missing sister Diamond. The whole family must be present for this triumph because the original casino was lost during the Cuban Revolution.

> *I cursed when I saw that it was my older sister Sapphire on the line.* Mierda! *It was barely six-thirty in the morning, far too early to deal with a family crisis.* (1)

Key features: First person narration; strong language in English and Spanish

Subjects: Cuban Americans; family businesses; family relationships; kidnapping; sisters

Similar titles: Lantigua's *The Ultimate Havana* is also about Cuban family businesses and intrigue.

Gaspar de Alba, Alicia (Mexican American, El Paso–Juárez border).

🖋 *Desert Blood: The Juárez Murders.* **Houston, TX: Arte Público Press, 2005. ISBN 1558854460. 346pp.**

Returning to the El Paso–Juárez border to adopt a baby was supposed to be relatively simple for Professor Ivon Villa. But the murder of the woman carrying the unborn child brings the Juárez murders home to Ivon. After her younger sister goes missing, Ivon knows she can no longer look the other way while women disappear.

> *The irony stung Ivon like a rock on the cheek. Water for Puerto de Anapra, the sign back there had said. A port without water. Not even the Rio Grande came to this god forsaken place.* (38)

Key features: First person narration; strong language in English and Spanish; sexual situations

Subjects: adoption; lesbian detectives; pregnancy; serial murders; Texas—El Paso; U.S.–Mexico border

Similar titles: *Cemetery Murders: A Mystery* by Marcy is another novel that features a lesbian detective investigating serial murders.

Awards: Lambda Literary Award; Library Journal Best Mystery Books; Latino Book Award for Best English Language Mystery, 2005

Latour, José (Cuban).

🔥 *Outcast: A Novel.* (*Mundos sucios,* 2002). **New York: William Morrow, 1999. ISBN 0060184884. 295pp.**

Schoolteacher Elliot Steil barely ekes out a living in Havana, Cuba. A chance meeting with an American gives Steil the opportunity to flee to America. The deal to leave the country goes awry when Elliot is left to die in the waters off the coast of Florida. Against all odds, he eventually reaches land, determined to find whoever left him for dead.

> *For an instant the teacher wondered why he felt so numb, so utterly exhausted. A sudden shove against his right shoulder brought him back to reality. A giant shark ripping out his side flashed in his mind, and his instinctive response was a horrid scream.* (62)

Key features: Strong language; sexual situations

Subjects: Cuba—Havana; Florida—Miami; sociopaths; suspense; teachers

Similar titles: *Spy's Fate* by Correa is another novel of suspense set in Havana and Miami.

Awards: Edgar Award nomination, 1999

Leto, Julie (Cuban American).

Naughty Girls Series.

In Tampa, Florida, Marisela Morales is a former gang member of Cuban descent who is using her skills as a bounty hunter to earn a living. She is recruited by the company that employs her ex-*novio*—a secretive outfit that works on international criminal cases involving weapons, drugs, and kidnapping.

Dirty Little Secrets. New York: Downtown Press, 2005. ISBN 1416501622. 315pp.

Set on *venganza* for the way he did her ten years earlier, bounty hunter Marisela Morales goes after her ex-*novio* Frankie when he tries to skip bail. But things are not what they seem as Marisela uncovers Frankie's secrets, including his work with a private investigative outfit that could put her on a path to job satisfaction (not to mention carnal satisfaction), if she has the *cojones.*

> *Marisela sighed, teasing his neck with her hot breath one more time before she slid onto the bar stool next to his. She'd been trying to track the man down for nearly a week. Who knew Frankie would turn up at an old haunt?* (2)

Key features: Strong language; sexual situations

Subjects: bounty hunters; Florida—Tampa; private investigators; sensual fiction; women's lives

Similar titles: The protagonist in *Picture Me Rollin'* by Black Artemis must also deal with prison and her ex-lover.

Dirty Little Lies. New York: Pocket Books, 2006. ISBN 1416501630 ISBN 13: 1416501633. 351pp.

Marisela Morales has her work cut out for her. She must contend with the death of a congressman and a female assassin, in addition to her lover/colleague/pain-in-the-ass Frankie Vega.

> *She swiped her hotel key through the lock and entered her room, with Frankie right behind her. She might have tried locking him out, but he'd only find a way to break in while she slept. Not that she minded a good invasion fantasy. (76)*

Key features: Strong language; sexual situations

Subjects: bounty hunters; female assassins; sensual fiction; women's lives

Similar titles: The <u>Stephanie Plum</u> series by Evanovich and *Running for Cover* by Montana also feature female bounty hunters and romance; *Burn* by Black Artemis also features a Latina bond agent.

Lucas, Frances.

If Looks Could Kill. **Norwich, VT.: New Victorian, 1995. ISBN 0934678634. 185pp.**

TV screen- and scriptwriter Diana Mendoza travels to LA to check on the progress of the TV series she is working on. It should be a simple trip, but that all changes when she meets Lauren Lytch at a party and recklessly agrees to help her out. Lauren's husband has been murdered, and Lauren is the prime suspect.

> *She'd always liked her life to be neat and orderly, but picking up a strange women from the side of highway, taking her back to her hotel for the night, then discovering that this woman was quite possibly a suspect in a murder investigation hardly qualified as neat and orderly. (33)*

Key features: First person narration; sexual situations

Subjects: California—Los Angeles; Costa Rican Americans; lesbians

Similar titles: *Desert Blood* by Gaspar de Alba is another novel about lesbians and murder.

Martin, Allana.

Texana Jones Series.

In the Big Bend area of the Río Grande on the border between the United States and Mexico, Texana Jones owns a little trading post in the village of Polvo (which translates as "dust" in English) near the town of Presidio on the Texas side of the border. The unique culture and beauty of the region play an important part in the mysteries Texana solves, with the sometime help of her veterinarian husband Cliff and her pet bobcat Phobe.

Key features: First person narration

Subjects: Chicanas; healers; murder; storekeepers; Texas; women detectives

Similar titles: *A Murderous Yarn* by Ferris and the <u>Tea Shop</u> series by Childs are also about women storekeepers and murder; the <u>Rafe Buenrostro Series</u> by Hinojosa is also set in the Texas–Mexico border region.

🌶 *Death of a Healing Woman.* New York: St. Martin's Press, 1996. ISBN 0312145810. 211pp.

> Trading post owner Texana Jones discovers healing woman Rhea Fair dead. When the sheriff makes no effort to find Rhea's killer, Texana takes it upon herself to right this wrong.

> *I stopped when I saw the toes of a pair of boots slanted up out of the tawny stems of needle grass. I felt as if my insides were disintegrating. In dread, I pressed my hand to my mouth and stepped closer.* (16)

Awards: Medicine Pipe Bearers Award, 1996

Death of a Saint Maker. New York: St. Martin's Press, 1998. ISBN 0312180827. 276pp.

When Texana travels south of the border to visit a church that is being rededicated, she finds the body of the old man who had carved the saints for the church. The presumed culprit is a pit bull, but Texana is not so sure.

Death of an Evangelista. New York: St. Martin's Press, 1999. ISBN 0312198531. 260pp.

When Texana encounters a dead body in the cab she hopes to take home after a dental procedure in Mexico, she finds herself at the beginning of a chain of macabre and deadly events that will take some work to unravel and involve more dead bodies.

Death of a Mythmaker. New York: St. Martin's Press, 2000. ISBN 0373263805. 272pp.

Texana decides to find out who murdered Julian Row, the fiancé of one of the Spivey sisters' (and possibly a gigolo). A Mexican photographer from the other side of the border has also been murdered and dumped in front of Texana's trading post. Could this be a warning to mind her own business?

Death of the Last Villista. New York: St. Martin's Press, 2001. ISBN 0312265735. 211pp.

A film crew comes to Polvo to make a movie commemorating a documentary made there forty years earlier about Pancho Villa, the Mexican revolutionary. At that time, a young man was murdered, and the killer was never found. Texana was an extra in the movie as a child and hosts the crew in the present day. This mystery has personal significance for Texana because her mother may have been involved with the young man and her father could be the guilty party.

Death of the River Master. New York: St. Martin's Press, 2003. ISBN 0312306857. 240pp.

Texana's husband Cliff has been arrested for killing the man responsible for allocating water on the border and is sitting in a Mexican jail! Can Texana find the truth and prove his innocence without being arrested herself?

Martinez, Michele (Puerto Rican American).

Melanie Vargas Series.

An up-and-coming prosecutor in New York City, Melanie Vargas is ambitious, smart, and sexy. Her personal life is in chaos after she separates from her philandering husband; struggles to provide a stable home life for her young daughter, and plays the power game she needs to get ahead in New York's legal system, often putting herself in danger of love (with a cute Irish FBI agent) and death.

Most Wanted. New York: William Morrow, 2005. ISBN 006072398X. 366pp.

Melanie Vargas is taking a midnight walk to soothe her little girl to sleep when she hears sirens. Being the consummate prosecutor that she is, Melanie can't resist the urge to see what is going on. A wealthy ex-prosecutor's house is on fire, and Melanie fights to get the case assigned to her. This may mean a promotion, if she can survive.

> *Suddenly she understood what the shape was. She opened her mouth to scream at the exact instant his hand shot out, fast as a bullet, to grab her by the hair. She listened as if from far away to the guttural, bubbling sound that emerged, not from her mouth, but from her slit throat. (107)*

Key features: Strong language; sexual situations; violence

Subjects: murder; New York—New York City; public prosecutors; Puerto Rican women; women lawyers

Similar titles: *Ida B.: A Novel* by Quinones Miller is another novel about Puerto Rican women and murder.

The Finishing School. New York: William Morrow, 2006. ISBN 0060724005 ISBN 13: 9780060724009. 387pp.

The death of two girls brings prosecutor Melanie Vargas and FBI agent Dan O'Reilly back together. Melanie must go undercover to investigate the private schools of New York, schools the dead girls attended. Even though she is undercover, the killer seems to know who she is.

> *The target was right there in front of her. Down, girl, down. She should stay where she was. Sit back and allow events to take their course without injecting herself. Let the agents do their job. (171)*

Key features: Strong language; sexual situations; violence

Subjects: New York—New York City—Manhattan; preparatory schools; public prosecutors; Puerto Ricans; women lawyers

Similar titles: Barbara Parker's <u>Gail Connor and Anthony Quintana Series</u> also features a woman lawyer protagonist.

Cover-up. New York: William Morrow, 2007. ISBN 9780060899004. 344pp.

After refusing to take on an overseas investigation, Melanie must redeem herself with her overbearing boss. Now, with the help of her FBI boyfriend, Dan, she does take on the gruesome case of celebrity scandalmonger Suzanne Shepard, who has been raped and murdered in Central Park. Suzanne had plenty of enemies, and Melanie has her hands full when the murderer begins to stalk her, too.

> *The park looked so different at night. Strange shadows loomed between the arcs of yellow light spilling from the lampposts, and branches flapped in the wet wind. What had happened to the old Melanie? Time was, she would've been eating this up instead of feeling the butterflies. (3)*

Key features: Strong language; sexual situations; violence

Subjects: celebrities; public prosecutors; Puerto Ricans; television personalities; women lawyers

Similar titles: Barbara Parker's <u>Gail Connor and Anthony Quintana Series</u> also features a woman lawyer protagonist.

Notorious. New York: William Morrow, 2008. ISBN 9780060899028. 336p,

This time Melanie must get to the bottom of a murder that takes place right before her eyes, making her a dangerous witness. The case involves a rap star, sleazy attorneys, and the Taliban. Melanie's love life is in disarray as well, *pobrecita* . . . .

> *The world erupted in fire and blood. Melanie's head hit the rough cement of the sidewalk, and she cried out in pain. All around her, pieces of flaming metal rained down.* (6)

Key features: Strong language; sexual situations; violence

Subjects: New York—New York City; public prosecutors; Puerto Ricans; rap stars; terrorists; women lawyers

Similar titles: Barbara Parker's <u>Gail Connor and Anthony Quintana Series</u> also features a woman lawyer protagonist.

Nava, Michael (Mexican American, San Francisco).

<u>Henry Rios Mystery Series.</u>

When the series begins, Henry Rios is an alcoholic in recovery and a brilliant public defender. By the end, he has weathered many personal losses as a gay man during the AIDS crisis and has had professional triumphs; he is about to be offered a judgeship. His cases delve into difficult social questions that dovetail with personal circumstances that Henry must resolve. He does so in a way that maintains his integrity and ultimate faith in the power of love, in whatever form it may take.

Subjects: California—Los Angeles; California—San Francisco; corruption; homosexuals; lawyers; murder; public defenders

Similar titles: Other mysteries featuring Latino lawyers who work overtime to see that justice is done are the <u>Luis Montez Series</u> by Nava and the <u>Melanie Vargas Series</u> by Michele Martinez.

The Little Death. Los Angeles: Alyson Books, 2001. ISBN 1-55583-694- 1.165pp.

Gay public defender Henry Rios must come to grips with the frustrating practice of the law. When suspicious circumstances surround the death of his lover, circumstances that seem to implicate an important member of the San Francisco community, Henry vows to find out the truth.

> *His eyes were focused but he still looked disheveled. I thought, irrelevantly, of a picture of a saint I had seen as a boy, as he was being led off to his martyrdom. There was a glint of purity in Hugh Paris's eyes completely at odds with everything that was happening around him.* (12)

Goldenboy. Los Angeles: Alyson Books, 1988. ISBN 1555831419. 215pp.

Henry takes on the seemingly hopeless case of a young man accused of murdering someone who had been blackmailing him about his homosexuality. Meanwhile, he meets someone special and his love life starts looking up.

All the green, she told me, was to provide subliminal encouragement to her clients to pay their bills. It must have worked because she looked sleeker by the day. (www.amazon.com/gp/reader/1555833667/ref=sib _dp_ pt#reader-link)

Howtown: A Novel of Suspense. New York: Harper & Row, 1990. ISBN 0060162074. 244pp.

> Henry has moved to Los Angeles to live with Josh, who has been diagnosed as HIV positive. He courageously takes on the case of a pedophile accused of murdering a child pornographer.

The Hidden Law. New York: HarperCollins, 1992. ISBN 0060167831. 192pp.

> Henry defends young Latino Michael Ruiz from charges of murdering Gus Peña, a rising star in the Chicano political arena. His investigation takes him into the dirty world of politics in Los Angeles while he faces difficult challenges in his personal life, as his lover takes a turn for the worse.

The Death of Friends. New York: G.P. Putnam, 1996. ISBN 039913977x. 232pp.

> An old friend of Henry's, California Supreme Court justice Chris Chandler, has been murdered. Chandler had been in the closet. His lover Zack comes to Henry for help, but is Henry prepared for what he might find out?

The Burning Plain. New York: G.P. Putnam, 1997. ISBN 0399143106. 305pp.

> Personal and professional lives collide when Henry is accused of murder. Seeking solace after Josh's death from AIDS, Henry spends the evening with a hustler, who is found brutally murdered a few hours later. He is cleared when other corpses show up, but the resulting case makes him a target while taking him into the sordid world of elite Los Angeles.

Rag and Bone. New York: G.P. Putnam, 2001. ISBN 039914708X. 289pp.

> The final title in the series brings Henry new family, new love, and new challenges. He has had a heart attack and finds himself questioning the point of it all. His newly found niece has shot her abusive husband in an apparently clear-cut case of self-defense. Henry isn't so sure, but he does feel the need to protect his great-nephew and decides to take on this one last case before beginning his new career as a Supreme Court justice.

Parker, Barbara.

Gail Connor and Anthony Quintana Series.

In Miami, Florida, these two smart and sexy lawyers make a formidable team. They navigate the legal system and their personal lives with romance and flair. The cultural differences between them make for an intriguing and dynamic relationship.

Suspicion of Innocence. New York: Dutton/Penguin Books, 1994. ISBN 0-525-93744-7. 343pp.

High-powered lawyer Gail Connor is forced to make some difficult decisions when her sister's apparent suicide is found to be murder, and she is the main suspect. She turns to the handsome and accomplished lawyer Anthony Quintana to take up her defense. Meanwhile, her world falls apart as her husband leaves her and she begins to uncover unsavory secrets about the sister she thought she knew.

> *Gail looked at him, trying to figure this out. She doubted he was coming on to her, not that her wedding ring would stop him. Maybe he truly had nothing better to do than spend an hour dawdling over coffee, which she could not for a moment imagine. Or maybe he was sincerely trying to get the case off square one.* (20)

Key features: Strong language

Subjects: Cuban Americans; Florida—Miami; lawyers

Similar titles: The <u>Britt Montero Mysteries</u> by Buchanan and the <u>Lupe Solano Mysteries</u> by García-Aguilera also feature Cuban Americans in Miami; the <u>Jack Swyteck</u> series by Grippando also takes place in Miami and has attorney protagonists.

Suspicion of Guilt. New York: Dutton Books, 1995. ISBN 0525937692. 388pp.

Gail agrees to take on the case of an old school buddy, Patrick, against the interests of her firm. Patrick's mother has died, leaving a will he suspects is phony. When the police determine she was murdered, Patrick becomes the main suspect.

Key features: Strong language

Subjects: Cuban Americans; Florida—Miami; lawyers

Similar titles: The <u>Britt Montero Mysteries</u> by Buchanan and the <u>Lupe Solano Mysteries</u> by García-Aguilera also feature Cuban Americans in Miami; the <u>Jack Swyteck</u> series by Grippando also takes place in Miami and has attorney protagonists.

Suspicion of Deceit. New York: Dutton Books, 1998. ISBN 052594401X. 358pp.

Attorneys Gail Connor and Cuban-born Anthony Quintana have become engaged, but Anthony has a secret that could tear them apart.

> *There are a couple of other things we need to discuss. You lied to me about what you did in Cuba. You did more than sing for the folks at the rundown theater in Havana.* (131)

Key features: Strong language

Subjects: Cuban Americans; Florida—Miami; lawyers

Similar titles: The <u>Britt Montero Mysteries</u> by Buchanan and the <u>Lupe Solano Mysteries</u> by García-Aguilera also feature Cuban Americans in Miami; the <u>Jack Swyteck</u> series by Grippando also takes place in Miami and has attorney protagonists.

Suspicion of Betrayal. New York: Dutton Books, 1999. ISBN 0525944680. 347pp.

> Gail Connor finds herself the victim of a stalker. Her ex-husband could be involved. The breaking point for Gail is the threat against her young daughter. Gail will have to face danger from all sides to protect herself and her child.
>
>> *Red. There were stripes of red on the trunk that dripped slowly onto the concrete floor of the parking garage. She walked closer, staring. Almost without knowing it, she reached out and touched the liquid, then studied the smear on her forefinger.* (112)
>
> **Key features:** Strong language
>
> **Subjects:** Cuban Americans; Florida—Miami; lawyers
>
> **Similar titles:** The <u>Britt Montero Mysteries</u> by Buchanan and the <u>Lupe Solano Mysteries</u> by García-Aguilera also feature Cuban Americans in Miami; the <u>Jack Swyteck</u> series by Grippando also takes place in Miami and has attorney protagonists.

Suspicion of Malice. New York: Dutton Books, 2001. ISBN 0525945423. 341pp.

> Although Gail and Anthony have broken up, circumstances force them to work together on the case of millionaire Roger Creswell when Bobby Gonzalez—Anthony's daughter's secret fiancé—becomes the main suspect.
>
> **Key features:** Strong language
>
> **Subjects:** Cuban Americans; Florida—Miami; lawyers
>
> **Similar titles:** The <u>Britt Montero Mysteries</u> by Buchanan and the <u>Lupe Solano Mysteries</u> by García-Aguilera also feature Cuban Americans in Miami; the <u>Jack Swyteck</u> series by Grippando also takes place in Miami and has attorney protagonists.

Suspicion of Vengeance. New York: Dutton Books, 2001. ISBN 0525946012. 359pp.

> A man is wrongly convicted and sentenced to be executed. Against the advice of her fiancé, Anthony Quintana, Gail Connor takes on the case. Now the two attorneys are on a race against the clock to find the real killer before an innocent man is executed.
>
>> *You presume. Let me tell you something, Ms. Connor. Guilt or innocence is not the point. The state is trying to kill my clients. I'm not asking that they be set free. I just don't want them dead.* (27)
>
> **Key features:** Strong language
>
> **Subjects:** Cuban Americans; Florida—Miami; lawyers
>
> **Similar titles:** The <u>Britt Montero Mysteries</u> by Buchanan and the <u>Lupe Solano Mysteries</u> by García-Aguilera also feature Cuban Americans in Miami; the <u>Jack Swyteck</u> series by Grippando also takes place in Miami and has attorney protagonists.

Suspicion of Madness. New York: Dutton Books, 2003. ISBN 0525946810. 369pp.

A trip to an island in the Florida Keys does not turn out to be the relaxing vacation attorneys Gail Connor and Anthony Quintana were hoping for. Instead, a former client of Anthony's is accused of murder and then tries to kill himself. Connor and Quintana try to find the true murderer AND survive a tropical storm.

> *Standing there silently, wondering what to do, aware that she had no right to interfere, Gail thought she heard a noise. It came from the hall. What had it been? A footfall, a shifting of clothing? Still holding her dinner plate she tiptoed to the door.* (254)

Key features: Strong language

Subjects: Cuban Americans; Florida—Miami; lawyers

Similar titles: The Britt Montero Mysteries by Buchanan and the Lupe Solano Mysteries by García-Aguilera also feature Cuban Americans in Miami; the Jack Swyteck series by Grippando also takes place in Miami and has attorney protagonists. *Rebel Island* by Riordan has a similar plot, with the sleuth's island vacation being interrupted by murder.

Suspicion of Rage. New York: Dutton Books, 2005. ISBN 0525948058. 373pp.

Attorneys Gail Connor and Anthony Quintana are on their way to Quintana's homeland of Cuba. Before they are able to get away, the CIA gives Quintana a message to pass on to his brother-in-law. The reason his brother-in-law is of such interest to the CIA will lead to a death, as well as to heartache for Gail and Anthony.

> *The image hit her brain before she could turn away, and she choked on the smell. A man seemed to be floating against the wall on the other side. His head was tilted, and his face was wrong—a thick tongue and slits for eyes.* (308)

Key features: Strong language

Subjects: Cuban Americans; Florida—Miami; lawyers

Similar titles: The Britt Montero Mysteries by Buchanan and the Lupe Solano Mysteries by García-Aguilera also feature Cuban Americans in Miami; the Jack Swyteck series by Grippando also takes place in Miami and has attorney protagonists.

Ramos, Manuel (Chicano; Mexican American, Colorado).

Luis Montez Series.

A lawyer in Denver, Colorado, Luis Montez is a Chicano who had an active youth participating in the civil rights movement. Now he spends his time righting wrongs one at a time.

The Ballad of Rocky Ruiz. New York: St. Martin's Press, 1993. ISBN 0-312-09271-7. 201pp.

Lawyer Luis Montez gets caught up in the intrigue surrounding the unsolved death of his close friend and fellow revolutionary Rocky Ruiz, who was murdered twenty years earlier during their college years.

> *Rocky's history of the movement, meticulously memorialized by him to maintain equilibrium in the heady days of youthful revolution, lay before me in a composite of yellowed paper and faded photographs. Newspaper clippings*

were mixed in with his poetry. I didn't know where to start. I picked out a thin spiral notebook and read. (116)

Subjects: Chicanos; Colorado—Denver; lawyers; rebellion

Similar titles: Nava's <u>Henry Rios Mystery Series</u> also features a Chicano lawyer investigating murder.

The Ballad of Gato Guerrero. New York: St. Martin's Press, 1994. ISBN 0312109350. 183pp.

Felix "el Gato" Guerrero needs a lot of help after suffering wrenching personal losses post–Vietnam War and getting romantically involved with the sexy wife of the local mobster boss. Of course, he looks up his old *amigo* Luis Montez to provide that help. Meanwhile, one of Luis's more problematic teenaged clients has been remanded to his custody.

Key features: First person narration; strong language; sexual situations

Subjects: Chicanos; Colorado—Denver; lawyers; organized crime

Similar titles: Nava's <u>Henry Rios Mystery Series</u> also features a Chicano lawyer investigating crime.

The Last Client of Luis Montez. New York: St. Martin's Press, 1996. ISBN 0312139977. 194pp.

Luis Montez gets his client off, only to be accused of that client's murder the next day. Montez's alibi skips town, making matters worse. Montez will have to work hard if he is to clear his name and stay alive.

Hey, I'm a lawyer. I make a living off the disasters of my fellow human beings. That's why we put up with lawyer jokes—tit for tat. If lawyers were actually offended by the jokes, we would have sued someone to shut up the so-called comedy. (9)

Key features: First person narration; strong language, sexual situations

Subjects: Chicanos; lawyers; murder

Similar titles: *Grim City* by Hensley and Nava's <u>Henry Rios Mystery Series</u> are also about Chicano lawyers and murder.

Blues for the Buffalo. New York: St. Martin's Press, 1997. ISBN 0312154801. 215pp.

A vacation isn't a vacation for lawyer Luis Montez. Feeling the effects of his last case, Montez travels to Mexico to relax, only to be caught up in the disappearance of a young woman. This mystery follows Luis back to Denver, where things turn even uglier.

How's the leg, Montez? Still gimping around, looking for sympathy from all the young senoritas? What an example of an officer of the court! You get in more heat than the birds in my kitchen. (112)

Key features: First person narration; strong language; sexual situations

Subjects: Chicano lawyers; Colorado—Denver; missing persons; murder

> **Similar titles:** Nava's <u>Henry Rios Mystery Series</u> also features a Chicano lawyer investigating murder.

Somoza, José Carlos (Cuban).

🖋 *The Athenian Murders.* (*La caverna de las ideas*, 2000). **Translated by Sonia Soto. New York: Farrar, Straus & Giroux, 2000. ISBN 0374106770. 262pp.**

In this dual mystery, the death of students from Plato's Academy brings crusty old Heracles Pontor to investigate, with help from the "Decipherer of Enigmas" and other teachers at the academy. The parallel story presents the translator working on the first story and eerily finding hidden meanings directed at him!

> *In Athens, the saying goes that to know the future, you need the Oracle of Delphi, but to know the past, you simply need the Decipherer of Enigmas.* (26)

Subjects: ancient Greece—Athens; murder; translators

Similar titles: The <u>Alexander the Great</u> series by Doherty is also about murder in ancient Greece.

Awards: CWA Gold Dagger Award, 2003

Taibo, Paco Ignacio, II (Mexican).

🖋 *Leonardo's Bicycle.* (*La bicicleta de Leonardo*, 1993). **Translated by Martin Michael Roberts. New York: Warner Books, 1995. ISBN 0892965894. 453pp.**

José Daniel Fierro takes a break from his writing to travel to Ciudad Juárez. He wants to help a young female basketball player after her kidney is stolen and she has been left for dead. Meanwhile, a former CIA agent from New York travels to Mexico in search of secrets that have something to do with Leonardo daVinci's idea of the bicycle and 1920s Barcelona.

> *His weakness was eating away at him from inside. A huge worm was crawling through his gut. He walked away from the hospital, trying to leave the images of the dead behind him, covered in sweat despite the freezing night.* (180)

Key features: Strong language

Subjects: basketball players—women; Mexico—Mexico City; writers—fiction

Similar titles: *The Lady in Blue* by Sierra is also about Leonardo and mysterious conspiracies.

Awards: Latin American Dashiell Hammett Award, 1994

Véa, Alfredo (Mexican American).

Gods Go Begging. **New York: Dutton, 1999. ISBN 052594513x. 320pp.**

After two friends/lovers are murdered in cold blood—an African American woman and an Asian woman—Vietnam vet and defense attorney Jesse Pasadoble finds himself defending the accused man, who is also a veteran.

> *It wafted down afternoon sidewalks and into nearby warehouses where greasy auto mechanics and squinting printers stopped working to anxiously peek at the time clock.* (6)

Subjects: California—San Francisco; defense attorneys; murder; veterans—Vietnam War

Similar titles: *The Speed of Light* by Cercas and *No Matter How Much You Promise to Cook or Pay the Rent . . .* by Vega Yunqué are other novels featuring Vietnam veterans.

The Silver Cloud Café. **New York: Plume, 1997. ISBN 0452276640. 343pp.**

The movement, people, and places of the *loco* history of the United States and Mexico converge on this *loco* café amid a *loco* cast of characters including priests, midget philosophers, angels, saints, martyrs, and transvestites. The mystery involves a priest's corpse found floating in the Bay, which is linked to another murder that happened decades before. Defense attorney Zeferino del Campo wrestles with these mysteries, which have something to do with his own migrant worker childhood and the Mexican Revolution.

> *They had both been rank neophytes to the mundane riddle of this place, but now they were seasoned sojourners who had hidden behind Lot's door, posed for Leonardo's brush, stayed the hand of Abraham, and they had followed the very first braceros.* (1)

Subjects: California—San Francisco—Mission District; ghosts; Mexican Revolution; murder; revenge

Similar titles: *The Lazarus Rumba* by Mestre is written in a similar mystical and grotesque tone.

Thrillers and Suspense

The novels in this section don't necessarily have a happy ending or a definitive resolution. They may leave the reader questioning his or her own perception of reality, justice, or good and evil. The protagonists here are more likely antiheroes, grudging participants in a situation they know little about, unwilling pawns who strive to turn the tables on their tormentors or uncover Machiavellian conspiracies. The authors in this section include some of the best writers of the Spanish-speaking world.

Arias, Arturo (Guatemalan).

Rattlesnake. **(*Cascabel*, 1998). Translated by Sean Higgins and Jill Robbins. Willimantic, CT: Curbstone Press, 2003. ISBN 1-931896-01-1. 245pp.**

American CIA agent Tom Wright travels to Guatemala to rescue Australian banker Mr. Gray, who has been kidnapped by guerrilleros, but he also aims to hook up again with the elegantly inscrutable, mysterious, tantalizingly aloof Sandra Herrera, who has an agenda of her own.

> *Regardless of the country's famed colors, everything seemed hazy and dull, as if cloaked under a veil of mist, giving it the appearance of a grainy black and white photo. Only the tremulous, melancholic image of the woman, idealized by the long separation, stood out in vivid color as the car moved erratically in the direction of his nondescript hotel, as impersonal as any other.* (5)

Subjects: CIA agents; Guatemala; guerrilleros; kidnapping; revolutionary struggles

Similar titles: *A Good Day to Die* by Coltrane is another novel about CIA plots in Latin America.

Bicos, Olga.

Dead Easy. **Don Mills, ON: Mira Books, 2004. ISBN 0-7783-2076-6. 377pp.**

Ana Kimble is a nice person with maternal instincts for her child prodigy friend, Rachel Maza (daughter of her ex-husband's megalomaniacal colleague). So she leaves LA to accompany Rachel on a Caribbean holiday. That holiday turns into a *pesadilla,* a nightmare, in which they are stalked by more than one shady character trying to steal Rachel's top secret computer program. One of the shady characters is a handsome detective.

> *Too much Kimble and not enough Montes. The observation came with affection from her mother, the Latin artist who had fallen in love with Ana's steadfast Yankee accountant father. "La americanita" the Montes side of the family had dubbed Ana—a comment on her accented Spanish and a body that, at five feet ten inches, was better suited for the runway than the rumba. She couldn't even cook rice.* (17)

Subjects: college professors; Cuban Americans; experiments; love stories; pharmaceutical companies; secret agents; stalkers; writers

Similar titles: *Turing's Delirium* by Paz Soldán also features a shady company and computer secrets; Scordato's <u>CellTech Series</u> also has a pharmaceutical company at the center of its action.

Black Artemis. *See also* Quintero, Sofia.

Explicit Content. **New York: New American Library, 2004. ISBN 0-451-21275-4. 332pp.**

Cassie, an up-and-coming hip-hop artist, and Leila, her best friend, have dreams of making it big in the hip-hop scene. After Leila is seduced by the generous offer of some very shady characters at the Explicit Content label, Cassie fights to make her own way, remaining independent and hoping finally to rescue Leila.

> *Leila has always been the ticket onstage, grabbing the audience's attention with her low-cut halters and stiletto heels and keeping it with those contagious chants. It was all good, because after the show while young girls were rushing Leila for her autograph and asking where she bought her gear, I was the one the other MCs stepped to saying, "Yo, your rhyme got me mad open" or "You got a tape I can cop?"* (3)

Key features: First person narration; reader's guide

Subjects: hip-hop; music industry; New York; Puerto Ricans; street lit; women's friendships

Similar titles: The <u>Naughty Girls Series</u> by Leto has a similar urban tone and setting, with a tough female protagonist.

Picture Me Rollin'. **New York: New American Library, 2005. ISBN 0-451-21513-3. 302pp.**

Esperanza (Espe) gets out after a year-long turn in jail after taking the fall for her boyfriend, Jesus, and the rest of the gang. Jesus expects her to fall back into her old role with the gang, but Esperanza's consciousness has been raised. Can Espe resist the pull of the gang and stay true to her newfound principles?

> [S]he hoped that Dulce might put aside her ill feelings toward Xavier to celebrate her release from prison. And Esperanza really did not want to face Jesus and the others by herself. But she would be damned if his crew and the wannabes partied in her name while she stayed home, especially when they owed her so much. (5)

Key features: Readers guide

Subjects: ex-convicts; New York—New York City; Nuyoricans; Puerto Ricans; Shakur, Tupac; sisters; street lit

Similar titles: *Maximum Insecurity* by Grady is also about ex-lovers and prison.

Carpentier, Alejo (Cuban).

The Chase. (*El acoso*, 1956). **Translated by Alfred MacAdam. Minneapolis: University of Minnesota Press, 2001, c1989. ISBN 0816638098. 121pp.**
A young man flees from henchmen intent on assassinating him for his off-the-cuff rebellion against the repressive regime of pre-Castro Cuba. His story and that of a worker in the ticket booth of the concert hall where Beethoven's *Eroica* symphony is being performed are intertwined when the man being chased finally takes refuge in the concert hall. This psychological thriller is told in exquisitely dense literary style, a precursor to the Latin American Boom generation. All the action takes place before the concert ends.

> She seemed unconcerned that the ticket seller behind her was a man, as she had just disengaged herself from the confinement of a most intimate garment—evidently not caring that he saw her do it—in one matter-of-fact, nonchalant movement. (4)

Subjects: Cuba—Havana; dictatorships; music—Beethoven; prostitutes; prostitution; rebellion; torture

Similar titles: *The Messenger* by Montero is also set in Havana, with a plot involving political intrigue and music; *The Wake* by Glantz is a similarly literary novel involving music that takes place over the course of an afternoon.

Chavarría, Daniel (Uruguayan).

🏆 *Tango for a Torturer.* (*El rojo en la pluma del loro*, 2001). **Translated by Peter Bush. New York: Akashic Books, 2006. ISBN 9781933354194. 341pp.**
Aldo Bianchi is a student from Uruguay, where he was tortured mercilessly by the military junta. He now lives in Italy but is on holiday in Havana. When he finds out that the man who tortured him, Alberto Ríos, is in town living under an assumed name, Aldo sets out to settle the score, with the help of his lover, Bini.

> Bini attracted one's attention not for her immediate physical beauty, but for her rough-and-ready Creole look. Nobody could catch sight of her sexy strut and resist turning around to give her behind a once-over. Tall, curvaceous, and feline. (17)

Key features: Sexual situations

Subjects: Cuba—Havana; prostitutes; revenge; students; torturers

Similar titles: *Dirty Blonde and Half-Cuban* by Wixon is also about prostitution in contemporary Cuba; *The Name of a Bullfighter* by Sepúlveda is about torturers and their victims.

Awards: Casa de las Américas Prize for Best Novel, 2000

Coltrane, James (U.S. American).

A Good Day to Die: A Novel of Cuba after Castro. **New York: Anchor Books, 2000, c1999. ISBN 0385498985. 155pp.**

Conflicted by earlier missions and personal traumatic history, Jorge Ortega is sent by the CIA to Cuba a year after Castro's death to lead a ragtag band in a farfetched plot to take over a radio station at the moment of a U.S. invasion, which may not take place.

> *The jungle had the same feel as El Salvador—the humidity, the same stench of decay—and he didn't like it. He could take it though, as long as he didn't start seeing Catalina. As long as he didn't start remembering.* (3)

Subjects: CIA agents; Cuba; U.S. invasions

Similar titles: *Goodbye Mexico* by Phillip Jennings is also about CIA plots involving Cuba.

Dorfman, Ariel (Chilean).

Blake's Therapy. **(*Terapia,* 2001). New York: Seven Stories Press, c2001. ISBN 1583220704. 175pp.**

Graham Blake is the CEO of a socially responsible company, and he suffers from insomnia and guilt. His therapist has prescribed a radical treatment involving active voyeurism in which Blake, as the patient, observes a Latino family, while he is being observed. The therapy has unintended consequences when Blake attempts to carry things over into his real life.

> *Graham Blake has more charm than is good for him, he covers up his mistakes with that smile, since he's been a child he's smiled his way out of every mistake he's ever made. Graham Blake may be used, therefore, to getting what he wants, but isn't willing to pay the price.* (12–13)

Key features: Second person narration

Subjects: dystopias; executives; psychotherapy; voyeurs

Similar titles: *Dr. Neruda's Cure for Evil* by Rafael Yglesias is another novel about psychotherapy gone wrong.

Fuentes, Carlos (Mexican).

The Eagle's Throne. **(*Silla del águila,* 2003). Translated by Kristina Cordero. New York: Random House, 2006. ISBN 1-4000-6247-0. 336pp.**

In a not-too-distant future, the letters of those surrounding the president of Mexico (who are forced to revert to hard copy communication after the United States has cut off all satellite connections) tell a story of power, passion, and corruption among Mexico's political elite.

You must know at once, Nicolás Valdivia, that with me everything is political, even sex. You may be shocked by this kind of professional voracity. But there's no changing it. I'm forty-five now, and ever since the age of twenty-two I've arranged my life around a single purpose: to be, to shape, to eat, to dream, to savor, and to suffer politics. (1)

Key features: Epistolary style

Subjects: epistolary fiction; foreign relations; futuristic fiction; Mexico; politics; United States

Similar titles: *Tarzan's Tonsillitis* by Bryce Echenique is also written in the epistolary style; *Turing's Delirium* by Paz Soldán looks at a dystopic future from a very different perspective.

García Márquez, Gabriel (Colombian).

Chronicle of a Death Foretold. **(*Crónica de una muerte anunciada,* 1981). Translated by Gregory Rabassa. New York: Alfred A. Knopf, 1983. ISBN 0394530748. 120pp.**

Young, handsome, and vital Santiago Nasar is going to be murdered. How can this happen when the whole *pueblo* is party to the plan to take his life?

I saw him in her memory. He had turned twenty-one the last week in January, and he was slim and pale and had his father's Arab eyelids and curly hair. He was the only child of a marriage of convenience without a single moment of happiness, but he seemed happy with his father until the latter died suddenly three years before, and he continued seeming to be so with his solitary mother until the Monday of his death. (7)

Key features: First person narration

Subjects: bachelors; dishonor; murder; *pueblos;* weddings

Similar titles: *The Chase* by Carpentier has a similarly literary structure and tone.

Giardinelli, Mempo (Argentinian).

Sultry Moon. **(*Luna Caliente,* 1983). Translated by Patricia J. Duncan. Pittsburgh, PA: Latin American Literary Review Press, 1998. ISBN 0935480927. 111pp.**

Back home in Argentina after a long sojourn of study abroad, Ramiro Bernardez is looking forward to a bright future in his *pueblito*—unfortunately, the hot, sultry moon unhinges him, moving him to rape and murder the teenaged daughter of his dinner hosts and become a fugitive. But what really happened? Why does Araceli keep showing up to torture him after he has killed her and gotten rid of her body?

Ramiro told himself that he might regret his own madness. He asked himself what he was doing. He hesitated a moment, petrified on the dirt road. But he gave in when he saw Araceli, at the second floor window, watching him. (14)

Key features: Sexual situations; violence

Subjects: Argentina; intellectuals; madness; murder; rape

Similar titles: *Night Buffalo* by Arriaga has a similarly dark nocturnal tone.

Lóriga, Ray (Spanish).

My Brother's Gun. (*Caídos del cielo,* 1995). Translated by Kristina Cordero. New York: St. Martin's Press, 1997. ISBN 0-312-16947-7. 119pp.

A murderer's brother tells the story of the almost random killing, subsequent flight and capture, and the resulting notoriety he and his mother "enjoy."

> When anybody, like the TV people for example, asks me about him, I always say that I don't think it was such a good idea what he did. Because it's the truth, and anyway, my mother would die if I said anything else. But, to tell you the real truth, he wasn't such a bad guy. (4–5)

Key features: First person narration; sexual situations

Subjects: alienation; brothers; mothers and sons; murderers; psychopaths

Similar titles: *White Leg* by Max Martinez also features a protagonist who is a criminal.

Marías, Javier (Spanish).

Your Face Tomorrow Series.

Jaime/Jacques Deza is recruited by England's MI6 intelligence agency thanks to his knack for interpreting people's actions and expressions. These novels are stylistically complex and thematically rich.

Volume One: Fever and Spear. (*Tu rostro mañana.1, Fiebre y lanza,* 2002). Translated by Margaret Jull Costa. New York: New Directions, 2005. ISBN 0811216128. 387pp.

Deza discovers his intuitive skills, and MI6 puts him to work investigating a potential coup d'etat in Venezuela. Meanwhile, he is indoctrinated by the strange and sinister Dr. Wheeler and followed by a woman with a dog.

> Telling is almost always done as a gift, even when the story contains and injects some poison, it is also a bond, a granting of trust, and rare is the trust or confidence that is not sooner or later betrayed, rare is the close bond that does not grow twisted or knotted and, in the end, become so tangled that a razor or knife is needed to cut it. (3)

Key features: First person, stream-of-consciousness narration

Subjects: England—London; interpreters; spies

Similar titles: *The Shadow of the Wind* by Ruiz Zafón is also about the Spanish Civil War and its secrets.

Volume Two: Dance and Dream. (*Tu rostro mañana. 2, Baile y sueño,* 2004). Translated by Margaret Jull Costa. New York: New Directions, 2006. ISBN 9780811216562. 341pp.

In the second volume of the trilogy, Jacques sees his boss violently assault a person in a nightclub. This event and the attitudes that attend it are juxtaposed with Deza's father's experiences during the Spanish Civil War.

> Because even there, far from Luisa and from our children, I would sometimes remember the young Bosnian woman and her two children, the small,

responsible, stateless optimist and his brother in the old stroller, none of whom I had seen and whom I had only heard about from Luisa. (16)

Key features: First person, stream-of-consciousness narration.

Subjects: Civil War—Spain; England—London; spies; violence

Similar titles: *The Shadow of the Wind* by Ruiz Zafón is also about the Spanish Civil War and its secrets.

Martinez, Max (Tejano).

Layover. **Houston, TX: Arte Público Press, 1997. ISBN 1558851992. 294pp.**

Priscilla Arrabal is a young woman who stops in a small town hoping for a chance to catch her breath from her hectic life. Instead, she is accused of murder and must run from the real killer and the police.

> *Priscilla felt her blood racing, throbbing at her temples. She kept driving, blinking repeatedly in counterpoint to the windshield wipers. She tried desperately to order her thoughts into the clear thinking she'd been trained to do.* (47)

Key features: Strong language; sexual situations

Subjects: Chicanas; murder; *pueblos*; sheriffs; Texas

Similar titles: The Dan Rhodes series by Crider is also about murder in small towns in Texas; the Ronnie Ventana series by White is also about Chicanas and murder.

White Leg. **Houston, TX: Arte Público Press, 1996. ISBN 1558850988. 253pp.**

Gil Blue thinks he has a pretty good career in robbing convenience stores. All this changes the morning Gil shoots and kills a Texas Ranger. Now not only is Gil wanted for the shooting, but his charming and cheating wife has also implicated him in a kidnapping.

> *The first thing I start with is my nerves. If it don't feel right, if my nerves ain't right, I wait until they do, or I stay put. It's all in my nerves.* (33)

Key features: First person narration; strong language; sexual situations

Subjects: kidnapping; murder; *pueblos*; robbery; Texas

Similar titles: *Still River: A Lee Henry Oswald Mystery* by Hunsicker and *A Mammoth Murder* by Crider are other novels about murder in Texas.

Murray, Yxta Maya (Mexican American, California; Central American).

Red Lion Adventures.

Bookstore owner Lola Sanchez has the lust for adventure in her veins beneath her unassuming exterior. She is an expert cryptographer and a specialist in arcane texts. Her adventures involve the entire eccentric and impulsive family.

The Queen Jade: A Novel of Adventure. New York: Rayo, 2005. 334pp. ISBN 0-060-58264-2. 366pp.

Lola's unconventional archaeologist mother Juana goes off to Central America after the elusive Queen Jade. She's following clues from an arcane Mayan text. When she disappears, Lola joins forces with Juana's rival professor, Eric Gomara. Lola's adventures take her deep into the mysterious past and the troubled present, as she is followed by shady characters, lost in labyrinths in a race against time to find her lost mother and the mysterious Queen Jade.

> *Mom gripped my legs as I stood on a ladder propped up against the bookshelf.*
>
> *"Watch it," she said. Whenever you get on this thing, I think you're going to break your neck.*
>
> *"And you want me to go play with scorpions and snakes in the jungle?"*
>
> *"It's safe in the jungle. But look at this place, books everywhere. It's a death pit."* (4)

Subjects: adventure; archaeologists; bookstore owners; college professors; Guatemala; Mayan Indians; Mexican Americans

Similar titles: *Rattlesnake* by Arias is another adventure novel set in Guatemala.

The King's Gold. New York: HarperCollins, 2008. ISBN 9780060891084. 406pp.

Right before her wedding, a stranger approaches Lola with a centuries-old letter that provides clues to Montezuma's lost gold. She cannot resist the possibility of finding the treasure, even if it means putting her entire family in danger.

> *I first realized that I was changing from a sedentary, word-mad bibliophile into a genuine biblio-adventurer on the Sunday evening a dark and dangerous man showed me that priceless piece of treasure.* (4)

Subjects: adventure; archaeologists; bookstore owners; gold; Mexican Americans; Mexico; Montezuma

Similar titles: Pérez-Reverte's novels are similarly full of adventure and puzzles to solve; see especially his *The King's Gold.*

Paz Soldán, Edmundo (Bolivian).

Turing's Delirium. (Delirio de Turing, 2003). Translated by Lisa Carter. New York: Houghton Mifflin, 2006. ISBN 9780618541393. 291pp.

In Rio Fugitivo, Bolivia, sits the Black Chamber, a somber edifice housing a cadre of cryptographers and codebreakers. Chief among these is the sinister Albert, possibly an ex-Nazi. Our hero, Miguel Sáenz, has been relegated to a corner office while holding on to the second highest security clearance, ostensibly in deference to his experience and longevity. The current task at the Chamber involves foiling a plot by the insurgent hacker Kandinsky, an idealist fighting globalization and transnational corporations. Can Sáenz survive long enough to find his own lost ideals and crack enough code to save civilization as we know it?

> *In Spain they call the screen saver* salvapantallas; *in truth it sounds ridiculous. Still, you shouldn't give up; it is worth going against the grain. The survival of Spanish as a language of the twenty-first century is at stake. Piratas informáticos, piratas informáticos.* (8)

Key features: Various points of view and shifts of perspective (second, first, and third person)

Subjects: codebreakers; codes; cyberguerrillas; globalization; hackers; revolutionaries

Similar titles: *The Absent City* by Piglia also features a futuristic Latin American setting; *Blake's Therapy* by Dorfman and *Blood on the Saddle* by Reig also have a similar weird ambience.

Peréz-Reverte, Arturo.

Captain Alatriste Adventures.

Iñigo Balboa is mercenary Captain Alatriste's ward. He narrates these adventures, which take place in the exciting and dangerous times of seventeenth-century Spain. Captain Alatriste is a great and astute swordsman who lives by his wits and skill. These novels are full of swashbuckling, thrilling adventures, in which many historical figures such as Quevedo and Calderón de la Barca make cameo appearances.

Key features: First person narration; sexual situations; violence

Subjects: historical fiction; mercenaries; Spain—Golden Age; swordplay

Similar titles: *Zorro* by Allende is another historical novel full of swashbuckling action. Modern-day swashbuckling adventure can be found in Murray's <u>Red Lion Adventures</u> series.

Captain Alatriste. (*El capitán Alatriste*, 1996). Translated by Margaret Sayers Peden. New York: G.P. Putnam, 1996. ISBN 0-399-15275-X. 253pp.

Taking place during Spain's Golden Age, this series of thrillers begins as Captain Alatriste, forced into retirement and out of work, is hired to scare a group of travelers into leaving Madrid. Because these travelers are deeply involved in the political intrigue of the time, Alatriste's simple job becomes a dangerous undertaking.

> *He was not the most honest or pious of men, but he was courageous. His name was Diego Alatriste y Tenorio, and he had fought in the ranks during the Flemish wars. When I met him he was barely making ends meet in Madrid, hiring himself out for four maravedís in employ of little glory, often as a swordsman for those who had neither the skill nor the daring to settle their own quarrels.* (1)

Purity of Blood. (*Limpieza de sangre*, 1997). Translated by Margaret Sayers Peden. New York: G.P. Putnam, 2006. ISBN 0399153209. 320pp.

Alatriste is hired to rescue a young woman from the clutches of an evil priest in a convent. The seemingly simple task becomes lethal when the Inquisition gets involved and Iñigo is put in mortal danger.

The Sun over Breda. (*El sol de Breda*, 1998). Translated by Margaret Sayers Peden. New York: G.P. Putnam, 2007. ISBN 0399153837. 304pp.

> Alatriste and Iñigo travel to Breda to help out his old regiment during this siege, which takes place near the end of the 100 Years' War.

The King's Gold. (*Oro del rey*, 2000). Translated by Margaret Sayers Peden. New York: G.P. Putnam, 2008. ISBN 9780399155109. 228pp.

> Alatriste is charged with rescuing a shipment of gold ingots en route from the West Indies. Iñigo's hormones put him in mortal danger.

The Club Dumas. (*El club Dumas*, 1993). Translated by Sonia Soto. New York: Harcourt, Brace, 1996. ISBN 0151001820. 362pp.

Mercenary book dealer Lucas Corso is drawn into a mysterious adventure filled with satanic cults and dangerous women when he begins to search for a book with the power to summon the devil.

> *Why are you so interested in the devil? I saw him once. I was fifteen and saw him as clearly as I'm seeing you. He had a hard collar, a hat, and a walking stick. He was very handsome. (222)*

Key features: First person narration; sexual situations

Subjects: book collectors; bookstore owners; devil; France—Paris; murder; occult; Spain—Madrid

Similar titles: *Death's Autograph* by Macdonald is another novel about murder and antiquarian book dealers; *The Shadow of the Wind* by Ruiz Zafón features antiquarian book dealers in Madrid, and Murray's <u>Red Lion Adventures</u> series features an antiquarian book dealer as the swashbuckling protagonist.

The Fencing Master. (*El maestro de esgrima*, 1988). Translated by Margaret Jull Costa. New York: Harcourt, Brace, 1998. ISBN 0151001812. 245pp.

A mysterious woman comes to fencing master Don Jaime to be taught the art of fencing. Don Jaime refuses, and the repercussions of this decision put him in the middle of political intrigue and murder.

> *"Forgive me, madam, but this . . . . It is a little unusual. I am the inventor of a secret thrust and I do teach it for the sum you have mentioned, but, please understand, I would never teach fencing to a woman, I mean." (24)*

Subjects: fencing; murder; Spain—Madrid

Similar titles: *The Tempest* by de Prada and *The Last Resort: A Moroccan Mystery* by Posadas are also about murder in Spain.

Painter of Battles. (*El pintor de batallas*, 2006). Translated by Margaret Sayers Peden. New York: Random House, 2008. ISBN 9781400065981. 211pp.

War photographer Faulques has retired to a reclusive tower on the coast of Spain, where he is working on a mural about war. The subject of one of Faulques's famous photos has come to kill him.

> *The whole formed an immense and disquieting landscape, no title, no specific time, where the shield half buried in the sand, the medieval helmet splashed with blood, the shadow of an assault rifle falling over a forest of wood crosses, the ancient walled city and modern concrete-and-glass towers coexisted less as anachronisms than as evidence. (5)*

Subjects: artists; love; photographers; Spain; war

Similar titles: *The Shadow of the Wind* by Ruiz Zafón also looks at the relationship between art and reality and the ugly consequences of wars.

***The Seville Communion.* (*La piel del tambor,* 1995). Translated by Sonia Soto. New York: Harcourt, Brace, 1995. ISBN 0151002835. 375pp.**

Vatican security has been breached, and a message is posted about The Lady of Tears, a church in Seville. Father Lorenzo Quart is sent to investigate the message and the church itself. Two people connected to The Lady of Tears have met with unfortunate "accidents." Now Father Quart needs to get to the bottom of these occurrences before anyone else meets the same fate.

> *"You have your mission." Absently he cleaned one lens, then the other. "Who Vespers is," he said, "isn't important. The message is a warning. Or an appeal to whatever there is that's still noble in the form that you and I work for." He put on his glasses. "A reminder that honesty and decency still exist."* (252)

Subjects: murder; priests—Catholic; Spain—Seville; Vatican City

Similar titles: *The Third Secret* by Berry and *The Lady in Blue* by Sierra are other mysteries set in Vatican City and featuring the Catholic Church and conspiracy.

Piglia, Ricardo (Argentinian).

***The Absent City.* (*La ciudad ausente: una opera en dos actos,* 1995). Translated by Sergio Waisman. Durham, NC: Duke University Press, 2000. ISBN 0822325578. 147pp.**

In a futuristic Buenos Aires, reporter Junior tries to locate a mysterious machine that holds the contents of the mind of a woman named Elena. His search for this "machine" takes him through many different stories, but in the end, only one matters.

> *Everything is scientific. Nothing evil. I met a Russian guy once who had invented a metal bird that could predict rain. This is the same. Pure science, no religion.* (29)

Subjects: Argentina—Buenos Aires; reporters; science fiction

Similar titles: *The Seven Madmen* by Arlt and the Honor Bound Argentine series by Griffin are other mysteries set in Argentina; *Turing's Delirium* by Paz Soldán has a similarly futuristic Latin American setting.

Posadas, Carmen (Spanish).

***Little Indiscretions: A Delectable Mystery.* (*Pequeñas infamias,* 1998). Translated by Christopher Andrews. New York: Random House, 2003. ISBN 0-375-50885-6. 305pp.**

Famous chef Nestor Chaffino is found frozen to death in the walk-in freezer at the resort. Who could want him dead? Just about everyone at the weekend house party, as it turns out, all of whom are hiding secrets—illicit affairs, involvement with Argentine torturers, suicide, and blackmail—that somehow involved Nestor. The solution brings the story

1 2 3 4 5 6 7 8 9

full circle, with fantastical elements, a clairvoyant, a ghost, and ubiquitous cockroaches with their wriggling antennae.

> *His mustache was stiffer than ever, so stiff a fly could have stepped out to the end, like a prisoner walking the plank on a pirate ship. Except that flies can't survive in a cool room at twenty below zero, and neither could the owner of the blond, frozen mustache: Nestor Chaffino, chef and pastry cook, renowned for his masterful way with a chocolate fondant.* (3)

Key features: First person narration

Subjects: chefs; humor; murder; Spain

Similar titles: *The Shadow of the Shadow* by Taibo is another mystery told from multiple perspectives.

Awards: Planeta Prize, 1998

Reig, Rafael (Spanish).

Blood on the Saddle. (*Sangre a borbotones,* 2001). **Translated by Paul Hammond. London: Serpent's Tail, 2005. ISBN 1852428708. 182pp.**

In the Madrid of the near future, where mega-genetic engineering conglomerate Manex rules over an Iberian–U.S. Federation, private detective Carlos Clot bumbles through a bewildering conglomerate of cases that have him searching for wayward spouses and wayward fictional characters, falling in love, and winning his spurs.

> *The year had begun with a series of wonders presaging earth-shattering events. In January the water in the canal was tinged with red, a swarm of bees had set up home in the dome of San Francisco el Grande, Chopeitia Genomics patented the new techniques of genetic modification, there were floods that inundated Legazpi and Vallecas, as well as a fall in the number of magistrates.* (4)

Key features: First person narration; sexual situations

Subjects: dystopias; humor; metafiction; private investigators; Spain—Madrid

Similar titles: *The Automatic Detective* by A. Lee Martinez is another humorous detective novel set in the future; *Solstice* by Silva also features fiction that gets out of control. *Turing's Delirium* by Paz Soldán and *Blake's Therapy* by Dorfman have similarly weird futuristic settings.

Rodriguez, Jerry A. (Nuyorican).

The Devil's Mambo. **New York: Kensington Publishing, 2007. ISBN 9780758217103. 292pp.**

Nicholas Esperanza, a former homicide cop and Navy SEAL, is a tough guy by any standard. Has he turned soft after winning $30 million in the lottery and living the high life as the owner of the hottest salsa club in New York City? Esperanza's childhood sweetheart, the incredibly hot Legs, is his partner in every sense of the word. Her *abuelita* pleads with Nick to find her missing granddaughter, the wild Alina. Nick's search for the teenager takes him into the grittiest, rawest stratum of the city, a place that forces Nick to grapple with his own taste for vice and evil.

All he knew was, the reaper had come for him disguised as a temptress. Death, in all of its seductive splendor, stood before him, ready to claim. He clenched his knees tight, tried to hold it in, but a puddle of urine gradually spread around his bare feet. Devona giggled lavishly. (15–16)

Key features: Author interview; graphic sexual situations; violence

Subjects: child pornography; murder; New York—New York City; rape; sex clubs; street lit; teen runaways

Similar titles: Leto's <u>Naughty Girls Series</u> also features sex and murder.

Sáenz, Benjamin (New Mexican).

The House of Forgetting. **New York: HarperCollins, 1997. ISBN 0-06-018738-7. 341pp.**

Gloria Erlinda Santos was rechristened Claudia by her abductor and tormentor, Thomas Blacker, who also happens to be an influential college professor. After twenty-three years of being his prisoner, she stabs him and escapes. Can her attorney, Cajun Jenny Richard, with the help of detective Alexander Murphy, give her the tools she needs to face Blacker in court?

> *As she watched the wind and its work, she tried to think of something calm. Her mother's face. But she no longer remembered—only remembered her mother had been dark and smelled like the pine soap she mopped the floors with. The color of her skin, the soap, the mop. Her hands. (3)*

Subjects: college professors; Illinois—Chicago; kidnapping; sexual slavery; women lawyers

Similar titles: *The Art of Murder* by Somoza is another novel about sexual slavery.

Salas, Floyd (Mexican American).

State of Emergency. **Houston, TX: Arte Público Press, 1996. ISBN 1558850937. 396pp.**

In the freewheeling 1960s, Roger takes off for Europe one step ahead (in his mind at least) of the conspirators seeking to take him out before he can publish his exposé of their grim plans to eliminate all voices of dissent. He is accompanied by former student and current lover Penny as they travel through Europe and down to Morocco. Is someone really following Roger, or is this flight inspired by drug-induced paranoia?

> *He looked across the table at Roger with what seemed a superior glint in his eyes, a smile like a thin line below the frosty surface of his glasses. But Craig sounded as if he were still annoyed over Roger saying the students thought he was a police informer. (27)*

Subjects: college professors; conspiracies; drugs; Europe; paranoia; tourists—American; writers

Similar titles: Riordan's Tres Navarre is another professor who solves mysteries.

Santos-Febres, Mayra (Puerto Rican).

Any Wednesday I'm Yours. (Cualquier miércoles soy tuya, 2002). **Translated by James Graham. New York: Riverhead Books, 2005. ISBN 1-59448-001-X. 273pp.**

After being fired from his copyediting job at the newspaper, would-be novelist Julian Castrodad takes a job working the late shift at the Tulán motel, where he encounters the dark underbelly of life in San Juan, Puerto Rico. Union organizers, illicit lovers, drug dealers, and the mysterious M. visit the motel, while murder takes place during his shift.

> *Walking back to the office it struck me that this job was double-edged. It immediately transformed me into an invisible being, less than a person, but at the same time, more: something like a reluctant ghost freed from the prison of its body.* (5)

Subjects: adultery; corruption; drug dealers; journalists; lawyers; motels; newspapers; unions; writers—fiction

Similar titles: *Night Buffalo* is a novel that also features drugs and its companions: corruption, adultery, and death; Gutiérrez's *Dirty Havana Trilogy* concentrates more on journalists and a decadent lifestyle.

Sepúlveda, Luis (Chilean).

The Name of a Bullfighter. (Nombre de torero, 1994). **Translated by Suzanne Ruta. New York: Harcourt, Brace, 1996. ISBN 0151001936. 211pp.**

At the center of this suspenseful tale is a treasure of golden coins stolen from the German treasury during World War II as two desperate men race to be the first to reach it, hidden somewhere in Chile. Juan Belmonte wants the money to pay for treatment for his girlfriend, who was ravaged by torture. Frank Galinksy, a former operative for the East German Stasi, is obsessed with recouping the treasure to recapture his lost status and self-respect.

> *A man can endure a great deal of pain. The astounding mechanism of the brain provides corners, empty stretches, where you can hide, and there's always the final option of succumbing to madness.* (13)

Key features: First person narration

Subjects: Chile; Germany; torture; treasure

Similar titles: *Tango for a Torturer* by Chavarría is another novel about a game of cat and mouse between a torturer and his victim.

Sierra, Javier (Spanish).

The Lady in Blue: A Novel. (La dama azul, 2005). **Translated by James Graham. New York: Atria Books, 2007. ISBN 9781416532234. 342pp.**

Jennifer Narody is having strange dreams about Sister María de Jesús Ágreda, a seventeenth-century nun supposed to have converted the Indians without ever leaving her convent in Spain by bilocating—that is, being in two places at once, Jennifer, part of a secret project having to do with psychic espionage, has much to deal with: an apparent suicide; a Spanish agnostic journalist and skeptic named Carlos Albert, who is investigating Sister Ágreda; a Cardinal who has studied paranormal phenomena for the Church; and time travel! Not to mention larcenous angels with code names and walkie-talkies!

> *And yet Baldi the old soldier had still other discoveries hidden in his study. His thesis was astounding. He believed, for example, that the ancients not only knew harmony and applied it, via mathematics, to music, but that harmony was capable of provoking altered states of consciousness that permitted priests and initiates in the classical world to gain access to 'superior' realms of reality. (3)*

Subjects: astral projection; bilocation; California—Los Angeles; Catholic Church; Italy; New Mexico; nuns; Spain—Madrid; spies; Vatican City

Similar titles: *Sor Juana's Second Dream* by Gaspar de Alba is another novel about nuns; *The Secret Supper* by Sierra and *Valley of Bones* by Gruber are other mystery novels that feature mysticism, murder, and the Catholic Church.

The Secret Supper. (La cena secret, 2004). **Translated by Alberto Manguel. New York: Atria Books, 2004. ISBN 978043287647. 329pp.**

Amid the intrigue and unrest of the Borgia papacy of Alexander VI, Dominican Agostino Leyre is sent to investigate Leonardo da Vinci and discover the identity of the soothsayer who has accused Leonardo of hiding heretical symbols from the mystical Cathar sect in his painting *The Last Supper*. Father Leyre must break codes, interpret symbols, and dig up secrets that make the fifteenth-century Church uncomfortable, which in turn could make Leyre expendable.

> *Unlike the rest of our brethren, I was far from certain that the departure of the Duchess of Milan meant the end of a long chain of irregularities, conspiracies and threats against the faith that had seemed to lurk in Ludovico il Moro's court and had for months caused unease among our network of informants. (13)*

Key features: First person narration; multiple points of view

Subjects: Catholic Church—15th century; historical fiction; Italy; *Last Supper, The*; Leonardo da Vinci; Spanish Inquisition

Similar titles: *The Da Vinci Code* by Brown also features Leonardo and secret codes; *The Shadow of the Wind* by Ruiz Zafón also deals with conspiracies and secret codes.

Ruiz Zafón, Carlos (Spanish).

The Shadow of the Wind. (La sombra del viento, 2001). **Translated by Lucia Graves. New York: Penguin Press, 2004. ISBN 1-59420-010-6. 487pp.**

Young Daniel embarks on a quest that includes political intrigue, forbidden love, and physical danger as he seeks to discover the fate of enigmatic author Julian Carax and the identity of whoever has been systematically destroying all copies of Carax's books. Daniel's journey takes us through the terrifying times of the Spanish Civil War and the subsequent oppression of his own time—the 1950s under the dictator Franco—as he seeks to solve a mystery that may best be left alone.

> *Once liberated from its prison on the shelf, the book shed a cloud of golden dust. Pleased with my choice, I tucked it under my arm and retraced my*

steps through the labyrinth with a smile on my lips. Perhaps the bewitching atmosphere of the place had got the better of me, but I felt sure that The Shadow of the Wind *had been waiting for me there for years, probably since before I was born.* (7)

Subjects: books; bookstores; Civil War—Spain; dictatorships—Franco; love stories; Spain—Barcelona; writers—fiction

Similar titles: *The House of Spirits* by Allende is also about love and political intrigue; *The Club Dumas* by Pérez-Reverte also features antique books and secret societies, as does Murray's <u>Red Lion Adventures</u> series.

Tusset, Pablo (Spanish).

The Best Thing That Can Happen to a Croissant. (Lo mejor que le puede pasar a un cruasán, 2001). **Translated by Kristina Cordero. New York: Canongate, 2003. ISBN 1-84195-715-1. 484pp.**

Pablo Mirelles is a philosopher king, underachieving bottom feeder, and hedonist, whose only care is to wander through life in an alcoholic-narcotic daze, coming down to earth only long enough to pick up his monthly dividend check. He unwittingly offers to help his overachiever brother in a deal involving a mysterious house. When his brother disappears and the family is threatened, Pablo finds himself right in the middle of a convoluted conspiracy involving secret societies, hard-nosed detectives, hackers, and beautiful women.

> *The day was not starting out brilliantly. I was out of coffee and clean shirts, and I had to turn the entire living room upside down before I found my keys. Then, just as I opened the downstairs door the sun hit me right between the eyes. But I hung tough, and managed to make it over to Luigi's bar.* (4)

Key features: First person narration

Subjects: computers; conspiracies; humor; philosophers; secret societies; Spain

Similar titles: *Palinuro of Mexico* by del Paso is another absurd and experimental novel; *The Lamentable Journey . . .* by Vega Yunqué and the <u>Silver Mendez Series</u> by Gary Soto also have slacker heroes as protagonists.

Vargas Llosa, Mario (Peruvian).

Death in the Andes. (Lituma en los Andes, 1993). **Translated by Edith Grossman. New York: Farrar, Straus & Giroux, 1996. ISBN 0374140014. 276pp.**

Army corporal Lituma and his deputy Tomás are assigned to a remote outpost in Peru. While on duty, they must investigate the disappearance of three men. The natural suspects would be the Shining Path guerrilleros, but there is a suspicious witch in town. She and her husband are suspected of engaging in cannibalism and wild, pre-Hispanic rites similar to the Dionysian rituals of ancient Greece.

> *Pedrito had gone down to the village to buy the two Civil Guards a bottle of beer, and he never came back. No one had seen them, no one had noticed any fear, apprehension, sickness in them before they vanished. Had the hills just swallowed them up?* (3)

Key features: Multiple points of view

Subjects: *brujas*; guerrilla warfare; Peru; terrorists

Similar titles: *The Uncomfortable Dead* by Taibo and Marcos is another literary-style thriller about a guerrilla movement.

1

2

3

4

5

6

7

8

9

Chapter 6

Fantastic Fiction: Science Fiction, Fantasy, Paranormal, and Magical Realism

La calavera tiene hambre

The time–space continuum and our paltry three dimensions are borders that Latino authors cross time and again. In these novels, the authors take us even further into other dimensions, alternate realities, alternate histories, potential futures, and worlds where dreams and fantasies are commonplace, and, in the case of magic realism, bring those dimensions into our world.

This chapter covers three traditional genres—science fiction, fantasy, and paranormal literature—as well as the literary genre magical realism. All share the use of speculation and supernatural elements that take readers beyond the mundane realities of everyday existence.

Science Fiction

Introduction and Appeal

Books about future worlds that could potentially exist fall in the realm of science fiction. Those who enjoy pondering the plausibility of an author's vision of a not-too-distant future will like the books in this section. Latino-style science fiction novels riff on contemporary problems such as "illegal" immigration and drug use.

These novels give us a vision of the future that can be funny and whimsical, as in the Hernandez and Martinez books, or dark and desperate, as in the Lóriga and Silva novels.

Hernandez, Jaime (Mexican American).

Maggie the Mechanic: A Love and Rockets Book. Seattle, WA: Fantagraphics Books, 2007. ISBN 1560977841. 271pp.

Maggie, a mechanic in the future, has many adventures. This volume contains the first five years of "Locas" stories in graphic novel form.

"Good work, little girl! Mighty quick, clever thinking how you activated the robot's magnetic field! Yessirree! POW!"

Save it for later, Duke . . .

"I think the little lady's had enough for today! It's about time to go home now!"

"Yes. . . . Home. . . . I'll never, ever do this again as long as I live!" (13)

Subjects: dystopias; graphic novels; mechanics; punk culture

Similar titles: *The Automatic Detective* by A. Lee Martinez is another humorous take on the future; *Turing's Delirium* by Paz Soldán is similarly dystopic.

Loriga, Ray (Spanish).

Tokyo Doesn't Love Us Anymore. (Tokio ya no nos quiere, 1999). **Translated by John King. New York: Grove Press, 2003. ISBN 0-8021-4147-1. 260pp.**

In the near future, a nameless Spanish narrator sells a drug that erases short-term memory. His travels take him from Arizona to Bangkok, in a bleak future full of narcotic-induced numbness, anonymous sex, and loss of identity.

> *Ever since the newspapers started saying that the world is going to end, songs have seemed shorter and the days longer. I called in at your house but they told me that you weren't there, they told me that you were somewhere else, in Tokyo.* (3)

Subjects: Arizona; drugs; dystopias; memory; pharmaceutical companies; Thailand—Bangkok

Similar titles: *The Cave* by Saramago also takes place in a dystopian future, and *Turing's Delirium* by Paz Soldán has a similar tone; Jaime Hernandez's *Maggie the Mechanic* portrays another version of the future.

Martinez, A. Lee (Tejano).

The Automatic Detective. **New York: Tom Doherty Associates, 2008. ISBN 9780765318343. 317pp.**

Mack Megaton is getting along just fine in Technotopia, biding his time nonviolently until his citizenship papers come in, although staying under the radar screen is a challenge for a robot created to be a killing machine. When Megaton finds out his aloof neighbors have gone missing, his nascent conscience kicks in, and he sets out to rescue them, and perhaps the world.

> *Traffic was rough as usual. I had skin of an indestructible alloy and even I feared for my safety once or twice. There was a buzzbug stall on Quantum Avenue. Happened all the time. Nothing got perfected in Empire before it was replaced by something better.* (25)

Key features: First person narration

Subjects: aliens; conspiracies; detectives; dystopias; kidnapping; robots; science fiction mysteries

Similar titles: The <u>Vincent Rubio Series</u> by Eric Garcia shares the hard-boiled tone and has a nonhuman protagonist and a sense of humor.

Saramago, José (Portuguese).

The Cave. (*A Caverna,* 2000). Translated by Margaret Jull Costa. New York: Harcourt, 2002. ISBN 0-15-100414-5. 307pp.

In a not-too-distant future, Cipriano Algor, a potter turned doll maker by the whim of a commercial society, escapes from the Center with his family after making a fearsome discovery. Cipriano and his family struggle to survive and conserve their humanity, constantly challenged by the inhuman forces of an increasingly alienating world ruled by marketing.

> *The hands grasping the wheel are large and strong, peasant's hands, and yet, perhaps because of the daily contact with soft clay inevitable in his profession, they also suggest sensitivity.* (1)

Key features: Stream-of-consciousness narration

Subjects: allegory; artisans—potters; dystopias; families; love stories; surrealism; widows and widowers

Similar titles: *People of Paper* by Plascencia also features flight in a dystopian society.

Silva, Ulises (Mexican American).

Solstice. Troy, MI: Tragical Mirth Publishing, 2007. ISBN 9780979451300. 344pp.

In a dark, dystopian world that is now being rewritten, Io (Yo, which translates as "I") is a tough and ruthless (in more ways than one) Editor who is sent on a mission to stop a Scribe named Nadie (which translates as "Nobody") from writing the world out of existence. Can she avert chaos and the destruction of the human race armed only with her wits and her deadly wakizashi?

> *Like a rapid fire sequence of grainy images playing on a flea market projector, she'd see her* wakizashi *slicing away with deadly grace as her entire body glided and danced along with the rhythmic strikes. All she'd remember were flashes. Pictures without context. Frozen images removed from any meaning or sense.* (4)

Key features: Graphic violence; sexual situations

Subjects: apocalypse; dystopias; languages

Similar titles: *The History of the Siege of Lisbon* by Saramago is another novel about the power of writing; *Tokyo Doesn't Love Us Anymore* by Lóriga has a similar tone and similarly dystopian setting.

Fantasy

Introduction and Appeal

In fantasy worlds, emotions and relationships take precedence over ideas and facts. These are worlds and circumstances that could never plausibly exist. Although traditional fantasy novels feature the classic struggle between good and evil, the novels in this section transcend that Manichean dichotomy. The

Latino style of fantasy is appealing to those who question the nature of reality and the official version of history. Those who enjoy reading about other worlds, other states of being, and alternative versions of reality will like these books.

In the world, or worlds, of the novels in this section, things do not proceed as one expects—history hasn't already happened but rather is happening, matter does not behave as we think it should, and nonhuman entities take on very human characteristics.

Antunes, António Lobo (Portuguese).

The Return of the Caravels: A Novel. (*As naus,* 1987). **Translated by Gregory Rabassa. New York: Grove Press, 1988. ISBN 0-8021-1708-2. 210pp.**

Antunes mixes the Lisbon of the 1980s with that of the Conquest, placing Cervantes and Vasco da Gama alongside a man named Luis; gives it all a good shake; and comes up with this zany novel.

> *He recalled the communal bathroom, a washbasin with a set of baroque faucets in imitation of fish that vomited out sobs of brownish water through their open gills, and the time he came upon a man on in years smiling on the toilet with his pants down around his knees.* (1)

Subjects: Angola; Cervantes, Miguel; conquest; da Gama, Vasco; historical fantasy; history—Portugal; Portugal—Lisbon; time-slips; writers—fiction

Similar titles: Del Paso's *Palinuro of Mexico* is another grotesque, scatological novel written in stream-of-consciousness with tongue-in-cheek style.

Chaviano, Daína (Cuban).

The Island of Eternal Love. (*La isla de los amores infinitos,* 2006). **Translated by Andrea G. Labinger. New York: Penguin Group, 2008. ISBN 9781594489921.**

Cecilia is a reporter in Miami on an assignment to investigate a mysterious house that disappears and reappears in different areas of Little Havana. She is a Cuban exile who feels alienated and restless. When friends invite her out for a night of merriment at the disco, she meets an old Cuban woman named Amalia. She returns night after night to hear Amalia's strange stories about love affairs that play out against the backdrop of Cuban history, with roots in Africa, Spain, and China, contending with otherworldly interference.

> *The visions conjured from the old woman's tale-the evocation of a Havana filled with music and life-had left her with an odd sensation of dislocation. She felt like one of those saints that can be in two places at the same time.* (10)

Subjects: Africa; China; Cuba—Havana; Florida—Miami; ghosts; love stories; reporters; Spain

Similar titles: *The House of Spirits* by Allende is another multigenerational story with fantastic elements.

Cortázar, Julio (Argentinian; French).

62: A Model Kit. (*62: modelo para armar,* 1968). Translated by Gregory Rabassa. New York: New Directions, 2000. ISBN 0811214370. 281pp.

This story begins where chapter 62 in the novel *Hopscotch* left off, taking the reader into a parallel universe in which a group of Latin American bohemians create the "model" for life in the "City" as they, and hence the reader, live it.

> *Of course, Juan was probably the only customer for whom the diner's request had a second meaning; automatically, ironically, as a good interpreter accustomed to the instant liquidation of all problems of translation in that struggle against time and silence which is an interpreter's booth, he had fallen into a trap.* (6)

Subjects: bohemians; cities; dystopias; languages; parallel worlds; surrealism

Similar titles: *Budapest* by Buarque and *Yo-Yo Boing!* by Braschi also experiment with language; *Budapest* has a similarly dark tone.

Gorodischer, Angélica (Argentinian).

Kalpa Imperial: The Greatest Empire That Never Was. (*Kalpa Imperial: La Casa del poder; El Imperio más Vasto,* 1983). Translated by Ursula K. Le Guin. New York: ibooks, 2003. ISBN 1-4165-0411-7. 246pp.

Composed of eleven connected stories (or chapters) told in the voice of a storyteller, this novel describes a fantastic empire at different phases of its existence. The empire is not technologically advanced and has more in common with the Middle Ages than with the present moment. Readers visit different moments in the history of the empire, and in almost every chapter an emperor/empress makes his or her appearance.

> *The storyteller said: Now that the good winds are blowing, now that we're done with days of anxiety and nights of terror, now that there are no more denunciations, persecutions, secret executions, and whim and madness have departed from the heart of the Empire, and we and our children aren't playthings of blind power.* (1)

Subjects: allegory; empires; epic fantasy; storytelling; utopias

Similar titles: *The Natural Order of Things* by Antunes also features the ups and downs of an empire, in this case, Portugal. The world created by Gorodischer in this novel has more in common with the one created by Tolkein in *The Lord of the Rings* than that created by Scott in the movie *Blade Runner.*

Goytisolo, Juan (Spanish).

A Cock-eyed Comedy. (*Carajicomedia,* 2000). Translated by Peter Bush. San Francisco: City Lights Books, 2002. ISBN 0872864502. 173pp.

Friar Bugeo, aka Father Trennes, transmigrates through the ages, from the medieval times of *El Cid* to the present, participating in literary adventures with authors, famous protagonists, and historical figures, including Jean Genet, whom "He worshiped . . . from afar but was intimidated by his rude ways" (8); Gregorio Samsa; Marguerite Yourcenar; Francisco de Quevedo; and Ernesto Cardenal.

> *He was preparing—or perpetrating—a novel that the author himself dubbed a door-stopper, tome or artifact—whose production required extensive reading and years of labor. A history of sexuality in the light of Catholic doctrine via a journey through the Spanish language from the Middle Ages to the present.* (8)

Key features: First person narration

Subjects: Catholic Church; historical fantasy; homosexuals; humor; literature; time-slips; transmigration

Similar titles: *The Best Thing That Can Happen to a Croissant* by Tusset is another Spanish novel that is both decadent and silly; readers will find another work of literary satire in *The Savage Detectives* by Bolaño.

Plascencia, Salvador (Californiano).

People of Paper. **San Francisco: McSweeney's Books, 2005. ISBN 1932416218. 245pp.**

In a futuristic dystopia, in which people made of paper mingle with people of flesh and blood, and the Glue Sniffers are a tribe of lost ones, Little Merced and her father, Federico de la Fe, travel from "the land of mud to the land of cement."

> *His hands were bloody, pooling the ink of his body on the floor, staining his pants. She stepped over her creator, spreading his blood across the polished floor, and then walked out of the factory and into the storm. The print of her arms smeared; her soaked feet tattered as they scrapped against wet pavement and turned her toes to pulp.* (15)

Key features: Multiple points of view in first and third person; text that has been blacked out or cut out, which implies censorship

Subjects: dark fantasy; dystopias; experimental fiction; immigrants; psychological suspense; surrealism

Similar titles: *The Cave* by Saramago contains a similar theme of flight from a dystopian society.

Ransom, Roberto (Mexican).

A Tale of Two Lions. **(*Historia de dos leones*, 1994). Translated by Jasper Reid. New York: W.W. Norton, 2007. ISBN 9780393329360. 114pp.**

The two lions, Cattino and Pasha, have extraordinary powers and interact with the humans around them in supernatural ways. Cattino's owner's husband becomes insanely jealous of him, and nobody can tell that Pasha is not stuffed. Both lions end up in Mexico City after finding their way to a circus.

> Devour my heart *she seems to be saying to Cattino when she presses his great head to her breast. This invitation does not include me, for while Cattino is firmly lodged in my wife's heart, I occupy something more like her large intestine.* (23)

Subjects: allegory; Italy; Kenya; lions; Mexico—Mexico City

Similar titles: *Two Brothers* by Atxaga also features anthropomorphic animals.

Paranormal

Introduction and Appeal

Paranormal stories present terrifying beasts and horrors that are echoed by our worst fears and give us a thrilling scare that we can manage on our own time and in the comfort and security of our own homes. The novels presented in this section will not terrify in precisely that sense, but they are creepy and terrifying in that they journey to the dark side of the human soul. Readers who enjoy a *frisson* of fear will like these books.

Ghosts, monsters, and other supernatural beings "people" these novels as the authors have us ponder if our worst fears of the supernatural may be but a pale shadow of the true horrors humans wreak on each other.

Andahazi, Federico (Argentinian).

The Merciful Women. (*Las piadosas*, 1998). Translated by Alberto Manguel. New York: Grove Press, 2000. ISBN 0-8021-1674-4. 188pp.

This translation of an Argentine novel presents a creepy take on the birth of the Gothic novel—a summer in a Swiss villa with Lord Byron, Percy and Mary Shelley, Mary's sister, and the mysterious (fictional) John Polidori, Byron's servant. They all compete to invent the best Gothic novel, while supernatural forces intervene.

> *The clouds were black cathedrals, tall and Gothic, about to topple at any moment on to the city of Geneva. Further away, on the far slopes of the Savoyard Alps, the storm was angrily whipping up the wind, unsettling the calm of Lake Leman. Trapped between the sky and the mountains, like a hunted animal, the lake fought back, kicking like a horse, clawing like a tiger and lashing out with its tail like a dragon.* (13)

Subjects: Byron, George Gordon; Gothic novels; Shelley, Mary; Switzerland—Geneva

Similar titles: *The Shadow of the Wind* by Ruiz Zafón is another dark, gothic-style novel.

Cerda, Carlos (Chilean).

An Empty House. (*Casa vacía*, 1996). Translated by Andrea Labinger. Lincoln: University of Nebraska Press, 2003. ISBN 080321524X. 245pp.

In present-day Chile, a dysfunctional family moves into a new house with high expectations of finding happiness there, only to be infected by the lingering horrors that permeate the empty place—remnants of the real terror everyone suffered under the dictatorship.

> *Yes, horrible, decrepit old ladies, letting such a lovely house go to ruin. No doubt they practiced witchcraft and burned incense in the girls' room—that explains the burn marks on the parquet.* (12)

Subjects: family life; haunted houses; terror

Similar titles: This novel is reminiscent of the classic horror tales featuring haunted houses, such as *The Fall of the House of Usher* by Poe and *The Yellow Wallpaper* by Gilman.

Ferrara, Alex, and José Levy (Argentinian).

Collateral Man. (*El garante,* 2003). Buenos Aires: Gráfica Andina, 2003. ISBN 987-43-6563-3. 336pp.

Martin Mondragon's late grandfather put up Martin's soul as collateral for a loan from the devil. When the devil's messenger comes to collect, Martin must engage in a desperate and thrilling fight for his soul.

> *When your grandfather came to us, of his own accord, and he signed this pact, Sagasti said, sliding his fingers along the bronze tube, he accepted the clause that named you his guarantor, his surety, his backup—in other words, his collateral man.* (18)

Subjects: adventure; collateral; dark fantasy; devil; loans; souls

Similar titles: *Turing's Delirium* by Paz Soldán and *The Absent City* by Piglia are thrillers with a similarly dark tone in an urban and futuristic setting.

Fuentes, Carlos (Mexican).

Aura. (*Aura,* 1962). Translated by Lysander Kemp. New York: Farrar, Straus & Giroux, 1980. ISBN 0374511713. 145pp.

Young Mexico City native Felipe Montero answers a cryptic classified ad in the paper that seems directed specifically at him and his unique qualifications as a historian. He enters the strange world of the beautiful Aura and her aunt when he is hired to edit the deceased uncle's papers, and then he is ineluctably drawn into their dark web.

> *You rap vainly with the knocker, that copper head of a dog, so worn and smooth that it resembles the head of a canine foetus in a museum of natural science. It seems as if the dog is grinning at you and you let go of the cold metal. The door opens at the first light push of your fingers, but before going in you give a last look over your shoulder.* (11)

Key features: Second person narration; bilingual edition

Subjects: classics; history; horror stories; Mexico—Mexico City

Similar titles: *The Uncomfortable Dead* by Taibo and Subcomandante Marcos is another novel that deals with the deceased in a macabre Mexico City.

Martinez, A. Lee (Tejano).

🌢 *Gil's All Fright Diner.* New York: Tom Doherty Associates, 2005. ISBN 076531-4711. 268pp.

Loretta manages the diner and is up against it when she asks Earl, a vampire, and Duke, a werewolf, to help her eradicate a zombie infestation for a hundred bucks. They agree to take on the job, but discover that Loretta's got a lot more trouble on her hands than a few zombies when some mighty unsavory and monstrous characters try to run her out of Rockwood.

Your average zombie is not a combat machine. Their fighting prowess springs from a single-minded determination and a certain walking corpse stick-to-itiveness. Your average werewolf is an unrivaled killing machine, vicious teeth and claws coupled with supernatural grace, power, and the ultimate predatory instincts. (18)

Subjects: humor; paranormal; vampires; werewolves; zombies

Similar titles: The <u>Vincent Rubio Series</u> by Eric Garcia also features nonhuman protagonists and a tongue-in-cheek tone.

Awards: Alex Award winner, 2006

A Nameless Witch. **New York: Tom Doherty Associates, 2007. ISBN 9780765318688. 320pp.**

Our Tejano author creates a witch who disguises herself as a hideous old crone to command more respect as she carries out her witchy routine, accompanied by her faithful crew—Gwurm, who is a troll, and her familiar, a duck named Newt. This routine is threatened by an oncoming horde of goblings that portend even greater catastrophe. The Witch enters into an unlikely alliance with a White Knight to save the world as they know it.

Being undead was not all that horrible a curse. Unfortunately, this was not the end of my worries. For besides being made a thing born to dwell in darkened misery, I was also made, in the infinite wisdom of fate, a girl. (10)

Key features: First person narration

Subjects: humor; witches

Similar titles: *The Lamentable Journey of Omaha Bigelow* by Vega Yunqué has a similar chatty tone, absurd situations, and witches, or in this case *brujas.*

Magical Realism

Introduction and Appeal

Magical realism as a concept came to the world from Latin America and is an important element in Latino culture as well as a worldwide literary movement. A good definition is found in *The Latino Encyclopedia of Popular Culture:*

[T]he style combine(s) naturalistic realism with elements of fantasy and supernatural motifs . . . . Writers of magic realism also seek to capture the common beliefs, grassroots customs, and unique imaginaries of people and cultures in their local settings as their everyday lives are affected by and collide with the policies and politics of governments and the powerful elites that run them. (Chávez Candelaria et al. 2004, 504–5)

In magical realism, animals and inanimate objects may be given human characteristics and perspectives; the deceased may take an active part in plots;

characters may have the ability to fly or leave their bodies; characters may use herbs or potions for their magic powers; characters might be possessed by spirits; and saints or other religious figures such as African gods may be appealed to and play an important part in plots. It is all taken as a matter of course, as the great Jorge Luis Borges said: "[T]he marvelous and the everyday are entwined . . . there are angels as there are trees" (Borges, cited by Hitchens in Allende, *The House of Spirits*, vii).

Readers who enjoy being kept off balance, enjoy the absurd and don't always need a neat resolution at the end of a story, enjoy looking at situations from strange perspectives, like to ponder the nature of life after death or the possibility of other dimensions juxtaposed and interacting with the one we are accustomed to, like to think that magic can influence circumstances and help even the score for the little guy and the downtrodden, and think justice can be done for the underdog, will enjoy the titles found in this section.

Allende, Isabel (Chilean).

The House of Spirits. (*La casa de los espíritus,* 1982). **Translated by Magda Bogin. New York: Alfred A. Knopf, 2005. ISBN 1-4000-4318-2. 488pp.**

The saga of the Trueba family spreads out over a century of strife in an unnamed Latin American country, pitting a progressive granddaughter against her tyrannical grandfather. This magical story features the gift of flight, ghosts, and apparitions.

> *Barrabás arrived on a Holy Thursday. He was in a despicable cage, caked with his own excrement and urine, and had the lost look of a hapless, utterly defenseless prisoner; but the regal carriage of his head and the size of his frame bespoke the legendary giant he would become. (7)*

Key features: Chronology and introduction by Christopher Hitchens

Subjects: dictatorships; families; family sagas; historical fiction; revolutionary struggles

Similar titles: García Márquez's classic *One Hundred Years of Solitude* is the touchstone for all the magic realism novels that intertwine the fortunes of a seminal family with its *pueblo* and country. A more contemporary example is *Cellophane* by Arana.

Amado, Jorge (Brazilian).

Doña Flor and Her Two Husbands. (*Dona Flor e seus dois maridos,* 1966). **Translated by Harriet de Onis. New York: Vintage International, 2006 (1969). ISBN 0307276643 (pbk.). 553pp.**

In Bahia, Brazil, Doña Flor puts up with her scalawag husband Vadinho, his rough treatment, and his irresponsible ways until his death in a brothel during Carnaval. Flor then marries an upstanding member of the community, Dr. Teodoro Madureria. Although Teodoro takes care of and respects her, she longs for Vadinho in bed, so she conjures him up, back from the grave. Doña Flor manages her cooking school while balancing a lively affair with her deceased husband and a deadly dull relationship with her living one.

> *Vadinho, Dona Flor's first husband, died one Sunday of Carnival, in the morning, when, dressed up like a Bahian woman, he was dancing the samba, with the greatest enthusiasm, in the Dois de Julho Square, not far from his house. (3)*

Subjects: apparitions; Brazil—Bahia; cooking; death; love stories; sex; widows

Similar titles: *Like Water for Chocolate* by Esquivel is another novel that serves up sex and ghosts with magic and cooking.

Arana, Marie (Peruvian American).

Cellophane. **New York: Dial Press, 2006.ISBN-13: 978-0-385-33664-2; ISBN 0-385-33664-0. 367pp.**

The Sobrevilla family patriarch's discovery of cellophane brings startling changes to the family and the magical *pueblito* of Floralinda in Peru during the second half of the twentieth century.

> *Imagine if you will that point where the great river begins its race to the sea. Imagine somewhere Señor Urritia's shop and Eiffel's colossus that, to this day, vaults from the mud of Iquitos. Imagine Floralinda as it was: a whirring miracle in the heart of the jungle, a glimmer of a new day.* (12)

Subjects: cellophane; families; humor; Peru

Similar titles: *One Hundred Years of Solitude* by García Márquez and Allende's *The House of Spirits* also revolve around families and *pueblos*, discoveries, and magic.

Atxaga, Bernardo (Spanish).

Two Brothers. **(*Dos Hermanos,* 1995). Translated by Margaret Jull Costa. London: Harvill Press, 2001. ISBN 1-86046-834-9. 118pp.**

Various animals from a village in Spain—birds and squirrels—and even stars narrate this tale about two brothers, Paulo and Daniel (who is mentally disabled), and two sisters, Teresa and Carmen (who is physically repulsive). As they suffer the throes of adolescent love, they find themselves capable of frightening depths of desire and cruelty.

> *There is a voice that comes from deep within ourselves, and just as summer was beginning, when I was still an inexperienced bird and had never strayed far from the tree where I lived, that voice gave me an order.* (3)

Key features: Anthropomorphic narrators

Subjects: brothers; disabilities; sisters

Similar titles: Valdés also uses anthropomorphic narrators in *Dear First Love*. Because of its disabled characters, this novel is reminiscent of Steinbeck's *Of Mice and Men.*

Belli, Gioconda (Nicaraguan).

The Inhabited Woman. **(*Mujer habitada,* 1988). Translated by Kathleen March. Willimantic, CT: Curbstone Press, 1994. ISBN 1-880684-17-9. 412pp.**

Lavinia is a privileged woman in the fictional country Fragua, which resembles Nicaragua in the 1980s. Returning to her native country after studying abroad, she finds that living as an independent female exercising her chosen career as an architect is not enough to quiet an awakening consciousness of the injustice surrounding her. However, a kindred spirit,

Itzá, lives in the orange tree that is blossoming in Lavinia's garden. Itzá becomes a part of Lavinia and narrates her own story of resistance during the Spanish Conquest and her perspective on Lavinia's inner struggle.

> She felt nostalgic again. Daydreaming, she sipped the orange juice and savored its bittersweet taste, similar to that of her memories; she thought of her grandfather. Plunging her eyes into her memory, she saw that tall, thin man with the long nose and small, clear, piercing eyes; she saw, through the translucence of his skin, the fine red veins like small deltas of great interior rivers. (55)

Subjects: Central America; dictatorships; love stories; revolutionary struggles; Spanish Conquest; spirits

Similar titles: *In the Time of the Butterflies* by Julia Alvarez features women's struggles during revolutionary movements; *Song of the Hummingbird* by Limón, *The Hummingbird's Daughter* by Urrea, and *Malinche* by Esquivel present indigenous women as protagonists.

Benitez, Sandra (Puerto Rican American).

A Place Where the Sea Remembers. **Minneapolis, MN: Coffee House Press, 1993. ISBN 1-56689-011-X. 163pp.**

The inhabitants of a village on the Mexican coast, like pieces of driftwood on the sea, are flung hither and yon by circumstances beyond their control. They are especially subject to the fickle nature of the *fuereños* that come from the big cities to exploit them. Remedios, *la curandera*, and the elements she uses in her healing—earth, air, fire, and water—provide the framework for their stories, beginning and coming full circle at the scene in which the villagers wait for a body to be washed back to shore.

> The old healer is weary, a result, in part, of the countless times she has cocked her head in the direction of someone's story. Remedios knows the town's stories. Just as the sea, as their witness, knows them, too. (1)

Subjects: *curanderas*; Mexico; *pueblos*; rape; seashore

Similar titles: Other novels structured as collective stories are *A Place Called Milagro de la Paz* by Argueta, *The Hive* by Cela, and *Cellophane* by Arana.

Castañeda, Omar (Guatemalan American).

Naranjo the Muse. **Houston, TX: Arte Público Press, 1997. ISBN 1558851925. 175pp.**

These interconnected stories center on literature professor Dr. Naranjo and his romantic pursuit of one of his students, Lori, who is also pursued by one Omar Castañeda. Dreams, delusions, and talking birds populate the stories.

> For a moment, he saw a young girl's face peer at him through the darkened rear window of the car. In that face, he remembered that virtually all species attack their older members. The old males weakened, hollowed without a fight or they died in bloody heaps. He waved at the ghostly face. (57)

Key features: Sexual situations

Subjects: fantasy; professor–student affairs; stories; writers—fiction

Similar titles: *Woodcuts of Women* by Gilb and *Brownsville* by Casares are other books by Latino men containing stories about love and lust.

Collignon, Rick (U.S. American).

Guadalupe Trilogy.

This trilogy depicts three key moments in the history of the magical *pueblo* of Guadalupe in New Mexico, where most of the residents are Mexican American. Stories are told from the perspective of three of those very different residents: Ramona, a middle-aged woman; Will, an Anglo outsider; and Flavio, a man at the end of life. The series is reminiscent of John Nichols's trilogy, which begins with the wonderful *The Milagro Beanfield War*, and Hinojoso's <u>Klail City Death Trip Series</u>.

The Journal of Antonio Montoya. Denver and Aspen, CO: MacMurray& Beck, 1996. ISBN 1878448692. 217pp.

Ramona Montoya, a middle-aged artist, lives alone in the *pueblo* of her childhood. When her sister-in-law and brother are killed in a car accident, she brings her nephew José to live with her—after her sister-in-law requests it from her coffin. Ramona and her nephew receive the journal of the title from her deceased grandmother, and the ghosts of deceased relations regularly appear in their daily lives, thus weaving together the generations and histories of the *pueblo*—both earlier residents and recent arrivals.

> *The burial of her father eight years ago was the last funeral Ramona had attended, and at least, Ramona thought, her father had had the decency not to sit up in his coffin and converse with her.* (18)

Subjects: ghosts; journals (personal); New Mexico; *pueblos*

Similar titles: *Canyon of Remembering* by Poling-Kempes also features an artist in a *pueblo*; *The Guardians* by Ana Castillo features a middle-aged single woman raising her nephew.

Perdido. Denver and Aspen, CO: MacMurray & Beck, 1997. ISBN 1878448765. 221pp.

In the town of Guadalupe, New Mexico (previously named Perdido), a long-time Anglo resident is intrigued by a hanging that happened decades earlier. When he starts digging into this old mystery, he stirs up old feelings and resentments with ugly racial overtones and finds he is still regarded as an outsider.

> *He shut his eyes, and a soft wave of dizziness washed over him. When he opened them again, he began to turn slowly in a circle. All about him were thousands of paintings.* (8)

Subjects: New Mexico; *pueblos*; race relations

Similar titles: Anaya's <u>Sonny Baca Mysteries</u> are also set in northern New Mexico.

A Santo in the Image of Cristobal García. New York: BlueHen Books, c2002. ISBN 039914921X. 271pp.

Flavio Montoya is accused of setting a fire that destroys the town of Guadalupe, New Mexico. As he sits in jail and remembers his life, ghosts appear, and the physical and sensual intertwine.

> *Flavio had first seen the santos thirty-five years before. They had appeared in this house as if from nowhere, and seeing them now standing in the corner made him suddenly feel as if they were the only remaining members of his family. Unfortunately, of all the family that had passed through his life, these were not relatives he had ever been fond of.* (11)

Subjects: arson; ghosts; memories; New Mexico; *pueblos*

Similar titles: *The Second Death of Única Aveyano* by Mestre-Reed also deals with memories and magic.

🎬 García Márquez, Gabriel (Colombian).

***The Autumn of the Patriarch.** (El otoño del patriarca, 1975).* **Translated by Gregory Rabassa. New York: HarperPerennial Classics, 1999. ISBN 0060932678. 261pp.**

During his final days—are they final, or is it another illusion of this seemingly immortal ruler?—an aged Latin American über-dictator relives the whole rotten, corrupt, and terrifying period of his reign.

> *Over the weekend the vultures got into the presidential palace by pecking through the screens on the balcony windows and the flapping of their wings stirred up the stagnant time inside, and at dawn on Monday the city awoke out of its lethargy of centuries with the warm, soft breeze of a great man's dead and rotting grandeur.* (1)

Key features: Stream-of-consciousness narration

Subjects: dictators; Latin America

Similar titles: *The Feast of the Goat* by Vargas Llosa and *The President* by Asturias also feature dictators as protagonists.

Awards: Nobel Prize for Literature, 1982

***One Hundred Years of Solitude.** (Cien años de soledad, 1967).* **Translated by Gregory Rabassa. Harper & Row, 1998. ISBN 0060740450. 458pp.**

This classic tale that introduced magic realism to the world is the story of the mythical *pueblo* of Macondo and the Buendía family. Their saga features unforgettable characters like Melquiades, the old gypsy who brings amazing inventions—like ice—to town; the hero Colonel Aureliano Buendía; the seventeen Aurelianos; the matriarch Ursula Iguarán; and Remedios the Beauty.

> *When they woke up, with the sun already high in the sky, they were speechless with fascination. Before them, surrounded by ferns and palm trees, white and powdery in the silent morning light, was an enormous Spanish galleon. Tilted slightly to the starboard, it had hanging from its intact masts the dirty rags of its sails in the midst of its rigging, which was adorned with orchids . . . . The whole structure seemed to occupy its own space, one of solitude and oblivion, protected from the vices of time and the habits of the birds.* (11–12)

Subjects: classics; families; Macondo; jungles; South America

Similar titles: Other magical family sagas that seek to follow in these footsteps are *Caramelo* by Cisneros and *Cellophane* by Arana, as well as the Guadalupe Trilogy by Collignon.

González Viaña, Eduardo (Mexican).

Dante's Ballad. (*El corrido de Dante,* 2006). Translated by Susan Giersbach Rascón. Houston, TX: Arte Público Press, 2007. ISBN 978155-8854871. 299pp.

In a small town in Oregon, Emmita's *quinceañera* is ruined for her dad, undocumented widower Dante Celestino, when Emmita runs off to Las Vegas with her boyfriend on his motorcycle. Dante promptly takes off after her with his donkey, Virgilio, and his dead wife Beatriz as his only companions, on a journey full of fantastic adventures and eccentric characters.

> He imagined that-in order to not be seen or heard-his daughter's friend hung from the roofs at night like a sinister pouch and that his wings covered him completely, nocturnal, fateful, ominous, evil, hanging, flying, silent, deadly. (8)

Subjects: animal companions; fathers and daughters; Nevada—Las Vegas; road trips; undocumented workers

Similar titles: In Escandón's *Santitos*, another parent searches for a child; *Don Chipote*, by Venegas, is also on a journey with a four-legged companion, his dog—Sufrelambre.

Llamazares, Julio (Spanish).

The Yellow Rain. (*La lluvia amarilla,* 1988). Translated by Margaret Jull Costa. New York: Harcourt, 2003. ISBN 0-15-100598-2. 130pp.

The last remaining inhabitant of Ainielle in the Spanish Pyrenees recalls his life and that of the moribund village as he awaits death—or is he already dead?

> And yet, those looking down on the village from the high pastures of Sobrepuerto will know that here, amid the utter stillness, the silence, and the shadows, I will have seen them and will be waiting for them. (2)

Key features: First person narration

Subjects: ghosts; memory; old age; *pueblos*

Similar titles: *Pedro Páramo* by Rulfo also features what may well be a ghost town; *A Santo in the Image of Cristóbal García* by Collignon has a similar magical tone.

Mestre, Ernesto. (Cuban American). *See also* Mestre-Reed, Ernesto.

The Lazarus Rumba: A Novel. New York: Picador USA, 1999. ISBN 0312199074. 486pp.

Alicia, the main protagonist, lives through the Cuban Revolution, with that experience touching everyone around her, even the mute fighting rooster, Atila. This novel has been compared to *One Hundred Years of Solitude,* in that it follows the fortunes of one family, in this case three generations of the Lucientes family in Cuba, using magical elements to tell the story.

Todo igual, coño. It's been two weeks and nothing has changed-all day locked in my room and wrapped in that musty old shawl she found the devil knows where. I think it was my mother's (la pobre, que en paz descanse). Y lo peor, now she has stopped eating altogether. (7)

Subjects: Cuba; Cuban Revolution; dissidents; families; family sagas; historical fiction; mothers and daughters

Similar titles: *One Hundred Years of Solitude* by García Márquez and *The House of Spirits* by Allende are similar magical tales of families and towns; *Kiss of the Spider Woman* by Puig has a similar political bent.

Rulfo, Juan (Mexican).

Pedro Páramo. (*Pedro Páramo,* 1955). **Austin: University of Texas Press, 2002. ISBN 0292771215. 161pp.**

The lonely narrator tells the story of the journey his dying mother sent him on—to find his father, settle a score, and receive his inheritance. He searches for the ethereal *pueblo* of Comala, and what he finds there is his own appointment with destiny.

Rulfo is one of the fathers of magical realism. This beautiful edition of the classic work is illustrated with photographs by Josephine Sacabo.

> *"It's hot here," I said.*
>
> *"You might say. But this is nothing," my companion replied. "Try to take it easy. You'll feel it more when we get to Comala. That town sits on the coals of the earth, at the very mouth of hell. They say that when people from there die and go to hell, they come back for a blanket." (16)*

Key features: First person narration

Subjects: classics; death; fathers and sons; ghosts; magical realism; Mexico

Similar titles: *When the Ground Turns in Its Sleep* by Sellers-García and *Dirty Blonde and Half-Cuban* also feature young people on a quest to know their fathers. *The Yellow Rain* by Llamazares is also set in a town populated by ghosts.

Sáenz, Benjamin Alire (New Mexican).

Carry Me Like Water. **New York: Hyperion, 1995. ISBN 0-7868-6135-5. 503pp.**

Dying Chicano AIDS patient Salvador transmits the ability to travel out-of-body to Lizzie, his nurse. Lizzie's newfound power helps her ferret out secrets from the past. It is the catalyst for changes in the lives of those around her—including Diego, a deaf-mute from El Paso; his stuck-up, yuppie sister Helen; and Jake and Joaquin, a gay couple also struggling with AIDS.

> *No one ever attempted to erase those pieces of graffiti. They had been there for as long as Diego could remember. He thought of them as landmarks, murals, voices of the people who lived there. The spontaneous letters on the wall were as solid as his hands, full of a brash humor that bordered on violence; loud, bright, but weak like the light of a waning moon. (9)*

Subjects: AIDS; astral projection; brothers and sisters; California—San Francisco; Chicanos; deaf mutes; homosexuals; race relations; Texas—El Paso

Similar titles: *The Wind from the East* by Grandes also has friendship and families at its center.

Vega Yunqué, Edgardo (Nuyorican).

The Lamentable Journey of Omaha Bigelow into the Impenetrable Loisaida Jungle: A Novel. **New York: Overlook Press, 2004. ISBN 1585676306. 352pp.**

Omaha Bigelow, a slacker hero, works at Kinko's and is frustrated with his love life. Enter Maruquita Salsipuedes, a bewitching Puerto Rican beauty who has the wherewithal to fulfill his wildest fantasies of potency IF he will remain faithful to her. Can he do it? Of course! Not! The narrator engages the reader in a lively dialogue about how these two and their adventures embody the forces in the U.S. culture wars of the twenty-first century.

> *Omaha Bigelow was very surprised to wake up and find a small monkey staring at him. It was a girl monkey, and she was holding a little flashlight and shiny black stick. He could see her cuchi-cuchi, tiny and pink, and that's how he knew it was a girl monkey. He blinked a couple of times and took a closer look, and it wasn't a monkey but a girl sitting cross-legged near him.* (21)

Key features: Some first person narration by the omniscient narrator

Subjects: humor; love stories; magical realism; New York—New York City—Lower East Side; Nuyoricans

Similar titles: *El Indio Jesús* by Chávez Ballejos, *The Brief Wondrous Life of Oscar Wao* by Junot Díaz, and *The Best Thing That Can Happen to a Croissant* by Tusset also feature slacker heroes and magic.

Yañez Cossío, Alicia (Ecuadoran).

Bruna and Her Sisters in the Sleeping City. (*Bruna, soroche y los tíos,* 1973). **Translated by Kenneth J. A. Wishnia. Evanston, IL: Northwestern University Press, 1999. ISBN 0810114089. 228pp.**

Bruna tries to make her own destiny while working through her family's centuries-long history in "the sleeping city" of Ecuador. She weaves through the illusion and reality of an eccentric family that shamefully hides its indigenous ancestry.

> *And if in the best circumstances she managed to sleep she dreamt of useless things, lacking in reality and interest; of things she hadn't suggested, or desired, that were later forgotten, never again to come to mind, or if they did come back, they were nasty experiences because they arrived unexpectedly.* (6)

Subjects: dreams; Ecuador; families; young women

Similar titles: *The Lazarus Rumba* by Mestre, *One Hundred Years of Solitude* by García Márquez, and *The House of Spirits* by Allende are other magical family sagas.

Anthologies and Collections

These volumes present a good introduction to the great tradition of speculative fiction in Latin America.

Agosín, Marjorie, ed.

Secret Weavers: Stories of the Fantastic by Women of Argentina and Chile. **New York: White Pine Press, 1992. ISBN 1-877727-15-6. 339pp.**

This anthology traces the contribution of women writers to the canon of fantastic literature in Latin America. The stories cover various styles, from magical speculative to futuristic and fey. Published in the second half of the twentieth century, many of these works are translated into English for the first time here.

> *My dreams already knew that I didn't obey them. Armindo came over to my bed, took out the knife and stuck it in my heart, the only way to kill me, but he didn't kill me and I felt no pain. I laughed at him until the tears were running down my cheeks. When I woke up, life went on. (33)*

Subjects: short stories; women—Latin American

Bell, Andrea L., and Yolanda Molina-Gavilán, eds.

Cosmos Latinos: An Anthology of Science Fiction from Latin America and Spain. **Middletown, CT: Wesleyan University Press, 2003. ISBN 0-8195-6633-0 (cloth); 0-8195-6634-9 (pbk.). 352pp.**

An anthology of science fiction stories translated from Spanish and Portuguese, from the early twentieth century to the present.

> *From a "Copernican" society, where industries depended upon external forces and had to maintain manifold relations with them, society became little enclosed universes, or Acronias, where each company was, definitively, a world. (103)*

Subjects: Latin America; science fiction; short stories; Spain

🏆 Bioy Casares, Adolfo (Argentinian).

Selected Stories. **Translated by Suzanne Jill Levine. New York: New Directions Books, 1994. ISBN 0811212750. 176pp.**

Ms. Levine selected these stories from collections published between the 1950s and 1980s as an introduction to Bioy Casares's work in which the fantastic mingles with love and passion.

> *If I had decided (shall we say) to fight Pierrot, the worst part wouldn't have been the dust of defeat but rather that I wouldn't even get to fight him. I'd be stuck at the end of his arm, punching and kicking the air. I had a nightmare about this. (7)*

Key features: Some first person narration

Subjects: love stories; magical realism

Awards: Cervantes Prize, 1990

Lugones, Leopoldo (Argentinian).

Strange Forces. (Fuerzas extrañas, **1906). Translated by Gilbert Al-**
ter-Gilbert. Pittsburgh, PA: Latin America Literary Review Press, c2001.
ISBN 1891270052. 126pp.

1

These twelve classic stories by one of the authors who created the fantastic
genre in Latin America—similar to what Poe did in the United States—explore the realm of the possible and the consequences that ensue when man
challenges the gods and nature.

2

> *Then a jagged virgule of fire streaked across the sky like a diagonal*
> *whiplash, and made a craterlet in the earth. Others followed, at long*
> *intervals.* (24)

Subjects: classics; occult; paranormal; science fiction; short stories

3

Similar titles: *Secret Weavers* edited by Agosín is another collection of fantastic
stories or stories of the fantastic.

References

4

Chávez Candelaria, Cordelia, Arturo J Aldama, and Peter J. García, eds.
2004. *Encyclopedia of Latino Popular Culture.* Westport, CT: Greenwood Press.

5

6

7

8

9

Chapter 7

Young Adult Fiction

Jessica Reed

Cada cabeza es un mundo

Introduction

The coming-of-age novel, often referred to as a bildungsroman, focuses on the development of the main character from youth to adulthood. Although not all coming-of-age novels can be labeled young adult fiction, many authors write with this population in mind to help guide teens through the difficult adolescent years. In many ways, coming-of-age novels can be looked at as the "teen angst" or issue books that have been around for a long time. They realistically represent the trials and tribulations of being a teenager and the period of social and personal growth that occurs as teens enter adulthood (Herald 2003, 15).

According to Vicky Hendel, "the major adolescent concerns of separation, exploration, validation and self realization are in some measure the central themes of all successful coming-of-age novels"(2007). As you look closely at the titles in this chapter you will see these themes appear repeatedly. Teenagers of all shapes and sizes experience a growing need for independence and acceptance as they mature, and teens of Latino heritage are no exception. Luckily, today the book industry is publishing more and more titles that represent the issues of all teens, which include the unique concerns of the Latino teenager.

Appeal

The appeal of coming-of-age novels for most young adult readers, many of whom are reluctant readers, is the fact that the situations encountered by the protagonist are similar to those they (and other teenagers) face in real life. These experiences are common to teenagers regardless of race—searching for independence, navigating complex relationships with friends, siblings, and parents, wrestling with budding and bewildering sexuality. Many teens must survive dysfunctional families, gangs, violence, and prejudice as a part of their everyday life. Coming-of-age novels represent these facets of twenty-first-century young adult life.

Latino teenagers benefit from the connections made with these types of novels, and seeing their own culture represented in the titles they read provides greater benefit and validation. Latino youth commonly experience many of the issues listed above while also facing challenges unique to their heritage and situation. The growing numbers of Hispanic youths in the United States, the fastest growing demographic in the country, find the coming-of-age novels written by Latinos about the Latino experience indispensable.

Evolution of the Genre

In the early 1990s, the interest in marketing to the ever-growing young adult population exploded in many industries, including publishing. Even more novels targeted at this population were published when interest in reading took off due to popular young adult novels, especially the <u>Harry Potter</u> series. The young adult coming-of-age novels themselves had been around in some form since the abundant "problem" books of the 1970s; however, the severity, grittiness, and despair of these books had by the 1990s changed to stories of hope and optimism (Herald 2003, 2–3).

Few materials were available that represented the multicultural experience prior to the mid-1990s. The increasing interest in the multicultural experience in the mid- to late 1990s, contributed to the rise of Latino voices in both adult and young adult literature (York 2001). Several awards recognizing the best in Latino literature for youth and children were commissioned, which further helped these voices be heard. Those awards included the Pura Belpré Award, the Américas Award, and the Tomás Rivera Mexican American Children's Book Award. Celebrating novels that present an authentic portrayal of the Latino/a experience, these awards advance a continuing interest in the Latino voice.

Publishing companies such as Cinco Puntos Press, Arte Público Press, and its imprint Piñata Books are well established in the Latino/a young adult publishing arena. But in the last five years, larger publishing houses such as HarperCollins and Random House have been increasing their participation in the world of Latino publishing, creating imprints such as Rayo and Random House Para Niños. Because teenagers are a key demographic for publishing, as well as for other business ventures, the number of novels dedicated to Latino teens and their dilemmas will certainly increase, given the upsurge in the Latino population in the United States.

Current Themes and Trends

Assimilation or Transculturation

Most Latino young adult novels focus on the protagonist's difficulties in coming-of-age within the clash of two cultures. At an age when one questions everything, these main characters struggle to find their place among familial and community expectations and those of friends and the greater culture. These protagonists may be new or second generation immigrants, yet they deal with similar issues surrounding their role in the world and as keepers of Latino traditions.

Gangs

Death and violence are frequently themes in Latino coming-of-age novels. The poverty of the barrio and its culture of gangs and drugs are described through the viewpoint of the boys and young men living in its boundaries. Not all novels feature bleak story lines, however. Many leave the reader with an uplifting message of hope for the future of the protagonist. The female voice is rarely heard in this subgenre, with the exception of *Party Girl* by Lynne Ewing.

Sexual Identity

As teens approach adulthood, their sexual identification and expression take on paramount importance. Books within the Latino coming-of-age genre often deal with these issues. The sexual situations in these novels can include heterosexuality, bisexuality, and homosexuality. Many approach the topic in a frank manner.

Magical Realism

Several young adult Latino authors also use elements of magical realism, following the tradition of their adult fiction counterparts, writers like Gabriel García Márquez and Isabel Allende. A twist of the fantastic is woven into the story as the teen protagonist embraces his or her cultural heritage from deceased grandparents or some other ethereal guide.

Chiquita Lit

The Latino coming-of-age novel is not immune to the overall industry Chick Lit explosion. Many coming-of-age titles aimed at young Latinas focus on hip, stylish young women, their friendships with other young women, and the humorous and heartbreaking pursuit of men, or in these novels, boys. In most cases, these novels lack the frank sexuality of adult Chick Lit (or *chica* lit) titles, making them more appropriate for a younger audience. The novels also tackle complex issues such as interracial relationships.

Unconventional Forms: Short Stories, Free Verse, and Letters from Home

The diversity of the Latino coming-of-age experience can be seen in the number of poetry and short story titles published each year. Individual authors or compilations featuring various important Hispanic authors are readily available from several publishers. Along with nonfiction titles, many young adult Latino novelists are also taking the initiative to create their stories in free verse. Award winners *CrashBoomLove* and *Cinnamon Girl* by Juan Felipe Herrera are excellent examples of this trend. The reader will also find many titles featuring diaries and letters (epistolary fiction), giving readers unique insight into the minds and emotions of the main character.

Scope and Selection Criteria

The materials selected for inclusion in this chapter were taken from a variety of sources. As part of the Tulsa City-County Library system, the Hispanic Resource Center was relied on heavily. The Center's young adult collection was perused for relevant titles and authors. Other relevant information about authors and their works was obtained from bibliographies available in databases and at Internet sites administered by public libraries and publishing companies. Organizations recognizing the best in Latino children and young adult literature were also utilized (e.g., Pura Belpré, Tomás Rivera, and Américas awards).

The authors chosen for this chapter are primarily of Latino heritage, with a few exceptions. This includes both authors born in Latin America and those born of immigrants to the United States. Young adult materials featuring foul language, violence, and/or frank discussion of sexuality are included. Notations have been made in the annotations in such instances. Title selection focuses on the last ten years of Latino publishing (1996–2006) and is representative of relevant materials printed in this time frame, but is in no way comprehensive.

Novels

Aira, César (Argentinian).

How I Became a Nun. (*Cómo me hice monja,*1993). **Translated by Chris Andrews. New York: New Directions, 2007. ISBN 9780811216319. 117pp.**

One of César's first memories are of his father forcing him to eat a dirty ice cream cone, then beating up the vendor and being sent to jail while César convalesced after having almost died from food poisoning. This experience shaped the person César will become—a writer with a rich fantasy life.

> *The memory of Dad in the ice-cream store made retching more real than reality itself; it was the thing that made everything else real, and nothing could withstand it. For me, ever since, it has been the essence of the sacred, the source from which my calling sprang.* (35)

Subjects: Argentina; fathers and sons; food poisoning; friendship; schools; writers—fiction

Similar titles: For more insight into a Latina writer's coming-of-age, read *¡Yo!* by Julia Alvarez.

Alegría, Malín (Mexican American).

Estrella's Quinceañera. New York: Simon & Schuster, 2006. ISBN 0689878095. 260pp.

Attending an elite private school on scholarship, Estrella finds it best to pretend to be someone she's not. Embarrassed by her family, barrio, and background, Estrella, about to turn fifteen, finds her mother in the midst of planning the most outrageous *quinceañera* ever. Caught between two worlds, Estrella must decide exactly who she wants to be.

> *Upon entering my parents' bedroom, I was blinded by a tangerine-orange color that was flashing before my eyes. My mother was holding Marta's gaudy quinceañera gown up to her body. It was still the most repulsive thing I'd ever seen. I imagined someone suggesting to Sheila that she wear that to a party. I choked back a laugh.* (60)

Key features: First person narration

Subjects: boarding schools; *chiquita* lit; friendship; Mexican Americans; mothers and daughters; *quinceañeras*

Similar titles: There are a number of similar titles featuring *quinceañeras*, including Osa's *Cuba 15*, Chamber's *Quinceañera Means Sweet 15*, and Bertrand's *Sweet Fifteen*. *The Tequila Worm* by Canales is also similar, featuring teenaged girls away at boarding school.

Sofi Mendoza's Guide to Getting Lost in Mexico. New York: Simon & Schuster, 2007. ISBN 9780689878114. 291pp.

Sofi has been invited to the hottest party of the year, but there's a hitch: it's in Mexico, and her parents won't let her go. Lying to get out of the house, Sofi and her friends head across the border anyway for a quick night of fun. On her return to the United States, Sofi is stopped by the border patrol and caught with a fake green card and refused reentry. Unbeknownst to Sofi, she and her parents are illegal immigrants. Sofi must remain in Mexico with her long-lost relatives until the matter is resolved.

> *Freaky, Sofi thought as she walked over to look at the different types of saints. There were women dressed in colorful robes, baby saints, and old men with pointy beards. The statues were arranged as if in the middle of a dramatic scene. Sofi kept glancing at the door. Her parents had to come, and quick. The stale, foreboding air of the room was suffocating her.* (87)

Key features: Glossary

Subjects: California; *chiquita* lit; family relationships; identity; Mexican Americans; Mexico

Similar titles: *Emily Goldberg Learns to Salsa* by Ostow is similar in the characters' search for identity and cultural heritage.

Alvarado, Lisa (Mexican American).

Sister Chicas. New York: New American Library, 2006. ISBN 0451217705. 264pp.

Tiana, Graciela, and Leni, three best friends who are as close as sisters, come to know themselves and their families as they embark on a year full of laughs, loves, and the search for independence.

> *This was so very Harlequin romance, not that I'm complaining. Thinking back, the fall should have hurt my butt, my back, my elbow, but I don't remember feeling anything but my heart pitter-pattering against my rib cage. God, more cliches? (9)*

Key features: First person narration

Subjects: blended families; *chiquita* lit; friendship; Illinois—Chicago; interracial relationships; Latinas; *quinceañeras*

Similar titles: Those interested in *chiquita* lit would also enjoy *Cubanita* by Triana, *Haters* by Valdes-Rodriguez, and *Honey Blonde Chica* by Serros.

Alvarez, Julia (Dominican American).

🎖 *Before We Were Free*. **New York: Alfred A. Knopf, 2002. ISBN 0375815449. 167pp.**
While many flee to the United States, twelve-year-old Anita de la Torre and her family remain in the Dominican Republic under the harsh dictatorship of General Trujillo. Situations grow increasingly dangerous as Anita learns about her family's involvement in a plot to kill Trujillo. Forced into hiding with her mother, Anita must grow up quickly and persevere until her country is free.

> *One time, right before she burned the trash in a coal barrel in the yard, I found a page all crumbled up. I uncrumpled it and read CALLING ALL CITIZENS on top—the rest was like a Declaration of Independence in Spanish, listing the freedoms that the country would now enjoy. (95–96)*

Key features: First person narration

Subjects: conspiracies; dictatorships; Dominican Republic; revolutionary struggles; Trujillo Molina, Rafael Leónidas

Similar titles: Other titles featuring life under repressive regimes include *The Cutter* by Suárez and *So Loud a Silence* by Jenkins. Revolutionary struggles are also tackled in Doval's *A Girl Like Che Guevara* and *In the Time of the Butterflies* by Julia Alvarez.

Awards: Pura Belpré Narrative Award, 2004; Américas Book Award for Young Adult Literature, 2002

Finding Miracles. **New York: Laurel-Leaf, 2004. ISBN 0553494066. 264pp.**
Fifteen-year-old Milly has always known she was adopted, but she has chosen to keep this deep secret from even her closest friends. The arrival of new student Pablo and his intense questioning of her background forces Milly to confront her conflicted feelings about her identity. As their relationship grows, Milly decides to join Pablo and his family on a journey to their mutual homeland, far from her Vermont home.

> *How tranquil and happy we'd been, not knowing what had happened in this place only months before. I felt my head spin in that way it always does when I take in too much and don't know where to put it. Some things, I thought, might be too big for the heart to feel all at once. (179)*

Key features: First person narration

Subjects: adoption; ancestors; Central America; high schools; transculturation; Vermont

Similar titles: *Breaking Even* by Grattan-Domínguez is another novel that follows a teen's search for family and identity.

How the García Girls Lost Their Accents. **Chapel Hill, NC: Algonquin Books, 1991. ISBN 0945575572. 290pp.**

Fleeing from the Dominican Republic in the 1960s, four sisters and their parents readjust to life in the United States. Each sister individually voices her struggles with being caught between cultures, as their lives carry them from the Dominican Republic, to New York, and back.

> *For the benefit of an invisible sisterhood, since our aunts and girl cousins consider it very unfeminine for a woman to go around demonstrating for her rights, Yoyo sighs and all of us roll our eyes. We don't even try anymore to raise consciousness here. It'd be like trying for cathedral ceilings in a tunnel, or something.* (121)

Subjects: Dominican Americans; family life; fathers and daughters; immigrants; transculturation

Similar titles: *Call Me Maria* by Ortiz Cofer, *The Flight to Freedom* by Veciana-Suarez, and Alvarez's sequel to *How the García Girls Lost Their Accents*, *¡Yo!*, tackle the challenges of cultural assimilation.

How Tia Lola Came to Stay. **New York: Alfred A. Knopf: Distributed by Random House, 2001. ISBN 0375802150. 147pp.**

Shortly after leaving their home in New York City and moving to Vermont, Miguel's mother invites her sister, crazy Tìa Lola, to visit and help Miguel and his sister, Juanita, adjust to their parents' divorce. But Miguel is more concerned with fitting in at his new school, and Tìa Lola keeps getting in the way.

> *Why would Tìa Lola have to go back? She's part of our family. Juanita's bottom lip quivers. For a moment, Miguel is not sure he can go through with it.*
>
> *She's been here one whole month. People are only allowed to visit for twenty-one days.* (30–31)

Subjects: aunts; divorce; Dominican Americans; family life; Vermont

Similar titles: For a similar tone of writing, try the <u>Marisol and Magdalena Duet</u> by Chambers.

¡Yo! **New York: Penguin Books, 1997, ISBN 0-452-27918-6. 309pp.**

This is the story of Yolanda García, successful novelist, as told by the many people her successful "novel" has upset, based as it is on many true anecdotes and quirky characters, mostly from her immediate, embarrassed, and angry family.

> *But to myself, I'm thinking, why can't she write about axe murderers or law-firm scams or extraterrestrials and make a million and divide it four ways, which by the way is what the other sisters suggest she should do with this book since we provided the raw material.* (9–10)

Key features: First person narration

Subjects: Dominican Americans; sisters; writers—fiction

Similar titles: For more adventures of the García family, read *How the García Girls Lost Their Accents* by Alvarez. For more insight into Latino writers coming of age, read Aira's *How I Became a Nun*.

Anaya, Rudolfo (Mexican American).

🏺 *Bless Me, Ultima*. New York: Warner Books, 1999 (1972). ISBN 0446675369. 290pp.

Young Antonio Marez is introduced to a different world of faith and kinship to nature by Ultima, a traditional healer, who was come to live with his family. Sensitive, Antonio is torn between his mother's urging him to become a priest and his father's desires for him to continue the family's cowboy heritage. Antonio relies heavily on Ultima's guidance as he comes of age and discovers his own destiny.

> *I thought about what he said as we walked to the bridge. I wondered if I would grow up too fast, I yearned for knowledge and understanding and yet I wondered if it would make me lose my dreams.* (77)

Subjects: Catholic Church; healers; magical realism; Mexican Americans; New Mexico

Similar titles: Other titles with magical realism elements and similar mystical tone include *Leaving Tabasco* by Boullosa, *Orange Candy Slices and Other Secret Tales* by Canales, and books by Allende.

Awards: Premio Quinto Sol Award, 1970

Berrocal Essex, Olga.

Delia's Way. Houston, TX: Arte Público Press, 1998. ISBN 1558852328. 186pp.

Delia and her sister María Elena share an intense rivalry. In fact, María Elena is a bully. The special bond between María Elena and their mother only contributes more angst to the girls' constant battle. When Delia learns the family secret of why they are so close, things finally start to go Delia's way.

> *Delia sat on her bed or on her floor observing, enjoying everything with amusement, but not really participating. She wasn't expected to join in. After all, María Elena had said once when Delia tried to express an opinion, "Oh, forget it! At thirteen Delia is still a little runt!"* (41)

Subjects: bullying; mothers and daughters; Panamanians; sibling rivalry

Similar titles: *Soledad* by Angie Cruz also tackles the tough relationship that can exist between a mother and a daughter.

Bertrand, Diana Gonzales (Mexican American).

Sweet Fifteen. Houston, TX: Arte Público Press, 1995. ISBN 1-55885-122-4. 296pp.

Seamstress Rita Navarro develops a friendship with fourteen-year-old Stefanie as she prepares a dress for Stefanie's *quinceañera*.

> *Rita smiled down at her great-grandmother. "Absolutely beautiful." Her heart was filled with so many emotions she couldn't name them all. It was as if she had stood with Stefanie, reaffirming her commitment to love, the source of all life, and taking from this special celebration the spiritual presence that would guide her choices in the years to come.* (287)

Subjects: *chiquita* lit; family life; friendship; Mexican Americans; *quinceañeras*

Similar titles: There are a number of similar titles featuring *quinceañeras*, including *Cuba 15* by Osa, *Estrella's Quinceañera* by Alegría, and *Quinceañera Means Sweet 15* by Chambers.

Trino's Duet.

Suffering adolescence in abject poverty, seventh grader Trino Olivares must survive the violent world of his Texas barrio and become a man, with little guidance from the adults around him.

Subjects: family relationships; gangs; high schools; Mexican Americans

Similar titles: Other novels that focus on gangs and the tough choices teens must make include *Behind the Eyes* by Stork, *Call Me Henri* by Lorraine López, and *Daisies in the Junkyard* by Enright.

Trino's Choice. Houston, TX: Piñata Books, 1999. ISBN 1558852794. 124pp.

Trino must make a difficult decision about where his allegiances lie when he witnesses others his age manhandling a local store owner. Does he turn his back on his old friends and turn gang leader Rosca in to the authorities? With his family barely making ends meet, Trino is tempted by the offers of quick cash from Rosca. Seeing nowhere else to turn, Trino falls in with the wrong crowd, which leads to trouble.

> *Fear had controlled everything then. He had been so busy running and hiding that nothing else mattered. Today he had time to think about how thirsty he felt, and how fast a bowl of cereal had disappeared inside his stomach, leaving only hungry, hungry in its place. And he had no money to get something to eat.* (32)

Trino's Time. Houston, TX: Piñata Books, 2001. ISBN 1558853162. 171pp.

The sequel to *Trino's Choice* has Trino learning even more about himself as he struggles with family responsibilities and the death of his friend during a botched robbery. He takes a new job to help out his struggling mother, and with the help of new friends and a new interest in education, Trino realizes time has changed him more than he ever realized.

> *Trino stood there in the hallway a moment, soaking in Hector's words. A school-type had called him "smart." A flicker of pride made him stand up straight and press his shoulders back. Here was a different reputation for Trino Olivares, but so far, Trino liked the way it fit him.* (64)

Boullosa, Carmen (Mexican).

Leaving Tabasco. **(*Treinta años*, 1999). Translated by Geoff Hargreaves. New York: Grove Press, 2001, c1999. ISBN 0802116841. 244pp.**

Raised by her mother and grandmother, Delmira Ulloa's adolescence is a magical world framed by her grandmother's nightly tales. In fact, it's not unusual for her grandmother to float above her bed when she sleeps and for the maid to develop stigmata. Surrounded by these tales, Delmira develops a vivid imagination and a strong sense of will. But when she becomes involved with local politics, Delmira is arrested and forced to flee her enchanting home to discover the real world.

> *It had already struck nine o'clock and the church was packed with both Indian and white parishioners, on this rare occasion mixed together, for they'd been waiting there for two hours in the midst of all sorts of rumors, some of which included Luz and some of which didn't. From the pulpit the*

> *priest explained how Luz had met her end, and how she had passed away in an odor of sanctity, omitting that it was an odor strongly tinged with urine.* (64)

Key features: First person narration; sexual situations

Subjects: family relationships; grandmothers and granddaughters; magical realism; Mexicans

Similar titles: Other titles with magic realism elements and similar mystical tone include *Bless Me, Ultima* by Anaya, *Orange Candy Slices and Other Secret Tales* by Canales, and books by Allende.

Canales, Viola (Mexican American).

🌹 *The Tequila Worm.* **New York: Wendy Lamb Books, 2005. ISBN 0-385-74674-1. 199pp.**

Sofia and her *comadre*, Berta, prepare for Sofia's biggest experience yet—a chance to attend boarding school eight hours away from her small barrio. But her family can barely afford the necessities she'll need while away, and her mother doesn't want to see her go. Upon her arrival, Sofia doesn't feel very confident in the strange new world of St. Luke's, and she worries about the people she left behind.

> *For the first time ever, I detected a sense of fear in Mama, that even her web of comadres was no match against these changes. And maybe, I thought, going away to school might help me help her someday.* (111)

Key features: First person narration

Subjects: boarding schools; family life; Mexican Americans; Texas; transculturation

Similar titles: *Estrella's Quinceañera* by Alegría also explores the difficulties of life at boarding school.

Awards: Pura Belpré Narrative Award, 2006

Cárdenas, Teresa (Cuban).

Letters to My Mother. **Toronto: Groundwood Books, 1998. ISBN 0888997205. 103pp.**

Following the death of her mother, a young African Cuban girl turns to her extended family, only to find herself surrounded by instability and abuse. The only release she has now is the letters filled with grief and loneliness she writes to her deceased mother.

> *I look for you in the ceiling tiles, but it's no use. You're never there.*
>
> *Before you used to glow in my room as if you were the moon.*
>
> *I'd like to be far, far away from here, with you, in heaven.* (37)

Key features: First person, epistolary narration; sexual situations

Subjects: Cubans; death; epistolary fiction; grief; letters; race relations

Similar titles: Other titles written in the epistolary form include *Call Me Maria* by Ortiz Cofer, *A Different Kind of Heat* by Pagliarulo, and *Luna's California Poppies* by Villanueva.

Chacon, Daniel (Mexican American).

And the Shadows Took Him. New York: Atria Books, 2004. ISBN 074346-6381. 339pp.

Talented Joey Molina has finally landed the lead role in the school play, only to find out that his father plans to move the entire family to Oregon. Living the barrio behind, Joey enters a new school and finds himself playing the most intricate role of his life. Being the new Latino kid from California, everyone assumes he is a former gang member, and Joey does nothing to disabuse them of this notion. Soon he really is creating a gang at the demand of his new friends, and of course comedy ensues.

> Gilbert Sanchez, a tough audience member, from the beginning seemed not to believe Joey. He questioned him about his gangbanger past, so much so that Joey had to keep his lies written down in a notebook, The Book of Lies he called it, so he would know how to answer a particular question. (201)

Key features: Strong language.

Subjects: actors; California; gangs; humor; Mexican Americans; Oregon

Similar titles: Another title with its own humorous take on gangs is Johnston's *Any Small Goodness.*

Chambers, Veronica (Panamanian American).

Marisol and Magdalena Duet.

Born and raised in Brooklyn, New York, best friends Marisol and Magdalena know very little about their Panamanian heritage. Together, with the help of neighbors and relatives, the two girls come to better understand their cultural identity, further solidifying their lifelong friendship.

Key features: First person narration

Subjects: *chiquita* lit; family life; friendship; grandmothers and granddaughters; New York—New York City—Brooklyn; Panama; Panamanian Americans; *quinceañeras*

Similar titles: *Pillars of Gold and Silver* by de la Garza is another excellent title featuring a young girl just learning about her heritage and its rich language. The *quinceañera* celebration can also be found in *Cuba 15* by Osa, *Estrella's Quinceañera* by Alegría, and *Sweet Fifteen* by Bertrand.

Marisol and Magdalena: The Sound of Our Sisterhood. New York: Jump at the Sun, 1998. ISBN 0786804378. 141pp.

> Sent to Panama for a year to better understand her heritage, Marisol worries that she might not fit in since she barely speaks Spanish. Plus, she will be miles away from her best friend, Magdalena. But all her fears are put to rest when she arrives and is welcomed wholeheartedly by her family and the community. Will she want to return to Brooklyn, and what will her friendship with Magdalena be like when she does?

> > I thought about the scene in the Wizard of Oz, when Dorothy says, "We're not in Kansas anymore, Toto. That was exactly how I felt, and I didn't even have a dog to tell it to. I was in this on my own." (88)

Quinceañera Means Sweet 15. New York: Jump At the Sun, 2001. ISBN 078680-4971. 189pp.

> The continuing story of Marisol and Magdalena has the two four-teen-year-olds preparing for their respective *quinceañeras*. However, in Marisol's absence, Magdalena has made two new friends who don't quite mesh with Marisol. Also, Marisol worries her *quinceañera* won't match the great party Magdalena can afford to throw. Can these two friends patch things up before their big day?

> > *As I prayed, I thought about my friendship with Magda. How could she be my mejor amiga and go to parties without me? How could she roll with a girl like Marisa and tell her things about me behind my back? I reached up to touch the little gold cross that I wore everyday, the one that was the exact replica of the one Magda wore. I hadn't changed since we were little girls, but Magda had. (55)*

Cisneros, Sandra (Mexican American).

🏆 ***The House on Mango Street.*** **New York: Vintage Books, 1984. ISBN 0679734775. 110pp.**

> Esperanza lives in the tough, poor Latino section of Chicago. While those around her only work to survive, Esperanza has big dreams of a world beyond her small neighborhood. She discovers that being able to communicate in English is key and begins recording stories of her neighborhood, friends, and everyday life, hoping one day to become a writer and purchase her dream home.

> > *You can never have too much sky. You can fall asleep and wake up drunk on sky, and sky can keep you safe when you are sad. Here there is too much sadness and not enough sky. Butterflies too are few and so are flowers and most things that are beautiful. Still, we take what we can get and make the best of it. (33)*

Key features: First person narration

Subjects: dreams; family relationships; Illinois—Chicago; writers—fiction

Similar titles: For more insight into Latino writers coming-of-age, read Aira's *How I Became a Nun. Call Me Maria* by Ortiz Cofer, *The Flight to Freedom* by Veciana-Suarez, and Julia Alvarez's sequel to *How the García Girls Lost Their Accents, ¡Yo!,* tackle the challenges of transculturation.

Awards: American Book Award, 1985

Cruz, Angie (Dominican American).

Soledad. **New York: Simon & Schuster, 2001. ISBN 0743212010. 237pp.**

> Forced to return home to her poor Washington Heights neighborhood to care for her sick mother, Soledad must face the family and past she tried so hard to put behind her and salvage some sort of relationship with her mother, Olivia.

> > *I keep wanting to apologize because of all the times I didn't believe her. I was selfish for shutting her out after she'd gone through so much. Maybe if I believed her we could have fought my father together. Maybe everything got so out of hand because we never talked about it. (179)*

Key features: First person narration

Subjects: Dominican Americans; mothers and daughters; New York—New York City

Similar titles: *Delia's Way* by Berrocal Essex also tackles the tough relationship that can exist between a mother and a daughter.

de la Garza, Beatriz Eugenia.

Pillars of Gold and Silver. **Houston, TX: Piñata Books, 1997. ISBN 1558852069. 260pp.**

Following the death of her father in the Korean War, Blanca Estela and her mother spend the summer in Revilla, Mexico, with her grandmother. Uncomfortable in her new small town surroundings, Blanca, who speaks little Spanish, finds it difficult to connect to the town and specifically to her stern grandmother. With a little encouragement from her grandmother, Blanca reluctantly joins the neighborhood children in their rural singing games. Such simple pleasures open Blanca's eyes to the small town charms of her grandmother's life in Revilla.

> *The moon had climbed to the middle sky, and its light, filtering through the bars, turned them into silver ingots. The moon, she thought as she drifted off to sleep, had always been their playmate, the companion of their games.* (241)

Subjects: grandmothers and granddaughters; Mexican Americans; Mexico; *pueblos;* transculturation

Similar titles: *Marisol and Magdalena* by Chambers is another novel that features a young girl who is just learning about her heritage and its rich language. A similar relationship with grandparents is also featured in *Orange Candy Slices and Other Secret Tales* by Canales.

de la Peña, Matt (Mexican American).

Mexican White Boy. **New York: Delacorte Press, 2008. ISBN 97803857-33106. 247pp.**

Danny survives in dual worlds. At his elite private school, everyone expects him to be the stereotypical Mexican and speak Spanish because of his dark skin, whereas he really lives with his Caucasian mother. With his father out of the picture, Danny's Mexican heritage is even more of a mystery to him. To gain a better understanding of his own identity, Danny spends the summer with his father's family, where he finds a perfect fit on the pitcher's mound.

> *Takes a deep breath and pictures the train over his head and then pictures nothing at all. He goes blank during his windup, like he does when it's just him and Uno at Las Palmas. Or at the train tracks. He lets go. And this time when he fires his fastball it rips right past a late-swinging Marzel and straight into Uno's new mitt.* (152)

Subjects: baseball; California; cousins; fathers and sons; identity; race relations; transculturation

Similar titles: *Dark Dude* by Hijuelos also discusses cultural stereotypes.

Diaz, Debra (Mexican American).

The Red Camp. Houston, TX: Arte Público Press, 1996. ISBN 1558851690. 126pp.

Once the booming home to hundreds of migrant citrus workers in Orange County, California, El Campo Colorado, or the "Red Camp" as it was known by the Mexican children, is now a poor barrio filled with little but heartbreak. Four sisters recount their youth living in this community with their alcoholic convict father and mentally ill mother, who were always at odds with each other.

> *I pulled the red velvet couch pillows over my ears and sank down into the couch. I didn't want to hear any of it. But Mom's sobbing, screeching voice cut through the cushions.* (70)

Key features: First person narration

Subjects: alcoholism; family life; mental illness; Mexican Americans; migrant farmworkers; sisters

Similar titles: *The Circuit* and its sequel by Jiménez also feature a bleak look at migrant farmworkers and their family life. In addition, *Esperanza Rising* by Ryan and *Under the Feet of Jesus* by Viramontes have similar themes from a female point of view.

Dole, Mayra Lazara (Cuban).

Down to the Bone. New York: HarperTeen, 2008. ISBN 9780060843106. 367pp.

Still coming to terms with her sexuality, Laura Amores is dealt a tough blow when Mother Superior discovers she is a lesbian and kicks her out of school. Unable to keep her suspension or the motive for it a secret from her mother, Laura finds herself on the street when her mother kicks her out as well. Luckily, Laura's best friend is waiting with open arms to become her new family.

> *I feel as if I've swallowed a baseball and it got stuck in my throat. Everything I've lost flashes in front of my eyes: Papi, Marlena, my reputation, Mami, my friends, my school, my old* barrio. *I want to console Mami, but instead I ask her if she has ice cream.* (256)

Key features: First person narration; strong language; glossary

Subjects: *chiquita* lit; Cuban Americans; Florida; friendship; lesbians; mothers and daughters; sexual identity

Similar titles: Novels that also feature lesbian characters are *A Girl Like Che Guevara* by Doval, *Trace Elements of Random Tea Parties* by Lemus, and *What Night Brings* by Trujillo.

Doval, Teresa de la Caridad (Cuban American).

A Girl Like Che Guevara. New York: Soho Press, 2004. ISBN 1569473587. 305pp.

Privileged Lourdes believes in the socialist ideals of her father and her beloved country of Cuba. When she and her classmates are sent to prove their allegiance to Fidel Castro in a government-run work study program, Lourdes works and comes of age in the tobacco fields of Cuba. The program opens her eyes to the divergence between her beliefs and their effect on the real world and brings about a sexual awakening Lourdes did not expect.

> *Che Guevara had stated that a loyal revolutionary must struggle against crime and injustice, and denounce them at once. But I was afraid of the principal. Afraid of Elena, too. And somehow Che's words didn't impress me as they used to.* (276–77)

Key features: First person narration; glossary

Subjects: Cuba; Guevara, Ernesto "Che"; lesbians; revolutionary struggles

Similar titles: Revolutionary struggles are also tackled in *Before We Were Free* and *In the Time of the Butterflies* by Julia Alvarez and *The Cutter* by Suárez. Novels that also feature lesbian characters include *Down to the Bone* by Dole, *Trace Elements of Random Tea Parties* by Lemus, and *What Night Brings* by Trujillo.

Draper, Sharon (African American).

Romiette and Julio. New York: Atheneum, 1999. ISBN 0689821808. 236pp.

This retelling of the classic Romeo and Juliet tale finds the star-crossed lovers, Romiette, an African American girl, and Julio, her Latino boy-friend, fighting to have their interracial relationship accepted by family and friends.

> "I never asked for any protection from some gang! I don't want it or need it." Romi was so angry she wanted to cry, but she refused to give Malaka the satisfaction.
>
> "Suit yourself. That Mexican ain't got a chance." (105)

Key features: First person narration

Subjects: African Americans; gangs; Hispanic Americans; Internet; interracial relationships; race relations

Similar titles: Interracial relationships are also addressed in *Accidental Love* by Gary Soto; race relations are also a focus of *White Bread Competition* by Jo Ann Yolanda Hernández.

Durbin, William (U.S. American).

El Lector. New York: Wendy Lamb Books, 2006. ISBN 0385746512. 195pp.

Growing up in Depression-era Florida, thirteen-year-old Bella always wanted to be a *lector* (a reader) like her grandfather. Daily he goes to the local cigar factory and reads news, poetry, and literature to the employees. Unfortunately, to help her family through these hard times, Bella must instead take a job at the cigar factory steaming tobacco leaves. Meanwhile, unrest grows in the factory as management replaces workers with machines and her beloved *lector* with a radio. When Bella's aunt is arrested for involvement with the union and the factory closes due to strikes, Bella must find a way to save the town, its history, and her dreams.

> The cigar workers smiled and tipped their hats as Grandfather and Bella started up the walk. For a moment she imagined she was wearing an elegant white dress and stepping onto a palm-lined boulevard lit by a golden sun. (53)

Subjects: cigar industry; Cuban Americans; Great Depression—1929; Florida—Ybor City; grandfathers; reading; unions

Similar titles: *Macho!* by Villaseñor also focuses on the plight of factory workers.

Enright, Michael (U.S. American).

Daisies in the Junkyard. New York: Tom Doherty Associates Book, 2002. ISBN 076530144X. 237pp.

College-bound seniors Tony and Carlos have done a good job of resisting the pressures of joining a gang. But having no gang allegiance puts both them and their families in a precarious position. After Carlos is shot and his younger brother is murdered, Tony and Carlos find themselves caught up in the violence of their Chicago neighborhood.

> *Usually it was a closed campus, but since it was such a nice day she let them stand out in front for a few minutes at their lunch periods. So, everyone goes out the front door at lunchtime and they're all standing around in front. Sure enough, the Stones come racing down Eighty-ninth Street in an old beater, shouting "Stone Love." Everyone was trying to get into the one door that was open when they started shooting into the crowd.* (156)

Subjects: friendship; gangs; high schools; Illinois—Chicago; Mexican Americans; murder

Similar titles: *Behind the Eyes* by Stork, *A Different Kind of Heat* by Pagliarulo, *Party Girl* by Ewing, and *Trino's Choice* by Bertrand all focus on the violence associated with gang life.

Ewing, Lynne (U.S. American).

Party Girl. **New York: Knopf: Distributed by Random House, 1998. ISBN 037580210X. 110pp.**

Best friends Kata and Ana are both part of the same gang in their Los Angeles neighborhood. Ana, who recently revealed she was pregnant, is tragically killed in a drive-by shooting. Kata seeks revenge for the death of her best friend, while learning to cope without her in a crime-filled neighborhood.

> *We used to sit on the playground and plan our weddings, tracing long flowing white gowns in the sand with sticks. In our imaginations the lace trains swept across the edge of the playground, carried by little girls in white ruffled dresses. Then in sixth grade—I can't remember the day it happened—a stone rolled in front of our futures. We dropped the sticks and our dreams and started planning our funerals instead.* (3)

Key features: First person narration

Subjects: California—Los Angeles; friendship; gangs; murder

Similar titles: The novels *Behind the Eyes* by Stork, *Daisies in the Junkyard* by Enright, *A Different Kind of Heat* by Pagliarulo, and *Trino's Choice* by Bertrand all focus on the violence associated with gang life.

Gilb, Dagoberto (Mexican American).

The Flowers. **New York: Grove Press, 2008. ISBN 9780802118592. 250pp.**

Fifteen-year-old Sonny Bravo is the new stepson of the landlord of The Flowers, an apartment building filled with an array of tenants from various walks of life. Assisting with building upkeep, Sonny entangles himself in the lives of the residents. When racial violence threatens his neighborhood, Sonny must save one young tenant who has nowhere to turn.

> *The stucco of the apartment building was painted a pale yellow, and bolted to its street side was a black wrought-iron sign, in a longhand-style lettering, two flood lamps in an ivy bed below aimed up at it: Los Flores. Beneath those words were three flowers branching out of one thick stem. I didn't know that much about flowers, but my mom told me they were margaritas, which I think are called daisies.* (75)

Key features: First person narration; strong language; sexual situations

Subjects: apartment buildings; landlords; Mexican Americans; poverty

Grattan-Domínguez, Alejandro (Mexican American).

Breaking Even. Houston, TX: Arte Público Press, 1997. ISBN 1558852131. 254pp.

> Tired of his boring small West Texas town, eighteen-year-old Val sets out on a journey to find not only himself but also the long-lost father he had believed died heroically years before. Upon meeting his father, Val becomes caught up in the world of high-stakes gambling and discovers that his father isn't all he had hoped.

> > *The picture had blurred over the years; yet it was Val's most prized possession, and about the only proof he had that there had ever really existed a man named Frank Cooper.* (37)

> **Subjects:** fathers and sons; gambling; Mexican Americans; Texas

> **Similar titles:** Another young woman's search for identity and family can be found in *Finding Miracles* by Julia Alvarez. Broken relationships between fathers and sons are also the theme of *Suckerpunch* by David Hernandez and *He Forgot to Say Goodbye* by Sáenz.

Griffin, Peni R. (U.S. Texan American).

The Music Thief. New York: Henry Holt, 2002. ISBN 0805070559. 154pp.

> Alma is having a hard time coping with all the devastating changes in her world. Her beloved *abuela* passed away; her brother, Eddie, is part of a gang; and her favorite Latina singer, Jovita, was tragically killed in a drive-by shooting. With all these troubles, Alma finds comfort in the music-filled rooms of her neighbor's home.

> > *"Jovita died," said Alma. A mockingbird sang in the stillness after her voice stopped; Silvita worked her way along the fence, rattling the link; Mrs. B. waited. "I didn't plan it. I was—I felt so—." She stopped, intimidated by the size of the feeling, the first huge and terrible feeling of this huge and terrible summer.* (147)

> **Key features:** First person narration

> **Subjects:** death; family life; gangs; grief; music; Texas—San Antonio

> **Similar titles:** Other novels that delicately address death and grief include *Sammy and Juliana in Hollywood* by Sáenz and *A Different Kind of Heat* by Pagliarulo.

Hernandez, David.

Suckerpunch. New York: HarperTeen, 2008. ISBN 9780061173301. 217pp.

> Marcus and Enrique's abusive father left the family over a year ago and is now pleading with their mother to allow him to return. Unhappy with this possibility, the brothers head to California to confront their father about his misdeeds.

> *I should've done something then as my dad kept yelling, his fury a black wind blowing through the living room, full of electricity. I should've said it was my fault, that I was the one who told Enrique to go to the flower beds and retrieve the ball. I should've done something, anything but cower in the corner and press my hands against my ears, which is exactly what I did. (65)*

Key features: First person narration; drug use; strong language

Subjects: brothers; California; child abuse; drug abuse; family life; family relationships; fathers and sons

Similar titles: Broken relationships between fathers and sons are also the theme of *Breaking Even* by Grattan-Domínguez and *He Forgot to Say Goodbye* by Sáenz.

Hernández, Jo Ann Yolanda (Mexican American).

White Bread Competition. **Houston, TX: Piñata Books, 1997. ISBN 1558852107. 208pp.**

After winning the spelling bee at her high school, Luz Rios finds herself the center of controversy in her culturally mixed neighborhood. Jealousy and racial prejudices are sparked in the community by the talented young Latina. The Latino community, including her own family, embraces but at the same time undermines her success. The Anglo community sees her as a symbol of the growing "Latino problem." To top it all off, as she prepares to represent her state at the national competition, her own friend accuses her of receiving the word list before the local event. Is going to nationals worth all this trouble?

> *Bad memories spill out from the back of your head, starch your neck muscles, and poison your whole day. Good memories sneak around your ears and tug the corners of your mouth into a smile. Angry memories can drive you crazy for a lifetime.* (173)

Subjects: competitions; languages; Mexican Americans; race relations; Texas; transculturation

Similar titles: Race relations are also a focus of *Romiette and Julio* by Draper.

Herrera, Juan Felipe (Mexican American).

🌟 *Cinnamon Girl: Letters Found Inside a Cereal Box.* **New York: Joanna Cotler Books, 2005. ISBN 0060579846. 164pp.**

Devastated that her uncle is in a coma after the terrorist attacks on September 11, Yolanda makes a promise to change her life for the better. She promises to stop drinking, clubbing, and smoking pot. As her family keeps a constant vigil at Uncle DJ's bedside, he awakens and asks Yolanda to save the others. Yolanda takes on the task of returning dust and rubble to the site of the World Trade Center.

> *We scoop voice dust from the bus seats, scoop more dust. Scoop. (77)*

Key features: First person narration in free verse form; drug use

Subjects: coma patients; free verse fiction; New York; Puerto Ricans; September 11, 2001; uncles

Similar titles: Herrera's other novels, *CrashBoomLove* and *Downtown Boy*, are also written in free verse form.

Awards: Américas Award for Young Adult Literature, 2005

🏆 *CrashBoomLove: A Novel in Verse.* **Albuquerque: University of New Mexico Press, 1999. ISBN 0826321143. 155pp.**

Written in narrative verse, this novel centers on seventeen-year-old Cesar Garcia and the difficulties of growing up as a young Chicano in California. Surrounded by gang members in a tough high school, surviving on welfare, and being almost completely illiterate, Cesar struggles to survive.

> *I want to run into the fields, maybe there*
>
> in the middle of the vines, in the arc
>
> *of grapes and star shaped leaves, I will*
>
> find a well, an ocean where I can jump
>
> *into its infinity, lose myself. Find myself.* (110)

Key features: First person narration in free verse form

Subjects: free verse fiction; gangs; high schools; Mexican Americans

Similar titles: For a similar look at barrio life and gangs, read *Parrot in the Oven* by Victor Martinez. Herrera's other novels, *Cinnamon Girl* and *Downtown Boy*, are also written in free verse form.

Awards: Américas Award for Young Adult Literature, 1999

🏆 *Downtown Boy.* **New York: Scholastic Press, 2005. ISBN 0439644895. 293pp.**

Through verse, a year of Juanito's life in the late 1950s is revealed. His existence is a roving one, as his small family continually moves around California in search of work. While Juanito and his mother board with family in San Francisco, his father continues to look. Always being the new boy in town is hard for the ten-year-old, and Juanito longs for his father to return so that together they all can establish a true home.

> *I drink.*
>
> *Let it cool me.*
>
> *Salty, green ocean*
>
> *swaying under the sun*
>
> *at the end of the world.* (199)

Key features: First person narration in free verse form

Subjects: California; diabetes; family relationships; fathers and sons; free verse fiction; Mexican Americans; migrant farmworkers

Similar titles: *The Circuit* and *Breaking Through* by Jiménez also highlight the relationship between fathers and sons and the demanding life of migrant farmworkers. Herrera's other novels, *Cinnamon Girl* and *CrashBoomLove*, are also written in free verse form.

Awards: Tomás Rivera Mexican American Children's Book Award, 2006

Hijuelos, Oscar (Cuban American).

Dark Dude. **New York: Atheneum Books, 2008. ISBN 9781416948049. 439pp.**

Fair-skinned, freckle-faced Rico Fuentes stands out like a sore thumb in his dysfunctional Cuban family. His light skin also causes strife at his Harlem high school, where bullies abound. He dreams of running away to his friend's Wisconsin farm for a life where he doesn't have to prove his strength or his heritage. Once in Wisconsin, he discovers the grass isn't always greener on the other side.

> *Just below the surface ripples, fish slithered like phantoms in and out of their secret hiding places. And in that quivering water, I saw my own face looking back up at me, but all distorted, and in an instant, it hit me that I looked a lot like my Pops.* (354)

Key features: First person narration; drug use, strong language

Subjects: alcoholism; bullying; Cuban Americans; family relationships; runaways; Wisconsin

Similar titles: *The Outsiders* by Hinton similarly addresses loyalty, rivalry, and friendship; cultural stereotypes are discussed in *Mexican White Boy* by de la Peña.

Hobbs, Will (U.S. American).

Crossing the Wire. **New York: HarperCollins, 2006. ISBN 0060741384. 216pp.**

With others around him leaving the failing land behind, Victor realizes that unless he too crosses the border to America, his family has little chance of survival. Without the assistance so many others have to guide them safely across the wire, Victor sets out on his own, encountering danger, dead ends, and hunger.

> *The patrolman was fast, very fast, even with his body armor, and he was gaining ground. But I had more reason to run than he ever would. I ran toward the trees with everything I had. My lungs opened up and my eyes widened to see like an owl. I put fear aside and ran, ran for my family.* (109)

Key features: First person narration

Subjects: friendship; immigration; Mexicans; Mexico; survival; U.S.–Mexico border

Similar titles: *Across a Hundred Mountains* by Grande and *La Línea* by Jaramillo also draw attention to the hardships faced by those immigrating to the United States.

Jaramillo, Ann (Mexican American).

La Línea. **New Milford, Conn.: Roaring Brook Press, 2006. ISBN 1596431547. 125pp.**

Following in his parent's footsteps, fifteen-year-old Miguel leaves his home in Mexico to journey to America. Plans are carefully made to ensure the journey across *la línea* is uneventful. However, unbeknownst to Miguel, his thirteen-year-old sister Elena has secretly joined him. Elena puts a kink in Miguel's plan, and together the siblings strive to survive the difficult journey to their new home.

> *They called it the mata gente, the "people killer." It was an ordinary freight train that passed through once a day, and it was the one way to get north without paying a peso.* (62)

Key features: First person narration

Subjects: brothers and sisters; immigration; Mexicans; Mexico; survival; U.S.–Mexico border

Similar titles: *Across a Hundred Mountains* by Grande and *Crossing the Wire* by Hobbs also draw attention to the hardships faced by those immigrating to the United States.

Jenkins, Lyll Becerra de (Colombian American).

So Loud a Silence. **New York: Lodestar Books, 1996. ISBN 0525675388. 154pp.**

Seventeen-year-old Juan leaves his life of poverty in Bogotá to live with his grandmother on her farm. Adjusting quickly to an improved lifestyle, Juan soon learns there is darkness just over the mountains. Guerrilla warfare has taken over the surrounding hillsides, and Juan must struggle to find his place in the fight without risking his or his grandmother's lives.

> *Then, slowly, Punta Verde began to grow and improve until my worries about my land, like other farmers' concerns, were mostly about the weather. She paused. "Now, in this country of ours, we farmers have turned into victims of 'vultures,' the name we give to the soldiers and guerrillas. We pray that these vultures do not destroy our work of a lifetime and our lives."* (78)

Subjects: Colombia; family life; grandmothers; revolutionary struggles

Similar titles: Other titles featuring life under repressive regimes include *Before We Were Free* by Julia Alvarez and *The Cutter* by Suárez. In addition, the relationship between grandsons and their grandmothers can also be found in *Drift* by Manuel Martinez.

Jiménez, Francisco (Mexican American).

❦ *The Circuit: Stories from the Life of a Migrant Child.* **Albuquerque: University of New Mexico Press, 1998. ISBN 0826317979. 134pp.**

Francisco and his family leave Mexico for north of the border and a life of endless migration as fruit pickers in California, ever on the run from "la migra" or migration officers. Just as Francisco gets acclimated to his school and new home, the family is once again on the move, which makes Francisco and his family stronger.

We unloaded the Carcachita, placed some cardboard on the dirt floor, and laid our wide mattress on it. All of us—Papá, Mamá, Roberto, Trampita, Torito, and Rubén, my baby brother—slept on the mattress to keep warm, especially during chilly nights when freezing wind pierced the canvas walls of our new home. (54)

Key features: First person narration

Subjects: California; family life; Mexican Americans; migrant farmworkers

Similar titles: Similar novels *Downtown Boy* by Juan Felipe Herrera and *Macho!* by Villaseñor feature a male perspective on the life of migrant farmworkers; *The Red Camp* by Debra Diaz features a female perspective.

Awards: Américas Book Award for Young Adult Literature, 1997

🌶 *Breaking Through*. Boston: Houghton Mifflin, 2001. ISBN 0618011730. 195pp.

Francisco Jiménez recounts more of his adolescent years in this sequel to *The Circuit*. Franciso must help support his Mexican American family by working in the fields with his father and by helping his brother with janitorial work. All the while, Francisco explores the joys and sorrows of high school life and begins to see his world widen with the idea of attending college.

> *He was a much faster picker than I was, so I lost every time, except when Papá helped me. Whenever Papá and I picked side by side, he handed me handfuls of strawberries. Papá never let on that he knew about our game, but I figured he must have known, because one time when I filled my crate faster than Roberto he glanced at my brother and winked at me.* (61)

Awards: Tomás Rivera Mexican American Children's Book Award, 2001

Johnston, Tony (U.S. American).

Any Small Goodness: A Novel of the Barrio. **New York: Blue Sky Press, 2001. ISBN 0439189365. 128pp.**

Arturo, who recently arrived in the United States with his family, is struggling with his new life in America. But his loving and supportive family helps him realize that to become a true American, he doesn't have to give up his heritage. This strong familial spirit also encourages him to keep on the right path in the difficult surroundings of East LA. Arturo and his friends heed their words and develop their own type of street gang intent on spreading joy in their barrio.

> *The world seems to wait while he arranges his thoughts. Then slowly he says, "In life there is bueno and there is malo. If you do not find enough of the good, you must yourself create it. A big speech for him. And I can tell he's not done." After a moment he says, "Remember this thing—any small goodness is of value."* (103)

Key features: First person narration; glossary

Subjects: California—Los Angeles; family life; gangs; humor; Mexican Americans; transculturation

Similar titles: Another title with its own humorous take on gangs is *And the Shadows Took Him* by Chacon.

Lemus, Felicia Luna (Mexican American).

Trace Elements of Random Tea Parties. **New York: Farrar, Straus & Giroux, 2003. ISBN 0374278563. 249pp.**

Escaping the traditional childhood she had growing up with her Nana, Leticia runs to Los Angeles and embraces her identity as a lesbian. There she discovers the joy and heartbreak of relationships, until she meets K. Their happy existence as a new couple is put on hold when Nana suffers a devastating stroke.

> *Popping bitter aspirin saviors into my mouth, I heard Nana over the years teaching me that it was the small things that count.*
>
> *Fine, if it's the small things that count, a small gesture just might have the power to bake life into peach pie.* (234–35)

Key features: First person narration

Subjects: California—Los Angeles; grandmothers; lesbian relationships; lesbians; Mexican Americans; sexual identity

Similar titles: Novels that also feature lesbian characters include *Down to the Bone* by Dole, *A Girl Like Che Guevara* by Doval, and *What Night Brings* by Trujillo.

López, Lorraine M. (Mexican American).

Call Me Henri: A Novel. **Willimantic, CT: Curbstone Press, 2006. ISBN 1-931896-27-5. 237pp.**

Tormented by his abusive stepfather and in over his head with household responsibilities, Enrique's life is filled with nothing but obstacles. After witnessing the shooting of a friend by a barrio gang, his life becomes even more complicated. But Enrique soon discovers that his passion for the French language just might be his ticket out of his rough-and-tumble life.

> *On it were pictures of old-looking stone buildings and a lot of snow-covered stuff. They reminded Enrique of a glass globe he was given for Christmas one year, a dome filled with water and tiny bits of white confetti that swirled about a gingerbread house when he shook it.* (169)

Subjects: California; family problems; gangs; high schools; languages; Mexican Americans

Similar titles: A similar title that shows knowledge as an opportunity to leave gang life is *Trino's Time* by Bertrand.

Martin, Eric B. (U.S. American).

The Virgin's Guide to Mexico. **San Francisco: Macadam Cage, 2007. ISBN 9781596922105. 238pp.**

Alma Price disguises herself as a boy and runs away from her suburban Texas home, seeking her mysterious Mexican grandfather and hoping to learn the truth about her cold mother. Aided by a detective, her parents follow hot on her trail, hoping to restore their family unity. But they may find out some surprising things about themselves.

> *This ground beneath her feet's flipflopped from Mexico to Texas to plain ol' USA, as feisty locals gave gringo's dream the finger and started their own damn city; planted a thriving Mex Jeckel United Hyde spleening smuggled cattle, weapons, booze, drugs, cars, casinos, migrants, maquiladoras. She knows all about it. She reads. The border has a long proud legacy of all fucked up.* (8–9)

Key features: Strong language

Subjects: family relationships; family secrets; grandfathers; Mexico; teenagers

Similar titles: *Esperanza's Box of Saints* by Escandón is another novel that features a road trip.

Martinez, Floyd (Mexican American).

Spirits of the High Mesa. Houston, TX: Arte Público Press, 1997. ISBN 1558851984. 192pp.

In a New Mexico *pueblo* just after World War II, Flavio must decide between new technologies and his small village's simple ways.

> They picked the middle of winter, and it was cold. The Rural Electrification Administration threw the switch from somewhere far away. Capulín stepped blurry-eyed into the electric lights. Long gone was the war against progress; the birds sat on the wires and didn't die, and everything the movie had said over a year ago was coming true. (71)

Subjects: grandfathers and grandsons; Mexican Americans; New Mexico; ranchers

Similar titles: Contrasts between the Old World and the new can also be found in *The Jumping Tree* by Saldaña.

Martinez, Manuel Luis (Mexican American).

Drift. New York: Picador, 2003. ISBN 0312309953. 244pp.

Sixteen-year-old Robert Lomos has had a rough family life. His father abandoned the family, causing his mother to have a mental breakdown. Seeing no other option, his mother leaves for Los Angeles with his little brother to recuperate, leaving Robert in San Antonio with his grandmother. Although his grandmother tries her best, Robert continues to find trouble until a particularly nasty incident convinces him to take off for LA to reunite with his family.

> You were right about me going crazy. But you were wrong about me going crazy like Mom. She went crazy from heartbreak and worry. I went crazy from feeling pent-up, like the bubbles in a boiling pot that keep lifting the lid up, popping and fizzing, needing somewhere to go. (84)

Key features: First person narration

Subjects: California—Los Angeles; family relationships; grandmothers; Mexican Americans; Texas—San Antonio

Similar titles: The unique relationship between grandsons and their grandmothers can also be found in *So Loud a Silence* by Jenkins.

Martinez, Victor (Mexican American).

🌲 *Parrot in the Oven: Mi Vida.* New York: HarperCollins, 1996. ISBN 0060267046. 216pp.

Fourteen-year-old Manual (Manny) Hernandez candidly recounts his adolescent life in the projects. Struggles abound for his Mexican American family, with his alcoholic, unemployed father, pregnant sister, and the ever-present threat of gangs and guns. But through it all Manny tries to keep an optimistic, trusting outlook about his childhood and his family.

> She thought schooling could graduate me into places that would make her eyes gleam. Dad thought I should cut school altogether and get a dishwashing job. Start on the bottom and work your way up, that's what he'd say. Only most of the people he knew started on the bottom and worked their way sideways. (38)

Key features: First person narration

Subjects: alcoholism; family life; gangs; Mexican Americans; teen pregnancy

Similar titles: *CrashBoomLove* by Juan Felipe Herrera and *Buried Onions* by Gary Soto take a similar look at gang life in California.

Awards: Pura Belpré Narrative Award; Américas Book Award for Young Adult Literature, 1996

Monroy, Liza (U.S. American).

***Mexican High*. New York: Spiegel & Grau, 2008. ISBN 9780385523592. 334pp.**

Milagro's diplomat mother moves the family to Mexico City, forcing Mila to finish high school at an elite private academy. The hallowed halls of the International School of Mexico are filled with the sons and daughters of Mexico's top politicians and executives. Maneuvering her way through the maze that is Mexican High is a challenge for Milagro.

> *Neither of our groups of friends would understand the relationship between the two of us—the Armani-wearing, Picasso-collecting slick-haired boy whose father had a multimillion-dollar art collection, and the nationless, purple-haired mystery gypsy girl who was fatherless, took acid, wrote confessional columns, and scrawled in her journal, smoking in the bathroom between classes.* (130)

Key features: First person narration; drug use; strong language; sexual situations

Subjects: Americans; *chiquita* lit; family secrets; high schools; Mexico—Mexico City; politicians

Similar titles: Another view of a privileged upbringing can be found in Serros's <u>Honey Blonde Chicas</u> series.

Ortiz Cofer, Judith (Puerto Rican).

***Call Me Maria*. New York: Orchard Books, 2004. ISBN 0439385776. 127pp.**

Maria chooses to move with her father back to his hometown in New York while her mother remains in Puerto Rico. Adjusting to life on a new island, Maria meets a myriad of interesting characters in her father's building and around the barrio. Through these encounters and writing lengthy letters to her mother, Maria discovers her voice as a poet.

> *I will go with Papi. I will explore a new world, conquer English, become strong, grow through the concrete like a flower that has taken root under the sidewalk. I will grow strong, with or without the sun.* (14)

Key features: First person narration

Subjects: identity; New York; poetry; Puerto Ricans; transculturation

Similar titles: Other titles written in the epistolary form include *A Different Kind of Heat* by Pagliarulo, *Letters to My Mother* by Cardenas, and *Luna's California Poppies* by Villanueva.

***Meaning of Consuelo*. New York: Farrar, Straus & Giroux, 2003. ISBN 0374205094. 185pp.**

In the 1950s, Puerto Rico is undergoing an intense Americanization, much to Consuelo's father's delight and her mother's horror. Among these culturally significant changes, Consuelo also sees smaller changes in the family around her, including the disintegration of her parents' marriage and her once lively sister Milli's descent into mental illness.

> *My island is so small it disappears on a globe or a map of the world. But as a child I could not see the end of the land from anywhere I stood, so to me it was as large as I needed my world to be.* (12)

Key features: First person narration

Subjects: family life; mental illness; Puerto Ricans; Puerto Rico

Similar titles: *Call Me Maria* by Ortiz Cofer, *The Flight to Freedom* by Veciana-Suarez, and Julia Alvarez's sequel to *How the García Girls Lost Their Accents, ¡Yo!,* tackle the challenges of transculturation.

Awards: Américas Book Award for Young Adult Literature, 2003

Osa, Nancy (Cuban American).

Cuba 15. **New York: Delacorte Press, 2003. ISBN 0385730217. 277pp.**

Born and raised in America, fifteen-year-old Violet Paz doesn't want anything to do with a *quinceañera*. But her Cuban grandmother insists; so reluctantly, Violet prepares for her upcoming "quince" and in the process discovers her Cuban roots.

> *I hadn't been fifteen a week, and I could see that it was going to be a very long year. After lunch, Mom and Abuela had reached an impasse in the clothing negotiations, nearly causing a scene in the After Five shop in Field's. Mom kept insisting on styles reminiscent of the fourth-grade corduroy jumper of mine, and Abuela couldn't stay away from the candy-frosting types.* (41)

Key features: First person narration

Subjects: *chiquita* lit; Cuban Americans; high schools; Illinois—Chicago; *quinceañeras*

Similar titles: There are a number of similar titles featuring *quinceañeras*, including *Estrella's Quinceañera* by Alegria, *Quinceañera Means Sweet 15* by Chambers, and *Sweet Fifteen* by Bertrand.

Ostow, Mical (Puerto Rican).

Emily Goldberg Learns to Salsa. **New York: Razorbill, 2006. ISBN 1595140816. 200pp.**

Raised in the suburbs of New York by her Puerto Rican mother and Jewish father, Emily Goldberg has never known much about her Puerto Rican heritage. Everything changes when Emily's maternal grandmother dies and the family attends the funeral in Puerto Rico.

> *I'm spending the afternoon with my mother, who's babbling cryptically about good fences and yadda yadda, and meanwhile I'm so disconnected from my boyfriend that he's off male bonding and I know nothing about it. I have stumbled into a Spanish-speaking wormhole in the time-space continuum.* (85)

Key features: First person narration

Subjects: *chiquita* lit; family life; identity; Jews; Puerto Ricans

Similar titles: *Sofi Mendoza's Guide to Getting Lost in Mexico* by Alegria is similar in the main character's search for identity and cultural heritage.

Pagliarulo, Antonio (U.S. American).

A Different Kind of Heat. **New York: Delacorte Press, 2006. ISBN 0385-73298-8. 181pp.**

Reeling from the death of her brother at the hands of the police, Luz Cordero has a problem with authority—and with controlling her anger. Now close to self-destructing, Luz lands herself in a group home. At the St. Therese Home for Boys and Girls, Luz develops friendships that help her begin to come to terms with her emotions.

> *When are they gonna understand that there's nothing to talk about? I'm too embarrassed about the way I acted. Too angry to think back on the whole experience.*
>
> *Just leave me alone, people. Let me burn.* (66)

Key features: First person narration; strong language

Subjects: brothers and sisters; death; diaries; gangs; New York; Puerto Ricans

Similar titles: Other titles written in the epistolary form include *Call Me Maria* by Ortiz Cofer, *Letters to My Mother* by Cardenas, and *Luna's California Poppies* by Villanueva. Death and grief are also addressed similarly in *Daisies in the Junkyard* by Enright.

Ryan, Pam Muñoz (Mexican American).

❦ *Becoming Naomi León.* (*Yo, Naomi León*, 2005). **Translated by Nuria Molinero. New York: Scholastic, 2004. ISBN 0439269695. 246pp.**

Abandoned by their alcoholic mother, Naomi and her little brother, Owen, live with their great-grandmother in California. One day, out of the blue, their mother surfaces to reclaim Naomi. She doesn't want Owen because of his birth defect and only wants Naomi for the welfare checks. Gram refuses and takes off with them for Mexico to find their long-lost father.

> *It was such a hard slap that my head turned and snapped against my shoulder. I didn't have to look in a mirror to know that the sting of her hand was perfectly imprinted. I felt it from the inside out.* (120)

Key features: First person narration

Subjects: brothers and sisters; family relationships; great-grandmothers; Mexican Americans; Mexico

Similar titles: *Pillars of Gold and Silver* by de la Garza is a similar work, as it focuses on family relationships, especially the special bond between grandparents and grandchildren.

Awards: Tomas Rivera Mexican American Children's Book Award, 2004

❦ *Esperanza Rising.* (*Esperanza renace*, 2002). **Translated by Nuria Molinero. New York: Scholastic, 2000. ISBN 043912042X. 262pp.**

Esperanza's beautiful life on her family's Mexican ranch is shattered by the murder of her father at the hands of bandits. Forced to flee to California, the once pampered Esperanza and her mother settle in a migrant camp and begin to work the fields. Not used to hard labor and financial struggles, Esperanza experiences prejudices and fears that she had never encountered before. The sudden sickness of her mother only increases her plight, as it is left to her to save their small family.

> *Esperanza smiled at him anyway, because she knew she would never spend a night in the same house with him and he would never be her stepfather. She almost wished she would be able to see his face when he realized that they had escaped. He wouldn't be grinning like a proud rooster then.* (55)

Subjects: California; Great Depression—1929; Mexican Americans; migrant farmworkers; mothers and daughters; transculturation; unions

Similar titles: *The Red Camp* by Debra Diaz and *Under the Feet of Jesus* by Viramontes both also provide a female perspective on the life of a migrant farmworker.

Awards: Pura Belpré Narrative Award, 2002

Sáenz, Benjamin Alire (New Mexican).

He Forgot to Say Goodbye. **New York: Simon & Schuster, 2008. ISBN 9781416949633. 321pp.**

Ramiro and Jake are two very different teens from El Paso, Texas. Ramiro lives in a predominantly Mexican barrio with his single, struggling mother, and Jake lives a privileged life across town with his own family. The knowledge that both boys were abandoned by their fathers at a young age fosters a valuable friendship through which tender scars can begin to heal.

> *I think I'm two people. One part of me just wants to be happy with everything I have and just fit right in to the life that's been handed me—including my father's last name. Embrace it, you know. I mean, you can dig that, can't you?* (88)

Key features: First person narration; drug use; strong language

Subjects: family problems; fathers and sons; Mexican Americans; Texas—El Paso

Similar titles: Broken relationships between fathers and sons are also the theme of *Breaking Even* by Grattan-Domínguez and *Suckerpunch* by David Hernandez.

🏵 *Sammy and Juliana in Hollywood.* **El Paso, TX: Cinco Puntos Press, 2004. ISBN 0938317814. 291pp.**

The small town life of his Hollywood, New Mexico, barrio is not as glamorous as the real Hollywood for Sammy. Life is hard for the sixteen-year-old as he struggles with the devastating death of his first love, Juliana, along with the demands of his friends and family during the tumultuous 1960s.

> *Because I'd lost my mother to cancer. Because I'd lost Juliana to a bullet and I carried her around with me and she was getting heavier and heavier and it made me tired and sad, but mostly sad. I couldn't stand it anymore because I'd lost Jaime to an exile I hardly understood. Because I'd lost Pifas to the army. Because I was running out of people to lose. Because I just couldn't stand losing one more damn thing. As if I wasn't poor enough already.* (201)

Key features: First person narration

Subjects: coming-of-age; death; grief; Mexican Americans; violence

Similar titles: Other novels that also delicately address death and grief include *The Music Thief* by Griffin and *A Different Kind of Heat* by Pagliarulo.

Awards: Américas Book Award for Young Adult Literature, 2004

Saldaña, Rene (Mexican American).

The Jumping Tree. **New York: Delacorte Press, 2001. ISBN 0385327250. 181pp.**

With family on both sides of his Texas–Mexico border town, Rey experiences both the Old World and the new in this tale of a boy anxious to become a man like his father.

> *I did. I couldn't look. I wanted to cry, but not in front of Apá. He'd taught me better. He had never told me "men don't cry," but I knew it was not a thing men did.* (48)

Key features: First person narration

Subjects: family life; fathers and sons; humor; Mexican Americans; Texas; transculturation

Similar titles: A similar look at contrasts between the Old World and the new can be found in *Spirits of the High Mesa* by Floyd Martinez.

Sanchez, Alex (Mexican American).

🎗 *So Hard to Say.* **New York: Simon & Schuster Books for Young Readers, 2004. 230pp.**

New kid Frederick becomes fast friends with Xio. But he quickly realizes Xio is on a mission to make him more than just a friend. Xio is really fun to be around, but Frederick is having thoughts about the captain of his soccer team instead. How can he break it to Xio that he might be gay, and what will that mean for how he is treated at school?

> *From outside Ms. Marciano's first-period class, I peered in the doorway. Xio's desk was empty. For a moment I sighed relief but then began new worries. Why wasn't she there? Had the shock of what I'd told her given her a heart attack? Had she felt so devastated she'd tried to commit suicide? I knew it was far-fetched, but it could happen.* (192)

Key features: First person narration

Subjects: California; friendship; high schools; homosexuality; Mexican Americans; sexual identity

Similar titles: Other novels that also feature homosexual (in this case lesbian) characters include *Down to the Bone* by Dole, *A Girl Like Che Guevara* by Doval, and *Trace Elements of a Random Tea Party* by Lemus.

Awards: Lambda Literary Award for Children/Young Adults, 2004

Santana, Patricia (Mexican American).

🏍 *Motorcycle Ride on the Sea of Tranquility*. Albuquerque: University of New Mexico Press, 2002. ISBN 0826324355. 270pp.

Eagerly anticipating her brother Chuy's return from duty in the Vietnam War, fourteen-year-old Yolanda is shocked by the man who comes home. Different in demeanor and appearance, Chuy has been changed greatly by his war experiences. Yolanda's world is turned upside down as her beloved brother comes to terms with his new demons.

> *His hair was down to his shoulders, brown and unkempt, and he now had a bushy beard—no sight of the clipped, immaculate soldier whom we met back in April. He was a metamorphosis from skinny green insect to wild, groovy, love child. My mother and father took one long look at their Vietnam veteran son and must have thought that the world was coming to an end.* (120)

Key features: First person narration

Subjects: brothers and sisters; California—San Diego; Mexican Americans; Vietnam War

Similar titles: *Jesse* by Gary Soto similarly addresses siblings surviving the turbulent 1960s and the Vietnam War.

Awards: Chicano/Latino Literary Prize, 1998–1999

Serros, Michele (Mexican American).

Honey Blonde Chicas.

Sophomore Evie Gomez struggles with peer pressure, puppy love, and parents as she lives a privileged life in a Californian beachside community.

Key features: Strong language; drug and alcohol use

Subjects: California; *chiquita* lit; friendship; identity; Mexican Americans

Similar titles: Those interested in *chiquita* lit would also enjoy *Cubanita* by Triana, *Haters* by Valdes-Rodriguez, and *Sister Chicas* by Alvarado. Another view of a Latina's privileged upbringing can be found in Monroy's *Mexican High*.

Honey Blonde Chica. New York: Simon Pulse, 2006. ISBN 1416915915. 298pp.

Evie and her best friend Raquel are part of the casual Flojo surfer set at her high school, where life is literally a beach. However, the return of Evie's former best friend, Dee Dee, wreaks havoc on Evie's laid back lifestyle. Should she join "Dela" as an ultrahip, wild and sexy Sangro, or stay true to her Flojo nature?

> *When Friday evening came around, Evie logged on to her computer to check her Myspace account just to reassure herself that she did have people in her life. "RioChica has 120 friends. Yeah, right. So where are they now?"* (127)

¡Scandalosa! New York: Simon Pulse, 2007. ISBN 9781416915935. 316pp.

Evie's life is perfect. She has a great boyfriend and the best friends a girl could ask for. That is, until her parents find out about her poor grades and threaten to cancel her *sixteeñera* party. The only way to raise her grades in time is to volunteer at the Southern California Horse Reserve. There she meets handsome ranch hand Arturo, and life gets complicated.

> *Charro boys in their snug charro suits were muy—how do you say*
> *FAF en español? Plus, tons of other guys were walking around in their*
> *own mariachi-inspired duds—bolero jackets and tight-fitting pencil*
> *pants with silver conchas stitched along the side seams. They were*
> *kinds sexy, in a mariachi-rocker sort of way.* (135)

How to Be a Chicana Role Model. **New York: Riverhead Books, 2000. ISBN 1573228249. 222pp.**

This collection of short vignettes offers a fictionalized account of Michele Serros's humorous struggle to find success and identity as a writer.

> *While I was in her bathroom I looked around at all the fancy tile in it and I*
> *started to count each piece. I gave up after I reached the first hundred and*
> *wondered how many words I would need to write in order to buy so many*
> *pieces of tile.* (45)

Key features: First person narration; strong language

Subjects: California—Los Angeles; humor; Mexican Americans; writers

Similar titles: For more insight into Latino writers coming-of-age, read Aira's *How I Became a Nun* and *The House on Mango Street* by Cisneros.

Soto, Gary (Mexican American).

Accidental Love. **Orlando, FL: Harcourt, 2006. ISBN 0152054979. 179pp.**

Hard-headed and hot tempered, Marissa is surprised when a chance encounter with nerdy chess player Rene stirs romantic feelings. It's undeniable that there is chemistry between the two. With this change, Marissa decides other changes need to be made as well. She transfers to Rene's school, loses weight, improves her grades, attempts to change her temper, and even moves out of the shadows to audition for the school play—all due to accidental love.

> *When she slapped his arm, she nearly lost control and steered the bike into*
> *a set of buckled garbage cans. She secretly thought she wouldn't have*
> *minded a crash because it would have brought him to the ground where*
> *she could kiss him until he was out of breath.* (128)

Subjects: actresses; high schools; humor; interracial relationships; love stories; makeovers; Mexican Americans

Similar titles: Interracial relationships are also the focus of *Romiette and Julio* by Draper.

Buried Onions. **San Diego: Harcourt Brace, 1997. ISBN 0152013334. 149pp.**

Eddie makes every attempt to live a good life while surrounded by gangs, drugs, and violence. But after dropping out of college at the insistence of his aunt, Eddie finds it even harder to stay out of trouble. His only chance to escape his violent neighborhood is to join the military and get as far away as he possibly can.

> *I knew the mortuary students would get good jobs because my cousin had*
> *died recently and my father and two uncles were dead, all of them now with*
> *arms like the arms of praying mantises, crooked and thin as whispers.* (1)

Key features: Glossary

Subjects: aunts; California; gangs; Mexican Americans

Similar titles: *Behind the Eyes* by Stork is another novel about escaping the gang life.

Jesse. Orlando, FL: Harcourt, 2006, c1994. ISBN 015240239X. 166pp.

In the shadow of the Vietnam War, Jesse leaves home to live with his brother, Abel. Together they attend Fresno City College and struggle to make ends meet by laboring in the fields picking the seasonal crop. Still maturing, Jesse hopes that college will be his ticket to a better life, as well as helping him learn how to talk to girls.

> *Minerva walked me to a back room and introduced me to her father, who pulled his eyes away from the television and extended his hand. When I shook it, I could feel the years of work. I could see in his lined face that he had stared over a continent of cotton plants, beets, and vineyards. "Mucho, gusto, señor," I said, trying to sound respectful. (90)*

Key features: First person narration

Subjects: brothers; colleges; Mexican Americans; migrant farmworkers

Similar titles: *Tex* by Hinton also features brothers facing life on their own in a difficult world; Santana's *Motorcycle Ride on the Sea of Tranquility* similarly addresses siblings surviving the turbulent 1960s and the Vietnam War.

Stork, Francisco X. (Mexican American).

Behind the Eyes. New York: Dutton Books, 2006. ISBN 0525477357. 246pp.

Always the quiet, studious child, Hector is pulled into the world of gangs and violence by his brother, Filiberto. In love with the former girlfriend of a gang leader, Filiberto gets caught in a gang war and is struck down. Hector soon finds himself the new target of the gang and realizes his only chance to escape is to go to reform school.

> *He had been raised to believe he was different. Now, however, as he strode on the dirt road toward cotton fields, he felt that he was becoming more like his dead brother and his dead father. He was going to let this new power take him wherever it wanted to take him. (158)*

Key features: Strong language

Subjects: brothers; family life; gangs; Mexican Americans; Texas

Similar titles: *Buried Onions* by Gary Soto is another novel about escaping the gang life.

Suárez, Virgil (Cuban).

The Cutter. Houston, TX: Arte Público Press, 1991. ISBN 1558852492. 152pp.

When his family tries to immigrate to the United States, Julian Campos is turned away at the border, while his parents are allowed to go on. To get his papers, Julian must "volunteer" to return to the sugarcane fields as a cutter to help harvest the tons of cane in Cuba. Forced to do backbreaking labor behind barbed wire fences, Julian struggles along until he is told he will be returned to the army. Seeing no other way out, Julian and some of his fellow cutters plan a daring escape to the United States.

On the round mirror over the sliding doors, he catches a glimpse of his tired face, his black sleepy eyes, pale cheeks, a thin bony nose, and colorless small lips, almost too small to be capable of smiles. (37)

Subjects: Cuba; immigration; sugar cane workers

Similar titles: Other titles featuring life under repressive regimes include *Before We Were Free* by Julia Alvarez and *So Loud a Silence* by Jenkins. Details about sugar cane workers are also brought to life in Doval's *A Girl Like Che Guevara*.

Triana, Gaby (Cuban American).

Cubanita. New York: HarperCollins, 2005. ISBN 0060560207. 195pp.

Seventeen-year-old Isabel is more than ready to leave behind her overprotective Cuban parents for college in Michigan. To avoid her mother and her constant nagging to embrace her Cuban heritage, she spends her last summer vacation teaching art at a summer camp and flirting with the boys.

Am I Cuban or American? Where do I belong? I was born here, but if I say I'm American, it'll draw no, mi vida looks from my folks. If I say I'm Cuban, that wouldn't make any sense either, since the closest I've come to seeing the island was with binoculars on a cruise ship one summer. (93)

Subjects: *chiquita* lit; Cuban Americans; Florida—Miami; mothers and daughters

Similar titles: Those interested in *chiquita* lit would also enjoy *Haters* by Valdes-Rodriguez, *Honey Blonde Chica* by Serros, and *Sister Chicas* by Alvarado.

Trujillo, Carla (Mexican American).

🎗 *What Night Brings*. Willimantic, CT: Curbstone Press, 2003. ISBN 1880684942. 242pp.

Twelve-year-old Marci Cruz's family life is tumultuous at best and full of secrets. Her womanizing father is an abusive alcoholic, and her codependent mother does little to stop him. Forced to grow up quickly for her own sake and her sister's, Marci questions everything and everyone as she tries to come to terms with her dysfunctional family and her budding sexual identity as a lesbian.

There's different ways to be scared. Like when you bike down a hill, or ride the Hammer at the fair, or when the teacher catches you stealing art paper to take home. These I could handle. But nothing is as scary as my dad getting mad. I can't remember the first time he hit me, only the sound of mad feet. (11)

Key features: First person narration

Subjects: abuse; adultery; California; Catholic Church; coming-of-age; domestic violence; family relationships; lesbians; Mexican Americans; sexual identity

Similar titles: Similar novels that also feature lesbian characters include *Down to the Bone* by Dole, *A Girl Like Che Guevara* by Doval, and *Trace Elements of a Random Tea Party* by Lemus.

Awards: Mármol Prize for Latina/o First Fiction, 2003

Valdes-Rodriguez, Alisa (Cuban; New Mexican American).

Haters. New York: Little, Brown, 2006. ISBN 0316013072. 351pp.

Forced to move with her cartoonist father to California for his big break, Paski becomes the new kid in a high school rife with elitist cliques. Attention from popular Chris puts Paski on the bad side of his girlfriend, Jessica, queen bee of the Haters.

> *Okay. So I've been here waiting by the bike rack at school for Chris, and now he's here, pulling up in front of me with a crazy cute grin on his face. Oh my God. I wish I could trust him completely. I wish I didn't feel scared and excited all at once. I never wanted to be one of those loser girls attracted to bad boys.* (232)

Key features: First person narration; strong language

Subjects: California—Los Angeles; *chiquita* lit; high schools; Mexican Americans

Similar titles: Additional titles deemed *chiquita* lit include *Cubanita* by Triana, *Honey Blonde Chica* by Serros, and *Sister Chicas* by Alvarado.

Veciana-Suarez, Ana (Cuban American).

The Flight to Freedom. New York: Orchard Books, 2002. ISBN 0439381991. 213pp.

Fleeing with her family to Miami in 1967 to escape Castro's Cuba, Yara Garcia must adapt to new and foreign customs. For one thing, teenagers like her and her sisters enjoy a lot more freedom in the United States than her traditional Cuban parents allow. As Yara and her family grow more accustomed to their new surroundings, Yara starts noticing marked changes in her parents. Her father becomes aggressively involved with the anti-Castro movement, and her mother grows distant and searches for independence. In a unique voice, Yara reveals her firsthand observations of the immigrant experience through her diary.

> *If I know both languages equally, in what language will I think? How will I dream? How will I pray?* (124)

Key features: First person narration

Subjects: diaries; emigration and immigration; Florida—Miami; immigrants—Cuban; transculturation

Similar titles: *Call Me Maria* by Ortiz Cofer and *How the García Girls Lost Their Accents* and *¡Yo!* by Julia Alvarez also tackle the challenges of transculturation.

Vega Yunqué, Edgardo (Nuyorican).

Blood Fugues. New York: HarperCollins, 2005. ISBN 0-06-074277-1; ISBN-13: 978-0-06-074277-1. 270pp.

Kenny Romero spends his summers working on a farm in upstate New York. The story of Kenny's summer job and his encounters with a sometimes hostile nature takes turns with the story of his Catholic parents—Irish mother and Puerto Rican policeman father—his mysterious boss, and Kenny's first love, Claudia.

> *And yet, inflexibly, they remained branded in their hearts, the one with a green shamrock and the other a blood-red flower, a flamboyant, each year their pride celebrated by marching pageants of ethnic excess.* (3)

Subjects: corruption; Irish Americans; New York; police officers; Puerto Ricans

Similar titles: *All the Pretty Horses* by McCarthy and *Pillars of Gold and Silver* by de la Garza present similar stories about the clash between different cultures.

Villanueva, Alma (Mexican American).

Luna's California Poppies. Tempe, AZ: Bilingual Press/Editorial Bilingüe, 2002. ISBN 0927534991. 238pp.

After the death of her beloved grandmother, Luna takes to writing faithfully in her diary to the Virgin Mary. Through these letters, Luna reveals that she has been abandoned by her mother and is left to fend for herself, until a kind stranger welcomes her into his home and encourages her to get an education. Sixteen years later, a grown Luna again picks up the diary and recounts her life as a married woman, struggling to raise children surrounded by bigotry.

> One night Darling brought out a HUGE BOOK that had thousands of pictures glued inside and there she was as a BABY WITH A BOW and then she was a kid, and she had her own PONY in Washington like she grew up on a ranch she said and she was a tomboy, and so that's what's so COOL about Darling right Virgen? (55)

Key features: First person narration; strong language

Subjects: California; coming-of-age; diaries; family life; poetry; race relations

Similar titles: Similar titles written in epistolary form include *Call Me Maria* by Ortiz Cofer, *A Different Kind of Heat* by Pagliarulo, and *Letters to My Mother* by Cardenas.

Villaseñor, Victor (Mexican American).

Macho! New York: Delta Book, 1991. ISBN 0385311184. 240pp.

A classic view of the migrant worker, this novel follows young Roberto García as he begins a journey from Mexico to California to make a better life for his family. Picking fruit in California, Roberto knows he can earn more in a week than he ever could have in Mexico. But the journey proves more difficult than he imagined, with overcrowded boxcars and locked trucks filled with desperate families. Once in America, Roberto works hard in the fields, encountering violence and exploitation while he labors to send his pay back to Mexico. Will he find the courage to join César Chávez and the United Farm Workers' fight for justice?

> With his back to the farmer's property as he faced the huelguistas, the strikers, who were calling, yelling, pleading, and begging for the workers not to go to the fields, but to quit and join them. Now. Quickly. To come to them, their brother, their fellow field workers, their brother campesinos. And not be afraid. (157)

Key features: Excessive violence, strong language

Subjects: California; Mexico; migrant farmworkers; unions

Similar titles: Similar novels *The Circuit* by Jiménez and *Downtown Boy* by Juan Felipe Herrera feature a male perspective on the life of migrant farmworkers; *El Lector* by Durbin also focuses on the plight of factory workers.

Villatoro, Marcos McPeek (Salvadoran American).

The Holy Spirit of My Uncle's Cojones. **Houston, TX: Arte Público Press, 1999. ISBN 1558852832. 298pp.**

The death of his Uncle Jack sends Tony to reminisce about the lessons he learned from his favorite uncle during the fateful summer of 1978. Depressed and in love at age sixteen, Tony makes a half-hearted suicide attempt and is subsequently sent to San Francisco to spend the summer with his pot-smoking, drug-dealing, womanizing Uncle Jack. Although Uncle Jack isn't exactly a good role model for the impressionable teen, he proves to be exactly what Tony needs. Under his influence, Tony becomes a man proud of himself and his Latino heritage.

> I stared out at this world that was gradually becoming more and more Latino, less and less a place where people like the Bee Gees and myself would feel comfortable. There were places in the world, I realized, where the Bee Gees did not reign. There were corners of the world that could strip me of the last slivers of control. (169)

Key features: Drug use; strong language; sexual situations

Subjects: coming-of-age; drug dealers; humor; uncles; writers—fiction

Similar titles: Humorous tales of eccentric relatives are also prominent in *How Tia Lola Came to Stay* by Julia Alvarez.

Viramontes, Helena María (Mexican American).

Their Dogs Came with Them. **New York: Atria Books, 2007. ISBN 9780743284661. 328pp.**

Interweaving stories of four young Latino women form a gritty portrait of East LA during the 1960s. Struggling with bigotry, poverty, gangs, and government entities, Turtle, Ana, Ermila, and Tranquilina manage to remain hopeful about their futures.

> The walls had absorbed so many years of disappointments, bad plumbing, strife, arguments, electrical shorts and temper outages that the wallpaper became unglued, the tiles fell from their grouting, the toilet chain in the water tank busted. Amá was part of the house, carelessly repaired with cardboard and duct tape like her cracked windows. (161)

Key features: Strong language

Subjects: California; gangs; homelessness; mental illness; Mexican Americans

Similar titles: Other novels that focus on gangs and the tough choices teens must make include *Behind the Eyes* by Stork, *Call Me Henri* by Lorraine López, *Daisies in the Junkyard* by Enright, and Trino's Duet by Bertrand.

Under the Feet of Jesus. **New York: Penguin Group, 1995. ISBN 0525939490. 180pp.**

Born into the world of poor migrant workers, Estrella, a young girl on the verge of womanhood, joins her family in the daily struggle to eke out an existence in the harsh climate of the California fruit fields. Backbreaking labor and extreme poverty almost pull the family apart, and Estrella's first love, Alejo, becomes ill after being poisoned by pesticides. Tired of the injustices and hardships, Estrella comes to realize only her inner strength can save her.

> It was always a question of work, and work depended on the harvest, the car running, their health, the conditions of the road, how long the money held out, and the weather, which meant that they could depend on nothing. (4)

Subjects: California; family life; Mexican Americans; migrant farmworkers

Similar titles: The female perspective on migrant farm work can also be found in *Esperanza Rising* by Ryan and *The Red Camp* by Debra Diaz.

Anthologies and Collections

Canales, Viola (Mexican American).

Orange Candy Slices and Other Secret Tales. **Houston, TX: Piñata Books, 2001. ISBN 1558853324. 122pp.**

The magical traditions of a Mexican community and its church are examined in this collection of short stories featuring a young woman and her beloved grandmother.

> *My mother was taught as a child that if she liked another's, say, eyes or nose, she had to touch them; otherwise, the person's eyes or nose would be cursed. Perhaps someone had liked my eyes, she said; perhaps what she was taught as a child is just Mexican superstition, I said.* (32)

Key features: First person narration

Subjects: Catholic Church; family relationships; grandmothers and granddaughters; magical realism; Mexican Americans; short stories

Similar titles: Readers who enjoy magic realism will also want to check out similar novels, such as *Bless Me, Ultima* by Anaya, *Leaving Tabasco* by Boullosa, or classic titles by Allende.

Ortiz Cofer, Judith (Puerto Rican).

🌺 *An Island Like You: Stories of the Barrio.* **New York: Orchard Books, 1995. ISBN 0531068978. 165pp.**

Twelve intertwined short stories reveal the lives of Puerto Rican teenagers in a New Jersey barrio.

> *Anita walks slowly past the familiar sights: shops, bodegas, and bars of the street where she's lived all her life, feeling like she's saying adiós, and good riddance to it all. Her destination is the future. She is walking toward love. But first she has to get past her life that's contained by this block. The barrio is like an alternate universe.* (131)

Subjects: coming-of-age; Puerto Ricans; short stories; transculturation

Similar titles: Another short story collection similar in tone and subject is *Crazy Loco* by Rice.

Awards: Pura Belpré Narrative Award, 1996

Year of Our Revolution. **Houston, TX: Piñata Books, 1998. ISBN 1558852247. 101pp.**

A collection of short vignettes recount the tales of young Hispanic women coming-of-age and rebelling against their immigrant parents.

> *I was taking a stand by refusing to decorate with angels and saints, and by disdaining everything my parents loved. My mother put the picture up in*

the hallway, right in front of my bedroom door so that I'd have to see it coming in and out. It came to be a symbol for me of our relationship in those days. (41)

Key features: First person narration

Subjects: family relationships; mothers and daughters; rebellion; transculturation

Similar titles: Esmeralda Santiago's memoir *Almost a Woman* similarly addresses family relationships and teenage rebellion.

Rice, David (Mexican American).

Crazy Loco. New York: Dial Books, 2001. ISBN 0803725981. 135pp.

The whole spectrum of childhood lessons, including the good (first kisses, dances, and summer camps) and the bad (bullies, lost dogs, and the death of loved ones), can be found in this collection of stories featuring Chicano teenagers growing up in southern Texas.

> *"Mom, where do you think Loco is?" I asked.*
>
> *"You know what? I think since we left the keys in the car, Loco turned it on and drove away. And I'll bet you he's in California somewhere."*
>
> *I smiled. "You think so?"*
>
> *"Oh, yeah," Mom said. "Loco wasn't a dumb dog, just a crazy one." (66)*

Key features: First person narration

Subjects: death; grandfathers; high schools; humor; Mexican Americans; short stories; Texas; transculturation

Similar titles: Another short story collection similar in tone and subject is *An Island Like You* by Ortiz Cofer.

Riding Low on the Streets of Gold. Edited by Judith Ortiz Cofer. Houston, TX: Piñata Books, 2003. ISBN 1558853804. 198pp.

A collection of poems and short stories by Latino writers, this title features young Latinos coming of age in a diverse world.

> *During lunch, we Chicanos hung out at the far end of the field, next to the chain-link fence that separated school grounds from the tall wooden fences of people's back yards, me, Johnny de la Rosa, who had long black hair in an Indian braid and wore a red bandanna, David Romero, and Gilbert Sanchez. We were too cool to be involved in anything that went on in junior high, too cool for junior high. (152)*

Subjects: coming-of-age; Latinos; poetry; short stories; transculturation

Similar titles: Collections similar in tone that also feature Latino teenagers coming of age include *Finding Our Way* by Saldaña and Gary Soto's novels *Petty Crimes* and *Help Wanted*; *Wáchale* is similarly comprised of both poetry and short stories from multiple authors.

Saldaña, Rene (Mexican American).

Finding Our Way. New York: Wendy Lamb Books, 2003. ISBN 038573-0519. 117pp.

The trials and tribulations of adolescence abound in this collection of short stories. Each story provides a glimpse into the daily lives of Hispanic teenagers across the United States and their attempts at self-discovery.

> *What if this were my dad stranded on the side of the road? I'd want someone to stop for him.*
>
> *"My one good deed for today," I told myself. "And I'm doing it for my dad really, not for Mr. Sánchez."*
>
> *I made a U-turn, drove back to where he was still sitting, turned around again, and pulled up behind him.* (9)

Key features: First person narration

Subjects: coming-of-age; Mexican Americans; short stories; transculturation

Similar titles: Collections similar in tone that also feature Latino teenagers coming of age include *Riding Low on the Streets of Gold* by Ortiz Cofer and Gary Soto's novels *Petty Crimes* and *Help Wanted.*

Soto, Gary (Mexican American).

Help Wanted: Stories. Orlando, FL: Harcourt, 2005. ISBN 0152052011. 216pp.

Teenagers search for help in many shapes and forms as they grow up in the gritty world of central California.

> *Maria's mouth twisted with fear. Unable to stop the words, she let her hands flop at her sides and let their mother have her say. Their mother's spirit was circling the house, their lives, with a last goodbye.* (168)

Key features: Glossary

Subjects: California; Mexican Americans; short stories

Similar titles: Collections similar in tone that also feature Latino teenagers coming of age include *Finding Our Way* by Saldaña, *Petty Crimes* by Soto, and *Riding Low on the Streets of Gold* by Ortiz Cofer.

🐾 *Petty Crimes.* San Diego: Harcourt Brace, 1998. ISBN 0152016589. 157pp.

Ten very different teenagers face adolescence head on as they struggle to find their place in the world while surrounded by the violence, poverty, and crime of the barrio.

> *Who in this class would get pregnant? Norma wondered. Lucy would because she was dumb. Dorotea and Alicia might because they liked boys more than anything in the world. Carolina would get pregnant because she liked babies. But me, she thought, no way.* (62)

Subjects: coming-of-age; Mexican Americans; short stories; transculturation

Similar titles: Collections similar in tone that also feature Latino teenagers coming of age include *Finding Our Way* by Saldaña, *Help Wanted* by Soto, and *Riding Low on the Streets of Gold* by Ortiz Cofer.

Awards: PEN USA Literary Award for Children's Literature, 1999

Wáchale! Poetry and Prose about Growing Up Latino in America. **Edited by Ilan Stavans. Chicago: Cricket Books, 2001. ISBN 0812647505. 146pp.**

Wáchale, Spanglish for "watch out" or "be aware," is a collection of short stories, memoirs, poems, and folktales by well-known Latino authors about what it means to be Latino in the United States. Poems are presented in both English and Spanish.

> *Growing up in Miami any tropical fruit I ate*
>
> *could only be a bad copy of the Real Fruit of Cuba.*
>
> *Exile meant having to consume false food,*
>
> *and knowing it in advance* (51)

Subjects: Latinos; poetry; short stories; Spanglish; transculturation

Similar titles: *Riding Low on the Streets of Gold* by Rice is similarly comprised of both poetry and short stories from multiple authors.

References

Hendel, Vicky. 2007. *An Approach to Teaching the Coming of Age Novel.* Available at http://novelst3.epnet.com/NovApp/novelist/results.aspx?sid=F01D9108-BA3F-4CE3-B20E-D6BBD326BD0F%40sessionmgr2&control=tr&rid=500815 (accessed November 9, 2007).

Herald, Diana Tixier. 2003. *Teen Genreflecting: A Guide to Reading Interests.* Westport, CT: Libraries Unlimited.

York, Sherry. 2001. "What's New in Latino Literature?" *The Book Report* 19: 19–24.

Chapter 8

Life Stories

Tracy Warren

El que es buen gallo dondequiera canta

Introduction

Biography, autobiography, memoir, and *testimonio*—all varieties of personal history —are works of nonfiction that focus on the lives of individuals. "Simply put, biography is a form of literature in which the stories of lives are recorded" (Cords 2006, 197). Biographies tell stories of lives and are not written by their subjects. Whereas an autobiography is an author's life story, written in his or her own words in a somewhat linear or chronological manner, the memoir is appropriately defined as

> a slice of life, remembered and recounted as much for the author as for the reader. The recollections can be quiet or significant, small daily battles or huge triumphs, but the point is to share a personal journey and in doing so widen out the story, like ripples on a pond, to make the individual universal. (Wyatt 2007, 82)

The ease with which autobiography and memoir are defined is not found with Latino *testimonio*. John Beverly and Marc Zimmerman define this genre as "a novel or novella-length narrative, told in the first person by a narrator who is also the actual protagonist or witness of the events she or he recounts" (quoted in Sklodowska 2004, 198). At the same time, Volek views the genre as a hybrid of "documentary writing, autobiographical report, eye-witness literature, the literature of resistance and protest, and the New Testament" (1997, 783). Schuessler echoes this sentiment, asserting that "testimonial literature is often considered a hybrid genre, because it incorporates both historical and literary qualities, straddling the areas of fiction and nonfiction" (1999, 385). Although no simplistic definition exists, certain features—first person narrative and commentary, within a political context, and allowing for the individual to represent the collective whole—are consistent.

Appeal

Readers are drawn to life stories because of the insight they provide into the lives and times of specific people, or they may be fascinated by a person, that person's milieu, or the times the person lived in and how he or she influenced or was affected by those times. These works provide detailed insight into the lives of individuals, such as entertainers and politicians, whom readers are curious to know about more intimately. Readers who are familiar with a celebrity's public life often thirst for more personal details—"what happened behind the personal persona" (Ross 2004, 116).

Furthermore, these works appeal to readers interested in a specific aspect of an individual's life. Because a person's life encompasses internal and external factors, personal histories often shed light on the private individual and his or her private world. Whether country of origin, field of endeavor, or familial relationships, personal histories provide insight into the individual's world as a whole. In this genre, readers can find examinations of a wide range of occupations, complex family structures, and fascinating historical happenings (Ross 2004, 116).

Alma Dawson and Connie Van Fleet characterize the genre as moving from a focus on self-definition to life as a hyphenated individual to larger cultural themes (2001, 252). Using this definition as a contextual framework, Latino personal histories are closely tied to their creators. The immigrant/refugee experience, familiar to many Latinos, has "left a permanent impression on the collective and individual experience of Latin Americans" (Lida and Zapata 2004, 503). The author's status as a first-, second-, or third-generation citizen, documented or undocumented resident, hyphenated American, and native or foreign-born individual is central to determining where a personal history falls in the aforementioned evolution.

Furthermore, the political realities of the mid- to late twentieth century have driven the evolutionary journey of the Latino life story. "Almost every writer in Latin America has taken part in the debate that attempts to heal the wounds of the post-dictator era in Argentina, Brazil, and Chile; also in smaller countries like El Salvador, Guatemala, and Uruguay" (Valdés 2004, 167). Latino life stories personalize and individualize the vestigial effects these political events have had on the collective Latino experience.

Organization

The three sections in this chapter cover *testimonio* (autobiography and memoir), biography, and anthologies and collections.

Testimonio: Autobiography and Memoir

The Latino life story is a thriving genre. Similar to those found in other cultures, many of these books focus on the lives of prominent Latinos. From trailblazing television personalities to political figures to authors, well-known individuals share their stories with the masses. The cult of celebrity is a driving factor of this trend.

The search for cultural identity, resulting from the immigrant/refugee experience, is a pervasive theme throughout many of these texts. Biculturalism and the reality of life as a hyphenated American are also popular themes. Many authors examine questions of language and bilingualism.

Agosín, Marjorie (Chilean American).

The Alphabet in My Hands: A Writing Life. **Translated by Nancy Abraham Hall. New Brunswick, NJ: Rutgers University Press, 2000. ISBN 081352704x. 187pp.**

Agosín's memoir, composed of more than 100 short vignettes, recounts her childhood in Chile as the granddaughter of Jewish immigrants, and later emigration to the United States after General Pinochet's overthrow of Salvador Allende. Agosin concludes by reflecting on returning to Chile and her present life in New England.

> *My entire family has been part of these far-flung, intermittent exiles, as if life were a journey in a ship of fools with no hope of return.* (59)

Subjects: Agosín, Marjorie; Allende, Salvador; Chile; immigrants—Chilean; Jews and Judaism; Pinochet, Augusto

Aguilera, Luis Gabriel (Mexican American).

Gabriel's Fire: A Memoir. **Chicago: University of Chicago Press, 2000. ISBN 0226010678. 291pp.**

With extensive use of provocative dialogue, Aguilera documents his teen years (ages thirteen to eighteen) as a Mexican American coming of age in a Polish neighborhood of Chicago.

> *I was in awe of him. Not only for his skills in detecting what was around, but for his ability to transform himself into a friend and to relate to us his insight.* (15)

Subjects: Aguilera, Luis; Catholicism; Illinois—Chicago; immigrants—Mexican; love affairs; Mexican Americans; Polish Americans; teenagers

Allende, Isabel (Chilean).

My Invented Country: A Nostalgic Journey Through Chile. **(Mi país *inventado: un paseo nostálgico por Chile,* 2003). New York: Harper-C ollins, 2003. ISBN 006054564x. 199pp.**

For Allende, the events of September 11, 2001, brought to mind the assassination of her uncle on September 11, 1973, and inspired her to make a nostalgic examination of Chile and the United States.

> *I often ask myself what exactly nostalgia is. In my case, it's not so much wanting to live in Chile as it is the desire to recapture the certainty I feel there.* (132)

Subjects: Allende; Isabel; Allende, Salvador; assassination; Chile; family relationships; immigrants—Chilean; military coup; September 11, 2001; terrorism; United States; writers

Alvarez, Julia (Dominican American).

Something to Declare. Chapel Hill, NC: Algonquin Books of Chapel Hill, 1998. ISBN 1565121937. 300pp.

> From the Dominican Republic to the United States, Alvarez explores her family and her two cultures in the Dominican Republic and United States, as well as her life as a writer.

>> *Once upon a time, I lived in another country and in another language under a cruel dictatorship, which my father was plotting to overthrow.* (133)

> Subjects: Alvarez, Julia; Dominican Americans; Dominican Republic; exile; immigrants—Dominican; military coup; New York—New York City; Trujillo Molina, Rafael Leónidas; writers

Anders, Gigi (Cuban American).

Jubana! The Awkwardly True and Dazzling Adventures of a Jewish Cubana Goddess. New York: Rayo, 2005. ISBN 0060563699. 298pp.

> The early 1920s immigration of her Russian Jewish grandparents to Cuba, and the 1959 immigration of her immediate family to the United States, underlie the experiences of this *Washington Post* editor's quest to balance her Jewish, Cuban, and American heritages.

>> *When you're bicultural, oops, make that TRIcultural (I'm American, too), not every message you're given by your family and Juban community is synchronized or harmonious.* (19)

> Subjects: Anders, Gigi; Cuba; Cuban Americans; editors; immigrants—Cuban; Jews and Judaism; Jubana; marriage; mothers and daughters; Russia

Arana, Marie (Peruvian American).

American Chica: Two Worlds, One Childhood. (*American chica: dos mundos, una infancia,* 2003). New York: Dial Press, 2001. ISBN 0385319622. 309pp.

> Deconstructing the marriage of her Peruvian father and American mother, the Washington Post Book World editor recalls a childhood shifting between two nations, two cultures, and two worlds. The contrast between her early life of Peruvian privilege and later life of American transculturation form the foundation of Arana's life as an American *chica.*

>> *Slip into my American skin, and the playground would never know I was really Peruvian. Slip into the Latina, and the Peruvians wouldn't suspect I was a Yank.* (272)

> Subjects: editors; family relationships; immigrants—Peruvian; journalists; Peru; *Washington Post*

Arellano, Gustavo (Mexican American).

Orange County: A Personal History. I've Been Taking Notes. New York: Scribner, 2008. ISBN 9781416540045. 269pp.

> Arellano examines his family's story alongside the history of Orange County. He deftly uses humor and a chatty style that shows how culture in the O.C. is a microcosm of national culture.

> *I've seen the Mexican future of this country, the coming Reconquista—and it's absolutely banal. Our looming takeover is spreading across America and will resemble the neighborhood where my parents live in Anaheim, California, Mexico. . . . Trembling yet? Really, the only way you would know it's a Latino neighborhood is due to a very American phenomenon called conspicuous consumption.* (1)

Subjects: California—Orange County; humor; Mexican Americans; Mexicans; racism

Belli, Gioconda (Nicaraguan).

The Country Under My Skin: A Memoir of Love and War. (El Pais Bajo Mi Piel, 2001). **New York: Vintage, 2003. ISBN 1400032164. 380pp.**

In fifty short chapters, Belli juxtaposes the upper-class Nicaraguan expectations of her family with the social realities that inspired her, as a young woman, to get involved in the Sandinista political involvement, all the while detailing her life of love, poetry, motherhood, and self-discovery.

> *In the United States, just as in Nicaragua, I am the same Quixota who learned through life's battles that defeat can be as much of an illusion as victory.* (369)

Subjects: Belli, Gioconda; Costa Rica; immigrants—Nicaraguan; love affairs; marriage; Mexico; motherhood; Nicaragua—Managua; poetry; revolutionaries; Sandinistas

Bell-Villada, Gene H. (U.S. American).

Overseas American: Growing up Gringo in the Tropics. **Jackson: University Press of Mississippi, 2005. ISBN 1578067200. 260pp.**

As an American Third Culture Kid growing up in Cuba, Puerto Rico, and Venezuela, Bell-Villada returns to the United States and struggles to define his country, identity, language, and culture. This memoir sheds light on the experience of being born American, but growing up abroad.

> *At times I begin to feel ever so slightly disenchanted with a country I'd long heard idealized by my father, my mom, and my Caracas schoolmates.* (175)

Subjects: Bell-Villada, Gene; Cuba; immigrants; languages; military school; Puerto Rico; Third Culture Kids; University of California–Berkeley; Venezuela—Caracas

Bentos, Carlos (Uruguayan American).

A Crew of One: The Odyssey of a Solo Marlin Fisherman. **New York: Jeremy P. Tarcher/Putnam, 2002. ISBN 1585421545. 204pp.**

Carlos Bentos, Voice of America contributor, details his love for the marlin, the sea, and the solitude he treasures as the world's only award-winning solo marlin fisherman—all the while providing the reader with an introduction to the nautical world.

> *[T]hat search for equilibrium—taught by example and learned by osmosis—may have something to do with the person I am today; an active observer of life at land, a roaming monk of the deep sea.* (66)

Subjects: adventure; Bentos, Carlos; fisherman; fishing; immigrants—Uruguayan; Voice of America

Betancourt, Ingrid (Colombian).

Until Death Do Us Part: My Struggle to Reclaim Colombia. (La rabia en el Corazón, **2001). New York: Ecco, 2002. ISBN 0060008903. 228pp.**

Betancourt relates her history, politics, and love of Colombia. She was a hostage of the Revolutionary Armed Forces of Colombia (FARC) from 2002 to 2008; her successful rescue from captivity makes her memoir even more important, because it provides the background to her life.

> *I believe we can't hand over the country's destiny to men who take no interest in the misery of the Colombian people, who think only about enriching themselves.* (42)

Subjects: Betancourt, Ingrid; Colombia; corruption; drug cartels; drug trafficking; France—Paris; hostages; immigrants—Colombian; legislators; Oxygen Green Party; politicians; Revolutionary Armed Forces of Colombia (FARC); terrorism

Bianciotti, Hector (Argentinian).

What the Night Tells the Day. **New York: New Press; distributed by W.W. Norton, 1995. ISBN 1565842405. 254pp.**

After thirty plus years of making his home in France, Bianciotti ponders the immigrant Italian experience of his parents, his childhood in Peron's Argentina, his Catholicism, his departure to France, and the reconciliation of these realities with his homosexuality.

> *There are some people and events you wait for without realizing it, and it is only when they finally appear or occur that you understand how long and how impatiently you have waited for them.* (222)

Subjects: Argentina; Bianciotti, Hector; Catholicism; France; homosexuality; immigrants—Argentinian; immigrants—Italian; priests—Catholics; sex; writers

Castro, Alicia (Cuban).

Queens of Havana: The Amazing Adventures of Anacaona, Cuba's Legendary All-Girl Dance Band. **As told to Ingrid Kummels and Manfred Schäfer. Translated by Steven T. Murray (from original German). New York: Grove Press, 2007. ISBN 9780802118561. 393pp.**

This is Alicia Castro's fascinating and delightful story of her band, Anacaona. She and her sisters made it to the top during the hard times of the Great Depression, which became the beginning of a glamorous, exciting, and revolutionary era.

> *In the 1930s, son was regarded in Havana's better circles as the vulgar music of the common people. Music for blacks. And certainly only played by men. When, all of a sudden, we young girls began playing these electrifying songs, with their suggestive lyrics, it shocked many an upright citizen.* (18)

Key features: Glossary

Subjects: Cuba—Havana; memoirs; music—big band; musicians; women's lives

Castro, Fidel (Cuban), and Ignacio Ramonet (Spanish).

Fidel Castro: My Life. (*Fidel Castro. Biografía a dos voces,* 2006). Translated by Andrew Hurley. New York: Scribner, 2008. ISBN 9781416553281. 714pp.

This is one of the few in-depth interviews Fidel Castro has given throughout his life, and possibly one of his last. Thus, this book contains a unique and eloquent perspective on key moments in the twentieth century from a world leader who has been successful at standing up to Washington at relatively close quarters.

> *In the winter of his life and now, due to health concerns, a little distanced from power, he is still driven to defend the energy revolution, the environment, against neoliberal globalization and internal corruption. He is still down in the trenches, on the front line, leading the battle for the ideas he believes in—which, apparently, nothing and no one will ever make him give up.* (21)

Subjects: Castro, Fidel; Cuba

Chavez, Linda (Mexican American).

An Unlikely Conservative: The Transformation of an Ex-liberal, or, How I Became the Most Hated Hispanic in America. New York: Basic Books, 2002. ISBN 0465089038. 262pp.

With unflinching honesty, Chavez details her political evolution, including trials and triumphs, from early work with socialists to cabinet nomination as George W. Bush's secretary of labor.

> *It was clear that Richard Nixon understood the Mexican American community better than any Republican before or—until George W. Bush—since.* (95)

Subjects: affirmative action; Bush, George W.; Chavez, Linda; Colorado; conservatism; Mexican Americans; politicians; secretary of labor

Chiang, Lynette (Australian).

The Handsomest Man in Cuba: An Escapade. Guilford, CT: Globe Pequot Press, 2007. ISBN 0762743905. 257pp.

Chiang recounts her experiences and adventures traveling throughout the Caribbean island on a bike. An Aussie and a Costa Rican resident, she immerses the reader in the Cuban culture and brings it into the reader's heart, dispelling the misconceptions spread by detractors of the communist country. The author's sense of humor and spontaneity will make readers want to go to Cuba!

> *Now, I must admit that I tend to respond in a friendly fashion to whoever happens to approach me, no matter who I am with, so I may well have been mistaken for a puta many times over, albeit one with poor nose for business.* (14)

Subjects: adventure; Cuba; humor

Cruz, Celia, with Ana Cristina Reymundo (Cuban).

Celia: My Life: An Autobiography. (*Celia: Mi Vida,* 2004). New York: Rayo, 2004. ISBN 0060725532. 260pp.

Posthumously published and based on interviews conducted months prior to losing her battle with cancer, Cruz's memoir tells the story of her Cuban childhood, exile in Mexico, immigration to the United States, and her triumphant career as the Queen of Salsa.

> *The United States has not only accepted us, it has given us the opportunities denied to us in the lands of our births without demanding that we lose our identities.* (125)

Subjects: Cruz, Celia; Cuba—Havana; Cubans; exile; Florida—Miami; immigrants—Cuban; marriage; Mexico; music—salsa; music industry; musicians; singers

De Ferrari, Gabriella (Peruvian American).

Gringa Latina: A Woman of Two Worlds. New York: Kodansha International, 1996. ISBN 1568361459. 176pp.

Gabriella de Ferrari's memoir, composed of short vignettes, recounts her early life in Peru as a gringa child of Italian immigrants, and her later American life as a Latina citizen.

> *Gringa Latina is a celebration of my growing up as a gringa in the land of Latinas and becoming a Latina in a land of gringos.* (1)

Subjects: De Ferrari, Gabriella; immigrants—Peruvian; Italians; Peru; women's lives

de Tagle, Lillian Lorca (Chilean American).

Honorable Exiles: A Chilean Woman in the Twentieth Century. Austin: University of Texas Press, 2000. ISBN 0292716060. 214pp.

An upper-class childhood spent as the daughter of a world-traveling diplomat was followed by a life of unexpected exile in the United States and a career in the private and public sectors.

> *But I had my ticket, my passport, and a permanent visa, courtesy of the American consul, who could afford such generosity in 1952.* (144)

Subjects: Chile; Chilean Americans; de Tagle, Lillian Lorca; Department of State; diplomats; immigrants—Chilean; languages; mothers and daughters; translators; Voice of America

Dorfman, Ariel (Chilean).

Heading South, Looking North: A Bilingual Journey. (*Rumbo al Sur, Deseando el Norte: un Romance Bilingüe,* 1998). New York: Farrar, Straus & Giroux, 1998. ISBN 0374168628. 282pp.

> Novelist and intellectual Dorfman explores the profound effects that the assassination of Salvador Allende has had on him, and the effect language and identity have had on his past pre-exile Chilean life and current life divided between the United States and Santiago.

> > *Could my writing in English make sense of this journey of identity into Latin America that was, of course, being carried out, primarily, in Spanish?* (195)

> **Subjects:** Allende, Salvador; Argentina; assassination; bilingualism; Chile; Dorfman, Ariel; exile; immigrants—Chilean; languages; Russia; writers

Esquivel, Laura (Mexican).

Between Two Fires: Intimate Writings on Life, Love, Food, & Flavor. (*Íntimas suculencias: tratado filosófico de cocina,* 1998). Translated by Stephen Lytle. New York: Crown, c2000. ISBN 0609608479. 153pp.

> In the style of *Like Water for Chocolate,* this book mixes a love of cookery with a love of life as it occurs in the kitchen among traditional Mexican women. Esquivel suggests that the true revolution in creating the New Man begins by restoring rituals and ceremonies, establishing a new relationship with the land and the planet, where everything is sacred.

> > *The hearth, my family's favorite place for entertaining visitors, was where I learned what was going on in the world, and where my mother had long talks with my grandmother, my aunts, and from time to time some now deceased relative. Held there by the hypnotic power of the flames, I heard all kinds of stories, but mostly stories about women.* (14)

> **Subjects:** cooking; Esquivel, Laura; food; Mexicans; women's lives

Fernandez, Alina (Cuban).

Castro's Daughter: An Exile's Memoir of Cuba. (*Alina: Memorias de la Hija Rebelde de Fidel Castro,* 1997). New York: St. Martin's Press, 1998. ISBN 0312193084. 259pp.

> Fernandez details her life as the illegitimate daughter of Fidel Castro, including his disjointed and strained relationship with her and her mother, behind-the-scenes political happenings, her love affairs and child, and her eventual immigration to the United States and Spain.

> > *By now I was the only person in the country with freedom of expression. I could speak freely about the lack of freedom, without having a police squad get me out of bed, beat me up, and take me to jail.* (221)

> **Subjects:** Castro, Fidel; Cuba; exile; family relationships; fathers and daughters; Fernandez, Alina; illegitimate children; immigrants—Cuban; love affairs; models

Fernandez Barrios, Flor (Cuban American).

Blessed by Thunder: Memoir of a Cuban Girlhood. **Seattle, WA: Seal Press; distributed to the trade by Publishers Group West, 1999. ISBN 1580050212. 244pp.**

Recounting her chaotic childhood during the Communist Revolution and subsequent immigration to the United States as a teenager, Fernandez Barrios provides a rare glimpse into Castro's Cuba and Cuban immigration—both from the perspective of a child.

> *Four decades later, I still freeze when I hear the sounds of a helicopter . . . . That sound! They're coming back! In an instant, I am a small child covering her ears to shut out the terrifying noise.* (13)

Subjects: Castro, Fidel; Cuba; Cuban Americans; Cuban Revolution; Fernandez Barrios, Flor; immigrants—Cuban

Fischkin, Barbara (U.S. American).

Muddy Cup: A Dominican Family Comes of Age in a New America. **New York: Scribner, 1997. ISBN 0684807041. 367pp.**

The oft-overlooked Dominican immigration experience is highlighted in this portrait of the Almonte family. From the early years in Dominican Republic under Trujillo's dictatorship to the family's eventual move from the island and settling in New York, Fischkin provides insight into the milieu of the family's many generations and New York's Dominican culture during the last five decades.

> *Señora Almonte, I can only give the visas to you and your eldest daughter. A wife and three children would be too much for your husband to support.* (31)

Subjects: Almontes; Dominican Americans; Dominican Republic; family relationships; immigrants—Dominican; New York; Trujillo Molina, Rafael Leónidas

Garcia, Manny (Cuban American).

An Accidental Soldier: Memoirs of a Mestizo in Vietnam. **Albuquerque: University of New Mexico Press, 2003. ISBN 0826330134. 278pp.**

The seemingly inconsequential act of enlisting in the army at age eighteen forever frames the life of Garcia as he travels from a log cabin in San Luis Valley to the front lines of Vietnam, and ultimately to civilian life as a defense attorney.

> *I joined up because I was working as a janitor and I figured I would be drafted soon and wind up in the Army anyway. So I thought I would choose to have some say in the matter. Dumb.* (25)

Subjects: Airborne Ranger; army; Colorado—San Luis Valley; Garcia, Manny; lawyers; *mestizaje*; Mormonism; Utah; veterans—Vietnam War; Vietnam War

Gonzalez, Rigoberto (Mexican American).

Butterfly Boy: Memoirs of a Chicano Mariposa. **Madison: University of Wisconsin Press, 2006. ISBN 0299219003. 207pp.**

Gonzalez's lifelong struggle to reconcile his sexuality with Latino machismo is further complicated by his childhood, which involves working as a migrant, the death of his mother, and becoming estranged from his father.

Everything I had learned to be and not to be, to accept and to deny, was finally derailed in the mid-1980s when Liberace began to attract suspicious attention. (152)

Subjects: California; Chicanos; death; family relationships; Gonzalez, Rigoberto; homosexuality; immigrants—Mexican; *machismo;* Mexican Americans; migrant farmworkers; sexuality

Greer, Pedro Jose (Cuban American).

Waking up in America: How One Doctor Brings Hope to Those Who Need It Most. **New York: Simon & Schuster, 1999. ISBN 0684835479. 202pp.**
Dr. Greer recounts his life as the son of Cuban immigrants, work as one of the leading advocates for Miami's homeless population, and the founding of Miami's Camillus Health Concern.

And there I was, a world away in med school, learning to save lives, yet I could not save one precious to me. (29)

Subjects: Cuban Americans; doctors; Florida—Miami; Greer, Pedro Jose; homelessness; immigrants—Cuban; medical school

Grillo, Evelio (Cuban American).

Black Cuban, Black American: A Memoir. **Houston, TX: Arte Público Press, 2000. ISBN 155885293x. 134pp.**
Grillo's journey from the Cuban Spanish town of Ybor City to the historically African American Xaviar University and an all African American unit in World War II sheds light on the process of transculturation undertaken by many immigrating to the United States.

For all our sharing of language, culture, and religion with white Cubans, we black Cubans were black . . . . School resolved all of my confusion about my color, my Spanish tongue, and my culture. I was a black boy. That's what was important. (39)

Subjects: African Americans; California—Oakland; Cuban Americans; Florida—Ybor City; immigrants—Cuban; race relations; transculturation; veterans—World War II; World War II

Guerra, Jackie (Mexican Americans).

Under Construction: How I've Gained and Lost Millions of Dollars and Hundreds of Pounds. **New York: New American Library, 2006. ISBN 0451217233. 259pp.**
Guerra, the first Latina to star in a network sitcom, shares her trials and triumphs with family, gaining and losing weight, and in show business, in this motivational memoir of self-love.

You can only play the role of the martyr for so long before you become the martyr who has been played out. Some people love to play the role of the martyr. That's a tough movie to be in. (207)

Subjects: actresses; comedians; death; dieting; gastric bypass surgeries; Guerra, Jackie; Mexican Americans; movies; self-esteem; television industry; weight

Guillermoprieto, Alma (Mexican).

Dancing with Cuba: A Memoir of the Revolution. New York: Pantheon Books, 2004. ISBN 0375420932. 290pp.

A lifelong love of dancing leads Guillermoprieto to journey from her native Mexico to study in New York, and eventually to teach in postrevolutionary Cuba at age twenty. After thirty years, the author contemplates the impact this six-month instructional period had on her politics and generation.

> *I think that particular combination of blind obedience and total rebellion embodied my generation's dilemma and gave it meaning and purpose.* (197)

Subjects: Castro, Fidel; Cuba; Cuban Revolution; dancing; Guevara, Ernesto "Che"; Guillermoprieto, Alma; Humphrey, Doris; Mexicans; New York; teachers

Hart, Elva Treviño (Mexican American).

Barefoot Heart: Stories of a Migrant Child. Tempe, AZ: Bilingual Press/Editorial Bilingüe, 1999. ISBN 0927534819. 236pp.

Journeying from south Texas to the beet fields of Minnesota in search of work, Hart vividly recounts her grueling and fascinating daily experiences as a child of migrant farmworkers.

> *I had never felt shame about being a migrant before, as my brothers and sisters had. My parents told us it was honest, clean work, working in the fields with the vegetables.* (217)

Subjects: family relationships; fathers and daughters; Hart, Elva Treviño; Mexican Americans; migrant farmworkers; Texas

Herrera, Juan Felipe (Mexican American).

Notebooks of a Chile Verde Smuggler. Tucson: University of Arizona Press, 2002. ISBN 0816522154. 186pp.

Utilizing poetry, screenplay, journal entries, letters, and prose, author and poet Herrera shares his life stories—including those about his childhood, family, and political involvement—and social commentary.

> *You keep on telling me that Chicanos are authentic Americans, that this is the first lesson. This takes me back to Pocho-Che days in San Francisco when we hoisted up Che Guevara and Lolita Lebron as our American figures.* (18)

Subjects: California—San Francisco; Chicanos; Herrera, Juan Felipe; poets; Tortilla Flats

Johnson, Kevin R. (Mexican American).

How Did You Get to Be Mexican? A White/Brown Man's Search for Identity. Philadelphia: Temple University Press, 1999. ISBN 1566396506. 245pp.

His relationships with his Mexican American mother and Anglo father frame Johnson's memoir, which highlights his childhood, academic life, and professional career and comments on the complex relationship of society and race.

> *If I got my Mexican American identity from my mother, my tolerance of racial difference unquestionably came from my father.* (64)

Subjects: California—Los Angeles; Chicanos; family relationships; Harvard University; Johnson, Kevin; lawyers; mental illness; Mexican Americans; mothers and sons; race relations

Kephart, Beth (U.S. American).

Still Love in Strange Places: A Memoir. **New York: W.W. Norton, 2002. ISBN 0393050742. 224pp.**

Visits to her husband's native El Salvador lead Kephart, an Anglo American, on a fifteen-year quest for deeper understanding of her husband, her in-laws, the family's land, and the nation as a whole.

> *The first time I went to El Salvador it was 1986. I looked for war; I found Tiburcio in Nora's garden. I looked for fear; I found only my own: fear of roads, fear of the dogs, fear of my husband's Spanish.* (170)

Subjects: cemeteries; coffee; El Salvador; farming; husbands and wives; immigrants; Kephart, Beth; marriage; plantations; St. Anthony's farm

Leguizamo, John (Colombian American).

Pimps, Hos, Playa Hatas, and All the Rest of My Hollywood Friends. **New York: Ecco, 2006. ISBN 006052071x. 280pp.**

With self-deprecating honesty, Leguizamo describes his life, from his early childhood in Queens, New York, to the world of stand-up comedy, Broadway, and the movies. Throughout the journey, he shares funny stories about friendships and family and opinions on and insights into the world of entertainment.

> *Most movie stars aren't very good. They're usually not talented. They're people who have a look the public likes, or they're clever enough businesswise to manipulate the system, or they're all drive and ambition. But they're not real actors.* (64)

Subjects: actors; Broadway; comedians; family relationships; friendship; Hollywood; humor; immigrants—Colombian; Leguizamo, John; movies; New York—New York City—Queens

Limón, José (Mexican American).

José Limón: An Unfinished Memoir. **Hanover, NH: University Press of New England, 1998. ISBN 0819563749. 207pp.**

Literally unfinished at the time of death, Limon's memoir traces his journey from Mexico when his family immigrates to the United States to the world of modern dance, where he finds his true calling and love.

> *There are things that one not only remembers but also cherishes with all fervor, for they are indispensable allies in the cruel yet splendid battle that artists must wage for their survival both as human beings and as artists.* (114)

Subjects: Arizona—Tucson; army; California—Los Angeles; choreographers; dancers; Humphrey, Doris; immigrants—Mexican; Limón, José; Mexican Revolution; New York—New York City

Liscano, Carlos (Uruguayan).

Truck of Fools. (*El furgón de los locos,* 2001). Translated by Elizabeth Hampsten. Nashville, TN: Vanderbilt University Press, 2004. ISBN 0826514642. 126pp.

> Liscano's poignant narrative recounts his thirteen years of incarceration and torture in the 1970s and 1980s in a Uruguayan prison as a political dissident. His story provides insight into the lives of countless Uruguayan political prisoners and their captors.

> > *After a long while I know: I am sitting down to wait for the armored truck of fools, that one day will take me on the absurd journey to liberty.* (118)

> **Subjects:** Liscano, Carlos; political prisoners; prison; torture; Uruguay

Lopez, George (Mexican American).

Why You Crying? My Long, Hard Look at Life, Love, and Laughter. (*Por qué lloras? Una mirada en serio a la vida, el amor y la risa,* 2005). New York: Simon & Schuster, 2004. ISBN 0743259947. 194pp.

> With expected humor, Lopez openly exposes an early life of parental abandonment and emotionally distant rearing by seemingly unloving grandparents, followed by a twenty-year struggle that culminated in comedic success at the helm of a top-rated prime-time sitcom.

> > *The truth of the matter is what makes this so special, so rewarding, so extraordinary, is this is the first Latino family sitcom that has been as successful as this one.* (125)

> **Subjects:** actors; comedians; family relationships; grandmothers and grandsons; Lopez, George; Mexican Americans; mothers and sons; television industry; television personalities

Lopez Torregrosa, Luisita (Puerto Rican American).

The Noise of Infinite Longing: A Memoir of a Family—and an Island. New York: HarperCollins, 2004. ISBN 0060534605. 286pp.

> The death of the family matriarch and resulting family reunion leads to remembrances of middle-class life in 1950s Puerto Rico and subsequent immigration to the United States and the world, as Lopez Torregrosa searches for a home.

> > *I know that for some of us who left it, the island is a remote place, a long-lost home we will probably not see again. But for others of us who left it, this is a place of dreams still, where we return time and again.* (282)

> **Subjects:** death; family relationships; immigrants—Puerto Rican; Lopez Torregrosa, Luisita; Puerto Rico; Puerto Rican Americans

Medina, Pablo (Cuban American).

Exiled Memories: A Cuban Childhood. New York: Persea Books, 2002. ISBN 0892552808. 135pp.

> Medina reconstructs his early years in middle-class pre-Castro Cuba, the subsequent revolution that enveloped his childhood, and the ultimate exile of his family to the United States.

After a few months, realizing that a return to the island was not forthcoming, we looked on a future where the sun was rising again. (3)

Subjects: Cuban Americans; Cuban Revolution; Cubans; family relationships; immigrants—Cuban; Medina, Pablo

Mejía, Camilo (Nicaraguan; Costa Rican American).

Road from Ar Ramadi: The Private Rebellion of Staff Sergeant Camilo Mejía. **New York: New Press, 2007. ISBN 9781595580528. 312pp.**

Mejía relates how he came to be a conscientious objector, convicted as a deserter who spent a year in jail for objecting to the war in Iraq. While in Nicaragua, he was the privileged son of Sandinistas and was brought up with strong ideological principles. At age eighteen he immigrated with his mother to the United States, where he fell victim to army recruiters and ultimately became an eyewitness to atrocities and cruelty.

> *I was supposed to be giving all my attention to watching out for insurgents, who had made the stretch of road we were on a death trap for the American forces. But then I would catch sight of the children running to the front gates of their homes to watch our vehicles rolling by and they would remind me of the children I had seen back in Nicaragua, my country of birth: barefoot kids with skinny bodies and dirty, weather-beaten faces.* (1)

Subjects: deserters; Iraq War; memoirs; pacifists

Mendez, Antonio J.

The Master of Disguise: My Secret Life in the CIA. **New York: William Morrow, 1999. ISBN 0688163025. 351pp.**

With striking detail, former CIA operative Mendez recounts his childhood in Nevada and shares twenty-five years of espionage work with the CIA, including serving as Chief of Disguise.

> *As I replaced the Intelligence Star in its velvet-lined case, I pondered the improbable sequence of events that has led me to this time and place. In some ways, I had been destined from childhood for a career in the shadow world of espionage.* (7)

Subjects: CIA; espionage; Mendez, Antonio J.; Nevada; spies

Mendez, Frank S. (Mexican American).

You Can't Be Mexican: You Talk Just Like Me. **Kent, OH: Kent State University Press, 2005. ISBN 0873388224. 76pp.**

From his upbringing as the son of an immigrant from Mexico to his life in Ohio, Mendez carved out a dual existence as American and Latino, with stints as a marine enlistee and professional engineer.

> *Mixing with gueros, I was Mexican. Living with Mexicans, I was an American. In high school I could not resolve these disparate pressures on my psyche.* (38)

Subjects: Chicanos; engineering; immigrants—Mexican; Mendez, Frank S.; Mexican Americans; Mexico—Michoacán; Ohio—Lorain; U.S. Marine Corps; veterans—World War II; World War II

Murguía, Alejandro (Mexican American).

The Medicine of Memory: A Mexica Clan in California. Austin: University of Texas Press, 2002. ISBN 0292752679. 228pp.

Shifting from the present to the past and back again, Murguía utilizes his clan's Chicano history to illustrate the larger indigenous experience in California. Covering more than two centuries, the memoir encompasses everything from early California history to the Chicano movement.

> *And now just as I claim my Spanish side, I also claim my Indian, indigenous side. I understand this commingling as the natural order of life. The biggest myth in our continent is the purity of blood.* (11)

Subjects: California—San Francisco; Chicanos; family relationships; *indigenismo; mestizaje;* Mexican Americans; Murguía, Alejandro

Pantoja, Antonia (Puerto Rican American).

Memoir of a Visionary: Antonia Pantoja. Houston, TX: Arte Público Press, 2002. ISBN 1558853650. 199pp.

With quiet candor, Pantoja reflects on her life as a Puerto Rican immigrant in New York, a founding member of the Latino youth organization ASPIRA, and a Presidential Medal of Freedom Award recipient.

> *Our family was one of the many families that grew up poor in Puerto Rico, surrounded by a society where privilege, abundance, and opportunities existed for others.* (24)

Subjects: ASPIRA; immigrants—Puerto Rican; New York; Pantoja, Antonia; Puerto Rican Americans; Puerto Rico

Paris, Margaret L. (U.S. American).

Embracing America: A Cuban Exile Comes of Age. Gainesville: University Press of Florida, 2002. ISBN 0813025451. 226pp.

Composed of edited transcripts from two years of interviews with Elena Maza Borkland, Paris's work reveals the effects of the little-discussed Operation Pedro Pan on Cuban families and children, who later reconnect and establish new lives in the United States.

> *Before boarding the plane, everyone including myself wondered if we would be turned back and not allowed to leave because they caught someone trying to sneak out. It was a day none of us in that plane would ever forget.* (7)

Subjects: Borkland, Elena Maza; Castro, Fidel; Cuba; Cuban Americans; Cuban Revolution; family relationships; immigrants—Cuban; Operation Pedro Pan

Pérez Firmat, Gustavo (Cuban American).

Next Year in Cuba: A Cubano's Coming of Age in America. New York: Anchor Books, 1995. ISBN 0385472978. 274pp.

Celebrating each Christmas in Miami's Little Havana, always with the expectation of the next year's post-Castro holiday in Cuba, Pérez Firmat struggles to reconcile his dual identities as Cubano and American.

> *Spiritually tied to Cuba, yet firmly rooted in the United States, I belong to a rare group of exiles that could, should Castro be overthrown in the near future, genuinely choose whether to return or stay.* (12)

Subjects: Cuba; Cuban Americans; families; Florida; immigrants—Cuban; Pérez Firmat, Gustavo

Quinn, Anthony (Mexican American).

One Man Tango. New York: HarperCollins, 1995. ISBN 0060183543. 338pp.

Receiving a package from his ailing first wife sends Quinn on a reflective ride, recounting his life, from a hut in Chihuahua, Mexico, to the top of the acting world.

> *My earliest memories are so deeply ingrained that I do not have to remember them to bring them to mind. They are there, always—below the surface and right to the top.* (16)

Subjects: actors; Hollywood; immigrants—Mexican; marriage; Mexican Revolution; Mexico—Chihuahua; movies; Quinn, Anthony; Texas—El Paso; Zorba the Greek

Ramirez, Juan (Mexican American).

A Patriot After All: The Story of a Chicano Vietnam Vet. Albuquerque: University of New Mexico Press, 1999. ISBN 0826319599. 179pp.

What begins as an undergraduate thesis becomes a personal examination of Ramirez's life before and after the Vietnam War, and ultimately a memoir of the oft-forgotten Chicano veteran.

> *My attitude about the war then was not to deny I have been there but to explain it away as bad history better forgotten. I had a lot of opinions about it but wouldn't necessarily volunteer them.* (157)

Subjects: California—San Francisco; Chicanos; drug abuse; Mexican Americans; Ramirez, Juan; U.S. Marine Corps; veterans—Vietnam War; Vietnam War

Ramos, Jorge (Mexican).

No Borders: A Journalist's Search for Home. (*Atravesando Fronteras: la Autobiografía de un Periodista en Busca de su Lugar en el Mundo*, 2002). New York: Rayo/HarperCollins, 2002. ISBN 0066214149. 302pp.

From his early life in Mexico to his stint at Noticiero Univision, Ramos details his life and the trials and triumphs of his career in the worlds of Spanish and English journalism.

> *Almost everything I am can be understood by looking at my childhood and adolescent experiences in that house in Mexico. In fact, I often act in marked opposition to the negative experiences I had back then.* (45)

Subjects: immigrants—Mexican; journalists; languages; Noticiero Univision; Ramos, Jorge; television industry; television personalities

Reed, Alma M. (U.S. American).

Peregrina: Love and Death in Mexico. **Austin: University of Texas Press, 2007. ISBN 9780292102394. 347pp.**

Michael K. Schuessler rescued this long-lost memoir written by Alma Reed, a U.S. American journalist who led a passionate life during the thrilling times of post-revolutionary Mexico. She was the fiancée of the revolutionary governor of Yucatán, Felipe Carrillo Puerto—who was tragically assassinated eleven days before their wedding—and became a heroine to all of Mexico.

> *The few dwellings along the dusty road that led to the railroad station were ugly hovels. It did not occur to me then that American enterprise was largely responsible for the crude, unwholesome aspect of Juárez and that, far from being a typical Mexican town, it was merely the messy backyard of Texas.* (85)

Subjects: Carrillo Puerto, Felipe; Mexico—Yucatán; Reed, Alma

Richardson, Bill (Mexican American).

Between Worlds: The Making of an American Life. (Entre Mundos: la Formacíon de una Vida Americana, **2005). New York: Putnam, 2005. ISBN 0399153241. 374pp.**

In a straightforward and easy style, Richardson relates the trials and triumphs of his life story, from its early beginnings in Mexico City to a Northeastern education and a fascinating political career in Washington, at the United Nations, and throughout the world.

> *I was not interested in becoming a professional Hispanic, but my heritage was central to my identity, and I was proud of it.* (96)

Subjects: ambassadors; Clinton, Bill; diplomats; governors; immigrants—Mexican; Mexican Americans; Mexico; New Mexico; politicians; Richardson, Bill; United Nations; Washington, D.C.

Rivers, Victor Rivas (Cuban American).

A Private Family Matter: A Memoir. **New York: Atria Books, 2005. ISBN 0743487885. 371pp.**

As an actor and the spokesman for the National Network to End Domestic Violence, Rivers details the harrowing childhood of violence he suffered at the hands of his father, the importance of strangers to his salvation, and his struggle not to repeat his father's mistakes.

> *He tied my arms and legs to the bed frame and hovered over me, choke chain in one hand. He beat me with the chain, off and on, for several hours, taking breaks for food and cigarettes or to answer the phone.* (171)

Subjects: actors; child abuse; Cuba; Cuban Americans; domestic violence; family relationships; fathers and sons; Hollywood; marriage; movies; National Network to End Domestic Violence; Rivers, Victor

Rodriguez, Richard (Mexican American).

Hunger of Memory: The Education of Richard Rodriguez. **New York: Bantam Books, 2004. ISBN 0553382519. 212pp.**

As the son of Mexican American immigrants, Rodriguez sheds light on his educational journey, from being a scholarship boy who only knew fifty words in English in California to becoming a student at a university in England.

> *The scholarship boy does not straddle, cannot reconcile, the two great opposing cultures of his life. His success is unromantic and plain.* (70)

Subjects: bilingualism; California—Sacramento; England; higher education; immigrants—Mexican; languages; Mexican Americans; Rodriguez, Richard

Sanchez, Reymundo (Puerto Rican American).

Once a King, Always a King: The Unmaking of a Latin King. **Chicago: Chicago Review Press, 2003. ISBN 1556525052. 286pp.**

Once a member of Chicago's Latin Kings, Sanchez struggles to carve out a new existence that does not include the life and family that he knew as a King, at times reverting back to his former gang life.

> *Even if I succeeded in making a positive contribution to American society in the streets of society, I would always be Lil Loco to some folks. I finally realized the true meaning of "once a King, always a King."* (137)

Subjects: drugs; gangs; Illinois—Chicago; Latin Kings; murder; prison; Puerto Ricans; Sanchez, Reymundo; Texas—Dallas

Santiago, Esmeralda (Puerto Rican).

Almost a Woman. (Casi una mujer, 1999). **Reading, MA: Perseus Books, 1998. ISBN 0738200433. 313pp.**

This compelling memoir recounts Esmeralda Santiago's journey to define herself as a young woman while also acclimating to a new country. While living in New York, Esmeralda discovers a passion for the performing arts.

> *In Puerto Rico I hadn't wanted any of those things. In Puerto Rico, I didn't know they were within my reach. But in Brooklyn every day was filled with want, even though Mami made sure we had everything we needed. Yes, I had changed. And it wasn't for the better.* (58)

Subjects: actresses; memoirs; New York—New York City; Puerto Ricans

Saralegui, Christina (Cuban).

Christina! My Life as a Blonde. (*Cristina!: Confidencias de una Rubia,* 1998). New York: Warner Books, 1998. ISBN 044652008x. 273pp.

In this candid memoir that is part private history, part motivational text, and part personal opinion, Saralegui shares her journey from an early upper-class Cuban childhood to her position as the host of one of the most popular talk shows in the world.

> *I began to formulate a definition of what liberation was for Latin women: We Latin women are liberated from the neck up, not the neck down. Our most important organ is located between our ears, not our legs.* (89)

Subjects: *Cosmopolitan en Español;* Cuba; Cuban Americans; Cuban Revolution; *El Show de Cristina;* Florida—Miami; immigrants—Cuban; journalists; Saralegui, Christina; television industry; television personalities; women's lives

Sepúlveda, Luis (Chilean).

Full Circle: A South American Journey. (*Patagonia express: apuntes de un viaje,* 1995). Melbourne, Oakland: Lonely Planet Publications, 1995. ISBN 0864424655. 192pp.

Sepúlveda begins this tale by recounting the horrors of prison and persecution in Pinochet's Chile. Bluntly and with humor, he takes the reader on this singular journey throughout South America, ending up in Spain. We meet people from all walks of life and vicariously enjoy adventures that include temporary academic jobs; casinos; and time spent rooming with random Canadians, Argentineans, and Uruguayans at a brothel called Ali Kan.

> *My colleagues had gone to the Ali Kan on account of a miracle that had occurred the previous night: the Canadian, having downed half a bottle of rum, had finally decided to ask the fat lady for a dance.* (59)

Subjects: adventure; South America; travel

St. Aubin de Terán, Lisa (European American).

The Hacienda: A Memoir. Boston: Little, Brown, 1997. ISBN 0316816884. 342pp.

The native Englishwoman de Teran migrates to her husband's Venezuelan estate and forges a life with the inhabitants of the hacienda, until her marriage disintegrates and she decides to leave her husband and the hacienda.

> *By throwing myself whole-heartedly into the lives of the gente, the work of the hacienda, my writing and my motherhood, I have managed to anaesthetize any other feelings or needs in myself.* (277)

Subjects: de Teran, Lisa St. Aubin; domestic violence; England; farming; immigration; marriage; mental illness; motherhood; plantations; sugar cane; Teran, Jaime; Venezuela

Stavans, Ilan (Mexican American).

On Borrowed Words: A Memoir of Language. New York: Viking, 2001. ISBN 0670877638. 263pp.

Stavans explores the centrality of languages—Yiddish, Spanish, Hebrew, and English—to his life and search for identity, from his childhood as a Mexican Jew to his student activism in Israel and work as a respected author.

> *My English-language persona is the one that superimposes itself on all previous others. In it are seeds of Yiddish and Hebrew, but mostly Spanish. (249)*

Subjects: Hebrew; immigrants—Mexican; Israel; Jews and Judaism; languages; Mexican Americans; Stavans, Ilan; writers; Yiddish

Suárez, Virgil (Cuban American).

Spared Angola: Memories from a Cuban American Childhood. **Houston, TX: Arte Publico Press, 1997. ISBN 1558851976. 159pp.**

Through seemingly disconnected poems, essays, and stories, Suarez exposes the first twelve years of his childhood in Cuba and later years as an immigrant in America.

> *You are a lucky man. Your parents did the right thing. When they took you out of Cuba, your parents spared you. Yes, you were spared. Spared Angola. (11)*

Subjects: Cuba; Cuban Americans; family relationships; immigrants—Cuban; Suárez, Virgil

Thomas, Piri (Nuyorican).

Down These Mean Streets. (*Por estas calles bravas,* **1998). New York: Vintage Books, 1997 (1967). ISBN 0679732381. 334pp.**

This classic coming-of-age autobiography recounts the harsh life of Piri Thomas, a man of African and Puerto Rican descent raised in Spanish Harlem. Caught up in the ways of the street, Piri embraces drugs, violence, and crime. Ultimately Piri finds himself headed to Sing Sing for the murder of a police officer. In prison he discovers that redemption can be found in the most unlikely places.

> *The world was getting tighter and tighter to wear. It was like I was outgrowing it. My God, the only thing I could do that the hacks couldn't stop was think. And I wished I could stop thinking about the free side. The free side—dig that! (254)*

Subjects: coming-of-age; drugs; New York; Puerto Ricans; violence

Urrea, Luis Alberto (Mexican American).

Nobody's Son: Notes from an American Life. **Tucson: University of Arizona Press, 1998. ISBN 0816518653. 184pp.**

His parent's constant struggle to define their son's ethnicity shapes author Urrea's coming-of-age—as a Mexican immigrant in the United States, yearning to be someone's son.

> *I'm not old enough to write my memoir. Yet I'd feel as if I'd cheated if I didn't try to share some observations. So many of us live in a nightmare of silence. We are the sons and daughters of a middle region, nobody's children, marching under a starless flag. (58)*

Subjects: Abbey, Edward; California—San Diego; family relationships; immigrants—Mexican; languages; Mexican Americans; Mexico—Tijuana; Urrea, Luis Alberto

Vilar, Irene (Puerto Rican American).

The Ladies' Gallery: A Memoir of Family Secrets. **New York: Vintage Books, 1996. ISBN 0679745467. 324pp.**

After awakening in a psychiatric facility, Puerto Rican American Vilar struggles to understand her relationship to her grandmother's participation in the 1954 attack on the U.S. House of Representatives and her mother's subsequent suicide.

> *Well, I am the product of repetitions. Of family secrets. Every family has its own; usually it is the untold family story a child is destined unwittingly to repress, or to repeat. We inherit these secrets the way we inherit shame, guilt, desire. And we repeat.* (4)

Subjects: diaries; family relationships; Lebron, Lolita; mental illness; Puerto Rico; suicide; U.S. House of Representatives; Vilar, Irene

Biographies

This section contains biographies, or life stories told by a third party, that focus on a wide variety of experiences—from the plight of the undocumented immigrant to the anguish of a tortured artist to the reality of life for runaway slaves in Cuba. Two of the titles in this section play a key part in the evolutionary history of the *testimonio*. Miguel Barnet's *Biography of a Runaway Slave* and Elena Poniatowska's *Here's to You, Jesusa!* are identified as foundational texts of the genre.

Barnet, Miguel (Cuban).

Biography of a Runaway Slave. (Biografía de un cimarrón, 1966). **Translated by W. Nick Hill. Willimantic, CT: Curbstone Press, 1994 (1968). ISBN 1880684187. 217pp.**

This classic *testimonio* tells the story of Esteban Montejo. Barnet wrote the book in Esteban's voice, based on extensive interviews done when Esteban was 105 years old and living in a nursing home. Esteban tells about his participation in key moments in Cuban history.

> *I began to realize everything was going backwards. It was getting darker and darker and then lighter and lighter. The chickens perched on the tops of posts. Folks were so scared they couldn't talk. Some died of heart attacks, and some were struck dumb.* (17)

Subjects: Cuba; revolutionaries; slaves; war

Breslin, Jimmy (U.S. American).

The Short Sweet Dream of Eduardo Gutierrez. **New York: Crown, 2002. ISBN 0609608274. 213pp.**

Breslin personalizes the typically dehumanized undocumented Mexican immigrant experience, shedding light on the early Mexican life and migratory journey of New York construction worker Eduardo Gutierrez. On November 23, 1999, Guiterrez's life ended in tragedy on a construction site.

> *Immigrants have to risk danger, and more of them die crossing the border, and the prize is the chance to go to work for below minimum wage and be lonely in America.* (33)

Subjects: construction workers; day laborers; death; Gutierrez, Eduardo; immigrants—Mexican; Mexico—San Matias; New York—New York City—Brooklyn; politics; undocumented workers; U.S.–Mexico border

Bretón, Marcos, and José Luis Villegas (Californianos).

Away Games: The Life and Times of a Latin Ball Player. **New York: Simon & Schuster, 1999. ISBN 0684849917. 272pp.**

Miguel Tejeda's journey into and through the world of professional American baseball illustrates the trials, triumphs, and exploitation potentially faced by every prospective professional athlete from the Dominican Republic and all of Latin America.

> *By the age of twelve, he spent nearly all of his time hovering around the sandlots where boys could be discovered, signed to professional contracts, and sent to the United States in search of millions.* (25)

Subjects: athletes; baseball; California—Oakland; Dominican Republic; Latin America; Oakland Athletics; Tejeda, Miguel

Fremon, Celeste (U.S. American).

G-dog and the Homeboys: Father Greg Boyle and the Gangs of East Los Angeles. **Albuquerque: University of New Mexico Press, 2004. ISBN 0826335365. 299pp.**

Fremon tells the story of Greg Boyle, a parish priest, and the saga of his involvement with the teenaged gangs of East LA. More than 800 youths lost their lives in gang-related activities in Southern California between 1990 and 1994. The author engages with G-Dog and those "kids" to offer insights into the root causes of violence and effective methods of taking kids to some kind of normalcy in adulthood.

> *I treated them as human beings . . . underneath all the tattoos, the dysfunction, and the bluster, gang members were adolescents who had the same hopes, fears, longings, and vulnerabilities as any other teenagers.* (3)

Subjects: Boyle, Greg; California—Los Angeles; gangs; Mexican Americans; teenagers

Gimbel, Wendy (Cuban American).

Havana Dreams: A Story of a Cuban Family. **New York: Vintage Books, 1999. ISBN 0679750703. 234pp.**

With the love affair of Naty Revuelta and Fidel Castro serving as a backstory, Gimbel shares the lives, loves, and losses of four generations of Cuban women, including the illegitimate daughter born of that relationship.

> *Why would she permit me—indeed encourage me—to tell her story? Memories are*
> *what she has to hurl against the bitter experiences of the last three decades—a span*
> *in which she has lost not only Fidel but both of her daughters.* (40)

Subjects: Castro, Fidel; Cuba—Havana; Cuban Revolution; Fernandez, Alina; illegitimate
children; love affairs; Revuelta, Naty; women's lives

Greising, David (Cuban American).

I'd Like the World to Buy a Coke: The Life and Leadership of Roberto Goizueta.
New York: Wiley, 1998. ISBN 0471194085. 334pp.

From modest beginnings at Coca-Cola in Cuba, Roberto Goizueta rose to become
the conglomerate's president and oversaw sixteen years of unprecedented success
for the company. All facets of Goizueta's life are covered in this accessible and
interesting read.

> *The depths of his personal allegiance to The Coca-Cola Company can probably be*
> *traced to the fact that his single most valuable asset when he arrived in the United*
> *States was his job at Coca-Cola.* (26)

Subjects: Coca-Cola; corporations; Cuba; executives; Goizueta, Roberto; immigrants—
Cubans

Malsch, Brownson (U.S. American).

"Lone Wolf" Gonzaullas, Texas Ranger. **Norman: University of Oklahoma Press,**
1998. ISBN 0806130164. 224pp.

Malsch thoroughly and accurately depicts the life and career of famed Texas
Ranger M.T. "Lone Wolf" Gonzallulas, while shedding light on early- and
mid-twentieth-century American law enforcement.

> *"Lone Wolf" is one of the best known and most respected peace officers in the south.*
> *He's quick on the trigger and all bad gun men know that, so seldom frequent his*
> *quarters.* (31)

Subjects: army; Gonzaullus, Manuel Trazazas; law enforcement; law enforcement officers;
"Lone Wolf" Gonzaullas; Texas; Texas Rangers; U.S. Treasury Department

Martínez, Rubén (Mexican American).

Crossing Over: A Mexican Family on the Migrant Trail. **New York: Henry Holt,**
2001. ISBN 0805049088. 330pp.

Martínez was inspired by the tragic death of the Chávez brothers to re-create their
journey from Michoácan to California, following up on the fate of the remaining
family members at the same time. The result is a lyrical defense of undocumented
migrants.

> *At five-fifteen the eastern sky is pale yellow. Shades of dusty pink rise into*
> *blue-greens and finally into deep blue at the zenith and in the west. A 1989 GMC*
> *truck, blue with sliver trim, equipped with a camper shell of darkly tinted windows,*
> *speeds westward down Avenida Del Oro. Twenty-seven people are inside,*
> *twenty-five of them in the camper and two in the front seat. All are undocumented*
> *Mexican migrants.* (5)

Subjects: families; immigration; Mexican Americans; transculturation; undocumented workers

Poniatowska, Elena (Mexican).

Here's to You, Jesusa! (*Hasta no verte Jesús mío*, 1969). **Translated by Deanna Heikkinen. New York: Farrar, Straus & Giroux, 2001, c1969. ISBN 0374168199. 303pp.**

Through the hardships that rough and ready Jesusa survives—beginning with a stabbing by her father's girlfriend and later fighting alongside him in the Revolution—this book vividly illustrates the reality of life for the majority of women in Mexico during the twentieth century.

> *When my husband's mission came back from the hills, he didn't find me at home. The boys told him that I had a place I went to! So when he opened the door he found me wrestling with the drunks. Uy, he was ready to kill me! He asked why I'd done it, and I told him that while he wasn't there I supported myself drinking: how else was I supposed to live since I didn't have an income?* (89)

Key features: First person narration

Subjects: family relationships; Mexican Revolution; Mexico—Mexico City; revolutionary struggles; *testimonio*

Prignitz-Poda, Helga (German).

Frida Kahlo: Life and Work. (*Frida Kahlo: die Malerin und ihr Werk*, 2003). **Munich, Germany: Schirmer/Mosel München, 2007. ISBN 978382960-1184. 261pp.**

Prignitz-Poda offers a new interpretation of Kahlo's work that takes a fresh look at the symbolism with which she expressed her pain, which the author traces to a shocking source.

> *The charged situation that Frida was born into could not have been more dramatic: the political unrest that ended only in 1917; the daily sight of wounded, hungry, and desperate people—fear and death underscored the first ten years of her life.* (12)

Subjects: art; artists; Kahlo, Frida; Mexico

Anthologies and Collections

Each of these books contains several life stories, usually grouped around a theme—such as immigration to the United States, learning English, or living as an undocumented worker. These collection are meant to bring attention to Latino contributions and experiences in the United States.

Garrison, Philip (U.S. American).

Because I Don't Have Wings: Stories of Mexican Immigrant Life. Tucson: University of Arizona Press, 2006. ISBN 0816525250. 149pp.

Garrison tells the stories of his Mexican immigrant neighbors, far from the border in the Yakima Valley of Washington state, and the trajectory of the Mexican migration to this area.

> The 1980s yielded the classic story of the illegal alien apprehended by the migra, the INS. "Hey messican, how come you took off running?" the agent leered through the van's protective screen. "Por alas no tener," replied our man. Because I don't have wings. (3)

Subjects: immigrants—Mexican; Mexico—Michoacán; race relations; undocumented workers; Washington—Yakima Valley

Hellman, Judith Adler (U.S. American).

The World of Mexican Migrants: The Rock and the Hard Place. New York: New Press, 2008. ISBN 9781565848382. 256pp.

The personal stories and testimony of fifteen Mexican immigrants about the conditions in Mexico that prompted them to emigrate, the difficult and dangerous journey, and the hostile situation they contend with in the United States.

> I ask whether it is unusual for someone from Nopal who has sacrificed to study and earned a university degree to find himself working in the United States in construction or landscaping or painting –the areas of concentration of Nopaleño migrants.
>
> "Not really," says Vicente. "I can think of a bunch of people besides my brother." (30)

Subjects: Mexico; undocumented workers

Marías, Javier (Spanish).

Written Lives. (*Vidas escritas,* 1992). Translated by Margaret Jull Costa. New York: New Directions, c1999. ISBN 081121611X. 200pp.

In this collection of short biographies of twenty acclaimed writers of various nationalities and languages (excluding Spaniards), Marías masters a unique style that affectionately "embellishes" anecdotes and episodes from these otherwise disastrous lives, to provide the reader with an interesting take on the known facts about these writers.

> [W]hen he [Oscar Wilde] was a student in Oxford, he received in his rooms the unwanted visit of four louts from Magdalen [sic] College who had come from a drunken party and went out to have fun at his expense. To the surprise of the more timorous members of the group . . . all came tumbling back down the stairs, one after the other. (124)

Subjects: writers—fiction

Martínez, Rubén, and Joseph Rodríguez (Latino; Salvadoran; Mexican American).

The New Americans. New York: New Press, 2004. ISBN 156584792X. 251pp.

> Rodríguez recounts the journeys of seven families into the United States. These families come from a wide range of nationalities, which allows Martínez to address issues such as national identity, immigration policy, racism, and death at the borders. The very nature of the topic makes the narrative complex and dramatic.

> > *Never in my entire life had I been so aware of my skin color and overall "ethnic" appearance as I was that morning in Maine. But clearly I was one of the lucky ones; there are dozens, perhaps hundreds—we have not been told by the authorities exactly how many—who remain in custody even as I write this, their constitutional rights suspended because, the Justice Department tells us, "we are at war." (4)*

> **Subjects:** death; identity; immigration; national security; racism; U.S.–Mexico border

Miller, Tom, ed.

How I Learned English: 55 Accomplished Latinos Recall Lessons in Language and Life. (Como aprendí inglés: 55 Latinos realizados relatan sus lecciones de idioma y vida, 2007). Washington, DC: National Geographic, 2007. ISBN 9781426200977. 268pp.

> From the athletes golfer Lorena Ochoa and baseball player Orlando Cepeda, to TV personalities Don Francisco and Christina Saralegui, to cultural icons the Ilan Stavans, Ariel Dorfman, and Coco Fusco, this collection presents thought-provoking, humorous, and touching stories of Latino immigrants' struggle with the language and ultimately, the culture of the United States.

> > *We also became great shape-shifters, turning on Latin politeness to impress our American friends' parents, and then reverting to little yanqui brats when we wanted to bewilder the latest nana. One of them, Rufina, fled the house after my parents refused to heed her pleas that we children be exorcised. "Traen el diablo por dentro," she cried. (They're possessed by the devil.) (29)*

> **Subjects:** languages; Latinos; memoirs

Molinary, Rosie (Boricuan).

Hijas Americanas: Beauty, Body Image, and Growing up Latina. Emeryville, CA: Seal Press, 2007. ISBN 9781580051897. 327pp.

> After surveying over 500 women and conducting more than 80 interviews, Ms. Molinary uses her own experience as a starting point to illustrate the conclusions that came out of this research. This is an emotionally challenging portrait of what it means to grow up Latina in the United States today, a struggle to reconcile two cultures to create a unique identity.

> *Sandra, thirty-seven and of Dominican heritage, grew up in Queens with a single mother. "She never talked to me about sex. She was very private. Her idea was that it came naturally and that nature would take its course. She never told me about my period. So it was traumatic for me when I got it. I thought I was dying." (41)*

Subjects: Latinas; transculturation; women's lives

Olmos, Edward James, Lea Ybarra, and Manuel Monterrey.
Americanos: Latino Life in the United States. **Boston: Little, Brown, 1999. ISBN 0316649147. 176pp.**

This is indeed a remarkable work of art in printed form, filled with carefully selected photographs that portray the life, culture, and spirit of Latinos/Hispanics in the United States—their contributions, achievements, dreams, and evolution. Bilingual essays, poetry, and commentary are included.

> *All the individuals who appear in this remarkable book need and are needed. They are picking the food we need on our tables, they are serving us our meals and taking care of our children, they are cutting our hedges and driving our buses and bringing dignity to the indispensable, never the "lowly," the indispensable tasks of life. (15)*

Key features: Bilingual edition

Subjects: identity; Latinos; *mestizos*; photography

Rivas-Rodríguez, Maggie, Juliana Torres, and Others.
A Legacy Greater Than Words: Stories of U.S. Latinos & Latinas of the WWII Generation. **Austin: U.S. Latino & Latina WWII Oral History Project, 2006. ISBN 0292714181. 344pp.**

The achievement and contribution of Latinos and Latinas during World War II is recounted in this carefully researched project through narrative, interviews, maps, and compelling oral histories.

> *Originally a Texas National Guard unit, the 36th (Infantry Division) boasted a large number of Latinos within its ranks, including the all-Latino Company E of the 141st Regimental Infantry Regiment. They landed on the beaches of Paestum near Salerno (Italy). (10)*

Subjects: biography; civil rights; Latinos; World War II

References

Cords, Sarah Statz. 2006. "Life Stories." In *The Real Story: A Guide to Nonfiction Reading Interests.* Englewood, CO: Libraries Unlimited.

Dawson, Alma, and Connie Van Fleet. 2001. "The Future of Readers' Advisory in a Multicultural Society." *The Readers' Advisory Companion.* Englewood, CO: Libraries Unlimited.

Lida, Clara E., and Franciso Zapata. 2004. "Signs of Identity Latin American Immigration and Exile." In *Literary Cultures of Latin America: A Comparative History*, Vol. 3. New York: Oxford University Press.

Loy, Pamela S. I. 1999. "Rigoberta Menchú: An Indian Woman in Guatemala." In *Latin American Literature and Its Times*, Vol. 1. Detroit: Gale Group.

Ross, Catherine. 2004. "Reading Nonfiction for Pleasure: What Motivates Readers?" In *Nonfiction Readers' Advisory*. Westport, CT: Libraries Unlimited.

Schuessler, Michael. 1999. "Massacre in Mexico." In *Latin American Literature and Its Times*, Vol. I. Detroit: Gale Group.

Sklodowska, Elzbieta. 2004. "In the Web of Reality Latin American Testimonio." In *Literary Cultures of Latin America: A Comparative History*, Vol. 2. New York: Oxford University Press.

Valdés, Mario J. 2004. "Social History of the Latin American Writer." *Literary Cultures of Latin America: A Comparative History*, Vol. 1. New York: Oxford University Press.

Volek, Emily. 1997. "Testimonial Writing." In *Encyclopedia of Latin American Literature*. London, Chicago: Fitzroy Dearborn.

Wyatt, Neal. 2007. *The Readers' Advisory Guide to Nonfiction*. Chicago: American Library Association.

1

2

3

4

5

6

7

8

9

Chapter 9

Narrative Nonfiction

Fernando Este and Sara Martínez

Atáscate ahora que hay lodo

Introduction

Narrative nonfiction that addresses Latino interests and concerns is a relatively new "genre" that has caught on like a *casa en llamas,* like a house on fire, *pues.* Sometimes called "creative nonfiction," these are books that use the literary techniques of fiction to present true stories or factual material. These books look at many aspects of society—health and beauty, history, politics, and self-help— through the lens of Latino cultural experiences. The authors empower, inspire, and instruct.

Appeal

These titles have varying appeal factors depending on their subject matter. Many bring the vicarious excitement and suspense of a good murder mystery. Others provoke strong emotions of empathy and indignation; still others are simply feasts for the senses. Popular themes address the current concerns that confront the community—especially those dealing with the difficult situation of people without documentation, the experience of discrimination and injustice, and the controversy over language.

Organization

The books in this chapter are organized under the following themes: business, culture, history, identity, sociopolitical issues, and sports.

Culture

Arellano, Gustavo (Mexican American).

¡Ask a Mexican! **New York: Scribner, 2007. ISBN 1416540024. 240pp.**

Choice excerpts from the iconoclastic and humorous column published in *OC Weekly* and many independent journals around this country. The "Mexican" answers any question, no matter how silly or offensive, with tongue in cheek and a firm grasp of history.

> *"How come Mexicans play soccer and not a real sport like hockey or football?"*
> *Ice-Cold Linebacker*
>
> *Dear Gabacho: Because soccer involves more running, and how else will we train for the midnight run across the U.S.–Mexico border?* (52)

Subjects: humor; Mexicans; race relations; racism; stereotypes

Bósquez, Mario (Mexican American).

The Chalupa Rules: A Latino Guide to Gringolandia. **New York: Plume, c2005. ISBN 0452286085. 242pp.**

Mario Bósquez shows that being born into poverty and experiencing domestic abuse, hunger, and discrimination does not have to be a barrier to a successful life. In *The Chalupa Rules* he shares the secrets he's learned from his Mexican American culture and ancestors.

> *The secret to his survival is the philosophy of life he calls "The Chalupa Rules." . . . So, while he goes about his work, trying to make it in the big city, no one has to know he feels like the newest chicken in the henhouse, has a beggar's body, and swims in two cultures.* (xiv)

Subjects: abuse; domestic violence; families; Mexican Americans

Poniatowska, Elena, and Amanda Holmes (Mexican).

Mexican Color. **New York: Stewart, Tabori & Chang, 1998. ISBN 1556708351. 160pp.**

In a truly magical feast for the eyes, the 200 full-color photographs and the exquisitely written essay will make the reader marvel and delight at the impact of color in Mexican culture, architecture, and society.

> *The cobalt blue that is often painted on the bases of the houses in small towns as a mud guard protects the paint from dirt, but even more importantly, it scares the evil spirits. It is a belief imported from Morocco.* (78)

Subjects: architecture; art; Mexico; photography

Rondón, Césara Miguel (Venezuelan).

The Book of Salsa: A Chronicle of Urban Music from the Caribbean to New York City. (El libro de la salsa: Crónica de la música del caribe urbano, 1980). Chapel Hill: University of North Carolina Press, 2008. ISBN 9780807858592. 340pp.

This is the story of salsa music—the music born out of a shared experience of urban poverty in marginalized *barrios* from the Caribbean to New York City.

> *Castro established the first Communist government in the hemisphere, a political fact that radically divided the global situation of Latin America. Music, which like any art reflects social conditions, would manifest the fullness and significance of the event. Musically speaking, things would never be the same.* (9–10)

Subjects: Caribbean; music—salsa; New York—New York City

Ruiz, Miguel (Mexican).

The Four Agreements: A Practical Guide to Personal Freedom. San Rafael, CA: Amber-Allen Publications, 1997. ISBN 1878424319. 138pp.

Ruiz discusses the four agreements he has gleaned from ancient Toltec wisdom, which lead to a fulfilled life, and invites us to abandon fear-based beliefs that rule our life and consume our energy to restore our personal power and freedom.

> *Ninety-five percent of the beliefs we have stored in our minds are nothing but lies, and we suffer because we believe all these lies.* (13)

Subjects: philosophy; Toltecs

Stavans, Ilan (Mexican American).

Spanglish: The Making of a New American Language. New York: Rayo, 2003. ISBN 0060087757. 274pp.

Stavans, in his always polemic and engaging prose, enthusiastically argues here that the evolution of a new language, the symbiotic encounter between the Hispanic and the Anglo civilizations, is already in progress and expanding rapidly, in spite of intellectuals' opinions to the contrary. This linguistic evolution is the expression of what's happening on the streets among common people and culture, and it challenges educated people who spend a lot of effort, some would say waste a lot of energy, on preserving the purity of both languages.

> *The lingo de la calle y la montaña, then, penetrates people's minds, and their vocabulary, at an astonishing speed. La revolución lingüística es imparable—the verbal transformation is unstoppable.* (14–15)

Subjects: bilingualism; languages; Spanglish

Vargas Llosa, Mario (Peruvian).

Wellsprings. Cambridge, MA: Harvard University Press, 2008. ISBN 9780674-028364. 202pp.

This is a collection of essays based on lectures given by the author in various venues. Vargas Llosa discusses the current state of Latin American literature, delving into the current state of Latin American society and then that of the world. He begins with an analysis of *Don Quixote* and ends by updating Karl Popper, with side trips to Ortega y Gassett and Borges.

> *However, its most magical and enduring feature continues to be that odd pair riding through its pages, brow-beaten, absurd, colorful, funny, tender, moving, indefatigable, who reveal to us, with each adventure, the marvelous abundance of the imagination in recreating human lives.* (25)

Subjects: literature; philosophy

History

Dorfman, Ariel (Chilean).

Exorcising Terror: The Incredible Unending Trial of General Augusto Pinochet. New York: Seven Stories Press, 2002. ISBN 1583225420. 223pp.

An unofficial advisor to top government officials of the Salvador Allende administration in Chile carefully documents the accounts of murder, torture, and disappearance during the twenty-seven years of Pinochet's regime. Dorfman retells with vivid and graphic details the reign of terror of one of the most brutal dictators in recent Latin American history.

> *Rodrigo Rojas Denegri, who on July 2, 1986, was burnt alive by a squad of soldiers and then transported to the other side of Santiago and left for dead in a ditch. Four days later—at the age of nineteen—he died of his wounds in a Santiago hospital.* (8–9)

Subjects: Allende, Salvador; Chile; dictators; disappeared; Pinochet, Augusto; torture

Goldman, Francisco (Guatemalan American).

The Art of Political Murder: Who Killed the Bishop? New York: Grove Press, 2007. ISBN 0802118283. 396pp.

A gripping account that delves into one of the bloodiest episodes in recent political history, the 1998 assassination of Bishop (Monseñor) Juan Gerardi, head of Guatemala's Recovery of Historical Memory Project and the Archdioceses's Office of Human Rights. Goldman fearlessly, and perhaps foolishly, uncovers the people who perpetrated this atrocity on the population and who continue to participate in Guatemala's civil life with impunity.

> *The REHMI report —whatever its flaws as strict social science—was by far the most extensive investigation of the war's toll on the civilian population that had ever been attempted. Guatemala: Never Again identified by name a quarter of the war's estimated civilian dead (the 50,000-plus names . . .) and documented 410 massacres.* (21–22)

Subjects: assassination; Catholic Church; Gerardi, Juan; Guatemala; Latin America; massacres

Gordon, Linda (U.S. American).

The Great Arizona Orphan Abduction. **Cambridge, MA: Harvard University Press, 1999. ISBN 0674360419. 416pp.**

On October 2, 1904, in an Arizona copper-mining boom town, a group of "white" Protestant vigilantes forcibly removed Irish Catholic orphans from the Mexican Catholic families who had taken the children into their homes. In this enthralling book, Gordon traces the racial and social tensions that brought the situation to a head—tensions that continue to resonate today.

> *They did not grasp that this trip was to offer them not only parents but also upward mobility. Even less did they know that mobility took the form of a racial transformation unique to the American Southwest, that the same train ride had transformed them from Irish to white.* (19)

Subjects: Arizona—Morenci; orphans; race relations; religion

Hurst, James W. (U.S. American).

Pancho Villa and Black Jack Pershing: The Punitive Expedition in Mexico. **Westport, CT: Praeger, 2008. ISBN 9780313350047. 198pp.**

The infamous raid by Francisco "Pancho" Villa on Columbus, New Mexico, during the violent Mexican Revolution of 1910 had repercussions that played out throughout the twentieth century. Hurst examines the myth, legend, and reality of this daring attack by the Villistas and what was previously considered General Pershing's bumbling countermove.

> *The campsite was reached in mid-afternoon, and all the serviceable mounts in the area were confiscated. Five beef cattle were killed to be distributed among the camps. Later in the evening orders were given that desertion would be punishable by death. The march to Columbus had begun, and there would be no turning back.* (12)

Subjects: Mexican Revolution; New Mexico—Columbus; Pershing, General "Black Jack"; Villa, Francisco "Pancho"

Kamen, Henry (U.S. American; Spanish).

The Disinherited: Exile and the Making of Spanish Culture, 1492–1975. **New York: HarperCollins, 2007. ISBN 9780060730864. 508pp.**

In this intriguing look at the trajectory of Spanish culture in exile, Kamen examines the Spanish *afán* (zeal) for deporting its best and brightest in its constant striving toward religious and social conformity. These exiles fertilized culture universally as they took their brilliance and creativity around the globe.

> *Spain was about to become a land of perpetual leave-taking, a nation that in order to enhance its own feeling of cohesion was prepared to drive into exile hundreds of thousands of its own native sons and daughters. For another four hundred years and more, to a degree that was unique in*

> *western civilization, exile became the spectre that haunted Spain's cultural destiny.* (4)

Subjects: exile; Spain; Western civilization

Ojito, Mirta (Marielita).

Finding Mañana: A Memoir of a Cuban Exodus. (El mañana: memorias de un éxodo cubano, 2006). **New York: Penguin Press, 2005. ISBN 1594200416. 302pp.**

Using firsthand accounts, including her own, Ojito documents the 1980 Mariel boatlift exodus, which brought 125,000 Cubans to southern Florida and the United States. This memoir sheds light on a cultural phenomenon that may be unfamiliar to many.

> *Today is the day I leave Cuba, I thought, and immediately I threw myself into action, because I knew that if I didn't, if I cried or hesitated or somehow crumbled under the ache of leaving, I might not go at all.* (168)

Subjects: Cuban Americans; Cubans; exile; Florida; immigrants—Cuban; journalists; Mariel boatlift exodus; Marielitas; memoirs; Ojito, Mirta; women's lives

Parker, Matthew (English).

Panama Fever: The Epic Story of One of the Greatest Human Achievements of All Time—the Building of the Panama Canal. **New York: Doubleday, 2007. ISBN 9780385515344. 530pp.**

Parker tells a compelling tale of intrigue, human suffering, and ingenuity, populated with fascinating characters, about the undertaking that marked the beginning of the American century.

> *There are many accounts of returning prospectors having their precious gold dust stolen from them. With the prospectors had arrived on the Isthmus not only cholera, gambling, and prostitution but also an epidemic of armed robbery.* (24)

Subjects: Panama Canal—history

Poniatowska, Elena (Mexican).

Las Soldaderas: Women of the Mexican Revolution. (Las soldaderas, 1999). **Translated by David Romo. El Paso, TX: Cinco Puntos Press, 2006. ISBN 978193-3693040. 93pp.**

The always wonderful Poniatowska presents a lyrical defense of the famous *soldaderas,* camp followers of the 1910 Mexican Revolution, accompanied by the luminous photos of the great Agustín Casasola, photographer of the Revolution.

> *In the photographs of Agustín Casasola, the women-with their percale petticoats, their white blouses, their delicate washed faces, their lowered gaze that hides the embarrassment in their eyes, their candor, their modesty, their dark-skinned hands holding bags of provision or handing a Mauser to their men—don't look at all like the coarse, foul-mouthed beasts that are usually depicted by the authors of the Mexican Revolution.* (15–16)

Subjects: Casasola, Agustín; Mexican Revolution; photography; *soldaderas*; soldiers; war; women's lives

Stavans, Ilan, and Lalo Alcaraz (Mexican American).

Latino U.S.A.: A Cartoon History. **New York: Basic Books, 2000. ISBN 0465082211. 175pp.**

Using Mexican pop culture as a format for this Latino history of the United States, Stavans offers a different and humorous perspective without compromising historical accuracy and veracity. The book offers a refreshing point of view, stripped of the romanticism found in many works of American history.

> *I myself have always been fascinated by the challenges of capturing the joys, nuances, and multiple dimensions of Latino culture within the context of the English language. . . . I was enthralled. Long-dormant adolescent memories surfaced, and Rius's art flashed into my mind.* (xiv)

Subjects: cartoons; humor; Latinos; undocumented workers; United States

Urrea, Luis Alberto (Mexican American).

The Devil's Highway: A True Story. **New York: Little, Brown, 2004. ISBN 0316746711. 239pp.**

The case of the Yuma 14 is a story of betrayal, survival, courage, and desperation, recounted by the author with incredible boldness and brutality. History and mythology weave together in a sort of magic realism in which tragedy, violence, and drama encounter shattered dreams and abandoned hopes within the merciless reality of the poor and oppressed as they struggle for a better life.

> *By 1850, he wrote, the Devil's Highway was "a vast graveyard of unknown dead . . . the scattered bones of human beings slowly turning to dust . . . the dead were left where they were to be sepulchered by the fearful sand storms that sweep at times over the desolate waste."* (12)

Subjects: death; desert; human trafficking; undocumented workers; U.S.–Mexico border; Yuma 14

Identity

Alvarez, Julia (Dominican American).

Once Upon a Quinceañera: Coming of Age in the USA. **New York: Viking, 2007. ISBN 9780670038732. 278pp.**

Novelist Alvarez writes an engaging report on the phenomenon of the *quinceañera* as it is observed by U.S. Dominican, Mexican, and Cuban American Latinas from Florida, Texas, and New Jersey, who invited her to their *quince* parties. She compares her own coming-of-age as an immigrant experience to that of the girls she visits. Alvarez places these experiences and observations into the larger context of young Latinas' current situation and prospects for a successful future.

> *In fact, you are not exceptionally beautiful or svelte and tall, model material. Your name is María or Xiomara or Maritza or Chantal, and your grandparents came from Mexico or Nicaragua or Cuba or the Dominican Republic. Your family is probably not rich.* (1)

Subjects: Latinas; *quinceañeras*; teenagers

Galvez, José, and Luis Alberto Urrea (Mexican American).

Vatos. **El Paso, TX: Cinco Puntos Press, 2000. ISBN 0938317520. 95pp.**

Decked with astonishing photographs by Pulitzer Prize–winning artist Galvez, this poem was written as a tribute to the forgotten, ordinary Latino man. The photographer exhibits his strong cultural and social connection to the Mexican man who has come to the United States and now struggles to find his own identity, whether as a father, grandfather, brother, or simply friend.

> *I begin to understand their wounds, and I find myself growing angry at those outside the picture, those who've forced them into segregated neighborhoods, forced them into fighting a war they did not choose to fight, forced them to become the warriors when they would have chosen more peaceful vocations.* (5)

Subjects: immigrants; Latinos; men; Mexicans; photography; poetry

Martin, Bruce T. (U.S. American).

Look Close See Far: A Cultural Portrait of the Maya. **New York: George Braziller, 2007. ISBN 9780807615898. 147pp.**

These photographs provide a visual context for the essays that bring the Maya culture and civilization out of the mystical, mythical, majestic past and into the living, and sometimes desperate, present.

> *Oppression is now centuries old, as pervasive and transparent as air and the words conveyed through it.* (11)

Subjects: Central America; Mayan Indians; photography

Morales, Ed (Nuyorican).

Living in Spanglish: The Search for Latino Identity in America. **New York: St. Martin's Press, 2002. ISBN 0312262329. 310pp.**

The multiplicity of nationalities, races, and ethnicities has made the search for a Latino/Hispanic identity a complex and difficult task. The author has come up with the term "Spanglish" to describe the situation, and with it attempts to address every aspect of the Latino/Hispanic community in the United States.

> *But Spanglish is altogether something else—it expresses something much broader and interesting than just a glitch in language. Spoken Spanish is only a verbal manifestation of a powerful force that has been incubating in America since the beginning of the postwar era, and will almost surely be a powerful determinant of U.S. culture in the twenty-first century.* (6)

Subjects: identity; *mestizos*; Spanglish

Sociopolitical Issues

Castañeda, Jorge G. (Mexican).

Ex Mex: From Migrants to Immigrants. **New York: New Press, 2007. ISBN 9781595581631. 222pp.**

Castañeda is a respected scholar of U.S.–Mexican relations who has taught at the University of California and served as the Mexican foreign minister during Vicente Fox's presidency. Here he presents the illegal immigration debate from the Mexican point of view, analyzing the motivation that drives Mexicans to the United States and making realistic suggestions of ways to mend the seemingly hopeless situation.

> *This explains the tianguis in the sky, on the beach, or in Dortmund, Germany: immigration and twelve years of economic stability and relative prosperity under presidents Ernesto Zedillo, Vicente Fox, and Felipe Calderón have created a new Mexican middle class that doesn't quite look or act the role, but that has become one of the country's best kept secrets and most sacred treasures.* (5)

Subjects: emigration; immigration; Mexican–U.S. relations; undocumented workers

Erikson, Daniel P. (U.S. American).

The Cuba Wars: Fidel Castro, the United States, and the Next Revolution. **New York: Bloomsbury Press, 2008. ISBN 9780596914346. 352pp.**

As the Cuban Revolution neared its fiftieth anniversary, in the year Fidel ceded power to his brother and the United States elected its first African American president, this volume examined the current situation between the two countries. The author presents the point of view of people from both sides of the relationship in a lively look at the current situation and the possibilities for change or probability of continuing stagnation.

> *In June, Bush told an audience at the U.S. Naval War College, "One day the good Lord will take Fidel Castro away," prompting Castro to respond, "Now I understand why I survived the plans of Bush and the presidents who ordered my assassination: The good Lord protected me."* (25)

Subjects: Castro, Fidel; Cuba; United States

Hutchinson, Earl Ofari (African American).

The Latino Challenge to Black America: Towards a Conversation between African Americans and Hispanics. **Los Angeles: Middle Passage Press, 2007. ISBN 9781881032229. 232pp.**

Hutchinson takes a look at the relationship between the black and Latino communities in the United States, especially after the revelation by the Census Bureau in 2002 that Latinos had become the largest minority group. He analyzes the issues that divide the two groups as well as opportunities for unity.

> *Though polls showed that blacks were generally more favorable toward illegal immigrants than whites, the polls seemed wildly at odds with the sentiments that many blacks privately expressed on immigration.* (11)

Subjects: African Americans; Latinos; race relations

Iglesias, David (New Mexican).

In Justice: Inside the Scandal That Rocked the Bush Administration. **With David Seay. Hoboken, NJ: John Wiley & Sons, 2008. ISBN 9780470261972. 246pp.**

Iglesias presents an engrossing account of being summarily fired from his position as a respected U.S. attorney and rising Latino star of the Republican Party during the Bush administration. He traces the events leading up to the firing and discusses the danger to the U.S. system of justice presented by the administration's blurring of the lines between loyalty to the administration and loyalty to the Constitution.

> *My world was anchored to faith and family and a fundamental belief that the work I did was righteous and had made a tangible difference for the citizens of my home state. Yet by the time I had fastened my seatbelt and felt the jet roll away from the gate, I was effectively a pariah, brought low by circumstances I didn't then understand and betrayed by those whom I counted as my friends and allies.* (18)

Subjects: Department of Justice; lawyers; memoirs; New Mexico; U.S. attorneys

Juarez, Juan Antonio.

Brotherhood of Corruption: A Cop Breaks the Silence on Police Abuse, Brutality, and Racial Profiling. **Chicago: Chicago Press Review, 2004. ISBN 1556525362. 307pp.**

With riveting descriptions, Juarez shares the intimate details of his seven-year career as a Chicago police officer, witnessing and participating in unspeakable acts of police corruption.

> *I was getting pretty good at juggling my two lives and making sure to keep them separate. With Ana I was the supportive, nurturing, and chaste boyfriend. At work I was a thrill-seeking, arrogant, skirt chaser. I was omnipotent and insatiable.* (64)

Subjects: corruption; domestic violence; drug abuse; higher education; Illinois—Chicago; Juarez, Juan Antonio; memoirs; Mexican Americans; police brutality; police officers; racial profiling; teachers

Mendoza, Plinio Apuleyo, Carlos Alberto Montaner, and Mario Vargas Llosa.

Guide to the Perfect Latin American Idiot. **Translated by Michaela Lajda Ames. Lanham, MD: Madison Books, 1996. ISBN 1568331347. 218pp.**

In thirteen chapters and one appendix, the authors present the delusions and dreams of the typical Latin American politician, supported by leftist cohorts from the economic, cultural, and academic worlds. They describe barriers to the continent achieving healthy development in today's world. Written in a witty style, this controversial book offers the reader a new perspective on the causes of underdevelopment in the struggling nations of the Latin American continent.

> *Thus our friend moves in the vast universe of politics, economics, and culture all at the same time, where each discipline supports the others and idiocy is propagated prodigiously as an expression of a continent wide subculture, blocking for us Latin Americans the road to modernity and development. A Third World theorist, the perfect idiot leaves us in Third World poverty and backwardness with his vast catalogue of dogmas presented as truths.* (8)

Subjects: Latin America; politicians; politics

Morgan, Lee, II (U.S. American, Texas).

The Reaper's Line: Life and Death on the Mexican Border. Tucson, AZ: Rio Nuevo Publishers, 2006. ISBN 9781887896979. 525pp.

The author recounts his experience as a Drug Enforcement Agent on the U.S.–Mexico border. He asserts that the time he spent confronting violence and corruption gives him the authority to provide context about illegal immigration and the government's ineffectual strategies in dealing with it.

> *But when you grabbed that ice-cold beer, leaned up in the shade against a now-silent, cooling tractor, and looked back over that cut field into an orange and purple Texas sunset, it all seemed so perfectly right. You knew your life had meaning and purpose.* (17)

Subjects: drug trafficking; memoir; undocumented workers; U.S.–Mexico border

Oltuski, Enrique (Cuban).

Vida Clandestina: My Life in the Cuban Revolution. (Gente del llano, 2000). Translated by Thomas Christensen and Carol Christensen. San Francisco: Wiley, 2002. ISBN 0787961698. 302pp.

Oltuski recounts the early events of the Cuban Revolution, with intimate firsthand memories as a Shell Oil executive and 26th of July Movement leader.

> *Fidel was in the Sierra Maestra, and we, the underground fighters in the cities, were working to strengthen the organization, propaganda, sabotage, and fundraising in order to acquire arms for the guerrillas in the Sierra.* (107)

Subjects: Castro, Fidel; Cuban Revolution; engineering; Florida—Miami; Guevara, Ernesto "Che"; Judaism; memoir; Oltuski, Enrique; Shell Oil; 26th of July Movement; University of Miami

Quinones, Sam (Mexican American).

Antonio's Gun and Delfino's Dream: True Tales of Mexican Migration. Albuquerque: University of New Mexico Press, 2007. ISBN 9780826342546. 318pp.

Quinones followed these stories while living in Mexico as a freelance reporter, working on issues having to do with Mexicans' migration to and from the United States.

> *Delfino carried himself with a brashness that Mexico doesn't always permit its people who are poor, short, and dark-skinned, all of which he was. Indeed, his brashness belied his place, which was at the bottom of Mexico City's economy.* (15)

Subjects: immigrants—Mexican; immigration; reporters; U.S.–Mexico border

True Tales from Another Mexico: The Lynch Mob, the Popsicle Kings, Chalino and the Bronx. Albuquerque: University of New Mexico Press, 2001. ISBN 0826322956. 336pp.

When Vicente Fox of the PAN party won the presidency from the PRI, it marked a sea change in Mexican politics. Quinones's stories follow these and the transcultural changes taking place at the same time in both Mexico and the United States, with the back and forth flow of workers/immigrants and *narcotraficantes.*

> *In the Mexican badlands, where the barrel of a gun makes the law, for generations dating back to the mid-1800s the* corrido *recounted the worst, best, and bloodiest exploits of men.* Corridos *were the newspaper for an illiterate people in the days before telephones and television. Corrido heroes were revolutionaries and bandits-people who had done something worth singing about.* (12)

Subjects: corruption; Fox, Vicente; immigration; transculturation; U.S.–Mexico border

Rivera, Geraldo (Nuyorican).

His Panic: Why Americans Fear Hispanics in the U.S. New York: Celebra, 2008. ISBN 9780451224149. 262pp.

The fiery investigative reporter and commentator Rivera takes a look at the controversy and high emotions that surround the debate on immigration and Latinos in the United States.

> *It is fear of America's changing face, masquerading as the immigration debate that has become our most divisive passion in the twenty-first century, surpassing even debates on the war in Iraq in vitriol. How will the nation cope with the dynamic growth of the Hispanic population?* (6)

Subjects: immigration; Latinos; race relations; undocumented workers

Rodriguez, Gregory (Mexican American).

Mongrels, Bastards, Orphans, and Vagabonds: Mexican Immigration and the Future of Race in America. New York: Pantheon Books, 2007. ISBN 9780375421587. 317pp.

Rodriguez traces the racial mixing process known as the *mestizaje*—the blending of races, or miscegenation—begun when the Spanish conquistadors set foot on the shores of Veracruz, and looks at its trajectory and future effects on the United States, as well as what it will come to mean to be "American."

> *Guerrero not only was no longer being held captive, he had married the daughter of Na Chan Can, a Mayan nobleman. Guerrero's response to Cortés's letter and to Aguilar's entreaties astounded his would-be liberator. Guerrero had assimilated so thoroughly into Mayan life that he no longer felt he would be accepted by his Spanish countrymen. His face was tattooed and his ears were pierced.* (4)

Subjects: *mestizos*; Mexican Americans; race relations

Rodriguez, Richard (Mexican American).

Brown: The Last Discovery of America. **New York: Viking, 2002. ISBN 0670030430. 232pp.**

With unique style, sophisticated use of literary language, and powerful insight, Rodríguez ponders his Hispanicity, its implications for his public and private life, and the "browning" of America. Not an easy read, this work will stimulate the curious mind and the philosopher in search of meaning and identity.

> *Brown as impurity. I write of a color that is not a singular color, not a strict recipe, not an expected result, but a color produced by careless desire, even by accident; by two or several. I write of blood that is blended. I write of brown as complete freedom of substance and narrative. I extol impurity.* (xi)

Subjects: *mestizos*; race relations

Sports

Madigan, Dan (U.S. American).

Mondo Lucha A Go-Go: The Bizarre and Honorable World of Wild Mexican Wrestling. **New York: HarperCollins, 2007. ISBN 9780060855833. 272pp.**

Full-color photos and lively reproductions of posters illustrate this exuberant celebration of Mexican *lucha libre,* a thrilling introduction to this controversial and little understood sport.

> *These masked men were walking, talking, flying, fighting superheroes and I thought the Mexican people were lucky to have them living among them. Instead of existing only on the pages of a comic book, these masked heroes or* enmascarados *(masked wrestlers) came to life in the middle of the ring.* (21)

Subjects: *lucha libre*; Mexico; professional wrestling

Wendel, Tim (U.S. American), and José Luis Villegas (Mexican American).

Far from Home: Latino Baseball Players in America. **Washington, DC: National Geographic Society, 2008. ISBN 9781426202162. 160pp.**

Baseball has become a path to glory for boys all over Central America and the Caribbean. Many of these young men dominate the sport today; others are callously exploited.

> *In some parts of Latin America, families still walk to the ballpark on Sundays dressed in their best clothes after a morning at church. Baseball and community, the game and faith, remain as intertwined as they were in Mays's day.* (27)

Subjects: baseball; baseball players; photography

Appendix

Publishers, Resources, and Awards

Selected Publishers of Latino Literature

Arte Público Press

> www.arte.uh.edu
> University of Houston
> 452 Cullen Performance Hall
> Houston, TX 77204-2004
> 800-633-ARTE

> Arte Público Press is "the nation's largest and most established publisher of contemporary and recovery literature by U.S. Hispanic authors. Its imprint for children and young adults, Piñata Books, is dedicated to the realistic and authentic portrayal of the themes, languages, characters, and customs of Hispanic culture in the United States. Based at the University of Houston, Arte Público Press, Piñata Books, and the Recovering the U.S. Hispanic Literary Heritage project provide the most widely recognized and extensive showcase for Hispanic literary arts, history, and politics" (www.arte.uh.edu).

Cinco Puntos Press

> www.cincopuntos.com
> 701 Texas Ave.
> El Paso, TX 79901
> 1-800-566-9072

> "Cinco Puntos Press (CPP), begun in 1985, is a nationally known, independent, literary press that specializes in publishing the literature (fiction, nonfiction, poetry, and books for kids) from the U.S.–Mexico border, Mexico, and the American Southwest" (www.cincopuntos.com).

Latino Imprints

Celebra

us.penguingroup.com/static/pages/aboutus/contactus.html
Penguin Group (USA) Inc.
Library Marketing Department (Adult Division)
375 Hudson St.
New York, NY 10014
Phone: 212-366-2372
Fax: 212-366-2933
librariansden@us.penguingroup.com\

Founded in 2008, Celebra is the first imprint to exclusively publish mainstream Hispanic personalities. Showcasing the appeal of today's most fascinating Hispanic personalities, Celebra publishes books by well-known leaders in a number of fields, including entertainment, politics, health, and business. Its goal is to publish books for mainstream readers that will also resonate with the vast population of Hispanics in the United States.

Penguin Group USA

www.penguingroup.com
375 Hudson St.
New York, NY 10014
(212) 366-2000

Urbano Book Publishing

PO Box 371641
Miami, FL 33137
www.urbanobooks.com
e-mail: Jeff@JeffRivera.com

Spanish Imprints

Rayo

HarperCollins
10 East 53rd St.
New York, NY 10022
(212) 207-7000
www.harpercollins.com/imprints/index.aspx?imprintid=517990

Rayo publishes books that embody the diversity within the Latino community, in Spanish-language editions, connecting culture with thought, and invigorating tradition with spirit.

Vintage Español

> Random House, Inc.
> 1745 Broadway
> New York, NY 10019
> (212) 782-9000
> www.randomhouse.com

Spanish Publishers and Distributors

Alfaguara

> www.alfaguara.santillana.es/index.php

Bilingual Publications

> 270 Lafayette St.
> New York, NY 10012
> (212) 431-3500

Lectorum

> www.lectorum.com/
> Lectorum has launched a new Spanish-language Web site for consumers, offering thousands of adult and children's Spanish-language titles. Visitors will be able to find that perfect book, whether it is the latest hot title, a classic, or a Lectorum staff pick. The site also offers information about authors and literature and book suggestions for readers of all ages.

Resources

Association of American Publishers

> Latino Voices for America
> www.publishers.org/main/Latino/latino_00.htm

La Bloga

> labloga.blogspot.com/
>
> Chicana, Chicano, Latina, Latino, and more. Literature, writers, children's literature, news, views and reviews. Contains links to Latino authors' Web sites.

REFORMA wiki

> reformaknowledge.wetpaint.com/
>
> REFORMA is the National Association to Promote Library and Information Services to Latinos and the Spanish Speaking. The REFORMA Wiki is a knowledge base of information about the Spanish language and services to Latinos in libraries. Contains "Resources for Public Libraries."

Web Junction

www.webjunction.org/spanish-collection-development/resources/wjarticles

Resources for libraries serving Spanish speakers; includes collection development tips for Latino youth, children, gay Latino teens, and their families.

Awards

In the United States

International Latino Book Awards are given by Latino Literacy Now, a nonprofit organization that supports and promotes literacy and literary excellence in the Latino community.

The **Mármol Prize** is awarded for a first work of fiction in English by a Latina/Latino writer that reflects a respect for intercultural understanding and fosters an appreciation for human rights and civil liberties. The prize is given by Curbstone Press.

The **Pura Belpré Award**, established in 1996, is presented to a Latino/Latina writer and illustrator whose work best portrays, affirms, and celebrates the Latino cultural experience in an outstanding work of literature for children and youth. It is cosponsored by the Association for Library Service to Children (ALSC), a division of the American Library Association (ALA), and the National Association to Promote Library and Information Services to Latinos and the Spanish Speaking (REFORMA), an ALA affiliate.

The last of the **Quinto Sol** prizes were awarded in 1975 by the publisher Quinto Sol, whose goals were to bring Chicano literature to the forefront of American culture and to unite all Chicanos in the United States.

Texas State University College of Education developed the **Tomas Rivera Mexican American Children's Book Award** to honor authors and illustrators who create literature that depicts the Mexican American experience. The award was established in 1995 and was named in honor of Dr. Tomas Rivera, a distinguished alumnus of Texas State University.

In Spain

The **Alfaguara Prize** is awarded by a Spanish publisher. It sets the best example, being a unique award on the Spanish literary scene, due to the transparency of its procedures as well as the enormous degree of circulation and the impact that the winning novels immediately have. These are simultaneously published in all of the countries where Alfaguara has offices and potentially reach more than 400 million readers.

The City Council of Gijón, Spain, awards the **Café de Gijón prize** to a novel in an effort to repay Gumersindo García, a Gijonés who in 1888 decided to name his café after his home town.

The **Planeta Prize** is given by the Spanish publisher Planeta for original novels written in Spanish (often published by them!). It is the highest paid prize for literature, after the Nobel.

In Latin America

The **Casa de la Américas** is awarded by the Cuban publishing house and is one of the most prestigious awards for literary creativity in Latin America.

The **Sor Juana Inés de la Cruz** (Premio Sor Juana Inés de la Cruz) is awarded to women writers in Spanish. It is organized by the Guadalajara International Book Fair in Mexico.

Awards from Non-Latino-Specific Organizations and Publications

Pulitzer Prize

Nobel Prize for Literature

PEN awards for literary fiction and literary translations

Booklist Editor's Choice

New York Times Notable Books

Library Journal Best Books List

American Book Award

Shamus award (Private Eye Writers of America)

Edgar award (Mystery Writers of America)

Alex (America Library Association for adult books that are appealing to young adults)

Hammett Prize (International Association of Crime Writers)

Medicine Pipe Bearer's Award (Western Writers of America)

American Fiction Writers Award (Christian Writers Association)

Lambda Literary Award

Glossary

abrazo: hug, embrace

abuelita: grandmother

afán: passionate zeal

amigas: friends

amor: love

amor con amor se paga: love should be repaid with love

arrimada: illegitimate daughter obliged to function as a servant due to her dependent, degraded status in the household

atáscate ahora que hay lodo: jump right in, the water's fine

barrios: neighborhoods

bisabuelo: great-grandfather

botánicas: stores where medicinal herbs and religious objects are sold, often purported to have magical properties

brujos: witches

burgués/guesa: bourgeois, middle class

cabrón: a Cuban immigrant and refugee fleeing the Spaniards before the War of 1898

cacique: locally powerful political boss

cada cabeza es un mundo: Every head contains its own little world.

campesina: country person

campo: country

casa en llamas: a house afire

chica: girl

cholo/a: Mexican American urban youth

cojones: balls

compañerismo: comradeship, camaraderie

compañero/a: comrade

compatriotas: fellow countrywoman, compatriot

compinches: buddies

conquista: conquest

cuidandera: keeper, caretaker

curandero/a: folk healer, "witch" doctor

de pilón: added value, lagniappe

el que es buen gallo dondequiera canta: He who is a good rooster can sing anywhere.

el viejo: old man

en el caso contrario: on the other hand

en gustos se rompen géneros: It takes all kinds.

final feliz: happy ending

fuereños: people from out of town, strangers

gato: cat

gente: people

gringo/a: foreigner, Yankee

grupo norteño: musical group that plays a style of music from Northern Mexico

guerrilla: unconventional and irregular battle strategy

guerrilleros/as: men and women soldiers who engage in guerrilla warfare

hacendado: landowner of large tracts

haciendas: large estates, ranches

increíble: incredible, unbelievable

jefe: boss

jineteras: people from Cuba's professional class who supplement their meager income by seducing international tourists

kout kouto: what the Haitians called the massacre of those Haitians found in the Dominican Republic, which was ordered by dictator Trujillo

la calavera tiene hambre: The skeleton is hungry. (This phrase comes from a song children sing in Mexico when they visit homes on *Día de los muertos,* a cross between Memorial Day and Halloween.)

la crema y la nata: the best of the best, la crème de la crème

la línea: the line; also refers to the U.S.–Mexican border

la mismísima Pelona: death herself

la raza cósmica: Mexican scholar José Vasconcelos's theory about a Latin American Cosmic Race, a mixture of all races

ladinos: acculturated Indians who often worked in Spanish *criollo* aristocratic households in Latin America

las muertas de Juarez: the female serial murder victims found near Ciudad Juárez, México

lépero: social lepers, beggars

loco: mad, insane

machismo: sexism, male chauvinism

macoutes: *See* tontons macoutes

mamá: mother

maquiladoras: foreign-owned factories located in Mexico near the U.S. border

más allá: the spirit world and the magical realm of intuition and dreams

más sabe el diablo por viejo que por diablo: The devil is wise thanks to his advanced age, not because of being the devil.

mestizaje: the process by which modern Mexicans became a people of mixed race, descended from the Spanish conquistadors and the native Indian population

mestizos/as: persons of mixed race

mujer que sabe latín . . . ¡claro que tiene buen fin!: a twist on the old saying, "Women who know Latin will not find a husband nor come to a good"; our version says that "Women who know Latin, will, of course, have a happy ending!"

nagual: animal alter ego

narcotraficantes: drug traffickers

ni tanto que queme el santo ni tan poco que no lo alumbre: When you shine a light on the saint, don't hold it so close that it will catch fire, nor so far away that you can't see it.

novio: boyfriend

pasión: passion

patria: homeland, mother country

pesadilla: nightmare

pícaro: rogue

pobrecita: poor thing

políticos: politicians

pueblito, pueblo, pueblos: village, small town

pues: then, so

quince: fifteen

quinceañera: fifteen-year-old girl; formal sweet sixteen–style birthday party

rendir cuentas: demand restitution

Rosas puras: pure roses

santera: faith healer

Santería: a religion practiced in the Caribbean and among Caribbean immigrants to the United States, based on West African deities and Roman Catholic saints, similar to voodoo

Semana Negra: Noir Week

Sendero Luminoso: Shining Path

soldaderas: camp followers of the 1910 Mexican Revolution

sucias: dirty girls

tambien: too, as well

telenovelas: soap operas

tertulia: social gathering, get-together

testimonio: testimony

tontons macoutes: the vicious volunteer "police" force in Haiti, answerable only to the dictator Papa Doc Duvalier

venganza: revenge, vengeance

References

The American Heritage Spanish Dictionary. Second Edition. 2001. New York: Houghton Mifflin.

Jarman, Beatriz Galimberti, and Roy Russell, eds. 2001. *The Oxford Spanish Dictionary: Spanish-English/English-Spanish.* Oxford; New York: Oxford University Press.

Gonzalez, Ralfka. 1995. *My First Book of Proverbs. Mi primer libro de dichos.* Emeryville, CA: Children's Book Press.

Author/Translator/Title Index

Book titles are italic; series titles are underscored.

Subject Index

About the Editor

Sara E. Martínez coordinates the Hispanic Resource Center for Tulsa City-County Library. She is responsible for collection development of Spanish-language materials. Sara works closely with the Latino and Spanish-speaking community in Tulsa. She received her MLIS from the University of Oklahoma and has a B.A. in comparative literature from the University of California, Berkeley. Sara did postgraduate work at the Universidad Nacional Autónoma de México in Latin American studies, with an emphasis on literature.

Photo by Elaine Lafón

About the Contributors

Brandi Blankenship has a bachelor's degree in liberal arts from the University of Oklahoma. She also received her MLIS from the University of Oklahoma. She currently works at the Mid-Continent Public Library System in Missouri, serving as branch manager for the town of Weston.

Fernando Este's first career was as a chemical engineer in Venezuela. He came over from the dark side to become a librarian, earning his MLIS from the University of Oklahoma while working for the Tulsa City-County Library System. Later he managed the Will Rogers Library in Claremore, Oklahoma, before moving to Vancouver, British Columbia with his life partner, Don, and his family, which includes Elvis, their four-and-three-quarter-year-old Chihuahua, Cosito ("Little Thing" in Spanish), and Delilah, their ten-year-old cockatiel. Besides working for the Vancouver and Burnaby Public Libraries, Fernando enjoys hiking, camping, and spending time in nature. He is engaged in peace work and Zen meditation.

Jessica Reed graduated with a B.S. in elementary education from Oklahoma State University and completed her MLIS at the University of Oklahoma. Upon completion of her degree, Jessica served as the Reference Department head at the Fort Smith Public Library in Fort Smith, Arkansas. In 2005 Jessica was thrilled to return to her childhood haunt, Martin Regional Library in Tulsa, Oklahoma, where she is an exceptional reference librarian. Jessica is in charge of Martin Regional's young adult and adult fiction collections and programming. She is also active at the state level, serving on the Oklahoma Library Association's committee for the Sequoyah High School Book Award.

Tracy Warren is the assistant manager at the Martin Regional Library, a constantly bustling branch serving the most ethnically diverse community in Tulsa, Oklahoma. Tracy received her MLIS from the University of Oklahoma and has a B.A. in anthropology from George Washington University. She is active at taking a leadership role in many committees at the systemwide level for the Tulsa City-County Library System. The Hispanic Resource Center's success owes a lot to her support and professionalism.

Genreflecting Advisory Series

Diana Tixier Herald, Series Editor

Genreflecting: A Guide to Popular Reading Interests, 6th Edition
Diana Tixier Herald, Edited by Wayne A. Wiegand

The Real Story: A Guide to Nonfiction Reading Interests
Sarah Statz Cords, Edited by Robert Burgin

Read the High Country: A Guide to Western Books and Films
John Mort

Graphic Novels: A Genre Guide to Comic Books, Manga, and More
Michael Pawuk

Genrefied Classics: A Guide to Reading Interests in Classic Literature
Tina Frolund

Encountering Enchantment: A Guide to Speculative Fiction for Teens
Susan Fichtelberg

Fluent in Fantasy: The Next Generation
Diana Tixier Herald and Bonnie Kunzel

Gay, Lesbian, Bisexual, and Transgendered Literature: A Genre Guide
Ellen Bosman and John Bradford; Edited by Robert B. Ridinger

Reality Rules!: A Guide to Teen Nonfiction Reading Interests
Elizabeth Fraser

Historical Fiction II: A Guide to the Genre
Sarah L. Johnson

Hooked on Horror III
Anthony J. Fonseca and June Michele Pulliam

Caught Up in Crime: A Reader's Guide to Crime Fiction and Nonfiction
Gary Warren Niebuhr